JUAN GRIS   HIS LIFE AND WORK

JUAN GRIS

HIS LIFE AND WORK

Daniel-Henry Kahnweiler

Translated by Douglas Cooper

HARRY N. ABRAMS, INC. · PUBLISHERS · NEW YORK

To the memory of my wife

Revised edition

Library of Congress Catalog Card Number: 69–11532
Copyright 1946 in France by Editions Gallimard, Paris
Printed and bound in West Germany

CONTENTS

PART THREE · WRITINGS OF JUAN GRIS

PREFACE

The division of this book into three parts is not just the result of an arbitrary decision. Originally it was imposed on me by circumstances. For, owing to the vicissitudes of the exodus in 1940, I was temporarily cut off from my reference files and note-books and therefore began to write Part II, "The Work of Juan Gris", without their help and in the only form which was then possible. However, as the work progressed, I began to feel that a division which had originally been unavoidable was in fact not without advantages and would allow more spontaneity in Part I and the elaboration of a solid basis of theory in Part II. The reader must decide for himself whether he shares my view.

Part III, which contains the collected writings of Juan Gris, needs no justification.

For many years Louise Leiris has helped me to assemble the relevant documents and to organise my reference files. Michel Leiris has very kindly read my manuscript at various stages; his comments and criticism have been of great assistance to me. To both of them is due my deepest gratitude.

PREFACE TO THE REVISED EDITION

The book that now appears in a new edition was written during the German occupation of France in the Second World War and was published soon afterwards. The question of corrections or additions has therefore naturally arisen. An American art historian exposed the major fault of the book when she called it a "catch-all". She was right: I had stowed into it everything I had to say at the time, for I was not sure that I should survive the war. I was in a hurry to set down all my thoughts.

Nevertheless, I think it desirable that this work reappear without any changes. I take back nothing of what I have written. There is not much I can add. Perhaps I should say that, more than ever, I am convinced that the so-called geometrical aspect of early Cubism is not essential. It is, at least in part, a reaction against the *linea serpentinata* of Art Nouveau. One must bear in mind that this characteristic of the "Style 1900" is just as evident in Seurat and Signac as in the Nabis. The Cubists reacted against the softness of this line, but what counted infinitely more with them was the different way of thinking, the new aesthetics. Today, Cubism is less understood than ever before. It seems to me that the disastrous consequences are manifest.

St. Hilaire, July 1, 1968

PART ONE · THE LIFE OF JUAN GRIS

INTRODUCTION

For many years I have been wondering how to recount the life of Juan Gris. The difficulty was evaded in the little book which I wrote about him in 1929,[1] for in that I emphasised particularly Gris' work and gave only a few essential dates. But in a work of greater scope devoted to this painter, it seemed essential also to give as full an account as possible of the facts of his life. How should this be done? I could not undertake a cold and purely objective narrative of the life of one who was a very dear friend and whose existence was for many years so intricately involved with my own. If I may borrow a phrase from Gertrude Stein, it seemed to me that I could not "be left out of him".[2] Yet I was frightened by the two dangers—untruthfulness and exhibitionism—which beset the autobiographical form.

Rightly or wrongly, I believe to-day that I have found both the correct form and manner. I have attempted to describe the life of Juan Gris just as he lived it during the all too short period of our intimacy, and to recount anything I have heard about his earlier life. I have faced this task with frankness and sincerity. I cannot yet tell all that I know about Gris' life—for some things it is still too early—but what I have set down is true.

I. RUE RAVIGNAN

After 1907 I often used to climb up to number 13 Rue Ravignan (now called Place Emile Goudeau). I will not attempt to describe once more, after so many others,[3] either the little sloping square planted with trees which was reached by a few steps from the Rue des Abbesses, or the curious wooden structure which was numbered 13, and was variously called "The Trapper's Hut", "The Wash-House", or something of the sort. The door was always ajar—the *concierge* lived in the house next door—and one went down stairs to reach the inhabitants of any but the two studios which faced the square. For the house, which was hung on the very sheer side of the hill of Montmartre, was entered by its upper storey.

I used to go there to see Picasso and also, a little later, Max Jacob. On the occasion of my first visit Picasso, wearing only a shirt and no trousers, opened the door and bade me enter. He already knew who I was, and when I saw him at home I remembered the small young man wearing dusty, worn-out clothes and muddy shoes who, a few days previously, had entered the shop which I had just opened at number 28 Rue Vignon, and whose return next day in a cab, accompanied by a bearded man older than himself, had so intrigued me. It had indeed been Picasso, who had brought Vollard to see the small new gallery which had just opened. I did not know either of them. As a matter of fact I knew no-one; I was only twenty-two and had just arrived from London to start my career as a picture-dealer, with the idea of taking up young painters. I knew nothing at all about them except for a few pictures which I had seen before going to London, or, on one of my numerous week-end visits to Paris, in the Indépendants, the Salon d'Automne, and the shop-windows of various private galleries which I had not dared to enter.

As I crossed the square before entering number 13, I often noticed the occupant of the studio which was on the left of the passage inside the front door. In spring and summer his two windows looking on to the square were always wide open, and in one or the other he would be sitting at work. He was very young and, I thought, handsome, with dark brown hair and an olive complexion. He was more than just "the Spanish type"; he was a real example of what is commonly called "the creole type", that is to say he had almost a mulatto appearance. What struck one about his face were his very large brown eyes, the whites of which were blueish. It was Picasso who told me that his name was Juan Gris, a name 11 which I had seen underneath drawings in *L'Assiette au Beurre*, *Le Cri de Paris*, *Le Charivari* and, later, in *Le Témoin*. I learnt that Gris was starting to paint and often used to call on him as I went past. His passion for work was unbelievable, and it was probably at this period that he made the remark attributed to him by Max Jacob:[4] "I only stroke dogs with my left hand so that if I am bitten I shall still have my right hand to paint with." In 1910 I saw the large naturalistic water-colours in which he 224, 225 worked out the basis of his formal vocabulary, in 1911 his first oil paintings, and in 1912 his *Homage* 237–239, 242 *to Picasso*.

Gris' studio[5] had an impoverished air, but I dot not remember being particularly struck at this time by its barrenness, its disorder or its dirt, for it looked like many another of the period. It was not noticeably different from the neighbouring studio of Picasso, with its pile of dead ashes beside the stove and the couch strewn with rolls of canvas and drawings covered in dust. In fact I only became aware of the picturesqueness—and the poverty—of the Rue Ravignan very much later as a result of the shocked comments of friends whom I took to visit Juan Gris. I was as accustomed to the wooden walls with, here and there, bits of paper sticking to them, to the floor strewn with cigarette stubs and spent matches, and to the two mean beds (there was one for the use of friends) with their broken mattresses, as I was to the seatless chairs, the tables daubed with paint and stacked with papers, empty tubes of paint and brushes. I remember particularly one of these tables, a small one with very long thick legs, which reminded me of a baby elephant. Gris kept it during the whole of his life; it was repainted and a place was found for it in his bedroom at Boulogne. There were no pictures on the walls, but on one wall hung a very beautiful hurdy-gurdy with marquetry inlay.

Gris did not give up this studio until 1922. Whether his health suffered as a result of the years he spent in this ramshackle, insanitary old dwelling I am not competent to judge, but it is at least probable. In any case, one thing is certain: Gris' taste inclined as little to picturesque squalor as it did to the bohemian life of Montmartre. True, he enjoyed his friends coming in and out, and a great deal of

Illustrations for " L'Assiette au Beurre "

his time in Montmartre was spent in serious discussion, either in their studios or in his own. But he was rarely to be seen "chez Azon" or in the other small eating-houses. He was not a leading figure in Montmartre life, and was never, for example, a "regular" at the "Lapin Agile". That he always disliked dirt, disorder or squalor, became apparent subsequently in his home at Boulogne. Yet he lived in this studio for over fifteen years without appearing to mind, and his life there was shared by two successive female companions. The first of these (who disappeared very early from his circle) bore him a son, Georges Gonzalez Gris. The child, too, lived in the studio with his parents and, as I told Georges one day, I remember seeing him suspended by his "nappies" between the window bars. Did I really see this? Or was it Gris who described to me this strange method of giving the baby an airing? Thinking it over now I cannot be sure. After Gris and Georges' mother had separated, the child was sent to his father's family in Madrid, where he was brought up by his aunt Antonieta and by one of his uncles. Georges did not return to Paris until 1926, when he was sent back at his father's request to continue his studies as a chemical engineer. He had begun these studies in Madrid and did not complete them until after his father's death.

After 1913 Gris lived with Josette, who remained his faithful companion to the end. They were in love, though there were frequent quarrels and reconciliations. Josette, who was intelligent, witty and shrewd, understood Gris and knew how to entertain him. He was a young man full of enthusiasm and of a very pleasing disposition. I remember comparing him to a puppy bursting with energy, affectionate and good-natured, but somewhat ungainly.

Posterity will inevitably see only the artist "*tel qu'en lui-même enfin l'éternité le change*", and its conception of him will be formed from the character of his work. Indeed, I myself gently chided my friend Maurice Raynal for what I considered a too highly coloured picture of Gris in his speech on June 13, 1938.[6] I have seen Gris somewhat inebriated at the end of an evening spent with friends, but he was in no sense a drunkard. For his art he had no need of that sort of stimulant, and his only excess was drinking coffee. In his youth he knew privation in all its forms; in later life he delighted in a good meal or a good bottle of wine. Yet when he was invited to friends' houses he was perhaps less touched by being given his favourite dish than by the fact of its having been specially cooked for him. He enjoyed female company, and the opposite sex found him attractive; however, he was discreet concerning his numerous conquests and never boasted of them. He was the very reverse of coarse and only swore or cursed at moments when he was roused to a terrible fury, a phenomenon which (as we learnt later) resulted from the slow poisoning of his whole system by defective kidneys. It would be a mistake, indeed, for posterity so to misinterpret the serious quality of his work as to form the totally false conception of a pompous and forbidding pedant. Picasso once made a remark to me which I find both pointed and profound: "Our friends who have died continue to grow older with us." Nothing could be more true. I have great difficulty to-day in visualising Gris, who was three years my junior and has now been dead for eighteen years, as anything but a solemn figure of almost my own age, that is to say nearly sixty. Yet his whole painted work was completed between the ages of twenty-three and forty, and I knew only a young man who, despite his fundamental seriousness, was both sociable and gay, except at those terrible moments when he was overwhelmed with gloom. So, since it is an effort even for me to think of Gris as young and smiling, I can well imagine that future generations will think of him as more serious than he was. It is therefore my duty to tell of the Gris I knew, whose tremendous laugh could shake a whole row of any cinema, who delighted in talking, joking and dancing and who loved to tell *gitano* stories (which, to a Spaniard, are the equivalent of Marseillais stories, Scottish stories or Jewish stories); in short, a delightful companion to his friends when his day's work was done. Without these aspects no picture of him would be complete.

II. GRIS' YOUTH

Jose Victoriano Gonzalez, called Juan Gris, was born in Madrid on March 23, 1887. He was the thirteenth of the fourteen children of Gregorio Gonzalez, a Castilian, and of Isabella Perez, an Andalusian.[7] Most of his brothers and sisters died young.

Juan Gris only adopted his pseudonym a short time before coming to Paris. It pleased him and there is, I think, a connection between the name and his work. Whether it has to do with the colour reference

Houses in Paris · 1911

(the word "gris" in French means "grey") or with the suggestion of modesty in the name I cannot tell. Almost all his drawings of the Madrid period are signed "Jose Gonzalez", but when he began to exhibit paintings his instinct was to sign them with a different name from that on his humorous drawings. I have seen some cubist drawings of this period signed "Victoriano Gonzalez", but evidently he decided to abandon this practice, and it is under the name of Juan Gris that he has passed into history.

Gris' family was prosperous and his sister Antonieta[8] has referred to their father as a "*rico commerciante*"; but at a later date, and in circumstances which are unknown to me, Gregorio Gonzalez was ruined. Gris, however, seems to have been brought up as a child of the bourgeoisie. The young Pepe, Pepito, Titito (he was called by all these diminutives) was playful and gay like any other child, and the fact that he was particularly addicted to playing at soldiers—he refused to wear anything but a "real" uniform which was specially made for him—is only interesting because when he finally left Spain he had not done his military service and so, being in no position to pay his exemption tax, was unable to obtain a passport. This caused him a great deal of trouble later in life when he was, at last, able to afford to gratify his desire for foreign travel and might have visited Italy, whose churches and museums he regretted knowing only through reproductions.

According to his sister, Gris' vocation began to show itself around the age of six or seven. "From the day when he was first sent to school," she writes, "he would fill the margins of his exercise books with sketches of his masters, of his school-fellows and of everything he saw, so that he made scarcely any progress with his studies and had to accept many a rebuke both from his teachers and from his parents." It seems, therefore, that there must have been a clash quite early in his life between his natural vocation and the career for which he was destined by his family. Nevertheless, he went on with his studies and finally entered the *Escuela de Artes y Manufacturas*.[9] While he was still there he used to send drawings to *Madrid Comico*, to *Blanco y Negro* and to other illustrated papers, though as a novice he was hardly paid at all. Finally he overcame his parents' opposition and left the school to devote himself

Still-life with Pitcher and Funnel

entirely to painting. It would, however, be a mistake to imagine that his studies had no influence on his mind. One has only to read what he wrote—particularly his lecture "On the possibilities of painting"[10]—to discover the depth of the impression left by his early training: he chooses comparisons from the fields of chemistry and physics, quotes examples from geometry, and in general has a scientific approach. His passion for books on biology was also the result of this education.

The next step was to study art. I often heard Gris talk of his first teacher as an old academic painter. His sister maintains that the man's name was Moreno Carbonero.[11] Gris sought the company of artists, of draughtsmen, and of writers, but of his friends of this period only Enrique Echea and Pedro Penzol kept in touch with him till the end. He met foreign painters who were spending a few years in Madrid; for example, Willy Geiger, a German for whom he designed a book-plate (which is extant), or Kars (from Prague), whom he saw again later in Paris. Then at the age of nineteen he began to feel himself too restricted in Madrid; he was no longer satisfied by what was around him and felt the need of a good breath of fresh air. To his sister Antonieta he confided the secret of his impending departure. They scraped together all the money they could between them, sold everything, including Gris' bed and mattress, and in the end had just enough to pay for his journey. "When he finally landed in Paris," she wrote, "he had just sixteen francs in his pocket."

III. THE PRE-WAR YEARS

The Paris of 1906 which Gris first knew was the Paris of men in top-hats and pointed boots, of women in leg-of-mutton sleeves and long tightly-fitting skirts, of horse-buses, and four-wheelers. He sat down to draw it and earn a living. His sister writes: "He never asked for any help from us and we never heard anything of his real life, his struggles and his privations. He can be called a rebel, but he was also a saint—*puede decirse que fue rebelde, pero un santo.*" Certain it is that he must have needed a great deal of strength to live his new life; but to keep it hidden from his family and never to ask for help must have called for a still greater purity of spirit. Quite apart from the actual labour, how much time must he have spent hawking his drawings from one editorial office to another, how often must he have been snubbed, and in the end how poor was the return! To-day, no such existence would be possible. Indeed it was only possible then because there was a certain ease about life, which bred a spirit of generosity and made it possible for young artists to get credit from landlords, grocers, wine merchants, and paint shops. The walls of Gris' studio were covered with long columns of figures scribbled in charcoal; they were his household expenses—and sometimes they were very long indeed. When the time came to pay he had to send for Reverdy to add them all up.

The growing fame of his compatriot, Picasso, had led Gris to number 13 Rue Ravignan, where he finally established himself. He carried on his work for the illustrated papers, which brought him in enough to live; but at the same time he began to work for himself, and to think. Four years passed before anyone saw his first canvases. Then Clovis Sagot bought some of them, and from that moment Gris gave up his old livelihood for ever. In the spring of 1912 he exhibited at the Salon des Indépendants, which was then held in the glass-houses on the Cours la Reine. In the autumn of the same year he exhibited with the society called the "Section d'Or", which had its headquarters at the Galerie la Boëtie in the Rue la Boëtie, to which it had transferred after one exhibition held in a mezzanine on the Rue Tronchet. With the exception of Braque and Picasso, all the practitioners of Cubism were represented, that is to say at this date not only Léger, Gleizes, Metzinger, Le Fauconnier, Herbin, Delaunay, Marcel Duchamp, Jacques Villon, and Duchamp-Villon, but also De La Fresnaye, Dunoyer de Segonzac, and Luc-Albert Moreau.[12] Besides this Gris had sent some paintings and drawings in the spring of 1912 to a "Cubist Exhibition" organised by the Galerie Dalmau in Barcelona.

It was during the winter of this same year that I became convinced that in this painter, whose development I had been watching for some time, I had in fact discovered an artist as great as I believed; accordingly I contracted with him to buy the whole of his future production, in addition to such pictures as he had in his studio. Henceforth, Gris' pictures were always to be seen in the Rue Vignon, and he gave up exhibiting at the various Salons, like all the other painters whose work I was buying. The first collector who bought a picture by Juan Gris from me was my old friend Hermann Rupf. After him came Gertrude Stein, Léonce Rosenberg, Alfred Flechtheim, the American sculptor Brenner, and some others, amongst them an Italian singer, who subsequently turned out to be the uncle of the painter Magnelli.

From then on Gris was free to paint without being constantly harried by material worries. That summer he left the Rue Ravignan to work in different surroundings for the first time and chose the Roussillon. At the beginning of August he moved to Céret, where he remained until the first of November. From the house where he lived he could see one of the gateways of the old fortifications. One day he sent me a post card, showing the massive towers of this gateway, on the back of which was written: "As you can see, my painting is well protected." In that summer of 1913 the "Mecca of Cubism" was also harbouring Picasso who, as a matter of fact, left rather suddenly about the fifteenth of August; Manolo lived there. Great discussions took place, to which Picasso, as was then his custom, contributed only occasional flashes of wit; on the other hand Gris, whose only concern was for the development of his art, argued every inch of the ground.

A reflection of these conversations can be found in the book by Josef Pla,[13] who reports Manolo as saying: "The one who explained Cubism was the poor Gris." By "the poor Gris", Manolo meant to describe not only his friend, who had died so young, but also the simpleton who explained so seriously his preposterous theories. A few years earlier, Manolo's way of criticising Cubism had been to ask Picasso in front of one of his own pictures: "And what would you say if your parents turned up to meet you on the station at Barcelona with faces like that?" He approached it in a spirit of simple good sense and confused the signs with the thing signified. So, despite his proverbial sharpness, Manolo was incapable of following Gris' arguments. Manolo's own art, a healthy, live growth, rooted in Catalan soil, is not in question; it is one of the sculptural achievements of our time. His art is classical—"Medi-

247

Self-Portrait No. 1 · 1909–10

Portrait of D.-H. Kahnweiler · 1921

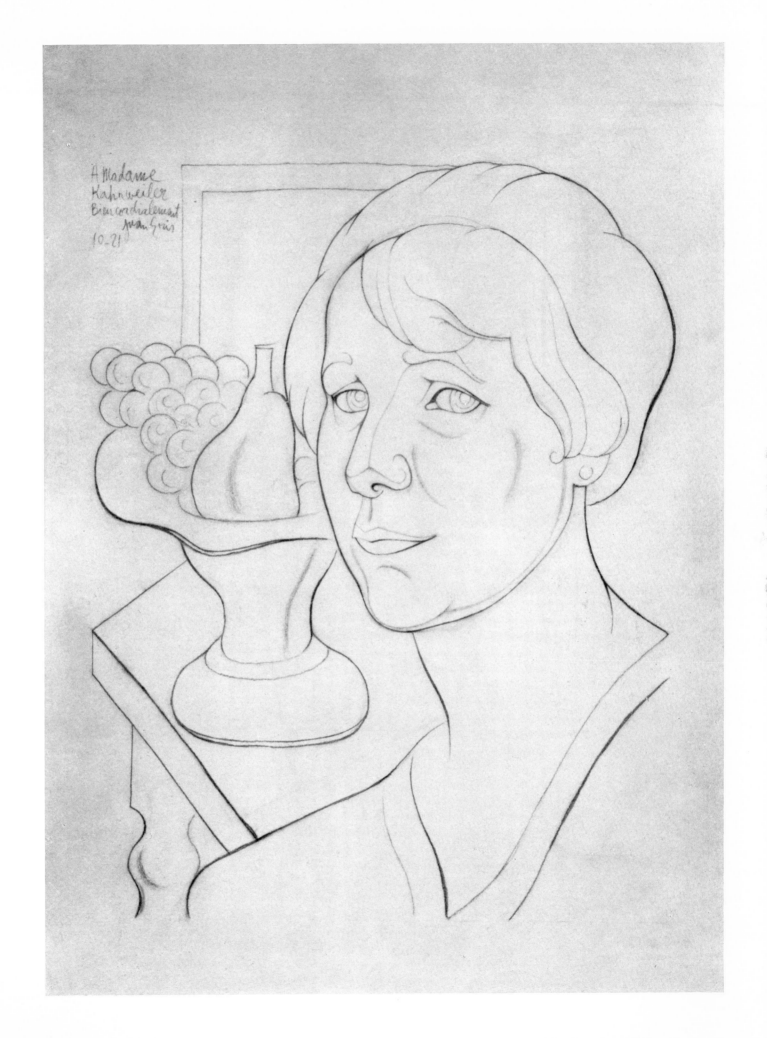

A Madame
Kahnweiler
Bien cordialement
Juan Gris
10-21

Portrait of Madame Lucie Kahnweiler · 1921

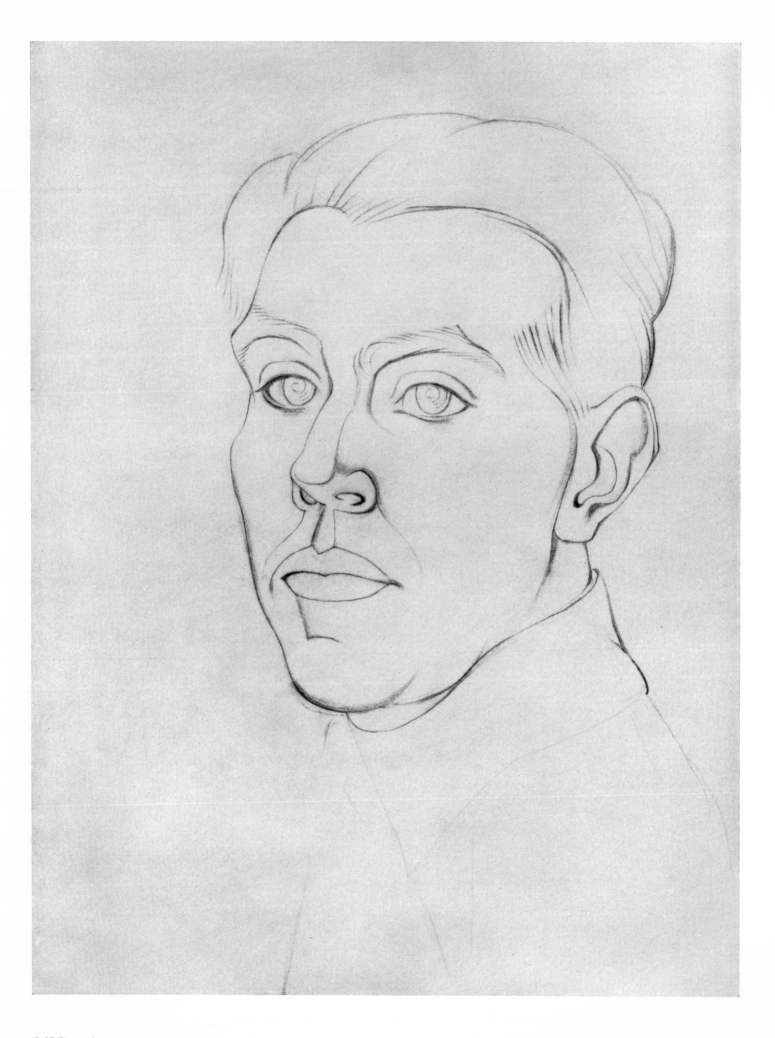

Self-Portrait · 1921

20

terranean art", as it is called in Barcelona—and his classicism is, in fact, justified by its own origins. All that I am disputing here is the intellectual claptrap which he used to justify himself, phrases which he had learnt during evenings spent at cafés like "Vachette" and "La Closerie des Lilas". There he had met Moréas, that other Mediterranean, who was the great admiration of his life. His literary ideal was the Roman School, and his aesthetic philosophy could be summed up in the words of André Chénier: "*Sur des pensers nouveaux, faisons des vers antiques.*"[14]

Cubism meant a complete break with the past and was diametrically opposed to any such outlook; so one can grasp how it must have shocked Manolo to hear Gris maintaining that a new state of mind necessitated a new form of outward appearance. But there was also a certain personal antipathy for, as Manolo was aware, the overscrupulous Gris could not really like his dissolute type of charm.

Gris worked with a will at Céret and wrote to me on September 17: "This is to tell you also that I am about to send off five pictures which I have finished: *The Bullfighter*, *The Banker*,[15] *The Guitar!!!*, *Landscape*, and *Violin and Guitar!!!* Tell me what you think of them, especially of the last two, *The Violin* and *Landscape*. I have worked particularly hard on the latter and cannot decide what I think about it. I like *The Violin* best. As soon as it is dry, that is to say in two or three days, I will send them both to you. I am very happy here and hope to remain until the end of October or the first of November. I am working hard and seem to see much more clearly certain things which I could not manage in Paris."

After the pictures had arrived in Paris I wrote to tell him how pleased I was with them, and also that Picasso had expressed himself favourably. To this he replied: "Thank you very much for your nice letter and the encouragement which it has brought me. You know that I am always worried about doing something foolish, even though I have put all my faith in a great effort. I am comforted to hear yours and Picasso's opinion."

The discussions at Céret were not wasted on Gris. They made it possible for him to become aware of many things touching his own painting. What he had gained showed itself in the far greater simplicity and enhanced clarity of the pictures which he painted after his return to Paris. From then on I saw a great deal of Gris. He would often come and fetch me in the evening from the Rue Vignon and walk with me to the Place de la Concorde, where I caught the steamer to Auteuil. He used to come to our house in the Rue George Sand. Sometimes I would spend the whole morning with him in the Rue Ravignan. I remember clearly one Sunday which we spent together. We had set out for a day on the Seine in our motor-skiff *L'Enchanteur*, named after the book *L'Enchanteur Pourrissant*, by Apollinaire, which I had published. (On the same principle our sailing-boat was called *Saint Matorel*, after a book by Max Jacob, which I had also published.) Besides Gris and ourselves, there was Vlaminck (joint owner of the two boats with us), his wife and three daughters. We were caught in a terrible storm, landed at Rueil in a soaking wet condition, and had to climb up to Vlaminck's home in St. Michel, where we were able to dry ourselves on front of a large fire. But when the good Gris opened his jacket we discovered that he had taken pity on and was carrying our little dog Holda, who found it difficult to walk through the tall wet grass.

47, 246

39, 247

The more I got to know this modest, though intransigeant young man, the more my affection and admiration for him grew. In this period of growing assurance, Gris' faith and his complete lack of scepticism were perhaps even more impressive than the self-confidence of Braque, of Léger, or of Picasso. For their assurance was born of confidence in their own talents, whereas Gris always tended to underestimate his, and had nothing but his heroic constancy on which to rely. Yet there was nothing stiff or priggish about him. By nature he was something of a vain young Spaniard who, whenever he left his studio, liked to be dressed as well as his very limited means would allow.

At that time he was, too, extraordinarily superstitious and was frightened of a hat being put on the bed (which signified the devil in the house), and of hundreds of other such dangerous omens. He, the thirteenth child, was afraid of the figure thirteen. He was buried on the thirteenth. . . . I should, perhaps, add that a few years later he completely overcame all these superstitions. Was this development in some way connected with the books on biology that he took to reading? Or was his enthusiasm for occult literature, which developed towards the end of his life, a sublimation of the mystic ideas which were so essential to him and which in youth assumed the primitive form of superstition? It is not easy to decide, for it is possible that what Gris derived from the works of Fabre d'Olivet and Saint Yves d'Alveydre had nothing to do with mystic contemplation, especially since he always displayed an active hatred of all religions, and particularly of the Catholic religion in which he was brought up. Later on he acquired a taste for table-turning, a taste indulged in with a breath of mockery when he called on "the spirit of Victor Hugo". Sometimes when we were all together of an evening at Boulogne he would try his hand at experiments in levitation and hypnotism. I might also mention here the attempts which he often made during his last few years to order his heart to stop beating. In one of the volumes of *The Men of Goodwill*, Jules Romains describes the astonishment of a certain doctor when confronted with a patient who successfully simulates this condition. It seems to me that Gris really succeeded in the same way.

IV. THE WAR YEARS: 1914–1920

On June 28, 1914, Gris set on a second time for the Roussillon. On the twenty-ninth he wrote to me from Collioure: "We have arrived, after a halt of several hours at Rivesaltes—a barbarous locality with no trees. We left by the first train. It is quite lovely here and I have already rented a nice house, which is marked on the post card." His house was in the Rue de L'Eglise, almost next door to the church, whose belfry rises sheer like a lighthouse from the waters of the harbour. In another letter, dated July 8, Gris wrote: "I have been meaning to write to you for several days, but time passes so quickly. . . . It is not that I spend my days on the beach or in the countryside, for as yet I have neither bathed nor been for even a short walk. I am living in such a charming house that I have not the slightest desire to go out. The house faces the harbour, where all the sailing boats are anchored, and in the early morning

Still-life with Bottles · 1912

(I get up at seven o'clock) I can watch the arrival of the sardine fleet. I spend the whole day on the roof or beside the open window. I have two studios: in one I work, and in the other I prepare and store my canvases. As for work, I have finished nothing so far. For the last week I have been wearing myself out in vain. One thing after another has had to be scrapped. It's no good, or maybe it's better, for everything seems to me topsy-turvy, and the things I was pleased with in Paris look ridiculous here." He also asked me for the address of Picasso, to whom he wanted to write.[16]

He continued to work even though the catastrophe was approaching. Optimists all, we had closed our eyes to the obvious warning signs. But on the first of August it was no longer possible to ignore the danger. Gris wrote me a letter which, like those which followed, I did not receive until several weeks later: "I have no idea where you are, nor whether amid all these troubles of war you will ever receive this letter. At all events, the fact is that in this part of the country the panic is increasing from hour to hour—perhaps the sun has something to do with it. The reservists have been called up, the foreigners, summoned to the Town Hall to declare their closest secrets, have been involved in a mass of fines and proceedings for not having their papers in order, and many of them have even been threatened with expulsion, while the local tradesmen are busy laying in stocks. We have even watched some rusty old cannons being cleaned, while some old things discovered in the artillery barracks were carried off in a large closed vehicle like a 'Black Maria'. Besides this, everybody is discussing the latest news, Jaurès' death and the attempt on Caillaux' life.[17] Is there any truth in it? Is it really true that war is imminent? Personally I do not know what to do. It seems to me more dangerous to return to Paris than to stay here. What do you think? If you really think the situation is getting worse will you please be so kind as to send me three hundred francs, as I have only enough left to keep me going for another three weeks. I apologise for troubling you with this new request, but events force me to anticipate."

The next thing was the declaration of war. Gris was profoundly affected. Everything seemed to collapse, and folly appeared triumphant. His friends were either at the front or scattered. He felt as if he had hardly achieved the possibility of being able to work steadily and to good avail before it had vanished. On August 3 he wrote to me: "I have been almost ordered to leave. That is to say that I was advised to leave, but on my declining to do so unless ordered I was told to hold myself prepared for this eventuality. Where and how shall I go? All the trains have been requisitioned for the mobilisation. Paris? It's risky. Spain? You know I'll have trouble. And then I'm short of money. Write and tell me what you think I had better do."

I had written to Gris from Rome, where I happened to be. Here is his answer, dated August 16: "Your letter which I was so anxiously awaiting has arrived to reassure me about your personal safety. As I said in my last telegram,[18] I have written you two letters and a post card addressed to the Rue Vignon. My letters were written about a fortnight ago, at a time when even I was still optimistic. My good friend, what is to happen to all of us? I have been profoundly touched by your letter, which has made me conscious of the gratitude and friendship I feel for you. It has also reminded me of all our friends who at this moment are fighting and of whom I have heard nothing. I have no news at all and am completely cut off. No news from anybody for at least three weeks and no newspapers from

Henri Matisse
Double-Portrait (Madame Juan Gris)
1914

Paris. I wish I knew whether it would be better for me to go back to Paris or to stay here. Please forgive me for having turned to you for money at this moment, but I don't know what else I could have done. The people in this part of the world are very kind but they don't know me. Sometimes I wonder whether, in order to be fed, I shall not be forced to enlist for a war which makes no appeal either to my nationality, my character, or my ideas. All those of us who had marked out our road through life must change temporally[19] (*sic*) and become I know not what. For I am well aware, my friend, that in the nightmare through which we are passing, previous engagements are no longer valid and each of us must make his own way. How, I do not know. That is why I turned to you as a friend and not as a dealer." At the top of the letter he added: "Where is Picasso?"

In Italy, I too was rather short of money, and not in a position to do much for Gris just then. However, he and Josette were luckily taken in by the parents of one of his friends, and on September 11 he wrote to me: "For the time being we are here and not too unhappy. I have discovered the family of a boy I used to know in Madrid, who has just been seriously wounded and is in a hospital close to the frontier. We are fed morning and evening, and this is a great help. If the war is short we can manage all right like this; but if it goes on very long I don't know what will become of us. Picasso wrote to me a few days ago. He is still in Avignon. It seems that he too has no news of Braque, Derain, or Vlaminck. Have you heard anything? Matisse arrived here yesterday. He tells me that Apollinaire and Galanis have enlisted, and there is talk of Derain having been wounded, because he has not written to his wife. I have also had a letter from Marcoussis. He is a clerk at H.Q. in Besançon; he's always lucky. Brenner has been in Paris, but I have had no news of him for three weeks. Don't worry about us, dear friend, for the moment. Later on, we'll see. For the moment there is no point in thinking too much about the future."

Despite the circumstances, he began to work again. A little later he wrote to me once more (the letter is undated): "We are very happy with this family, who are charming and full of kindness towards us. Ever since I have been in this house I have [started] to work again with enthusiasm. I'm full of new energy; so I should be, after doing nothing for a month. Our hosts were rather astonished by my type of painting. It has been rather tiresome making my *excuses*, but now I have almost broken them in: to the extent indeed that they were so pleased with a canvas, size 25, which I have just finished, that I gave it to them. I have not been very well during the last few days: frequent bouts of faintness and a slight temperature. It will be very annoying if I am ill, as it will upset the whole household. I see a lot of Matisse. We talk painting relentlessly, while Marquet listens and shuffles along. No news of our friends; nor have I had any news from Picasso. No more from Brenner either since the letter which I sent to you. Have had a card from Gertrude Stein. She is in London. Oh, Paris! Paris! Now that my return ticket has expired my last hope of getting back is gone."

One can imagine the sort of discussions that occurred between Gris and Matisse, both of them men inclined to think a great deal about their art, and to talk of it. Both, I am sure, must have benefited by these conversations. It may seem surprising to suggest that Matisse, who was so much older, was somehow influenced by Gris; but if one looks with an unprejudiced eye at the large canvases which Matisse began at Collioure, while he was with Gris, or at those which he painted immediately afterwards, one cannot, I think, fail to notice a certain quality—especially in the structure—which does not appear in his painting either before or after. One might almost call it a new vision; and I am convinced that this new vision was the fruit of his conversations with Gris.

Materially Gris' position was getting worse. Matisse had shown an extraordinary devotion and had tried to arrange with a few collectors that they should each guarantee a small monthly sum so that Gris could eke out a modest existence and carry on with his work. On October 30 Gris wrote to me: "I have not written to you before because I wanted to give you my *latest* news, and this was not possible before to-day. The time has come to leave this household which has been harbouring us; we have been here so long and we cannot abuse their hospitality. But where to go? I thought first of Manolo, in view of what he offered me through Terrus[20] not long ago. So, three weeks ago we went to Céret—Matisse, Marquet, Terrus, and myself—and Manolo suggested in front of the others that I should come to him. He would rent a small house for me and he and Haviland[21] would supply me with vegetables. 'I'll write to you in a couple of days,' he said, 'as soon as I have taken the house.' I am still waiting for his letter. Not only that; I wrote to him reminding him of his promise, but he has not even bothered to answer me. Gertrude Stein, hearing of my difficulties, has been so kind as to send me two hundred francs. Matisse, who has gone to Paris for a few days, has succeeded in arranging with Gertrude and Brenner that, between them, I shall receive one hundred and twenty-five francs a month. Although it is very little for two of us, we intend going to Paris as soon as Matisse gets back here." There was also news of various painters in the army. "Matisse writes from Paris . . . that Derain is in the front line . . . Vlaminck is painting for the army in Le Havre . . . Gleizes has been wounded, and Segonzac too. De La Fresnaye, who volunteered, is at the depot and sick. I have no news of Braque, about whom I am most concerned."

This was followed by a sudden return to Paris (on the very day, in fact, on which this letter was posted), resulting from his discovery that his railway tickets were still valid until the following day. I was informed in a letter that he wrote on November 6: "We arrived last Sunday, after a journey lasting thirty-three hours, during which we were unable either to sleep or to eat owing to the number of people on the train. I am very happy to be back again in my old studio, which has been repainted." But unfortunately the arrangement which had been fixed by Matisse broke down, because Gris, who was so scrupulously honest, could not reconcile what was asked of him in exchange with the rights which he considered were still mine. He was dropped—temporarily—by Gertrude Stein, though not by Brenner.

As I had moved to Bern in the meanwhile, I was again able to pay Gris' living expenses. Then other collectors began to make him offers. On January 14, 1915, he wrote me the following: "M. Rosenberg visited me with the intention of buying something. He was very discreet and did not insist when I told him that I considered myself as still bound by our agreement. He fully understood and approved of my behaviour." But other people were of a different opinion. In a letter written on March 26 Gris says: "Let me tell you that the troubles of a painter who refuses to sell anything are worse than those of a painter from whom no-one will buy. I emphasise this because, before you came along, there was no-one who wanted to buy the very pictures which are now causing me so much trouble." Finally, in April, we had to bow to the fact that our business arrangement could not be continued and it was annulled by common agreement. On April 19 Gris wrote to me: "Believe me, life at this time is not much fun, and I who was so fond of Paris would be glad to leave it. I do nothing but fret and am bored all the time."

We kept in touch by letter until the end of the year, but then our correspondence ceased. On June 1 Gris wrote to me: "Apart from unpleasant things I too have nothing to tell you. You asked for news of Braque. He has been badly wounded but is now out of danger. Yesterday he was moved to a hospital here and I hope to see him to-morrow. He got a bullet in the head and has been trepanned. We have known for the last fortnight that he had been wounded, but no details. He did not want anybody to know so long as he was on the danger list. He is a wonderful man. I have been terribly worried for, as you know, I am very fond of him. Derain is still well behind the front line." On August 4 he wrote again: "Life is as monotonous as ever and full of privation. I am hard at work and see hardly anyone. I desperately wish it were all over and keenly regret the past. What's more, I wonder whether the evil which the present has brought us can ever be put right. Braque is recovering. He is still in hospital but can go out every day. I often think of you and of all the good you have done me. There are times now when I think that it is all over and that after the war it will be impossible ever to sell a picture. You know that I am always pessimistic."

On September 7: "It is very kind of you to give me encouragement as you did in your last letter. I see only too well that, knowing me as you do, you are thinking of how I must be worrying. At times I too am as optimistic as you are and believe in a rosy future. But that is only when the sun shines. Right now I live in fear, especially of the approaching winter. ... Nowadays, when I have finished my work I don't read blood-and-thunder novels [in an earlier letter he had talked of reading Alexandre Dumas *Ed.*], but work at portraits from life. They are very good likenesses, and I will soon have acquired as much skill as any winner of the *Prix de Rome*. It's fun for me all the time to learn how it is done. I can't get over it: I always thought it was far more difficult."

Modest as ever, Gris underestimated his gifts. At a later date—when he was working for the Russian Ballets—I, too, was astonished at the extreme dexterity which he possessed, in addition to his other more important gifts.

His letter goes on: "I do not see many people, for I hardly leave Montmartre. I scarcely ever go to Montparnasse. Those bohemian cafés, the Rotonde and the Dôme, become more and more horrible. I'm all for the domestic life of Montmartre, where one can meet in friendly studios without ever going to cafés. Braque is improving."

In Part II of this book I have quoted an important passage from the last of this series of letters, which is dated December 14, 1915, and ends as follows: "I must apologise to you for discussing things which, at the present grave moment, must appear to you purely silly. But I have worried so much that I am now going to shut myself off and think of nothing but my work. I don't want to hear anything more, especially as everything which is now happening seems to me both useless and devoid of good sense."

The fact that Gris was able to carry on at all with his work was due to Léonce Rosenberg. This dealer, who had previously bought from me pictures by Picasso and Gris, took over during the war—and it is to his lasting credit—the role which I could no longer fulfil, that of the patron of Cubism. He took over in difficult circumstances—for he was in the army—and posterity should not overlook his five years of tireless effort. He began to buy pictures from Gris in the spring of 1915 and signed a contract with him in 1917.

Gris' monotonous and baneful existence, which is reflected in his letters, was broken in the summer of 1916 by a holiday in Josette's native Touraine, at Beaulieu near Loches. Gris was enchanted by the nobility and softness of this corner of France. Then it was Paris again, with its restrictions, artists' canteens, and lack of heating. One day Josette, with a group of other women, helped in "acquiring" a lorry full of coal. Next came the air-raid warnings, the Zeppelin raids, and the nights spent sheltering in the underground tunnel between the stations Abbesses and Lamarck-Caulaincourt, or watching the Zeppelins, the searchlights, and the anti-aircraft fire from a friend's studio in the Rue Caulaincourt, which looked out over all the northern suburbs. Gradually there was built up in Paris during the last years of the war a strange, frenzied atmosphere in which those who had remained lived, which was feverishly fanned by those on leave and which reached its zenith in the orgies of November 11, 1918. There was Montparnasse and the night walks back to Montmartre through icy, unlighted streets. But there was also another form of excitement in the ardent intellectual life: little reviews like *Nord-Sud* and *SIC* made their appearance, and the Russian Ballet, revived with the collaboration of Picasso and Satie, at last emerged from the shadows and became a focus for *Les Six*. Apollinaire, Max Jacob, and Reverdy got a hearing. Reverdy had become an intimate friend and (since he lived in the Rue Cortot) neighbour of Gris. So too had Max Jacob. Both paid frequent calls, bringing with them many other

The Watch (The Sherry Bottle) · *1912*

painters and poets. People came and went all the time at the Rue Ravignan, and the animation was only interrupted for a few months when the bombardments by "Big Bertha" caused many of his friends temporarily to abandon Paris. In April, Gris and Josette left Paris to spend the spring and summer at Beaulieu, where they were joined by various friends such as Lipchitz, whose seriousness appealed to Gris, Maria Blanchard, and Metzinger. They bathed and went for walks. I have heard from Lipchitz that Gris, who was as modest in his daily life as in his art, had an extreme distaste for undressing in public when they went bathing. In the autumn they all went home. Then came the Armistice, and the nightmare was over.

We resumed our correspondence in the summer of 1919. Gris' first letter, dated August 25, begins thus: "Your letter, which I received this morning, after such a long time without news, has brought me great pleasure." There follows news of our mutual friends, and then the passage about his painting, which is quoted in Part II of this book. In April 1919, Rosenberg had exhibited Gris' latest works. I had written to tell him how impatient I was to see them. On September 3 he replied: "I have been greatly touched by your letter and by the interest in me which you expressed in it. Still, you must not think of my painting as being better than it in fact is. If I am sometimes able to push a picture to a successful conclusion, it is due more to my understanding of the language of art than to my experience of actual painting. This lack of experience means that, though my feelings and my thoughts are well under control, the same is not always true of the point of my brush. My work in its present stage can be likened to Seurat's pictures, in which the harshness and the fumbling are due to inexperience and not to incompetence. I could not say the same of Braque, whose experience is now beginning to be considerable and sufficient to enable him to bring off some masterly works. (It is perhaps wrong of me to speak so well of him, for he has not behaved well towards me.) Picasso is still doing fine work, when he has time in between a Russian ballet and a society portrait. As for the others, nothing very exciting. Léger still has fine qualities, but he inclines more and more towards dadaist excesses. We have a new recruit in Severini, who has given up Futurism during the last two or three years. There is the sculptor Laurens, a friend of Braque and to some extent his pupil. Of the young ones, the sculptor Lipchitz is probably the most serious and has the nicest character. In my opinion he has a great future, for he is developing well and has made great progress in a very short time.

"The most astonishing thing is the sudden crop of poets. Reverdy is one of the leaders and one of the best; he has influenced a great many of the younger ones. There are some extraordinary ones like Radiguet, who is barely seventeen, and has written some charming things. It is the Reverdy school which is most akin to our painting; they are breaking away more and more from Cendrars and Tzara. There are some young musicians too, but I don't understand anything about music. For instance, there is Auric, who is only twenty but is much admired."

On November 15 he wrote again: "I have not been to the Salon d'Automne but I have been told by friends that there is nothing of interest. It appears that Matisse is the only one who is any good. … The cold and the lack of coal prevent me working, and I am very bored."

Then on December 22: "I apologise for not having answered your letters sooner; I have been prevented from doing so by the fit of hard work which is upon me just now. For, when I have put away my easel, I am very tired. For more than a month I have done nothing, and now I have to catch up. ... The Salon des Indépendants opens in February and I mean to exhibit there."

Indeed this Salon of 1920 was to be a sort of common (though passing) Cubist front. With the exception of Picasso, both the greater and the lesser Cubists exhibited. The worm was, however, already in the fruit, and this unity was no more than an appearance, as one can now see. On January 8 Gris wrote to me: "I have been working hard during the last few days, finishing my pictures for the Indépendants, which is to open in the month of February. I am only showing two, both canvases of 30, a Seated Man and a Still Life. I am not displeased with the colour, but I am afraid on that account, for it seems to me my weakness." Then, after the opening, he wrote to me on January 31: "The Salon des Indépendants opened with something of a success for the Cubists, who were taken seriously by almost the whole of the press. Even Monsieur Vauxcelles admitted that he had wronged us. Braque and Léger have been well received because they took a good deal of trouble about it. As for Metzinger, he has been almost re-established, although his contribution is not remarkable; I am almost overlooked because I am a foreigner.

"However, several people have been loud in their praise of me. Picasso has given me a lot of support and Gertrude Stein, with whom I have not been on good terms, told me that one of my pictures was the best in the whole Salon. On the other hand, Braque refused to be hung in the same room with me, and is decrying me for all he is worth. But after all, none of these troubles are serious, for, if I am satisfied with my work, nothing can dishearten me; and if I am dissatisfied, no amount of praise can comfort me."

On February 7 he wrote: "It is very kind of you to think of writing something about me, especially now when I have been overlooked at the Indépendants. There is no explanation for Metzinger's success, and even he must be rather surprised. Here are a few details about myself: born in Madrid on March 23, 1887; studied something of physics and mathematics. Never attended the School of Fine Arts but spent a very short time—less than two years—in the studio of an old official artist, who promptly gave me a distaste for *good* painting. Arrived in Paris in 1906 and fell straight into the studio of Picasso, where I met the gang of Apollinaire, Max, Salmon, etc. ... Sold the first things to Sagot in 1911; exhibited at the Indépendants in 1912 and at the 'Section d'Or' in the same year."

What Gris worried over was not the future of his own work, but that of the common cause. It is even possible that his view was right and that we are so blinded by the brilliance (not to say genius) of certain individuals, that we do not yet realise that the collective impulse which might have developed into a true style was shattered by the war of 1914-18. And by "style" I mean a form of common plastic expression whose idiom would have been strong enough to support the ventures of even the weaker exponents. There can be no question but that the works of the masters of Cubism still hold good as imperishable masterpieces, which have left their mark on the whole field of contemporary art. They have not, however, produced any stylistic concentration, but have given rise to a considerable diversity of outward appearance. Cubism contained, perhaps, the seeds of a truly creative style, a quality which seems to have disappeared since the days of the Renaissance with its concept of plastic illusionism. Yet if this quality is absent, painters will only be surrounded by imitators and will never find worthy disciples. However, be that as it may. Nothing communal developed out of Cubism, despite its potentialities, so that, in contrast to a Cimabue or a Giotto, Braque, Gris, Léger and Picasso remained isolated figure-heads.

On December 2, 1919, Gris had written to me: "As for the future of our painting, I am distinctly alarmed lest a serious effort be swallowed up in the waves of Dadaism and Futurism. I have been looking through the numbers of *Der Sturm*,[22] which Raynal showed me, and it makes me sick. What a wrong direction all that has taken! It is nothing but wild stylisation.[23]

"Courbet is much in vogue this year. Somebody is trying to put him across and send up the prices, and the painters are following like a lot of sheep. Courbet is their only god. As for Delacroix, Cézanne, Ingres and Renoir—nothing but horse droppings."

Feeling the lack of a real "style", which could have given to our own time that unity which we admire so much in some of the great periods of the past, and despairing of its birth, Gris detached himself from all who, in his opinion, had taken the wrong turning. He began to concentrate only on his own work and gradually discovered his strength. On February 17 he wrote to me: "I have seen some recent works by Braque, which I find soft and lacking in precision. He is moving towards Impressionism. It is with some pleasure that I register my dislike, and it takes a great weight off my back; for I was such an admirer of his painting that I was crushed by it."

A few days later I arrived in Paris and our meeting was a very happy one. I had recently seen a Cubist

Guitar and Glass · 1918

Exhibition organised by Léonce Rosenberg at the Galerie Moos in Geneva, and had been struck by Gris' enormous progress. Now, both in his studio, at Léonce Rosenberg's, the "Section d'Or", and the Indépendants (there were exhibitions at both), I saw still later pictures which bore witness to continued progress. I had left behind a young painter whose works I liked. I had returned to find a master.

V. FIRST ILLNESS

Gris was looking very ill. In his letter of December 22 he had complained of being tired at the end of the day's work. Yet he continued to work until he took to his bed at the beginning of May 1920. Josette sent a note informing me of his illness, which was at first thought to be pneumonia. In the end it developed into pleurisy. At the start Josette looked after him in the studio with great devotion and did everything possible. A sheet was stretched with string across the skylight to tone down the hardness of the light and shut out draughts. But, as his condition got worse, it was no longer possible to leave Gris in such unhygienic conditions amid dirt and discomfort. So he was moved to the Tenon Hospital, where a doctor whom he knew had been able to get him a private room. I often used to go and see him. In order to get to his room one had to go through a large ward in which moribund, consumptive old men lay coughing and spitting. Gris' room, luckily, was not unpleasant, and although he was very depressed he bore bravely and with resignation his long and complicated illness, the shattering cough, and the fixation abscess which was induced. In July, at last he started to get better, and on August 12, the day after he left the hospital, we accompanied him and Josette to the Gare d'Orsay, where they took the train to Beaulieu.

He wrote to me from Beaulieu on August 15: "I stood the journey better than I had expected, but I have been suffering from an exhaustion which is only beginning to pass off to-day. However, I can feel that the air here is doing me good, for I have a large appetite and sleep better than in the hospital."

Again on August 26: "As I am beginning to feel stronger I shall try to paint. To-day Josette brought me two canvases from Loches. I can't walk yet, because my leg has not healed. Until now I have been drawing every day and have filled about twelve pages of my sketch-book. I don't know how it will be with my painting, and am keen to begin. I think it will be impossible to take up my work again exactly where I left off more than three months ago. I am very glad to hear that you are opening the gallery on the first of the month. Indeed, it was a real pleasure to see your notepaper printed with the gallery heading."

He gave away this first series of pencil drawings to friends, an action which perhaps expressed his gratitude to the Fates who had spared his life. He was aware, as we have seen, that his painting would not be the same as it had been before his illness.

On September 25 he wrote again: "Nothing new to tell you since my last letter. My pictures are getting on and so is the time of year. The weather is poor and it begins to feel cold already."

His last letter from Beaulieu was dated October 21: "We have decided to leave because, after the dampness of the last few days, I begun to feel my chest a bit, and am afraid to stay. We will take the train on Saturday and get to Paris in the evening."

When he left "Les Fourneaux"[24] Gris was cured, but clearly his chest was still weak. It was, therefore, impossible for him to spend the winter in Paris, especially not in the Rue Ravignan. So, towards the end of November, he and Josette moved to Bandol in the Var, where they stayed *chez* Mme. Toucas, 4 Rue Nationale.

Both Gris and I had felt during our new meeting that nothing should be allowed to part us again. Yet Gris would certainly not have broken his contract with Léonce Rosenberg. He had even sent to me in Bern, in the autumn of 1919, those pictures of 1914 and 1915, to which he thought I was entitled, and which he had faithfully kept for me. He told Rosenberg, whose three-year contract with him was due to expire in the spring of 1920. When Rosenberg renewed his agreement, he only contracted for canvases of specified dimensions, so that I was able to arrange with Gris to take all the others. But Gris and Rosenberg quarrelled at the time of the former's illness, and as a result Gris painted nothing of a size to which Rosenberg was entitled, because he did not want to sell anything more to him. So all Gris' subsequent work came straight to the gallery which I had just started with my friend André Simon: the Galerie Simon, 29bis Rue d'Astorg. This arrangement lasted until Gris' death.

After his arrival at Bandol, Gris wrote to me on December 1: "The sun is wonderful, but what a sinister landscape! Everything is as beautiful as can be, but how sad! We could not stay in the house where we had taken rooms, for it was in a narrow street with a tall house in front, and the rooms were dark. However, we found a single room right on the edge of the sea; it is not very light either, but it is more pleasant than the other place. It is not too well furnished and costs one hundred francs, but I have only paid for one month. In front of the room is a sort of verandah, not very large, enclosed with trellis like a tea-garden, where I shall try and work. There is running water, a W.C., and electricity. Since yesterday, when the electric wiring was put in, I have counted four breakdowns already. Last night and tonight, three times. As I write, it is six o'clock in the evening. So we must expect a few little interruptions before we go to bed. To-morrow I am going to have a look at one of the attics in the house to see about working up there. The temperature here is very agreeable, but in the bright sunlight the landscape looks gloomy. It is warmer beside the harbour, where we are living, than in the streets or on the roads running away from the sea. We have found this out during some of our long walks." Then he adds: "Half-past six, fifth breakdown; light came on again at seven-twenty. Half-past seven, sixth breakdown; light came on again five minutes later." Across this is written, in Josette's handwriting: "It is all due to the mistral, which breaks the wires."

Gris was more encouraging in a letter to me of December 6: "No, no, my friend, I'm not bored. When I first arrived I found this part of the world rather sad, but I'm beginning to get used to it. Besides, I have a large attic to work in." He then went on to discuss his work on the illustrations for *Ne Coupez Pas*, by Max Jacob.

324

Gris and Josette had begun to settle down to the life of Bandol, and now tried to find some amuse-

35

ment. In his letter of December 27 Gris wrote: "We spent a fine Christmas Eve in the Grand Casino of Bandol. We might almost have been at the Opera in Paris. It cost us ten francs a head. Supper was delicious, with *tripes Lyonnaises*. There were not many people, but we were quite amused."

On December 30 he wrote again: "You don't know how pleased I am that you liked the lithographs.[25] On the strength of it we'll go out and celebrate New Year's Eve at the Grand Casino (this time the supper is down to eight francs)."

Besides this letter we had a post card with best wishes for the New Year. He had drawn a still-life over a view of Bandol harbour, making use of the given forms (ships, etc.).

All his letters at this time contain directions for printing the lithographs, and on January 10, 1921, he adds: "I am working on several things, including two seascapes, real ones, with boats. I am not sure yet whether they will be successful. I am not dissatisfied with the still-lifes, for they look rather good. In the next few days I am going to start on a picture, size 40,[26] which I have had in mind for a long time."

Bandol proved favourable for his painting, and on January 15 he wrote to me: "For once I am happy about my work. To-day I finished a still-life, size 12, with which I am quite pleased. Others are coming along nicely. The seascapes, alas, are much more difficult to control. I have also begun a canvas, size 40M, a still-life with the sea and hills in the background. There seems so be nothing wrong with the composition, but I don't yet know whether it will be a success. Generally speaking, the canvases at which I am working are well composed, and the colour contrasts are less strong than before. I like these colour schemes better, though they are more in related than in strong tones."

Again on January 21: "As a matter of fact I am quite pleased with the things that are more or less finished, though one of the seascapes is a failure and has had to be abandoned, and the other is causing me a lot of trouble. The large picture has been filled in and won't be bad. The work was done by my pupil, a boy of eleven, who is astonishingly gifted and says he only wants to paint like that. He is the butcher's son.[27] I shall have finished four or five pictures (not including the big one, obviously) in the next week or ten days, and unless anything unforeseen occurs will send them to you right away. You must not form too high an opinion of them in advance, for I may be mistaken in my judgement and then you will be disappointed when you see them." 323 (3)

Four pictures were sent on February 2. "Tell me what you really think about them," he wrote. "Personally I am quite pleased and think they are better than the last Paris ones, but perhaps I am mistaken. One seascape has been destroyed, and I am so ashamed of the other that I did not want to send it to you. The canvas of 40 is progressing gradually and I am starting on other things."

I wrote and told him how much I liked his pictures, and on February 10 he replied: "You can't imagine how delighted I was to hear that you liked the pictures. I have no bad memories, either of them or of the remorse which so often seizes me after I have despatched some pictures." The continuation of this letter will be found in Part II of this book, but it concludes with some news of his health: "Although I am not very strong, my health is good. I feel terribly exhausted at times, but that is all."

His letters reveal unmistakeably the gradual return of his *joie de vivre*, which brought with it the need for work and for recreation. It was at this time that he developed his passion for dancing: "My pupil is very lazy, like everybody here be it added, and there's no way of getting him to do anything. I have been filling his head with all sorts of ideas about painting which he probably can't understand, but they will be of use to him one day no doubt. The remaining seascape—I have destroyed the other—is not good enough, and there is nothing to do about it. I am having a lot of trouble too with the 40 canvas. I'm afraid it will end in a catastrophe. ... Last Sunday night I put on fancy dress to go to a dance: it was Carnival. I had a fine Senegalese costume, quite authentic, with a head-dress and weapons, which had been lent to me. My face was painted like a fetishist mask."

On February 25, 1921, he announced that he would shortly be sending me three small canvases: "You must tell me what you think of them and whether they are as good as the earlier ones. I am not very happy about the small one with the flowers. If you don't like it, don't hesitate to say so, and chuck it out. I am more certain of the others, for I am better able to judge them. The size 40 has been resting lately but I am going to take it up again. I am also starting a size 31, that is to say a canvas of 95 × 61. I have made a drawing of my pupil's head from which I shall probably make a lithograph. ... I have learnt to dance, more or less, and we go every Sunday night to the Bal des Joyeux Bandolais. I need hardly tell you that, now we have got to know a number of people, there are several who come to look at my pictures; and they don't appear too horrified."

He was a little worried to learn from the newspapers of an exhibition of his pictures at Léonce Rosenberg's. I was able to reassure him that the exhibition consisted of earlier pictures, but was very fine.

"Here there is a procession to look at my pictures," he wrote to me on March 1. "In general, people approve; but yesterday I had a violent discussion, which almost ended badly, with an old painter from here who was up in arms against such pictures. He told me the perspective was all wrong. Indeed, it was rather painful, for I trounced him in front of a large audience. What ignorance and what folly! On the other hand, the local butcher has become a great friend of mine and is very enthusiastic about my work. He even wanted to buy one of the pictures which I am sending to you: the one with the jug and the curtains in the background. He hesitated when I told him that he would have to buy it from you, and gave him an approximate estimate of the price he would have to pay. By way of consolation, I have promised him a photograph of the picture. He is my pupil's father and, though he is an ignorant, uncultured man, he has a rare intelligence."

The new consignment of pictures was a long time on the way, so Gris, who was worried, telegraphed to me. Then on March 12 he wrote to me: "Please accept my apologies, old man, for the telegram. Your letter arrived at the same time as the reply. I was so worried at the lack of news about the pictures that, for two days, I was unable to work; and so Josette decided that, to allay my fears, she would send you a telegram. I am greatly relieved by what you say about these pictures. Although I feel that things are going well, I am nevertheless afraid of storing up a shock for myself. The canvas of 40 has given me a lot of trouble, but yet I have brought it off and, except for a few small details, it is so to speak 323 (2)   finished. I have, too, almost completed the portrait of a very pretty woman; I will soon be sending you 323 (3)   the lithograph,[28] and the portrait of the child. I think, by the way, that I will do some more figures from life in lithograph. ... I have been a bit on edge recently owing to my pictures and to the news in the papers. But don't think, because of that, that I'm fed up. Quite the contrary! I'm very happy here, and when work is over we go off and dance with the neighbours, one of whom is the young lady of the portrait. ... I can't say the same for my health, for it is still not what it used to be. I often have difficulty with my breathing and sometimes have twinges of pain in the back; so I don't think it would be wise to return to Paris."

His letter of March 30 reads: "I am delighted by what you say about the 40 canvas. As a matter of fact I'm rather pleased with it. On the other hand, the 31, the figure (Spanish woman with a guitar), is in a very bad way and I don't know whether I can rescue it. I am starting on a new 40, of which I have hopes. ... We have been dancing a lot during the Easter holidays. After the ball on Sunday a whole party of twelve or fourteen of us went to supper with the fair Marcelle[29] and stayed dancing until three o'clock in the morning. Marcelle is the cousin of the young musician whom I sent to you."

323 (1)
323 (4)

Again on April 9: "I have finished a canvas, size 40 Marine. It is rather free in style and has a not unpleasing popular look, but that does not mean that I have employed a popular idiom. It has, if I am not mistaken, a sort of Derain air." He was thinking of experimenting with a new process for reproducing drawings "by ferroprussiate, like engineers' drawings". But in the end he did not use it.

This calm life of work and amiable distraction was broken into by a telegram from Diaghilew, and on April 14 Gris wrote: "I have this minute received a telegram from Diaghilew asking me to do the sets and costumes for a ballet. He has invited me to go to Monte Carlo on Monday to discuss it with him. It is an awful nuisance, because if I refuse I will be chucking away a golden opportunity, since a ballet will help to make me known and bring me admirers, whereas if I accept I will be chucking away my glorious tranquillity. What is your opinion?"

Next day he wrote again: "This question of doing a ballet is disturbing my peace of mind, but really I dare not refuse. It can make my name known to a certain public which is not to be despised. I shall have to come to Paris on this account, but hope not to be there long; indeed, for as short a time as possible."

The ballet project was abandoned, but not without upsetting Gris. On April 26, 1921, he wrote me from Monte Carlo: "I have been here since Monday, and am very bored. The ballet project has not come off.[30] Diaghilew told me that my reply to his telegram arrived too late and so he made other arrangements. I don't rightly know what happened. ... I was so disappointed that I wanted to go back at once to Bandol, but Diaghilew asked me to do portrait drawings of the leading male[31] and female[32] dancers for the souvenir programme of the season. ... So I am still here doing the two drawings, which I shall transfer to lithographic paper when I get back to Bandol, that is to say in three or four days. ... I am in a great hurry to get back to Bandol, for I can't stand this sort of Universal Exhibition landscape, where one sees nothing but bad architecture, people with idiotic expressions or intriguers. True, I spend a great deal of time with Diaghilew, Larionow, or the dancers, but they are all Russians, that is to say eccentrics of one sort or another. Then there is the new Spanish star whose portrait I am doing. So I need not tell you that I go to bed almost as bad-tempered as I get up."

He was back at Bandol on April 29 and wrote to me: "I returned the day before yesterday, very

Violin and Guitar · 1913

tired after eight days in Monte Carlo, drawing and being bored. I have transferred the portraits on to lithographic paper here and sent them off immediately to Diaghilew. The portraits of Larionow[33] and Slavinsky are, I think, pretty good, but I am not very happy about the one of the Spanish dancer. However, I sent it all the same. Diaghilew will visit you to look at the lithographs which you have and discuss the colours in which these are to be done."[34] Gris added that he had met Gertrude Stein at Monte Carlo, also Matisse, "who has done for the same programme the portrait of a Russian musician whose ballet is being given".

In his letter of May 18 Gris first mentioned the accident which was to spoil the end of his stay at Bandol: Josette had pricked her right thumb on an aloe leaf, and a whitlow had begun to form. They had also been visited by Gertrude Stein and Miss Toklas. "Kisling has written me an enthusiastic letter about some pictures of mine which he has seen in the gallery. I was not expecting that."

"I am really very worried about Josette," Gris wrote on May 24. "Her finger is not improving at all. It is no laughing matter I assure you, more especially as I myself am not awfully well and am having trouble with my breathing."

On May 28: "Josette is just back from Toulon, where she had an operation yesterday in a clinic. She is very dejected. They gave her an anaesthetic and amputated the terminal phalanx of her finger."

A fortnight later they were preparing to amputate the rest of the finger, but luckily this operation was postponed and, ultimately, proved unnecessary. Gris, however, wanted to work, and on June 10 he wrote: "I shall be very sorry to leave here for, despite everything which has happened, I feel greatly set up by my work and in a mood to tackle all sorts of things." Nevertheless, Gris left Bandol on June 22 and, after spending a few days at Le Cannet, arrived in Paris in the middle of the summer. This summer he was alone and, as we too were in Paris, he spent many days in our garden at Boulogne, where he drew the portraits of my two sisters-in-law, my wife, and myself.   18,19

There could be no question of spending the winter in the Rue Ravignan; anyway, his doctors were absolutely against it. So, towards the end of October, Gris and Josette left for Céret. They missed their connection at Perpignan and were held up for five hours; but they discovered a public dance hall and spent the time dancing, "to loosen up our limbs" as Josette described it. Having reached Céret, they took rooms in the Hotel Garretta, and on November 6 Gris wrote: "We have been here a week and I am beginning to get accustomed to it. I was very depressed for the first few days, but now it is all right and I have already done a little work. No doubt the air is doing me good, for I have a large appetite and I think I'm getting visibly fatter. However, there is nothing to let in this neighbourhood and so we are, and will be, in a hotel for a long time yet. Our room, it is true, is large enough and light enough for me to work in, and the food is not too bad. It costs twenty-two francs a day for the two of us, which is reasonable; but this hotel life is unaccountably boring, I don't know why. We see the Manolos every day; they are very nice and have received us most kindly. I think we shall stay here, for I could not bear living in a smaller place where I knew no-one."

Although he knew a great many people, Gris had very little real contact with the inhabitants of Céret. On December 11, 1921, he wrote to me: "This part of the world is not at all sympathetic and is certainly more deadening than Provence or Touraine. I'm not bored, because I work from morning to night and am satisfied with what I have done. I never go out and am cut off from all intellectual contacts, for there is no-one here to whom one could talk—not even Manolo, for he hates my painting and everything else I like. I even keep off risky topics for fear of violent arguments. So you can guess how much I miss our discussions on aesthetics and the intellectual stimulus I derived from them. To keep my mind from absolute stagnation I read books on biology which are lent to me by the Sub-Prefect. I wanted to read some novels, but I just can't swallow them, no matter by whom they are."

I have mentioned earlier Gris' predilection for works on biology. In literature he only liked volumes of poetry. His work continued to prosper. "I have just finished a canvas of 31 and another of 12, with which I am quite pleased," he wrote on December 23. "I have a 40 and a 12 under way, but I am really enthusiastic about a picture I am beginning of the white peak of the Canigou covered with snow. ... My best wishes to all of you for Christmas; I am sorry indeed, my friend, that I cannot be with you." But Gris and Josette were able to indulge their passion for dancing even though, despite Gris' protests, no Ball was given by the Sub-Prefect.

On January 3, 1922, Gris wrote again: "Thank you for your kind letter. There has not been much jollity here over the holidays and I would very much sooner have spent them with you. On New Year's Eve we won the fox-trot prize. Josette was very proud of the bag of sweets which she won." Then, turning to his real preoccupations, Gris went on: "Yes, Waldemar is mistaken about the meaning of induction and deduction.[35] He says: 'Gris works by induction, for he goes from the general to the particular.' But this is deduction. It is a mistake in words but not in understanding. By the way, Severini has gone rather too far in *L'Esprit Nouveau*, claiming the deductive theory as his own, and even taking as an example the cylinder and the bottle which I used in the E.N.[36] Needless to say, he has quite forgotten to mention my name (I am writing to Ozenfant about it). I have received the copy of *Kunstblatt* with Raynal's article about myself, and a very nice card from Westheim. It is a pity that they have not put the dates under the pictures."

He felt very cut off at Céret, and on January 12 he wrote: "No-one but you writes to me from Paris. It is very annoying to feel so forgotten." Then on January 26: "It is still cold here and the oil-stove gives us headaches. I am working at three compositions with figures; I am hopeful. You must tell me what you think of the last canvases, for I am sometimes afraid of losing the thread down here." In a second letter, written that same evening, he continued: "It is very disappointing not to have had a letter from you and I am afraid that you do not like my last pictures but cannot bring yourself to say so. Maybe I was wrong, but I was rather pleased with those pictures."

The fact was that my letter, in which I told him of my pleasure at his latest work, had been delayed; I also mentioned my distress at the feeling of isolation to which he gave expression in his letters. In a letter of February 5 he reassured me: "Don't think I am as bored as all that. Time passes quickly and we can hardly realise that we have been here more than three months already. The climate evidently suits me for I have got fatter. Last Sunday I weighed myself and am now nearly eighty kilos.[37] True, the only exercise I take is dancing. At present I am giving lessons to those ladies of the sub-Prefec-

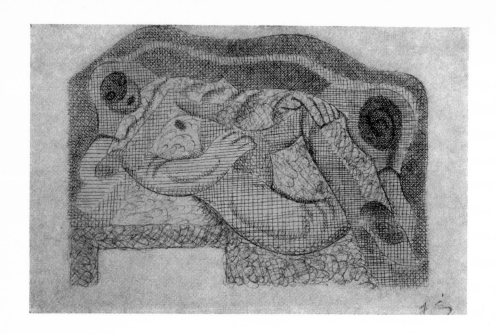

Reclining Harlequin · 1923

ture who want to cut a good figure at the Carnival balls. I am working at a picture of a seated pierrot; it is quite far advanced and looks rather good. I think it is much better than the one I did in Paris.

"I have not yet heard anything about the Salon des Indépendants, except from your wife's letter to Josette enclosing the circular from Picabia. Was there any good picture there? This isolation encourages me to feel less unhappy about my own work, but I wonder whether that is due to atrophy or to the fact that I am more completely master of my art. Whichever it is, I no longer feel such disgust for my own painting as I used to."

"Gertrude Stein has not written to me as you said she would," he wrote on February 13. "And I would have liked to know what she thinks about the pictures. The Pierrot is finished, a Harlequin is very nearly so, and I am working on a third figure. I still have no news from anyone. It is rare for the postman to bring me any letter. I have seen some reproductions of the Indépendants in the E.N. None of it looks very good; in fact, it discloses great confusion."

Then on February 22: "The weather here has begun to get nice and I am beginning to soften under the impact of springtime indolence. Twice we thought we had found an apartment, but it has fallen through.... There's no getting away from the hotel.... An astonishing request from the *Revue de l'Epoque* : they ask me—me!, if Cubism is dead!"

The social life of Céret was unusually brilliant during the Carnival days. One ball followed another, and in this little town "where previously they had danced the Lancers and the Skaters' Waltz" and "a lot of dances which I have never seen anywhere else", as Josette had written in one of her first letters, the new dances introduced by Josette and Gris were all the rage. "Jean is a great success here you know," Josette wrote. "All the girls put on fancy dress and masks, and that gives them courage. Then they come and ask him for every dance; and there is one who confessed to him that she had been wanting to dance with him for a long time. What annoys him is that not one ever takes off her mask."

Josette, too, put on fancy dress "but", Gris wrote on February 22, "she looked very embarrassed and rather idiotic in her pierrot's costume. She has not got the right amount of nerve." Then it was her turn to write: "The Carnival festivities are very gay. Everyone is masked and behaving extravagantly, both the straight-laced, the little working girls and the young ladies."

But Ash Wednesday followed, and on March 9 Gris wrote: "We do not intend to stay here after April. It is a boring part of the world and we have almost had enough. With the coming of Lent the inhabitants, who are Catholic to a ridiculous degree, put on funeral airs. Anyone who stays here must turn into a fossil. There is nothing to do to dispel one's inertia and indifference for everything. Here there is none of the sunbaked, gluttonous sloth of Provence; it is all smug, sententious sobriety. Everyone is bored, but no-one does anything about it. Really it demands a great deal of courage or cowardliness to take the decision to settle down here for the whole of one's life. I hardly ever get a letter, and I too have almost lost the habit of writing. I, too, drift on into idleness, and that is why we must get away before long, as soon as the fine weather comes."

However, work kept Gris at Céret until the middle of April. The holiday had been very good for his health; the pure, bracing air of the Tech valley with its snow-capped mountains suited him, and he returned to Paris an apparently healthy man in April 1922.

VI. BOULOGNE-SUR-SEINE

Every year we had worried at the thought of Gris returning to live in the studio, but while he and Josette were at Céret my wife found a small flat to let at number 8 Rue de la Mairie, Boulogne. We ourselves lived at number twelve in the same street, now called Rue de l'Ancienne Mairie. Number eight was a house with two floors. The proprietor, a plumber, had his workshop, office, and living-room on the ground floor, besides which he occupied one room on the first floor. The little three-roomed flat which was to let was also on the first floor, and the proprietor was willing to put in a bathroom. The second floor was occupied by an old couple and a sort of box-room. Behind the house was a yard dominated by a lovely fig-tree, which yielded fruit every year; beyond the yard was a shed where the proprietor stored his materials. From the window of the room which was to serve, at first, as his studio, Gris looked out over a green landscape ending in the hills of St. Cloud. Later on, the landlord agreed, for an increased rent,[38] to put a skylight in the roof of the attic, which then made an excellent studio. So the earlier studio was turned into a bedroom.

Gris and Josette, who had learnt from us that, since the death of an old woman, the flat was vacant, wrote from Céret giving us full power to act; so we rented it in their name. They both seemed delighted: "We are anxiously awaiting the decision about the flat. Hurry up and give me the answer, old man," he wrote on March 31. A few days later came a letter from Josette: "So it's all settled and I am to have a real house, and close to you into the bargain. You don't know how happy it makes me. I didn't sleep all night for thinking about it. I'm longing to get there. ... I don't know whether, as far as his work is concerned, Jean will be better off in the new flat, but I shall certainly be glad not to be with him while he is working. He heaves such heavy sighs, and that depresses me."

As soon as they returned from Céret they moved from the old studio into the Rue de la Mairie. Josette combed the antique shops. Gris made an imitation negro head (like an Ogoué mask) out of cardboard, and some fine lighting fixtures out of paper; the elephant-like table was given a new coat of paint, and the worn-out pieces of furniture were discarded.

Gris never used to hang his own paintings on the walls. It only happened once (in 1926) when a small picture, *The Eggs*, which he had given to his son, was hung in Georges' room. In the dining-room were the two still-lifes which I mentioned earlier, by his young pupil Marmaronne, an imposing chromolithograph advertisement for the firm of Pernod (a picture of a table on which were a bottle of absinthe and the *Gazette de Pontarlier*), and some etchings by Matisse of Josette, which later gave place to a picture by Lascaux, *Les Ruines de Ventadour*. In the room with the divan, which served as the living-room, were another picture by Lascaux, *Vue de Tulle*, and two by Suzanne Roger, *Tête de Femme* and *Groupe de Femmes cousant*.

We were under no illusions about the disadvantages attaching to Gris' move into the suburbs, but the state of his health required it. And Boulogne was not devoid of charm in those days, for it had not then become as industrial as it is to-day; the invasion by Renault and Farman was only just beginning on the farthest side towards Billancourt—and Boulogne seemed more like a sort of lower middle-class appendage of Auteuil. There were few large houses, and the place consisted of small private villas and bungalows surrounded by gardens which, on the northern side, adjoined the Bois de Boulogne and the park belonging to Edmond de Rothschild (formerly the Cambacérès property), and on the southern side ran down to the Seine, on whose other bank was the park of St. Cloud. (Coming back from Paris by steamer—as one still did occasionally—one landed at St. Cloud. It was on one of these river steamers that Gris saw the nun who was the subject for one of his pictures.) But, on the other hand, Boulogne was a long way from Montmartre and Montparnasse. And it was obvious that very few of those casual visitors to the studio in the Rue Ravignan, who used to drop in and pass their comment on a picture, or recount the latest from the art world, would make the journey often to Boulogne. How, we asked ourselves, would Gris take this semi-isolation? Nevertheless, he got used to it. He and I would meet every day, sometimes to go out together in town, sometimes to go to the local cinema. Josette and he often spent the evening in our house, which was full of life. My two young sisters-in-law lived with us, and Gris had a sort of brotherly affection for "the two little ones", as he called them, for whom he would write little poems or make up cross-word puzzles; some of these figure in his pictures. His intimate friends, of course, used to come out to Boulogne to see him.

We kept open house every Sunday for a large circle of friends. There were the regulars like André Simon, Germaine and Maurice Raynal, Odette and André Masson, Suzanne Roger and André Beaudin, Charles-Albert Cingria, Elie Lascaux, Antonin Artaud, Georges Limbour, Michel Leiris, Roland Tual, Lucienne and Armand Salacrou; and occasional visitors like "our good master", the great and dear

300

Satie, or my old friend Max Jacob (on the occasions when he escaped for a few days from his seclusion at St. Benoit-sur-Loire), Tzara, Desnos, and many another. Gris was present at all these gatherings. There would be dancing to the gramophone which he brought with him—in the garden in summer, in the hall in winter. People came and went between the two houses as in turn they visited the studio to look at his latest pictures. After supper we talked, played, and sang. The pearl of Gris' repertoire was his creole version of the sailors' song *Nous étions deux, nous étions trois, Embarqués sur le Saint François*. But he also did a duet with Germaine Raynal, the song about Molcourt de Mauléon, who:

> "*Quitte ses épaulettes*
> *Son sabre et son ceinturon*
> *Son épée (?) et ses aiguillettes*
> *Non, ce n'est plus, non, ce n'est plus le fier dragon*
> *C'est le père Timoléon.*"

who confesses his love, discovers that he too is loved, and bursts out with:

> "*A vos genoux, à vos genoux, ce capuchon*
> *Je le quitte, redeviens dragon.*"

Max Jacob, too, had a lovely piece which he had picked up from Apollinaire, *De vos jardins fleuris, fermez les portes*, also an English song, *Le pauvre Milady*.

There was also the variety turn of Lascaux, whose range ran from Nadaud and Macnab to Maurice Chevalier, taking Mayol (the funniest) by the way. Cingria would sometimes play the piano. There were the sessions of table turning and hypnosis to which I have already referred. Artaud's speciality was imitations—or rather, I should say, incarnations. He would lie down on the divan and ask to be left alone in the dark for a few minutes. Then, when the lights were turned on again, he was found lying motionless looking for all the world like the model he had chosen. One day Gris wanted to try the same thing. He failed completely, but the sight of him lying there frightened me. This scene came back to my mind five years later as I saw him lying fully dressed upon his death-bed.

On weekdays Gris received very few visitors, but now and again a friend would call: Gertrude Stein, Raynal, Doctor Allendy, or some of the young painters. Gris' day did not begin very early, for on those evenings when he stayed at home he would sit up until very late into the night drawing or reading. He got up between nine and ten o'clock in the morning, drank a cup of coffee, and slipped on an old paint-covered jacket and trousers over his night-shirt. He put his bare feet into a strange pair of slippers, which he had made for himself by cutting the uppers of some old shoes with a razor blade. Then he went upstairs to his studio, where he smoked all the time he was working. At about half-past one Josette would call him for lunch, which he ate rapidly, and then went back to work until the evening, or until about four o'clock if he was going into town. He used not to wash or get properly dressed until he stopped working. Often, if he went into Paris, he would call and fetch me in the Rue d'Astorg, and we travelled back together. After dinner, as I have said, he and Josette would frequently come to our house. It is my chief regret that I did not write down, day by day, the conversations we had together. It was not that I failed to attach to them the importance they deserved, but simply that I imagined I would not forget them. One always thinks that everything by which one is struck will be engraved on one's memory, but that is not the case at all. However, I hope that the main lines of his thought will yet be made clear in this book, though for actual statements we have nothing but his letters and his other writings.

We felt his friendly presence, his affection, always about us. If any help was needed he came at once. I can still see him on hands and knees underneath our piano—one of the "square" kind—lifting it up on his back so that a leg could be screwed on. I remember, too, another day when I was ill. It was only a few weeks before his death, and Gris was very exhausted, but he came round at once because, as he said: "Cavélère [he pronounced my name like that] was always there when I was ill." His kindness and affection was extended even to dogs. Our German sheep-dog Porthos would lick the hand of anyone whom he liked, so we did all we could to break him of this habit. One day, however, as I came downstairs I heard Gris in the hall, saying to him: "Here, old man, lick my hand quickly while they are not looking." When Porthos died, on January 17, 1927, I received the following note from Gris, who was then very ill himself: "I am very sorry about the death of Porthos, a beautiful and charming animal which I really loved. I can well understand your attachment to him." A few weeks later, just before his own death, he said to me one day: "All our troubles began with the death of Porthos."

His jealousy went hand in hand with his affection, and the idea that another friendship could count beside his own made him really unhappy. Dear Jean! . . . It is by this name that he lives on in the memory of his intimate friends. Only Gertrude Stein used to call him Juan. He chose to be called Jean and not Juan as a way of expressing his love for everything French. He was infatuated by France, French civilisation and culture, and the French language. He spoke French extremely well and with a great sense of the vocabulary but, like all his compatriots I think, with a noticeable accent which he never lost. At the time of his death he was on the point of naturalisation, and yet he was always a Spaniard. Despite the fact that he took hardly any interest in music, I have seen him moved to tears while listening to a concert in the Salle Adyar at which a singer, accompanied by Joaquin Nin, sang Spanish popular songs from the different provinces.

His passion for dancing remained, and he made a point of learning all the latest dances. In fact his studious approach was the subject of many a friendly joke between us. I taxed him with studying everything seriously, even these dances. Actually he learnt them from little handbooks which were published at that time, but there was some truth in what I said all the same. In a letter from Céret dated November 27, 1921, Gris wrote of a certain X: "This man is yet another example of the axiom that seriousness is divorced from will-power; some people are naturally serious in everything they do without making an effort, while others never achieve it no matter how they try. X is as serious in intention about his business as Z is, for example, about his religion." Gris was serious in everything he attempted without making any effort.

We would all be taken off by him to the Elysée Montmartre, to the Moulin Rouge, or to the dance-

The Torero · 1913

halls of St. Cloud, such as L'Impérial, the Tête Noire, or Maurice et André. At this time also there were still a few "bohemian" dance-halls (last vestige of the giddy post-war life), for example the Bal Suédois in the Maison Watteau, and the Bal Russe in Bullier. We went together to the Bal Suédois wearing similar paper masks.[39]

In spring and in autumn we never missed the fair at St. Cloud. One day when Gris had won a bottle of red wine in one raffle and a bowl in another, he ran around offering everyone a sip from his bowl. Needless to say the bottle was quickly emptied. On Sunday mornings we used to go to Saint Ouen, to the "Flea Market". At this time the market was still held in the open and its unusual wares were displayed over a vague area outside the fortifications and not, as happened later, in the slums of Saint Ouen. Josette had the same passion for it as ourselves; Jean made fun of it and used to talk of buying a second-hand toothbrush.

Above all there were our visits to the Louvre, to Chantilly, and to the exhibitions. Jean had a particular admiration for Ingres, Cézanne, and Seurat, but he was also fond of Delacroix, Corot, and Renoir. He was very attached to Raphael, to the Ferrarese painter Cossa (whose works he only knew by reproduction), to Fouquet, to the painters of the Fontainebleau School, to the brothers Le Nain, to Chardin and Boucher. In front of a picture there was no-one better able to describe its structure and the artist's intentions. He it was who brought home to me the simple grandeur and inventiveness inherent in the realism of Murillo's *Miracle of San Diego*. I also learnt to share his taste (perhaps not very surprising) for Philippe de Champaigne. We both had an admiration for the dignified *Portrait of Mère Arnaud*. Il Borgognone (Ambrogio da Fossano) was another of Gris' enthusiasms and we would always stop in front of this painter's impressive work in the Grande Galerie of the Louvre. Gris was, naturally, interested by El Greco, but he was not one of his favourites. Nor was he as fond of Mantegna as one might have expected, for there is a certain similarity between them. Perhaps this was due to his never having seen the magnificent frescoes in the Eremitani church in Padua. Clouet and Holbein he really disliked. He had a certain appreciation of the Italian painters of the thirteenth, fourteenth, and fifteenth centuries, but I would say that he had a higher opinion of those of the two centuries following.

He was a great reader and particularly addicted to Gongora. (He did a watercolour sketch, *Hommage à Don Luis*, for the cover of the special number of the Spanish review *Litoral* devoted to this poet.) I remember him telling me that among more recent Spanish writers whom he admired especially were Valle-Inclan and Ruben Dario. He worshipped Mallarmé, whom he greatly preferred to Rimbaud, and I shall not forget a heated argument he once had about this with some young poets. Michel Leiris remembers hearing him many times recite with glee the line beginning, "*Dans la considérable touffe...*" from Mallarmé's sonnet *Quelle soie aux baumes du temps....* In the letter in which he refers to this, Leiris writes: "To be exact, Jean's pleasure was derived from the simple combination of a substantive and an epithet of this kind. And I believe that it reflects one of his chief preoccupations; for in talking about his own painting he often used the words 'qualifying', 'substantive', 'adjective', etc.... What appealed to him about this phrase—and I am sure it is not my imagination—was the pure conjunction of two words irrespective of the image."

Gris was very fond of Reverdy, whom he preferred, I believe, to Apollinaire. Radiguet, too, he liked, as one of his letters bears witness. He delighted in the novels of Pigault-Lebrun (a sort of French Smollett who is all too little known), especially *Mon Oncle Thomas* and *L'Enfant du Carnaval*. In quite another way Dumas *père* helped him in 1915 to conquer his boredom, as he once mentions in a letter. But he hardly ever mentioned this author later on, and instead often praised Gaboriau. Like everyone

261   of our own generation, and of the one which followed, Gris had a strong taste for *"Fantômas"*, whose powers of invention fascinated him. I have already mentioned his taste for occult literature, and I will come back to it in Part II of the present book. The sad thing is that he was prevented by death from reading those works of philosophy about which he had been thinking for so long, for I am convinced that they would have taken the place of biology in his mind. He was preparing to read Kant when he died; it might have given him the spiritual nourishment for which he sought.

VII. INTERLUDE: THE RUSSIAN BALLETS

The telegram from Diaghilew, that Gris had received at Bandol, had not resulted in a ballet. In the autumn of 1922 Diaghilew returned to the charge. Gris, happy to be back in Paris and finding himself fairly comfortably settled at Boulogne, spent the summer at home and did not intend to go away that winter. We were preparing an exhibition of his work, which was held in the Rue d'Astorg from March 20

162, 163   to April 5, 1923. Diaghilew asked Gris to design the *décor* and costumes for a ballet of the Louis XIV period, to music by Montéclair arranged by Henri Casadesus, and Gris accepted. As we have already seen in his letters from Bandol and Monte Carlo, the idea of doing a ballet did not really interest him, but he suffered from the feeling of being lost in obscurity. He was not jealous of the fame of Picasso, nor of the success of Braque and Léger, but he was amazed that he should be overlooked. During his fits of depression, he was seized by a real despair. I would do all that I could to cheer him up, but his modesty only made the task more difficult. "No-one pays any attention to me," he said one day, and recited to me the names of all the painters, even the younger ones, who, in his opinion, were more successful. I tried to console him by reminding him how late fame had been in coming to many a great painter, and instanced Cézanne. "But I am not Cézanne, old man, I am not Cézanne," he exclaimed in horror. "No," I replied, "but you are Juan Gris." I think that I comforted him on many occasions: "but," he once said to my wife, "what if Cavélère is wrong?"

It was, then, in the hope of attracting new admirers for his work that he agreed to collaborate with Diaghilew. He was not attracted by the material profit, for he received only a small sum—four or five thousand francs, if I remember rightly—such as might suffice for a hack, but which meant nothing in terms of the amount of time that Gris was forced to take off from his real work. For, as one would imagine, having once agreed to do a ballet, he was eager to put his best into it. I have already said that he was incapable of doing anything by halves, and the ballet, like everything else, developed into a serious undertaking which proved to be a thoughtful, coherent piece of work. From this moment, Diaghilew came regularly to number 8 Rue de la Mairie, and it became a current joke to say: "Ah! That's Diaghilew!" whenever, from our house, we heard Gris' front-door bell ringing. It was often true.

Gris made an exact model of his set, done to scale, and did a large number of pastels and water-colours for the costumes. I was astonished at the ease or rather mastery of it all. Diaghilew used to come and discuss with him. I was frequently present during those talks and I must admit that I can imagine nothing more demoralising. Diaghilew, with an air of friendly charm, would scrap, or at least modify, all Gris' original ideas. I remember the lovely device of a figure of Venus, which was to be gradually inflated so that it rose up, simultaneously with a jet of water, from the bed of a fountain and then slowly subsided. It seems to me, looking back, that it was probably the sight of the egg dancing on the top of its column of water in the shooting gallery at the St. Cloud fair which inspired this idea. Diaghilew was at first sight most enthusiastic over the scheme, as over so many others. Then he began to discuss the details, and at the end of a quarter of an hour it was dead and buried.

Gris, nevertheless, designed very beautiful scenery and costumes. Diaghilew was delighted, and asked him to arrange the setting for the "Fête Merveilleuse" that he was organising on June 30, 1923, in the Hall of Mirrors in the palace at Versailles. An enormous scaffolding had to be erected, and Gris practically lived at Versailles while carrying out this architectural work. It was a brilliant evening. As Louis XIV climbed up to his throne, which was at the top of a long flight of steps, his blue cloak covered the whole stairway from top to bottom. The effect, amid Gris' scenery and costumes, was magnificent.

Diaghilew, whose fancy had certainly been caught, then asked him to do the *décor* for an opera by Gounod, *La Colombe*. He also executed the model and designs for this at Boulogne. Then, on October 9, 1923, he left for Monte Carlo, hoping to be able to combine work on the ballets with work at his own painting. He and Josette visited the museum at Marseilles, and Gris sent me a post card of Millet's *Mother Giving Soup to her Child*, which he did not usually greatly admire. On the eleventh they installed themselves at Beausoleil, in the Villa Tosca, 3 Rue du Marché.

The difficulty of combining his own work with the necessity of supervising the scene-painters very soon became apparent. On October 20 Gris wrote to me: "I have not yet completely settled down to work, though I am trying to. Every day, however, I have to call in at the scene-makers' studio to see that they do not make stupid mistakes. For, despite the model, which incidentally they have half destroyed, and despite the plans, they still find some way to go wrong. Up to now I have succeeded, with my watchful eye, in preventing any mishaps. ... I have not danced once since we arrived—you see what a sober life I lead! Monte Carlo is as boring as a sanatorium. All one sees are people wandering about aimlessly, not knowing what to do. I hope I don't set foot in the Casino; I am disgusted by this atmosphere of gambling. On the other hand, Nice seems to be charming."

On November 5: "The sets are nearly ready, thank goodness. Three more days would have seen them finished altogether if we hadn't had to stop to-day for lack of canvas. Diaghilew should arrive to-morrow, bringing some more with him. I don't yet know whether I shall stay on here for a while

163

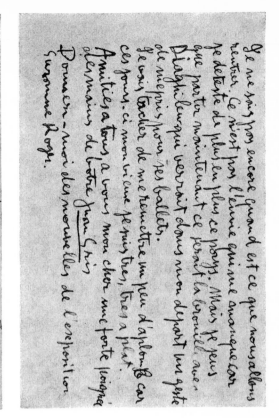

Letter from Juan Gris to D.-H. Kahnweiler, December 9, 1923

or return as soon as the scenery is finished. If I work well here, perhaps we shall stay; but if not, it's the first train for us. I am terribly bored here. Poulenc arrived the day before yesterday and finds Monte Carlo delightful. He's lucky."

On November 26: "Yes, I am still bored and I wish it were all over. I have not yet seen the set as a whole, but only a section which has been roughly put up for the dancers to rehearse in. What's more, the lighting was very bad. I haven't yet seen anything set up for *Colombe*. I went to Nice yesterday with Gertrude. She is leaving for Paris to-morrow. She will tell you all sorts of things about what goes on here which would take too long to explain in a letter. At all events I have had no amusement whatever—the moment I'm not looking something goes wrong. I am working regularly now, or almost so, as I only bother about minor details which still need attention. The weather is vile: it has rained without ceasing for a week and it is even cold."

December 9: "I have had a lot of trouble with *Colombe* as, on the day we put it up in the theatre—last Tuesday—I saw that the colours were nothing like those of the design. The painters have got to repaint all the scenery. I hope I don't get a similar shock with the Montéclair! I have given permission here for the photographs of *Colombe* and the Montéclair, which I have slightly touched up, to be reproduced in the programme. Diaghilew has also asked me for a drawing for the cover and two others for the inside. I have done them, but I don't think they are very good. I am wondering if it wouldn't be better to reproduce some of the drawings that you have at home. I still don't know when we are coming back. It is not for lack of wanting to. I loathe this part of the country more and more, but I feel that to leave now would mean a split with Diaghilew, who would read into my departure a gesture of scorn for his ballets. I must try to recover my equilibrium, for during the last few days, old man, I have been feeling very, very flat."

December 20: "I have had to leave my painting aside just now, as I have suddenly been called on to do a setting and two costumes for Diaghilew. They are for *L'Education Manquée* by Chabrier, which Picasso was to have done but at the last moment has not. They took four days. In addition, everyone has begun to be irritable in anticipation of the approaching 'first nights'. As one might expect, nothing is ready. They began to rehearse Auric's ballet to-day. He worries so much about it that he spends all his time at the gambling tables. At any rate I have to some extent saved the situation over the *Education Manquée*, and Diaghilew was very touched, at least for two hours. By now he has forgotten. I *must* escape soon from this centre of incompetence and hysterics where, as you can imagine, I am in a nervous state the whole time. I am very annoyed at not being able to celebrate the New Year with you, but really it is impossible for us to return just now."

January 6, 1924: "I have had too much to do these last days before the *premières* and, now they are over, activity has been followed by a wave of depression which has prevented me from writing to you. I have received a number of compliments on *La Colombe*, although the piece is too long and tedious. The costumes look well with the scenery, although they have been badly made. Barrientos' dress is very nicely done, but it is nothing like my design and does not look right. The Montéclair ballet has been a great success. The costumes for it are also badly made but they go well with the setting. I had to take a curtain call, and Nijinska says that she has never seen such a complete harmony. But Oh! how frantic I was during the last days. Except for Nijinska, who takes her work seriously, and Diaghilew who knows his job, nobody uses his brains or foresees anything. No-one has any common sense. I cannot wait to get away from this infuriating *milieu*. If one doesn't keep one's eye on every little detail, something is certain to go wrong; and if one keeps one's eye on everything, one is interfering. What an unbearable atmosphere! The *décor* I have done here is to be put on on the thirteenth. I have not yet seen it in the theatre. Poulenc's *Les Biches* [40] has been a great success. They have begun to rehearse the Auric ballet. Satie has been here for several days. But what a frightful life the theatre is! I assure you I have no desire to go through it all again. One lives in an air of perpetual misapprehension, and it is impossible to get people to understand. And above all what caddishness! I will tell you all about it when I have the pleasure of seeing you again. For the moment, I am taking up my painting once more as I have begun several canvases."

January 21: "The third *décor, Une Education Manquée*, was put on on the seventeenth and *Les Fâcheux*, by Auric and Braque, on the nineteenth. I am delaying my return because I have not yet been paid in full. I still have 2500 francs to come, which I would not like them to forget on account of my departure. I am also waiting for the railway permits which have been sent to Paris for renewal, as they have expired. I don't know if Satie [41] has told you how unhappy I am here. The countryside irritates me and so does the way the ballets are managed. I will explain all that. My time has been spent either losing my temper or worrying. As for the inseparable friends, Cocteau and the composers have been remarkably distant, and so has Braque. Not that it is of any importance, but still it has helped to make life here unpleasant. It is difficult to achieve anything in such a bad frame of mind. I assure you that if I haven't written more often to my friends, it is because I have been depressed and in a bad temper most of the time. However, I hope to return soon and look at it all from a distance."

Gris returned to Boulogne at the end of January. His health and his work had suffered from this contact with the Russian ballets. He was tired, and in Part II of this book the reader will learn from relevant passages in his letters of the very serious crisis that his painting went through during these months. This crisis certainly had to come, but its development might have been infinitely less painful. In the tranquil atmosphere of his normal work it would have been confined to a struggle within himself.

However, yielding to entreaties, Gris designed one more setting, this time for a Red Cross Fête organised by Diaghilew on May 28, 1924, in the Grands Magasins du Printemps. It was an architectural work, after the style of his construction at Versailles. That marked the end of his collaboration with Diaghilew.

VIII. LAST YEARS OF WORK AND DEATH OF JUAN GRIS

At Boulogne he resumed the peaceful routine of normal work. His first need was a clear vision, so Gris spent some time reflecting on his art and on the crisis through which he had just passed. On May 15, 1924, he read a paper "On the Possibilities of Painting" at the Sorbonne, to the Society of Philosophic and Scientific Studies, founded by Dr. Allendy. In this he summed up the essence of his own art. It was published in various periodicals in French, German, Spanish, and English, and the name of Gris soon became known. The public began to appreciate this pure art with so few "snags". Success was, for him, a great moral support, not because of the modest material benefits it brought but because of the encouragement he derived from the idea of being watched. His fame spread, in France and also abroad, notably in Germany where, for many years, Alfred Flechtheim[42] had indefatigably supported him. This period witnessed the creation of works of a noble purity, for he knew, better than ever, the goal towards which he was striving, and set out for it with the renewed courage which comes of no longer feeling alone.

In the summer of 1924 Gris left Boulogne only for a short visit to Nemours, where he and Josette spent a week, from August 17 to 23, basking in the sunshine and having a gay time with André and Odette Masson, Armand and Lucienne Salacrou, Michel Leiris and Roland Tual.

The year 1925 brought further successes. The great supporters of Cubism—such as Dr. Reber and others—realised Gris' importance.[43] Gris wrote to me from Boulogne on August 18, 1925 (I was at Cap d'Antibes), to tell me what pleasure a visit from Alphonse Kann had given him. "He came to-day and was very pleased with everything he saw. He overwhelmed me with praise and told me to ask you to reserve a picture for him. This has made me very happy, for you know how unpleasant I found the thought that Kann did not buy my work."

His fame reached the ears of Paul Rosenberg, who requested Gris to call on him and then made a point-blank offer to buy his work. When Gris refused, pointing out his commitments to myself, Rosenberg replied: "I will pay for your freedom." Gris, who had always felt free precisely because of our agreement, was astounded at this attitude. But Rosenberg insisted, trying to dazzle him with the high prices that he was prepared to pay. Picasso was present at the interview. But Gris did not give way; he turned the offer down and came to tell me about it, content at the thought of his importance.

During the summer of 1925, the Exhibition of Decorative Arts, with its Amusement Park, was the object of frequent visits. A certain "chute", down which terrified couples were precipitated, made Jean laugh till he cried. His health, however, was not really good. "I hope that you are having a nice holiday," he wrote on August 18. "For myself, life is not too bad and I am working well enough. But I feel rather tired and I shall have to go south this winter."

At the end of August, he and Josette took a short trip with Lucienne and Armand Salacrou. They went down the Seine estuary by boat, from Rouen to Le Havre, where they stayed for about a week. The captain of the little steamer greatly impressed the travellers by his old "sea-dog" look. His appearance was perpetuated in one of the etchings for the *Mouchoir de Nuages*.

326, 327

At the beginning of December they left for the south. They installed themselves at Toulon, *chez* Madame Ollivier, Boulevard Sud des Casernes, Sainte Anne. Gris wrote to me on December 10: "Yes, we have found quite an attractive house in, so to speak, the Boulogne of Toulon. We are a quarter of an hour's walk from the centre of the town. We go out every evening. I have hunted everywhere for an easel but it has been impossible to find one. Eventually I discovered a huge three-legged apparatus which was used to support a blackboard in a school. After a little adjustment it will do reasonably well. I have begun to work, and the two canvases for Lucie[44] are done. What an unsympathetic town Avignon is! I only spent a few hours there but I should hate to live in it. The Giovanetti frescoes are very striking, but there are certain figures by Memmi that I like more. As for the *Rural Pleasures*[45]—they are not up to much. I found some very interesting things in the Avignon museum—(I don't know if you have been there). An admirable Gallo-Roman sculpture, some very lovely pieces of mosaic, and a few good pictures. There is an Entombment by Simon de Chalons which isn't bad, and a portrait by one of the brothers Le Nain—also some other quite good things."

He did not find Toulon too isolated. Friends who were passing through came to see him. On December 29 he wrote: "I have already settled down to work, which I do regularly, as in Paris—that is, for the whole day. We only go out in the evenings. The Raynals and Simon stayed here for three days, which we spent together very pleasantly. We had great fun on Christmas Eve and they are coming back again to-morrow to celebrate New Year's Eve with us."

Differences with his family caused him to send for his son. Gris' brother was angry that Jean should be on the point of becoming a Frenchman, for he thought it would adversely affect his son's future in Spain. On January 14, 1926, Gris wrote to me: "My plans to become naturalised have produced

Teacups · 1914

unexpected reactions in my family. In one letter I have been strongly censured by my brother and, in another, my sister has expressed her approval. My son, for his part, has written me a letter without their knowledge asking to be allowed to come and join me. From what he says, he appears to hate Spain as much as I do. As his wish is my wish, I have decided to send for him. I would never have done it against his will, but since he wants it . . . Besides, I am better able now to have him with me without his being too unhappy. What do you think of this decision? He should arrive in April, as soon as I return to Paris."

Besides the friends who passed through, there were those who lived in Toulon. Jean wrote on January 4: "The Fords[46] are here and spent New Year's Eve with us. I am terrified by the amount of alcohol that he always drinks. I did not think it was possible to drink so much. I don't regret missing the binge you describe. Villette, a *bal musette* and the X are not at all in my line." Nevertheless, he was not idle. On January 14 he wrote: "At the moment I have two Still-lifes, sizes 10 and 30, finished. Two figures, one size 30 and the other size 40, are well advanced, and two small Still-lifes just begun. I cannot as yet really tell whether they show any progress. At any rate, they do not strike me as being inferior to my last works, and perhaps technically they are richer."

January 26: "I have on hand some ten paintings, of which only three are finished. There is still something to be done to the others. The canvas I buy here is very absorbent, and I am being driven mad by tonal values which are constantly changing. I can now see some progress in what I am doing. There is a greater ease and maturity. I have just started on two figures, one size 30—a woman with a lyre— and one size 20—a woman with drapery—which I think indicate a step in the right direction. There is a Pompeiian look about them, but more like David than Poussin. In my enthusiasm for working on these canvases, I have for the time being put aside the water-colours that I had begun for Lucie. I will finish them soon and send them to her."[47]

His health, unfortunately, left much to be desired. He wrote to me on February 6: "For almost a month now, we have been going out much less, as I am not satisfied with my health. My temperature goes up regularly every afternoon to nearly thirty-eight, and that is rather too high. I have written to Allendy and he has just replied with a letter in which he tells me not to worry, but advises a complete rest after lunch. He has also sent me a new prescription which I have already ordered from Paris. And, in fact, I lay down after lunch to-day and did not get a temperature. I think it is high time I took more care of myself, for this temperature, together with a slight spitting of blood that I have had occasionally, forbodes no good. You must admit, all the same, that it is no fun for me to resign myself to the rôle of an invalid. . . . Apart from the woman with the lyre, all the pictures are more or less finished and I am starting on some others. The woman with drapery, now that she is finished, is more like something from Fontainebleau than from Pompeii. It is a bit smooth and the paint is not very thick, as it was done in almost one sitting, but it has a very fresh look and a certain purity which I find pleasing."

A few days later there was an improvement. "I believe now," he wrote on February 17, "that with my daily rest things are going better. As a result of lying down for two hours between two and four o'clock my temperature remains normal." I advised him to take a walk in the morning, to which he countered with the remark: "If I went for a walk in the morning as well, what time would there be left for my work?" He took to living in still greater seclusion. "I don't see many people here, except for Ford and Latapie, whom I see occasionally of an evening. I have not seen Cocteau and Stravinsky, nor Manolo either. I forgot to say that we met Marguerite Matisse and her husband,[48] with whom we spent an evening. Believe me, I am taking great care of myself. I declined to go to the Carnival Ball at the theatre for fear of tiring myself."

March 1: "I am getting better. I have had rather a long and sharp attack of bronchitis, revealed by an analysis of my spittle, which proved to be full of bronchitis germs. This analysis has comforted me, for there were no Koch bacilli as I had feared. It also disclosed a serious condition of anaemia. For the last week I have felt stronger and have been looking much better. As soon as I have finished the three or four things I am working on, we shall think of leaving. Some of the paintings I have done here do not displease me, and I regard them with a certain satisfaction. I am less sure about others, and we will decide together on what must be discarded."

March 18: "As I am not painting much now, I have begun to do a few water-colours. The last pictures of any series are always a painful business for me. I haven't much taste for work. One's interest seems to run out, leaving only the boredom of execution. We have spent two evenings with Matisse, who has come to visit his daughter. He was nice and not at all superior. . . . The local 'Rotonde' will soon be closing down. Duthuit is charming."

March 30: "We expect to get back to Boulogne on the fifth or sixth. . . . I am anxious to return as I am not doing very much here. I have done nothing apart from some water-colours and I don't want to start on anything whatever. I am thinking of stopping at Lyon. Kann spoke very highly to me of the museum there, and I should like to see it. I have been feeling rather exhausted lately and lacking in ideas for my work. I hope that the change will shake me up again. I realise now that it is impossible for me to work continuously. I have to stop after about twelve paintings, otherwise I fail in whatever I attempt."

Gris returned to Boulogne at the beginning of April. Satie's death had occurred in the previous summer. Jean and I had walked side by side in the procession which followed his coffin to the cemetery at Arcueil. But I had never thought that within two years I would be following Jean to the cemetery. I did not realise what his condition was, and I should add that even the doctors, as must be apparent, did not believe that he was seriously ill. Moreover, nothing in his work indicated illness. The paintings which he produced during that spring and summer were sublime in their perfection. Yet, there were certainly days when he was very sick. I remember on one occasion coming home by car from La Roche Guyon, where we had lunched at an inn beside the Seine; Jean, usually so animated and an indefatigable talker, slept in the back of the car during the ride home. He consulted various doctors. Dr. Valette, at Boulogne, who had accurately diagnosed high blood pressure, had completely dropped the idea of a threat of tuberculosis, which the doctors had for a long time been fighting by intensive feeding, in which there was, apparently, a certain danger.

His son arrived. His sister Antonieta and his nephew, young Guillermo, spent several weeks at

Boulogne. Gris was also visited by his boyhood friend Pedro Penzol, accompanied by his wife. As soon as it turned cold, he left Paris with Josette and Georges. They installed themselves on November 21 at the Villa Germinal, Quartier Mont Fleuri, at Hyères—that sleepy town full of large, empty hotels, which seems to be haunted by the ghosts of many an English spinster who has died there of consumption. This choice was to prove a great misfortune.

No sooner had they arrived than Georges developed a serious attack of tonsilitis. "He is getting up for the first time," wrote Gris on November 28, "but what is so infuriating is that, in nursing him, I have evidently caught the infection, in spite of all my precautions. For the last three days I have had a very sore throat, which I am fighting as best I can. So I have not been out since Monday, but I get up every day at eight o'clock and follow my diet very strictly. The weather is lovely and the rooms are full of sunshine. The house is not unpleasant, although too congested with useless objects. I have been able to clear one room to work in and I have been lent an easel with three legs which I hope will do. If my sore throat does not get worse, I shall go to Toulon tomorrow or the day after to buy such painting materials as I need."

December 2: "We are leading an exemplary life. ... We have also begun to take walks in the countryside which is close at hand and very beautiful. With my diet, which is very strict—I have entirely given up coffee—my temperature seems to be going down a little. I have also begun to work, for Josette has fetched me all I need from Toulon. Things should go well in the room I have prepared, as it is quite large and almost white."

December 10: "A touch of bronchitis has got me down these last few days, but with the help of mustard plasters things are improving. There can be no doubt that my diet and the climate here are doing me good. I am making good progress with some small canvases which are no worse, I think, than the last ones I did in Paris, but as yet there is nothing very sensational. ... I hardly recognise myself here. I go out every day for a walk, but never in the evenings. I drink no coffee, only lime tea, and hardly smoke at all. Let's hope it lasts!"

December 20: "We are still leading the most sober and orderly existence imaginable. We never go out in the evenings and have completely given up the cinema. We have no diversions apart from our daily walk from half past one to three. The country is so beautiful that I am becoming quite a nature-lover. As for the town, it is odious—without charm or interest. I am beginning to feel more like working, and have embarked on some larger canvases. I don't yet know what the result will be. My health is, I think, better. My temperature is normal almost all the time, except for odd occasions like to-day, when it went up a little. But I haven't told you that since I arrived in the south I have been having attacks of asthma which cause me much pain. Sometimes at night I have to sit up in an armchair for two or three hours as I am unable to lie down. Josette has just brought me, from Toulon, an apparatus for spraying up my nose, which is said to bring effective relief. I am so afraid of these attacks that I hardly dare to move. They generally occur when I go to bed. I imagine that this will put an end to my dancing days for ever. In all, I lead a futile existence, and the funniest thing about it is that it doesn't bore me."

Man Reading · 1925

December 30: "The doctor came to examine me the other day. My blood pressure, despite all the care I have taken, seems rather to have increased. I don't know exactly by how much, as this time it was taken with a different apparatus, and the doctor did not really know how the two sets of figures correspond. I find it discouraging, for I cannot follow a more severe diet than the one I have been on since I came here. Meat, wine, coffee, tobacco, even my evening outings, have all been firmly abolished; what more can one do? I am taking new medicines, which have a vile taste of decay, to counteract my emphysema, and I have ampoules of morphia for the bad attacks. You can see that all this is no laughing matter. But the most surprising thing is that I'm not miserable. I am growing accustomed to the life of a perfect invalid. I work hard for three hours in the morning and in the evenings I do a bit of drawing by lamp-light. I have completed some small canvases with which I am quite pleased, and a figure, size 30, which to my mind isn't bad, but which I loathe and shall probably begin all over again."

I found his news extremely disquieting, and in a letter of January 12, 1927, I told him: "I repeat once again: are you sure that the climate of this Hyères country isn't bad for you? Far from getting better, your health seems to be less good down there. As for the asthma, you never had it before. Why not go somewhere else? Or why not seek diversion and a change of air by a short sea voyage? Anyway, I hope that the spring will bring some improvement, but I am really beginning to think that the south does you no good."

He replied on January 17, 1927: "I see you are getting very anxious about my health. It is very kind of you and I am most touched. But I cannot say I am any worse than in Paris, apart from the asthma attacks, which give me little respite, as I have more or less heavy ones every evening. When I don't take any exercise my temperature is normal; but if I go out or exhaust myself with walking it sometimes rises to thirty-eight. Above all it is the bad attacks which pull me down. The day after one of them I can do nothing, I am so exhausted. I have thought, like yourself, that the climate here might be bad for me, but frankly I can think of no reason why it should be unhealthy. It hardly ever rains, the sun shines almost every day, and the sea breezes don't reach as far as here. Furthermore, I take every precaution against dampness, as I never go out after four o'clock. I think that these attacks have come on here as they would have done anywhere else. Valette told me that I had asthma, but he did not warn me about possible attacks. I attribute them rather to the fine dust and the pollen floating in the air, which irritates the respiratory tract and even the eyes. And what is still more curious is that people actually come here to relieve their asthma; for example, my landlord's wife. But the most annoying thing is that though one can relieve asthma it can never be cured. It is a real infirmity which wrecks the nerves and the heart.

"However, believe me, my friend, I lead the quietest life imaginable—an almost monastic life, which I am astonished I am able to bear. I work for two or three hours each morning, but then there are the days after an attack when I haven't the strength. However, the few small things that I have done do not seem to me any worse than those I did in Paris, although I sometimes ask myself if they haven't got a sickly look. ..."

The same letter continues—"Monday: last night was again a very bad one. To-day I sent for the doctor once more, but he does not rightly know what causes these cruel attacks. He has given me some new medicines and we shall judge of their effect on Saturday when he comes again. In any case, he too is beginning to have doubts about the climate. He even talked of giving me a pollen injection, as for hay-fever. So we are thinking of leaving if all this comes to nothing. But it means a great deal of money wasted, and, with the little I can work, it is not at all funny. I hope next time to be able to give you better news, old man."

A letter which arrived next day (January 18) really alarmed me. In it Jean said: "It is impossible to go on. Last night I had a series of attacks which followed one on top of another. I slept a little after taking some morphia. We must leave as quickly as possible, as I cannot bear it any more. But where can we go? I am trying to find a place not too far from here but a long way from the sea and high up. Please send me by return of post 5000 francs. We shall then leave straight away. I have finished four pictures, but they are not sufficiently dry to send off. I also have some others half done, which I shall take with me to finish. Believe me, old man, I don't exaggerate: I am suffering a great deal. To-day, for example, the morning is not yet over and I already find it difficult to breathe. My nerves and heart are in a sorry state."

Knowing how fatal morphia was for his kidneys, I hurried to Dr. Valette, who confirmed my fears. I sent Gris a telegram to this effect. His reply was as follows: "Hyères, January 19, 1927. I have this moment received your telegram and the money-order. Thank you a thousand times; to have a friend like yourself makes up for many sad things. I am deeply touched by your alacrity. Yes, I must go away from the sea as speedily as possible, for now the feeling of suffocation never leaves me. To-day the doctor came and we both agreed on this point. I also had thought of the Basque country, but I cannot undertake such a long journey in my present condition. We are going to a little place in the Alpes Maritimes, eighty kilometres from Nice and five hundred metres high. The doctor thinks that is high enough to bring relief. Anyhow, my blood pressure increases as my asthma gets worse. In fact, the one seems to almost be the cause of the other, for the blood pressure has increased ever since I left Paris. In two days I hope that we shall have left this horrible Côte d'Azur which is so bad for me. For I assure you, I am leading the life of a veritable martyr. I cannot lie down; I can only sit bolt upright, and if I incline my body ever so slightly, things become impossible. Last night I managed to sleep lying down for three hours after an injection of morphia. Thank you, thank you once again. The address we are thinking of going to is the Hotel Laugier at Puget-Théniers (Alpes Maritimes). If that is no good we shall move on up towards Savoy."

On the twenty-second, I received the following telegram from Puget-Théniers: (10.50 A.M.) "Have had good journey, hoping for improvement, regards." Another telegram on the following day, however, announced his immediate return to Paris. On January 24, I received a telephone call in the morning from Boulogne to say that they had arrived. I hastened round. Jean was in bed. He stretched out his arms and embraced me with tears in his eyes, crying: "They have killed me, old man, they have killed me!"

At Puget-Théniers a young country doctor had immediately diagnosed Jean's trouble as an attack of uremia and had satisfied himself that the fits of suffocation were merely the result of high blood pressure and a dilated aorta. Puget-Théniers, he said, was too high for Jean and recommended him either to go to Vence or to return to Paris. Josette and Jean had hesitated a while but finally decided to return.

It was the crisis. "A square chest is trying to fasten itself to my round one," he moaned in his delirium. Oxygen cylinders were fetched, he was cupped, and finally Jean recovered sufficiently to get up. He was able to go out again and once more took up his work. He had a very strict diet and, as he insisted on not being entirely deprived of tobacco, saying that he could not work without smoking, he was occasionally given half a cigarette. Nevertheless, a second slight attack occurred. After it, he started to work once more. He went out very little. One day in March he came and sat in our garden, but the sun tired him and he had to go in again. Then came the third crisis. At first he stayed indoors. Lascaux, Beaudin, and other friends would come and talk and play cards with him. Then he had to take to his bed. He was hopeful, however, and did not feel he was going to die. He talked of Bains-les-Bains, where he was to go for a cure in June, picturing how well he would be in such surroundings, composed as he imagined of large trees casting their shade over fresh little streams among the hills. I discovered with amazement the accuracy of this description when I myself went to Bains-les-Bains for a cure some months later.

Jean was soon suffering terrible pain. We could hear his cries from our garden. All the same, I was inclined to be hopeful, despite the evidence. He was so young! The finest possible doctors had been called in. One of them, Professor Achard, had shown considerable optimism, unfortunately unjustified. The other two, Dr. Laubry and Professor Bezançon, had foretold the worst. I clung to the hope offered by Professor Achard. A nurse assisted Josette in looking after Jean. His friends did all they could to help and his landlords, the good Bruyères, were a great stand-by.

Jean became silent, neither speaking nor crying any more. He lay motionless. His head seemed to have shrunk. It reminded me of those minute heads made by the Jivaros. Day after day he went on in this condition. Every night a woman who was in love with him telephoned to me from a remote foreign city for news. Everyone who knew him came to inquire.

On the evening of May 11 we heard a faint and very gentle hissing come from his lips. I had never heard the death-rattle of a dying man and did not realise that it was the end. We left Josette and Georges to go home for dinner, but we had hardly sat down at the table when Georges rushed in, pale and trembling, and said: "I believe Jean has died." We ran back—it was about half-past eight. Juan Gris was dead. Picasso and his wife, Beaudin, and Suzanne Roger soon arrived, followed by Maurice and Germaine Raynal and other intimate friends as soon as they heard the news. It was Elie Lascaux who closed Jean's eyes, assisted by my sister-in-law Jeanne. Suzanne Roger, Beaudin, and Lascaux watched over him that first night.

He was buried on May 13, in the morning. Only a few of the wreaths were on the death-bed, the rest were piled against the wall of the house and on the pavement. One large wreath bore the following inscription: "To Juan Gris, from his companions in the struggle." This inscription puzzled many of those present, as it was not sent by his fellow artists.

There were neither speeches nor a religious ceremony, but in the procession which filed down the Avenue de la Reine to the old cemetery of Boulogne were all those who had known Gris—painters, sculptors, poets, and musicians. The chief mourners were his son Georges, Lipchitz, Picasso, Raynal, and myself.

Thus died the purest of men, the most faithful and tender friend I have ever known, and one of the noblest artists ever born.

Bunch of Grapes and Glass · 1922

INTRODUCTION — 1. AESTHETICA IN NUCE

The artistic movement which was called by its early opponents Cubism (the name by which it has passed into history) met at the outset with general hostility. The Cubist painters were accused of being practical jokers, madmen, and even ingenious swindlers. It must be admitted that their pictures, which differed considerably not only from those in museums but even from the work of the artists of the preceding generation, were bound to come as a shock to those who saw them. For they defied habits of vision and thought which had been established for many centuries.

By their brilliant gifts four great painters—Braque, Gris, Léger and Picasso—finally established their work in the admiration of all who possess a feeling for the plastic arts. They were trusted, and then people became accustomed to the appearance of their pictures. Nevertheless one cannot help wondering whether all the admirers of Cubism, despite their ardour, really understand the causes of this appearance which so shocked their fathers. I believe therefore that a book devoted to one of these four painters should begin with an explanation of this appearance. In this way the historical position of Cubism will also be clarified. But first of all one must dispel any possibility of misunderstanding. The upheaval which Cubism caused in western art has been amazingly far-reaching and, if this movement is to be seriously studied, a preliminary understanding of certain elementary notions is indispensable. Many expressions, in fact, owing to the imprecise way in which they are used, are easily interpreted in a sense derived from the very tendencies against which the Cubists were struggling. And as the creation of Cubism was really the fact which proved that our understanding of them was one-sided and in-adequate, there must be no uncertainty.

We are concerned with *Painting*. The creator of a painted work—be it oil, water-colour, pastel, or drawing—the painter, that is, is a man who feels an overpowering need to record his emotion[49] on a flat surface by means of lines and forms of one or more colours. I say "his *emotion*" and not an object apart from himself, because the object only exists for him in the tangible world through his emotion, to which he attributes a particular quality which drives him to perpetuate it so that everybody, through communication, can share it. This emotion often appears directly linked with an optical sensation, but it can equally well be of a different nature. Even then, however, it can only be communicated in paint if it is objectivised, that is to say amalgamated with elements which will take on objective significance for the spectator. This fusion will take place right away in the creative imagination of the artist: it is the very sign of his plastic gift. For the painter, every emotion ends in a plastic image and it is this image which he attempts to transmit.

Let us be clear. The true painter does not coldly *copy* a mental image; this would be mere duplication. It is true that many painters state that they *see* in advance their completed canvas in all its detail. I well remember that this was van Dongen's boast in about 1908. But I do not believe that such foresight is a healthy sign in an artist. Picasso, on the contrary, has often told me that "one must have an idea of what one is going to do, but only a vague one". Fear of repetition has always prevented Picasso, as much as Gris and Braque, from working out precise drawings in preparation for pictures; for the lazy repetition which results from this habit and ends in the Ecole des Beaux-Arts practice of "squaring up" always seemed to them to kill the enthusiasm which is the essence of fruitful work. What is more, I have frequently seen pictures by Picasso completely change their appearance during the course of execution, as though several mental images had fought for the honour of coming to life. With Juan Gris, as will be seen, the autonomy of the act of creation was so great that, at the end of his life, contact with the emotion in which the work originated was ostensibly only resumed upon completion of the picture. In short, with the true artist it is as if the mental image, fruit of the emotion, defines itself for the painter himself only as it gradually takes shape on the canvas—as if he himself only discovered this image gradually. The excitement of this enthralling quest can well be imagined.

Van Dongen's method, with its "journalistic" flatness and its "reportage" of the mental image, appears so cold when compared with this uninterrupted process of "becoming". It precludes in effect all "inspiration", all possibility of being swept beyond the control of reason, from the moment the picture is begun. That is why van Dongen, although gifted as a colourist, has never advanced; for, provided that the work is really creative, the real progress is made on the canvas.

To be brief: the mental image which has formed in the creative imagination of the artist exists for him alone. The new factor is that it is going to exist for others by taking shape. This materialisation is the crucial moment; the real struggle takes place during the transformation of the "internal image", still vague and undefined, into the "external image", clear, firm and visible to all on a flat surface of given dimensions.

This is the origin of a work in paint, which, like all works of art, is a new object which has never existed before and which will always be unique. This entity has a two-fold existence. *It exists autonomously in itself, by itself and for itself, as an object : but outside itself it has a further existence—it signifies something.* Its lines and forms are there to compose certain signs, and by virtue of this the painting is a representation of thought by means of graphic signs—*writing*. The painter in fact tries, through these signs, to reproduce his emotion in the imagination of the spectator by inducing a re-creation of the image which appeared in his own. He will succeed if the spectator "reads" the picture. The spectator will then "see" what the painter intended to represent: *he will have identified the sign with the object signified.*

Transmission of thought has only been possible since the discovery of the *possibility* of such identification; this is the basis of painting and of every other form of writing, and also of language. The identity of the graphic, plastic or vocal sign with the thing signified appears complete to primitive man—an identity of fact, with all the "magical" consequences which ensue. For civilised man this identity is only imaginary, except in the case of painting and sculpture, where a trace of ancestral beliefs

The Sun-blind · 1914

lingers on in the attitude of the simple spectator. The simple spectator is unable to think of a work of art as a sign; for him it is linked to the object it "represents" by an identity which he feels to be "true" when the work of art resembles it, whereas he denies all *raison d'être* to the work which does not. To his mind a work of art can only exist as a reflection, a "replica" of the object represented. He would certainly not feel this about the graphic signs that he learnt to make at school, for he does not believe that the written word is identical with what it signifies. But it would never strike him that a painting, drawing or sculpture might have some connection with his own scribbling.

Writing, however, is always involved when thought is transmitted by graphic or, for that matter, plastic signs. Thus, not only painting, but also sculpture, is writing. Besides, the use of plastic signs goes back to the very beginnings of what is normally called writing. Mnemonic signs (which I shall discuss shortly) are often objects which take on meaning through their mere presence, or by the way in which they are arranged.

The reader must not regard this definition of painting as a paradox or an exercise in rhetoric. I am convinced that it is only by analysing the essence of painting that we shall arrive at an understanding of the profound aims of Juan Gris and his friends (aims hidden to the artists themselves) and consequently of the appearance of their works; and so we shall prove that they are not plastic freaks or the subtle pastimes of clever men. It is then imperative for us to examine, without prejudice, the different ways in which thought can be transmitted through graphic or plastic signs.

It is usual to refer, under the name of "pictography", to a certain number of works (paintings, drawings or engravings) which should undoubtedly be classed also as painting. Some writers even regard many sculptures as "pictography". "In various parts of the world," writes Robert Lowie,[50] "we can observe a particular form of realism known as pictography. Strictly speaking, it does not fall under the heading of art, for its essential aim is not the creation of beauty but the recording or passing on of information. Nevertheless it is difficult to separate it from art, firstly because it uses the same technique, and secondly because it expresses ideas which are also conveyed by unquestionably aesthetic processes."

No-one could fail to see how confused and ambiguous this definition of pictography is. Lowie declares that pictography does not fall under the heading of art because its essential aim is not the creation of beauty: he adds, however, that it is difficult to separate it from art. It is the practical function of pictography which forces Lowie to separate it from art, because he is faithful to the old theory that art is "the creation of beauty". Hence, his ambiguity and subsequent contradiction.

Now my purpose is to prove that this old theory is wrong, that never in any period has the object of painting (or for that matter of any other art) been "the creation of beauty", but that this quality has been mysteriously incorporated in certain works painted for purely practical ends. Every plastic work of art is produced in response to the requirements of the spiritual community.

The practical purposes of painting can be most varied, and one of the commonest is that very purpose which Robert Lowie feels to be foreign to art, namely the "recording or passing on of information". The purpose of "historical painting" has been just this, from earliest times down to Delacroix. Velazquez' *Treaty of Breda* is information recorded or passed on.

If it now seems established that pictography is an integral part of painting, the difficulty still remains of defining those works which we can unquestionably call pictographic. The real aim of pictography, which will be confused with historical painting as long as Lowie's definition is accepted, can only be accurately defined by stating that it concerns information intended to *provoke an action*. Pictographic information is in the nature of a command or advice. This limitation will at once disqualify a large number of works at present regarded as pictographic. Thus, Lowie quotes as examples "the shirts and robes of the Prairie Indians, the bas-reliefs in the Palace of Abomey, and the messages carved on birch-bark by the inhabitants of Northern Siberia".[51] Of all these, only the "messages carved on birch-bark" are without doubt "pragmatic" information. As regards the shirts of the Indians, a magic purpose seems the most probable,[52] whilst the bas-reliefs of Abomey are mainly historical paintings. In any case, any classification will clearly remain uncertain which finds no objective support in the works themselves, but is forced to deduce their nature from the supposed intentions of their creators. Let us then be content with saying that primitive man made use of painting, drawing and engraving for many purposes, one of which was the communication of practical messages. Such messages are called pictography, but this term is only permissible if the practical nature of the message is indisputable. The use of painting, drawing and engraving for these messages certainly offered considerable advantages: they could be read in any language. But because of this, they often lacked the desired precision. On the other hand, the use of pictorial means limited the number of possible "scribes", since artistic gifts were necessary to "write" these messages.

I have used the word "pragmatic" in connection with true pictographic messages. The writings of all races are, in fact, "pragmatic writings". By using this word I am deliberately rejecting the idea that writing developed owing to a need to express abstract ideas. I cannot share the opinion of Jacques de Morgan, who writes:[53] "When man, with the gradual refinement of his intellect, emerged from a purely material existence, he felt the need to record his thoughts in order to transmit them through signs intelligible to all; and the first means he found was to represent by drawing the simple ideas that occurred to him. This first attempt gave birth to representative pictography: but soon, when the field of pictography became too narrow to cope with even the simplest abstract ideas, conventional symbols were added to it." To my mind it was not "abstract ideas" which primitive man first felt the need to transmit, but rather the most concrete information which was useful in his struggle for life. It was not in a world of "images" but in one of "forces" that he turned for support to writing as a means of communication with his fellow-men. It is to this very purpose that painting does not easily lend itself; but it is not fundamentally incapable of transmitting abstract ideas, which it does by means of signs which we call symbols. I shall return to this later on.

Pragmatic writing necessitated signs which everyone would be capable of making after some instruction, signs which could be executed rapidly and which, by convention, acquired a definite and invariable meaning. All these qualities are lacking in painting, which I will call "formative writing"[54] for reasons which I shall explain.

The difficulties which stand in the way of a regular use of painting as pragmatic writing did not exist in the case of the other primitive form of writing called *mnemonic signs*. These are signs, or even objects, to which a conventional meaning was arbitrarily given. Signs of this type dating from the Stone Age are thought to be found on the painted stones from Mas d'Azil and the engraved bones from the caves at Lorthat. They occur frequently in the primitive art of America and Oceania. Indeed, the tradition still carries on in the secret signs of gipsies and tramps, a practice which the Boy Scouts try to copy. Certainly a magical meaning is often inherent in mnemonic signs. Moreover, this coincides with their pragmatic, utilitarian aim. What is important for us is that mnemonic signs are, like pictography, *information giving commands or advice*. Nevertheless, it has often been established that the information they convey is necessarily rather limited; so that, if difficulties of execution did not exist and their meaning was fixed by convention, the defect of this "writing" was its poverty of expression.

Neither pictography nor mnemonic signs were adequate for less primitive civilisations. More subtle methods were needed. There can clearly be no question of showing here how the graphic sign in different forms of writing came to correspond more or less to the vocal sign, nor, for even better reasons, how the vocal sign is connected with the object. Our subject only requires a description of the various sorts of writing, so that we can analyse the way in which they work.

The systems of pragmatic writing that man has developed for his use are generally classified as ideographic and phonetic. Now I maintain that there is a discrepancy between these two systems which makes a common origin impossible. I believe that this discrepancy is such that, according to which system is used for figuration, even the languages (and particularly the poetry of these languages) bear the stamp of the system they have adopted. Ideographic writing goes with concrete languages, for their basis is the image; phonetic writing with abstract languages, for their basis is the idea. It is not for me to say (and it has little bearing on our study) whether writing formed the language, or *vice versa*; what is interesting for us is that this connection exists.

It is my belief that any interpretation which ignores this fundamental difference is the victim of a mistaken occidental conception—that writing is merely as faithful a transcription of the language as possible. This is certainly not true of one language which is still spoken and written to-day—Chinese. Granet writes:[55] "The chief merit of figurative writing is that it permits graphic signs, and through them words, to give the impression of having the value of active, real forces." Thus, Granet here affirms the supremacy of writing over language, whereas in western writing the pre-eminence of language is evident, the purpose of writing being merely to transcribe it as faithfully as possible.

Once this is clear, we should ask ourselves whether man did not arrive at the invention of pragmatic writing along two entirely different lines, making a choice according to the particular qualities of his cultural environment, according to his needs and his ways of thinking and feeling, according to whether they were more or less abstract or concrete—true, this is contrary to the still very prevalent opinion that evolution has been an unbroken progression. The supporters of this hypothesis regard the mnemonic sign as an abortive attempt, doomed by its own nature to failure and inevitably destined to disappear without any possible continuation. The whole evolution starts, thus, from pictography. Vendryes writes:[56] "A great step forward was taken when man learnt how to draw and so make the

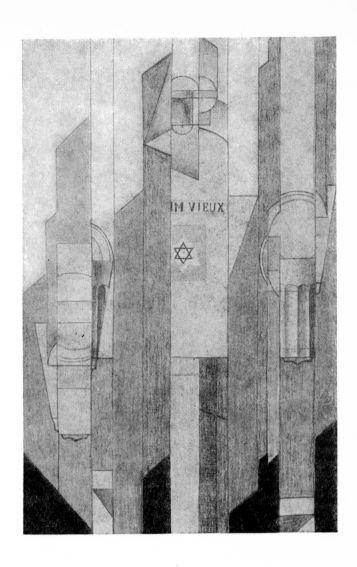

Rum Bottle · 1912

image into the emblem of the object. ... From this there was born ideographic writing ... which is at the root of every system of writing used by mankind." Some people try to bridge the gulf between ideographic and phonetic writings by proving (to quote the prevailing theory) that the alphabetical writing of the Phoenicians was derived from the ideographic writing of the Egyptians. Kurt Sethe, in particular, believed he had found the missing link in the inscriptions discovered in the Sinai Peninsula by Sir Flinders Petrie, in 1905, which Gardiner and Peet described in 1917. However, in a pertinent postscript to Sethe's posthumous work which puts forward this point of view,[57] Siegfried Schott completely destroyed the assumption. His argument is not only based on the most recent discoveries and on a technical analysis which I could not give here, but also on a very clear perception of the basic difference between the two languages. He proves that, contrary to common belief, Egyptian writing, in its "inner" form as he calls it, remained ideographic to the end. He denounces attempts to prove a gradual evolution as an abuse of historiographic tendency, which is only justified when it groups together what are really members of the same family.

Proof of the theory that all writing has one origin having failed, it seems legitimate to propose another based on the discrepancy which we have just been examining.

Ideographic writings derive from painting. There can be no doubt of this, since they are obviously a rationalisation of pictography which, as we have seen, is essentially painting. Their signs are pictorial ones, whose meaning is frozen by convention, but which nevertheless retain a sort of immediate efficacy. These signs are read in images. Their power of direct evocation persists even when two ideograms are combined in one. For proof I need only quote an example given by Granet:[58] "The character 'wou' (warrior) is formed with the elements *stop* (image of a foot) and *the spears* (image of a spear)." From this one can see the plastic force which the sign retains.

Egyptian writing kept the image as its base even when, at a certain stage in its development, it adopted the form of so-called puns, that is to say as if it wrote "bedlam" by depicting a bed and a lamb. Thus, it signifies the syllable and not the word. Even so, whilst aiming in this way to transcribe the vocal sign more precisely, it juxtaposes ideograms, frozen pictorial signs. The Egyptians did not think of using *arbitrary* signs, which they would doubtless never have come to identify with the thing signified.

The peculiarity of *phonetic writing* lies in the *choice of entirely arbitrary signs*. The relationship with *mnemonic signs* is here so close that I do not hesitate to regard them as a perfection of the latter. Like mnemonic signs, the signs of phonetic writing are conventional, arbitrarily chosen and with no autonomous power. Like them, they indicate a mentality less responsive to the image than to the idea, or, to put it differently, less to the appearance of things than to their effect. Like mnemonism, phonetic writings require "initiation": they too are pure cryptography with no visual "key".

One need not here enquire whether the first phonetic writing (Phoenician) replaced a writing with mnemonic signs. Anyway, it is most unlikely. What I believe is that a very special state of mind is necessary to conceive of a possible identity between signs deliberately chosen and the thing they are meant to represent, and that such a state of mind will lead in an inferior stage of civilisation to mnemonism, in a superior stage to phonetic writing. This phonetic writing could even take over certain signs from an ideographic writing (which is exactly what happened with Phoenician and Egyptian writing). It is precisely by using these signs in the wrong way, by giving them quite another meaning to that which they had before, that it shows itself indifferent to their direct action; it transforms them into mnemonic signs.

These new mnemonic signs transcribe the vocal sign in every detail. Therein lies the innovation of alphabetical writing. The old mnemonic signs necessarily remained subject to a rather variable vocal transcription. In this respect they were "fluid"; they were only precise in their practical meaning.

In place of one writing which, despite all its varied aspects, is always essentially the same, we have discovered two graphic families. This duality should be visible in the action of writings, for it should reflect their foundation. Ideographic writings should inevitably have something of the character of the message transmitted by painting; phonetic writings should operate quite differently. What then is the action of the message in "formative writing" and in the two great branches of "pragmatic writing"?

The *painter* drew the sign which for him meant "tree". It would not be quite correct to say that this sign has *no* conventional value, for (as we shall see later), without some convention (or, perhaps, familiarity for the "reader", which is absolutely the same thing), the sign would remain unintelligible. This conventional value, however, remains fluid, vague, and the painter has complete freedom to vary and enrich it after his own fashion. The initiated spectator will certainly read "tree", but this idea will be completed with countless details and will be surrounded with an aura. The tree may be slender or bushy, shapely or twisted, smooth or gnarled; it may exist at a certain hour of day, at a particular season. The sign will release a flood of impressions. What is read will not be a *word* but an *image* with its limitless possibilities. Painting, in so far as it is writing, transcribes images, not words. The painter tries to transmit images; the spectator first "reads" them and then transforms them into ideas.

The progress of the message could be shown as follows:

> Graphic sign
>
> Image
>
> Vocal sign
>
> Idea

The image which appeared in the spectator's mind on reading the graphic sign was translated into a word which became fixed as an idea.

The man who uses *ideographic writing* draws his sign. This has an established, conventional value, but its plastic origin is not entirely forgotten. Of Chinese writing, Marcel Granet writes:[59] "Confucius, it appears, declared that the sign representing a dog was a perfect drawing of one. If we look at this sign, it is clear that, for the philosopher, a representation can be adequate which does not seek to reproduce all the object's characteristics. It is enough for it to reveal, in a stylised fashion, an attitude considered characteristic or judged significant of a certain type of action or relationship."

Chinese writing, like cuneiform writing, can be read by people who speak a different idiom. Its signs have a direct action very similar to that of pictorial signs. Now the term *graphic emblem*, which Granet uses for them, seems to me to apply so well to pictorial signs that I think it will be useful to adopt it here to describe pictorial signs with a single meaning; we can then reserve the term *symbol* for signs with a dual meaning—that is to say, representing objects of two-fold identity. By this I mean the Paschal Lamb or the Fish of the early Christians which "is" Christ at the same time.

In the remainder of this chapter I shall show that the effectiveness of graphic emblems and symbols in painting is partly defined by Granet's statement about the signs in Chinese writing. However, the stages of communication differ, for in Chinese writing it must end in vocal emblems, which are considered identical with the graphic emblems. Here is the process:

> Graphic sign
>
> Image
>
> Idea
>
> Vocal sign

We must now examine the action of the graphic sign (that is, the group of signs assembled to transcribe a succession of sounds) in languages with *phonetic writing*. The group of signs is "spelt", for its *appearance* has no meaning, no effective power of its own. Its equivalent is reconstituted in the form of a word, a vocal sign. The word inspires an idea and this idea finally produces the image. Thus, the method is as follows:

> Graphic sign
>
> Vocal sign
>
> Idea
>
> Image

It is perhaps not irrelevant to explain how the mnemonic sign also is read, as it will confirm that this sign really is at the root of phonetic writings. Their non-visual, that is to say abstract, character —for the image alone is concrete in the action of writing—is even more deeply marked in the mnemonic sign, which never ends in an image. It is the archetype of pragmatic writing, of writing which only knows and is concerned with "forces". It proceeds as follows:

> Mnemonic sign
>
> Idea
>
> Vocal sign

The image—which is not necessary for the action desired, advised or ordered—never appears. Because they have not remained purely pragmatic, because they have lent themselves to the transcription of *poetry*, phonetic writings create images when the act of reading is complete.

I have already referred to the influence of the system of writing on the *poetry*. And we shall find, if we class the various arts according to their medium, that there is a kinship between poetry and painting, for both are writing. The poet, like the painter, seeks to make the "reader" share his emotion by using graphic signs. Nevertheless the intervention of these in poetry is only secondary, for before there was any written literature there was a great body of spoken literature, whereas the very existence of painting is bound up with its signs, which in consequence have a value of their own. Not only do the *products* of painting exist autonomously, but also its *signs* work by virtue of a power inherent in them. Graphic signs retain some of this power in the poetry of a language which uses ideographic writing, for they retain, albeit feebly, some *formative quality*: that is to say, the power to create images. The great painter invents new signs. So does the Chinese poet. "Chinese writing," says Granet,[60] "has served to increase the vocabulary. Since earliest times the writers' art, and *above all that of the poets*," he adds, "has seemed to consist partly in the great number of graphic signs employed in their manuscripts. This fact discloses the domination exercised by the system of writing over the development of the language. It must be supposed that the poems when recited *spoke*, if I may use the phrase, *to the eyes*, owing to the stimulation of a graphic memory echoing the verbal memory. It is hard for us to understand this process, but it clearly had a decisive effect: the words never became mere signs. Figurative writing helped most of the words to retain full power of concrete expression, together with a kind of freshness and the character of *living words*."

Here, then, the poet creates the graphic sign equivalent to the vocal sign: the image is the primary

Bottle and Glass · 1914

factor. In the poetry of *languages written phonetically*, on the other hand, the written signs are merely a simple transcription of the vocal signs. The images only appear later, after the spoken text has been reconstituted. The *painter*, finally, has absolute command over images to the point, as we shall see, of determining through them even the world-image of the spiritual community to which he belongs.

Not long ago an attempt was made to endow French poetry with powers similar to the Chinese; I allude to Guillaume Apollinaire's *Calligrammes*.[61] When he revived in his poems what, in the seventeenth century, had merely been fanciful decoration—a typographical arrangement forming one or more graphic signs—he intended to restore to French phonetic writing the "power to solicit or compel".[62] At the same time, Apollinaire came near to painting by his attempt to arrive directly at the image, for in phonetic writings the message normally has to cross the no-man's land of abstractions (vocal sign, idea) before becoming an image. His experiment was confined to a small number of poems of his own and of the few disciples who copied him, for it is impossible deliberately to alter the nature of a language. But this enrichment had its limitations, for it then became impossible to read the poems aloud and so they were deprived of the *musical* quality which all western poetry possesses. Apollinaire used a trick of typography: it seems that there is no other way for the occidental poet to create *new graphic signs*. As a general rule he feels no need of them, since for him graphic signs only serve to transcribe the vocal signs on which his work depends. And he does not need to create *new vocal signs*.[63] His task is to restore real meaning to words which have become stale through constant use. The tendency inherent in phonetic languages is for words to be reduced to abstractions, after which they become empty shells. The poet strives to give them back concrete meaning.

I shall refer only briefly to *music* here, as I must return to it later. It should be mentioned because it too employs writing; but in this case the graphic signs have no autonomy, simply an entirely conventional meaning. When read, their immediate significance is for musicians only; communication of the message really only occurs when the music is performed, translation into sound being necessary before most people can understand it. This is a more serious limitation than that of poetry, which need only be read aloud to illiterates. Thus, even more than the graphic signs of phonetically written languages, the "notes" in music are a conventional figuration without any existence of their own, serving only to preserve and transmit the musical thought. Music does not seek to re-create either images or ideas in the listener. We shall see that the art most comparable to it is architecture, which is also based on rhythm.

The arts which to-day are grouped with painting under the common heading of *the plastic arts* are sculpture and architecture. Like poetry and painting, sculpture endeavours to transmit an emotional experience. But whereas poetry only exists in space through its medium (because writing has no existence of its own), painting and sculpture are closely related through a characteristic common to their products:[64] they "exist" autonomously as objects in the outer world. Sculpture, however, is the creation of "plastic emblems" (to use a phrase which is etymologically pleonastic but excusable), three-dimensional objects existing in space and exposed to its light, whereas painting takes shape on a flat surface; that is to say, it refuses to exist in the three-dimensional world, and in each work space and light are simulated by means of graphic emblems. It follows that only *sculpture in the round* is essentially sculpture. High-relief is sculpture which dares not venture further into space. It clings to a fixed background and has no cubic existence. Then there is bas-relief, which cuts itself off completely from space and is painting done with the tools of a sculptor. It exists in the imaginary space which it creates, but sculptural technique compels "real" light to illuminate this fictitious space which is pictorially conceived.

There are so many possibilities of interpenetration between the techniques of painting and sculpture that it is important to adhere firmly to the definition of sculpture as something which has a cubic existence in space. Picasso, for example, often attempted to make use of sculptural methods in his pictures during the period when he was striving to find a substitute for chiaroscuro. In 1909, in a still-life (*The Piano*), he tried to produce the effect of light by means of slight projections on the flat surface of the canvas; one might call them an almost imperceptible sort of bas-relief. These projections were made with lumps of plaster which were then painted over. He hoped in this way to be able to achieve the "true" colour of an object, its "local colour", and to leave the representation of volume to these projections, since in daylight they cast slight shadows which replaced chiaroscuro.

These attempts, which he considered unsuccessful, led to "superimposed planes". I shall deal more fully with all these experiments later on. Since then, the whole of this frontier-region between painting and sculpture has been widely explored and the phrase "Sculpto-Painting" invented. Among those who have obtained successful results, first place must be given to Picasso himself, and to Braque, whose paper sculptures have, however, disappeared. Léger painted and sculpted a bas-relief of Charlie Chaplin which deserves mention here. Gris' sculpture, although polychrome, was sculpture in the round, true sculpture.

The experiments of the Cubist painters have been carried on by various sculptors, notably Laurens and Lipchitz. Archipenko was the first to apply the term "Sculpto-Painting" to his work.

During the period from 1910 to 1930 there was a definite tendency for artists to express themselves in forms which made use of the technique of more than one art. I have in mind particularly Apollinaire's *Calligrammes*, which has already been discussed, and other similar attempts: Huidobro's "painted poems", that is to say poems inscribed on coloured bands; coloured typography on a coloured background (Cendrars' and Delaunay's *Transsibérien*; *La Fin du Monde* by Cendrars and Léger); and lastly, Picasso's sculpto-architecture, which exist as pictures but were never executed owing to lack of financial backing. These were to be erected beside the Mediterranean and were buildings, which were at the same time sculptures representing female heads.

There may be a technical mixture, but the works themselves cannot be simultaneously two kinds of art. Sculpto-painting is painting, *Calligrammes* and similar attempts are poetry, and Picasso's sculpto-architecture is sculpture.

At this point it must be stated that the plastic emblems by which sculpture is expressed are plastic emblems in true space. This enables us to class relief in the domain of painting. Picasso's sculpto-architecture is legitimately called sculpture because it makes use of vast plastic emblems in space; because, standing out grandly against the sky, it "signifies" women's heads.

Architecture, like sculpture, exists in real space, but it exists only as itself and signifies nothing outside of itself. From this point of view it may fairly be compared with music; but whereas architecture remains immobile in space, music, like poetry, moves forward in time. Architecture and music have no graphic character, since they do not create signs. They are "egocentric", abstract arts, as opposed to the representational arts (painting, sculpture, and poetry), which are not limited to their own existence and strive to signify something. There have indeed been attempts at "significant music", but these were based on a misunderstanding of its true nature. To-day hardly anyone can be found who supports this movement. We have seen that interpenetration has gone on between painting and sculpture, sculpture and architecture, poetry and painting. During the same period there was a further attempt at combination: efforts were made to enrich poetry by musical means, recitation by several voices, spoken choruses, etc. This attempt did not last long: a few public performances proved its useless and hybrid character. The real solution would have been to set the text to music.

At this point it is essential to say something about ornament, which is wrongly termed "decorative art". We must be clear that this is *not* art, and then ornament will not be mistakenly classed as one of the abstract arts. All art, as we have seen, is the creation of new objects which are unique. The purpose of ornament is quite different: it is purely hedonistic. It is intended simply as an embellishment of an object which already exists. Cosmetics, for example, are a form of ornament. In some civilisations ornament is a stylisation derived from painting, through the hedonistic petrifaction of certain pictorial signs. More frequently it does not derive from painting, which is formative writing, but from pragmatic writing, and is purely and simply calligraphy, an emblem of ideographic writing (or even a sign of a phonetic writing such as Arabic script) whose meaning and power have been forgotten and whose sole function is to embellish and make pleasing some existing object—carpet, wall or vase.

Like all true art, the abstract arts (architecture and music) create new objects. These objects, however, live by themselves alone, whereas the representational arts have a function beyond the particular existence of the works themselves. To fulfil this function these arts became graphic. Within each art the writing has a very varied appearance—a fact easily explained in the case of poetry, but which is surrounded with mystery in the case of sculpture and painting, where the diversity becomes alarming. This curious phenomenon, however, presented no difficulty to an undeveloped aesthetic, which held that a picture was only the reflection of the outer world, and therefore only admitted the one form of writing which it regarded as a faithful reproduction of this world, and rejected any other as the work of men incapable of exact imitation.[65] Such an aesthetic could only prevail in the west so long as an absolute ideal—Greek art in the fifth century B.C.—seemed to correspond alone to reality; any style that was different was regarded as the product of a period or of an artist who had not succeeded in reproducing reality. To-day the painting and sculpture of all ages and civilisations has entered our aesthetic orbit and our museums, and it has become very difficult to uphold this simple-minded and presumptuous opinion any longer. How can one, in fact, believe either that Pericles' contemporaries were the only men capable of reproducing the outer world or that, therefore, this can only be achieved by copying them? Still more, how can one explain why so many periods which *might* have copied

Glass and Carafe · 1917

them did nothing of the kind? Let us take sculpture, since Greek art has mainly survived in this form. The public squares of Byzantium, until the Crusaders' conquest, were full of Hellenic statues, some of which, owing to the difficulty of removing them, even survived until the Turkish conquest. The same was true of Rome throughout all the Middle Ages—a letter from Cola Rienzi to Petrarch bears this out. Why then did artists refuse to imitate the models which were in front of their eyes? Inability? But between 1233 and 1240, the sculptors of Apulia succeeded in erecting for Frederick II the Triumphal Arch at Capua, in the Roman style, as the busts adorning it, some of which have survived, can prove. When the desire to imitate was present there was no lack of ability.[66] Besides, plaster moulds and bronze castings were known, so mechanical duplication would have been perfectly feasible. We are left, therefore, with only one possible explanation for the multitude of different "styles" that we know to-day: the desire of their creators to transmit their message *in their own way* and no other. What then is the meaning of the enormous diversity of these records, all of which purport to describe the same outer world? How is it that, when faced with most of them, the average Occidental cannot even manage to form an image corresponding to the outer world as he knows it? Is it because of difficulty in reading an unknown writing, as with a poem in an unknown language? In a small way yes, as we shall see later. But let us remember that the signs of poetry written in an occidental language only act through words which themselves signify objects and ideas, whereas the connection between pictorial writing and the result when read, the image of the world in the spectator's mind, is direct. Consequently, in the latter case the difficulty of reading is less.

Now that we have discarded any idea of inability to imitate, and since extensive proof can be found that men have always seen in the painting and sculpture of their time an exact representation of the outer world,[67] only one explanation is to my mind possible: that since such divergent writings, many of which do not agree with our own vision, "signified" the outer world for hundreds of millions of men, then *this outer world itself can appear to mankind in many different guises*. To understand this axiom, which I consider fundamental to any serious analysis of the essence of painting, a brief discussion of *vision* is indispensable.

For the animal, the outer world is a group of active forces, good or evil, which it knows only by their effect on itself. Recognition and knowledge of them merely serve it to live and move amongst them. The faculties of a young child are not developed beyond this *pragmatic vision*, which even remains as the basis in the adult stage, ready to assist us in case of danger. Research into the development of vision is usually limited to this pragmatic vision. Now it is this vision which has need of the tactile sense in order to develop, for in life we need to "know" the bodies with which we come into contact. Without this pragmatic vision man would behave as if blind, but even its possession merely gives him an instrument whose use is limited to the facts of day to day existence. It makes no effort to explore or know any but a world of *forces*—something fairly similar to the physicist's world—and not a world of *images*.

This pragmatic vision is dominant among primitive beings, whose "aesthetic vision" (as I call it) is scarcely developed and is only composed of a small number of "created images". It is only by sharing the vision of contemporary painting that the aesthetic vision achieves totality. He alone *sees* clearly and fully who is familiar with the painting of his time. For him alone the outer world takes on form and colour, and becomes an image, in imitation of the pictures which he is accustomed to see. Painters do not *imitate* an outer world which we know but vaguely, within the limits of our senses; painters *create* the outer world in visible form, they make us *see* it in the likeness of their works, where the animal or small child, who is plastically blind, only feels the play of obscure forces. One must under-stand that aesthetic vision implies practical indifference. Many philosophers, particularly Schopenhauer, have shown this. The vision of most men is almost perpetually confined to the domain of utility.[68] Hence, their great difficulty in attaining to an aesthetic vision on the rare occasions when they try; for they have so little material with which to construct their image of the outer world.

Now what exactly is the role of painting in this construction? It provides the materials. The "graphic emblems" which it creates are stored up in the spectator's imagination: with them he builds his outer world, and will perhaps later enrich other groups of graphic emblems with the image-memories thus built up—a sort of give-and-take, the basis of which, however, is painting. And this is what one might call the biological function of painting.

It follows that, in painting, differences in handwriting create differences in the outer world. And this helps us to understand how the most varied forms of record (for example, during the Christian era, the frescoes of Pompeii, Byzantine seventh-century mosaics, the works of Rembrandt and those of Courbet) have each in turn represented perfect "likenesses" for contemporary spectators. It is only our own period which has fallen behind in its ability to read. The average spectator has not been able to read the writing of his time. This happened with Impressionism, Pointillism, Post-Impressionism, Fauvism, and Cubism, each time growing less marked afterwards until, with the second generation of spectators, the difficulty had vanished. But it has not yet entirely disappeared in the case of pictures by Picasso and Braque of the 1909–13 period, which in consequence is often called their "hermetic period".

In a normal, untroubled civilisation the spectator can always "read" the art of his time and recognise the outer world herein. For him this art is representative. Why, from Impressionism to Cubism, has the art of our time only been comprehensible to certain people? The fault lies with the Academies of the various western countries. Many people are still inclined to regard the teaching of these schools as normal and the work of unofficial painters as abnormal in its novelty. They are wrong: what is normal is the "becoming", the perpetual evolution and alteration of style, for it is by inventing new graphic signs to replace those that are worn out that the painter proclaims his greatness and truly fulfils his role. We shall see in a minute why the need for such renewal has undoubtedly been more urgent during the past century than ever before. In the old days, teaching, practical teaching through apprenticeship to a master, was not an attempt to impose an aesthetic outlook but merely an effort to impart a craft. True, the weak pupil imitated the style of his master, but the real painter made his personality felt directly he left the studio. In spite of the name "Academy", this teaching of a craft continued as successfully amongst the painters who were members of Italian institutions such as The Academy of St. Luke in Rome, as in the Académie de Peinture Française, which was founded in imitation by Le Brun in 1648. It was only at the beginning of the nineteenth century, and especially in Napoleon's Ecole des Beaux-Arts, that direct teaching in the master's studio, which meant evolution, the advocation of no particular form of appearance or style, began to be abandoned (for the *atelier* of the Ecole des Beaux-Arts is one in name only) in favour of a bureaucratic, state-run organisation. With the reform of the Ecole by Viollet le Duc, in 1863, the rot finally set in.

From the opening of the Ecole the graphic emblems petrified. Confusing the emblems of formative writing with those of pragmatic writing, the Ecole declared that only the emblems of the classical heritage of the Louis XVI period were valid and thereby established a perpetual convention. But owing to short-sightedness, the Ecole overlooked the most vital element in the art of a David: composition. And here I will make use of a term which we shall often come across in the writings of Gris, and which I shall have to employ frequently: it insisted on an imitation of the handwriting and ignored the *architecture*, for which it substituted a vague, pseudo-geometrical arrangement, whose miserable recipe it taught. [69]

The reader may have noticed that when the State took over the teaching of the Fine Arts this also marked the beginning of the decay in architecture and the applied arts. A certain cohesion was of course evident up to about 1850. There was the "Empire style" and the "Louis-Philippe style" which developed from it, and painting and sculpture can be related to these styles. Everything changed with Napoleon III. There was no true "Second Empire style" in architecture and furniture nor, *a fortiori*, in painting and sculpture. And when, in the applied arts, this designation is used it covers merely a vague eclecticism based on the "Louis XV style". The destruction of aesthetic unity in every branch of artistic creation coincided with the reform of the Ecole des Beaux-Arts by Viollet le Duc. This reform was a codification of the artistic sanctions which had been imposed on art fifty years previously by a State which, by arrogating to itself the right to impose an immutable vision of the outer world (*ne varietur*), ended by making even the creation of a period style impossible.

By its teaching, the Ecole artificially kept alive a vision that had been dead since the beginning of the nineteenth century, and thereby petrified the outer world for contemporaries and slowed up the reading of any new writing. This is not the place to discuss whether the State should undertake the teaching of the Fine Arts or not. The present system is only one hundred and fifty years old, but it is during this very period that the regrettable split has occurred between the true painters of the time and their contemporaries. Would a change of personnel, and consequently of method, produce other results? The Weimar Republic attempted a regeneration of Official Art by appointing real painters to professorships. Thus, Klee was a Professor at the Düsseldorf Academy, and before that at the Bauhaus of Weimar and Dessau, a semi-official institution. The fall of the Weimar Republic put an end to this experiment too soon for results to be judged. All we know are the products of the bureaucratic Ecoles des Beaux-Arts, whose professors are always selected from amongst former students. What have they produced? They have manufactured an "ideal beauty", which is just a heavy and crude distortion of the noble if somewhat dry art of David, and he has thus become the father of an Official Art which quite dishonours him. They have managed to impose their miserable, frozen vision on the public. Whilst "Modern" Museums and Salons have swamped society with works by the official academy spokesmen, the poor have merely received, in place of the popular print and the tuppence coloured, the cheapest objects such as chromolithographs, almanacs, postal calendars and illustrated papers like the supplements to the *Petit Journal* or the *Corriere della Sera*, the work of the unsuccessful products of this very teaching. The Church has ceased to be what it formerly was, a sacred museum, a figurative teacher of all things. The simple spectator stands between the pitiful view of the outer world in the pseudo-works of art surrounding him on all sides, and the work of true painters. And if he compares them he sees "distortion" in the work of the new painters, assuming, that is to say, that he can interpret them.

Lately, it is true, there has been a tendency towards change. The modern poster, on which Léger has left his mark, the window displays and catalogues of the chain stores, are accustoming even the provincial spectator to the appearance of Cubist and later painting, thus slowly re-creating for him the outer world in the image of the new art. There is therefore reason to hope that we shall soon see the end of this isolation of the painters from their contemporaries, a separation unparalleled in history.

Fruit-bowl and Carafe · 1914

Now although it is not given to all men immediately to assimilate the art of their time, they can usually at least read it without difficulty; for, in general, contemporary painting is representational to contemporary eyes, and it is only when a man compares other styles with *his own* outer world, which is the creation of the painting of his own day, that he decides whether these other styles are representational or not. The old theory that plastic art is the mirror of the world must be reversed: *it is the outer world which is the mirror of plastic art*.

One may wonder, of course, why the handwriting of different periods and civilisations is so disparate. But one must not go to the extreme of always supposing that there is a multiplicity of "outer worlds" behind the multiplicity of graphic emblems to which we are unaccustomed. This can be avoided by always bearing in mind the characteristics of plastic writing and not assuming that what are only graphic *tricks* are part of an imaginary outer world; such tricks were correctly read in their time, but the simple mind of the average modern spectator does not recognise them as part of *his* outer world and believes them to be "distortions".

The simple spectator describes as "distorted" every object, or part of an object, which he "reads" in a picture and which to his mind does not conform with that object as he imagines it in the outer world. We have already seen that the terms of this comparison must be revised. In reality, the object in the picture does not conform to the objects which are stored in his memory and which have taken shape according to the style of his period.

The causes of distortion can be legion, its significance most varied. It may be that the creator of the picture wished to emphasise by a flourish some particular detail. His contemporaries could easily read this sort of writing. When the painter *underlined*, as it were, some detail, when he wrote in capital letters or in italics, his contemporaries perfectly understood the meaning of these graphic tricks. They knew quite well that the individual depicted as being larger than the others was in fact not so, but simply more important; they knew that the arm which seemed too long was really of normal length but that the gesture needed emphasising. This type of distortion we can call *expressionistic*.

As an example of expressionistic distortion which has been digested, that is to say is no longer noticed by the spectator of to-day, I would cite linear perspective as it has been practised by the painters of the Occident from Uccello to the Impressionists. The occidental spectator "sees" this system of representation, which necessitates innumerable distortions, as absolutely identical with the appearance of the outer world.

Constructivist distortion is quite different, although one must hasten to add that, at quiet times, it too passes unnoticed by its contemporaries because they make the same sort of mental adjustment as they do for expressionistic distortion. In dealing with constructivist distortion we turn away from writing (through which painting is related to poetry) and come down to the picture as an object which exists in the outer world. As we have seen, the written or printed page, which is the graphic form of occidental poetry, only exists in the outer world as a means for the artificial transmission of words. In reality, poetry is communicated aurally (in which it is related to music) whilst painting is communicated visually, in which it is related to sculpture and architecture. It is this existence in the visible world, this obligation to take on a shape, which it has in common with these two arts, and it is precisely this obligation which imposes constructivist distortion on painting. Architecture knows no distortion, for its products do not "signify" anything and demand no comparisons. There can therefore be no contradiction. A piece of architecture is an "object" without a "subject", and is therefore free from expressionistic distortion. It shapes matter freely and with absolute authority, and is therefore also free from constructivist distortion. Sculpture, on the other hand, shares the lot of painting.

Constructivist distortion is born of the contradiction between the subject as presented by the artist's emotion and the form, proportions and substance of the object in which the subject is to materialise. The pillar-figures of Romanesque art and the figures carved within the rectangles of capitals, on lintels and on spandrels, are examples of this; likewise the paintings and mosaics made to fit triumphal arches, cupolas, or some other specifically defined area. I have merely noted the most striking examples. As a matter of fact, the fitting of the subject into the rectangle of the modern easel-painting presents difficulties which are scarcely less great.

Our examination of this problem of distortion has clearly revealed the dual role of a picture. It is *writing* whose purpose is to transmit the painter's emotion to the spectator; but to accomplish this it must take shape, it must become a visible object with its own existence, a flat surface of given dimensions and proportions covered with lines and forms. The fusion of the graphic emblems into a whole must be achieved by what, like Gris, I shall call *architecture*, despite the inconvenience of describing pictorial construction by the name of another art. Gris, however, has forcefully shown that this term alone describes the way in which the details are swallowed up by the whole.[70] The spectator first sees the flat surface. It may please or displease him, even before he has begun the closer examination which ends by his reading the message contained therein. A hedonistic aesthetic is content to limit "beauty" to this slight, skin-deep sensation of pleasure or displeasure. This is no way to appreciate art. "Do you then believe," said Berlioz to Adolphe Adam, "that one listens to music for pleasure?" A *psychological* study of individual reactions of this type would not, in any case, provide a basis for the *philosophical* definition of "beauty". For, instead of setting the bounds, it would have to take into account the oddest sensations simply because they claim to be reactions in front of a work of art. Now we are in the habit of using the word "beautiful" about a woman or a mountain as well as about a painting, thus often confusing our sexual emotion or the sense of well-being due to the proper functioning of the lungs with our aesthetic emotion. It can, of course, be claimed that this adjective will sometimes apply to a sort of ephemeral work of art which appears for a few moments in the creative imagination of the spectator, a vision formed by image-memories of works of art previously seen and which respond immediately to the stimulus of a new optical sensation. This aspect of the problem cannot be denied, for it explains the enhancement that painting brings to objects, whether natural or manufactured. Without Cubism no-one would ever have seen the *beauty* of the simple objects that the Cubists painted. It is the image of them in the work of these painters which has given them a new appearance for a generation which has assimilated Cubist painting. So it is evident that we have to reckon with a sort of reflected or second-hand beauty. However, it is too much to hope for a clear distinction between what is beautiful and what is pleasing in the mind of the average spectator; and therefore a poll of this sort will never be of any help to us in discovering "the beautiful". The average spectator can only state his likes and dislikes. A picture, or some other cause of optical sensation, will either be pleasing to him or not; but that has nothing to do with beauty. To make it clear that beauty has no concern with sentimentality or arbitrary taste, it must be emphasised that ugliness is the opposite of "prettiness", but that "beauty" has no antonym.

So far the question of beauty has not entered into our examination of artistic creation. In my attempts to elucidate the process of this creation we have nowhere been concerned with it. Why? Because, contrary to current aesthetic belief, the artist does not think of beauty at the time of creation. We have seen what is his aim: to record an emotion which he has experienced, to transmit his *Erlebnis* to other men. Beauty only reveals itself upon completion of the message. He who can read the message will be aware of its special quality, a sort of aura which will make itself mysteriously felt in his apperception. This quality cannot be discovered to reside in any particular part of the work itself, nor can it be defined. It forms part of the whole message received by the spectator worthy of its reception. It is a simple *Wertform*, to use Rickert's phrase.[71] The creator himself thought only of enabling his emotion to be shared. It is, then, without his knowledge that the work has acquired this indescribable quality whose presence cannot be proved.[72]

Is it this value which the spectator confusedly recognises in the picture which "pleases" him? I think not. So long as he is content to allow himself to be passively affected by coloured forms, he cannot make any contact with beauty. The sensation he feels originates in a pre-aesthetic vision, and his reaction is similar to that of a child which reaches out for the coloured form which pleases it and turns away in tears from the one which frightens it. This rectangle which "pleases" him is not the work of art but merely its unformed embryo, for the work of art is only complete in the spectator's mind after it has been read. The complete work of art as it was imagined by the artist cannot exist until its message has been deciphered. Beauty is little known or appreciated if it is thought to exist in anything but the completed work. The sensations provoked by the picture's appearance, before its completion by the spectator, belong to the "pleasing" category and are essentially different from those provoked by contact with beauty. How can this contact be described? None but the language in which mystics describe their ecstasies is adequate for communicating this vivid joy, this absolute revelation. Here, as with mystics, it is a question of communion. The spectator's soul is united, through space and time, with the soul of the creator in an ineffable embrace.

Nevertheless, I would not like to set up this constantly recurring miracle as a definition of beauty. Ecstasy knows no rules and the soul is not always in a state of grace, but even when we are incapable of union, some immanent faculty makes us aware of this transcendental quality which is beauty. An "aesthetic conscience" imposes its decision on us, as does our ethical conscience before another transcendental quality "goodness", or our logical conscience, otherwise called reason, before "truth". Its decision is final. It takes no account of our personal preferences and does not ask if the work "pleases" or not. I can think of many a work of art that I do not like, but which my aesthetic conscience tells

Harlequin · 1919

me is glowing with beauty. There are marriages of reason; but when the marriage becomes a real union, then ecstasy is born.

The quality of beauty is, as we have seen, only present when the work of art attains completion through the apperception of the spectator. From this, like the concentric circles made by a pebble thrown into a pond, radiate associations of images and ideas, widening the complex by what Kant calls *anhängende Schönheit*. And so questions of kinship, comparisons and analogies arise, thus creating those reciprocal ties through which painting fulfils its biological role, the creation of man's outer world.

It is possible that some of the ideas expressed in this book may be considered either trivial or useless. I do not think they are. They have a direct bearing on the study we are making, and I believe that the false definition of the idea of "beauty" is the source of an error which has been disastrous for contemporary painting.

Amongst the first admirers of Cubism, there were those who said that it was enough for them to "like" these new pictures without being concerned with what they represented. They claimed to be satisfied with their feeling of pleasure in front of a given picture. As a matter of fact, they did not even know this picture, since it did not exist unless they had taken the trouble to understand it. I consider that the laziness of certain spectators, no matter how sympathetic they were towards the Cubist painters, was at the root of that state of mind from which so-called "abstract painting" was born. I shall refer to this later. The spectators who were satisfied with their little sensuous emotion soon discovered painters as lazy as themselves who provided them with objects calculated to titillate this emotion, that is to say flat surfaces pleasantly decorated. Thus, the patrons who believed that they had found beauty when their senses were merely agreeably titillated, and the painters who, consciously or unconsciously, created painted canvases whose only purpose was to please, were victims of a confusion which might have been avoided by clear and precise definitions.

2. HISTORIA IN NUCE

It will be apparent from the preceding chapter that artistic activity oscillates between two poles. It emanates from the artist's *emotion*, which seeks to perpetuate itself, and comes to realisation in the *work of art*, by which the emotion is communicated to other men. In the final result, one or other of these poles will be dominant. Those artists who tend to sacrifice form to their need to express themselves without restraint we call "Romantic"; those who set the unity of the work itself above the expression of their emotion we call "Classical". This interpretation of the two terms, based on a distinction between two kinds of creative approach and not on differences in subject matter, is by far the most satisfactory. Nor is it new; it was enunciated by Taine, as follows:[73] "Human thought is an operation in two stages; the Classical artist sets more store by the second stage than by the first. In fact the second is harmful to the first; and the obligation always to say things well prevents him from saying everything that he should. To the classical mind the form is more beautiful than its content, and the original impression, which is the source of inspiration, loses its force, its depth and its effervescence because of the mould into which it is compressed."

As an ardent Romantic, Taine speaks with disdain of "form", which he thinks impoverishes expression; but he does not mention that disregard for form destroys the work itself, and therefore the means by which the artist communicates his emotion to other men.

The artist is not concerned simply with expressing his emotion in a more or less pleasing form, but is engaged in a veritable struggle between this emotion and the particular material in which it is to take shape and become perceptible to other men. In the case of painting this emotion has to materialise on a flat surface of given dimensions. No sooner has the painter drawn a line on this surface, no sooner has he introduced a form, than *a rhythm* is established between the proportions which he has thus created. It is this rhythm which constitutes the law peculiar to the newly created object, which is for ever unique. It is only by obeying this particular law, and not some imaginary predetermined general law, that the artist can fulfil his work and preserve that unity which is its very life. If the Classical artist runs the risk of transmitting an emotion weakened by a too servile and mechanical acceptance of a law, the Romantic artist runs the risk of transmitting nothing at all, because he allows the disintegration of the work itself, the one means by which his emotion is assured of life and reality in the eyes of others and which is, to use a Hegelian phrase, "the being for others" of this emotion.

The main characteristic of the Romantic it seems to me is his need for self-expression. It is the artist's self which pours forth so freely in the lyricism of the Romantics; in tragedy or the epic, however, characters and even objects serve the artist as pegs on which to hang those of his own sentiments which he wishes to be shared. It therefore appears that the lyrical form of expression is the one best suited to the Romantic, for it allows him to indulge his irresistible urge to self-confession. Hence, a lyric work seems to him one into which he can put the whole of himself, whereas an epic or a tragic work seems to him like something apart. Herein lies the explanation of what the German Romantics called "irony", which is simply a manifestation of the author's need to defend himself against his own creation, to make himself felt from within. When, in *Der Gestiefelte Kater*, Tieck brutally destroys the whole theatrical illusion by scenes played in the auditorium and by the appearance on the stage of the author reasoning with the audience, he is not indulging in an idle game but is giving way to his fear of being destroyed by his own creation. Grabbe does the same in *Scherz, Satire, Ironie und tiefere Bedeutung*. Pitilessly they tear their own creations into shreds. However, we must not extend the limits of Romantic Irony too far. When Heine, for example, introduces into the middle of one of his lyrics a prosaic triad which brutally recalls both the poet and the reader from their rapture to reality as:

"Doktor, sind Sie des Teufels?"

it is a matter of simple fun, disagreeable perhaps, but nevertheless fun. The author is not trying to impose himself on his creation, but is laughing at his own emotion *which has become a part thereof*. This is a case of a Romantic ashamed of himself.

Thus, we can formulate the difference in the relationship between the artist and his creation as follows: the Classical artist thinks only of the work of art and suppresses himself for its sake, whereas the Romantic wishes to project his personality and regards the work of art as a means to this end.

Here then we have a fundamental—and most important—cause of the infinite variety of appearance of the pictures which have survived from past ages. It is the character of the individual, the artist's temperament, which counts. This is a permanent factor, but there are others of a temporary kind, which are only active at one particular time. Why is one conception of the outer world abandoned in favour of another? I am not referring here to something which is common to one or to several painters, but to a more general phenomenon whose influence makes itself felt in everyone of the period. The painters merely give it visual expression, for the spirit speaks through the mouths of all artists, as well as through the philosophers and scholars. A new vision is born because fundamental changes have taken place in the spiritual life.

Insofar as it is a record, painting is a direct expression of the spiritual life of a period, and therefore it reflects without delay in plastic terms any change in that spiritual life. It is, of course, tempting to maintain that these changes are reflected only in the writing and that the architecture of pictures remains unchanged, because that enables one to maintain the thesis that the "architecture" is identical with "beauty" as the element which is stable and eternal in any work of art. This claim has indeed been made by the numerous supporters of formalism, an aesthetic which is the basis of the so-called "abstract" art of our own day. The *demonstrable beauty* which is thus created is, in my opinion, a philosophical error. Moreover, the practical application of such a dogma leads to a new standardisation of beauty in a geometric or mathematical form. When applied seriously, both numerical beauty and the "ideal beauty" postulated by fifth-century Greek art end by excluding from art history numerous artistic manifestations which we have come to know and admire. I for my part am no more prepared to uphold the "divine proportions" than I am the Greek ideal of beauty; for I cannot subscribe to any theory which is not valid for the whole range of plastic creation.

Yet there must be some permanent element which makes a work of art, some element which is not subject to passing influences; for there are works of art which have survived from the remotest past and which, although they express pre-occupations which no longer signify, are still capable of moving us as strongly as they did the original spectator. This element, which we can neither define nor analyse, but of whose presence before our eyes we are conscious, can only be the "quality" which the artist's genius has mysteriously and unwittingly given to his creation and which we call beauty. In Kantian terminology one can call it "the thing in itself", that element which is active, permanent, free, but unknown, as opposed to that other element "the appearance", which is neither free nor spontaneous and is conditioned by the spirit of the time. This latter element serves a practical purpose.

From this it results that art history (insofar as it is history) is only concerned with what I have just called "the appearance" of works of art. "The thing in itself", since it is timeless, is not within the art historian's competence; nor is it capable of any investigation, since it is unknowable and indefinable. It remains for me to establish that this "appearance" really corresponds to a projection of the spirit of the time. There is no room here to pursue the proof of this through the whole course of history; but we can find sufficient evidence in the history of painting during the Christian era.

In an age of faith the plastic arts are used to create images of the Gods, that is to say to make the Gods themselves visible; unless, of course, the God is invisible (the case with the Hebrew and Moslem religions) when not only the representation of God but the creation of all images is forbidden. The attitude of Christianity to the plastic arts is less dogmatic because its God is incarnate. Thus, mediaeval Christianity, except during the century of Byzantine iconoclasm when images were banished from churches and art became profane, was content to forbid sculpture in the round[74] (the creation of corporeal idols) while permitting in churches bas-relief and painting, which were used to depict Holy

Writ, to make the myth living and visible to all, to represent figuratively the lesson of the earthly life of Christ, his apostles and the saints. This continued to be the role of painting from the triumph of Christianity in the fourth century until the time of the great schism between Catholics and Protestants, when the former accepted the worship of images and provided for it a metaphysical justification, while the latter stuck rigidly to the Bible and continued to abhor this practice.

It is impossible really to understand the art of the Middle Ages unless one is always aware of the absolute supremacy of the Christian faith during this time. To quote E. Gilson:[75] "All consciences lived on the memory of a historical fact, in relation to which all previous history was ordered and from which dated the beginning of a new era. It was a unique event of which one might almost say that it was a date in the life of God Himself: the incarnation of the Logos, the birth of Jesus Christ." The whole of life was dominated by faith. As Christopher Dawson writes:[76] "The modern European is accustomed to look on Society as essentially concerned with the present life, and with material needs, and on religion as an influence on the moral life of the individual. But to the Byzantine, and indeed to mediaeval man in general, the primary society was the religious one; economic and secular affairs were a secondary consideration. The greater part of a man's life, especially a poor man's, was lived in a world of religious hopes and fears, and the supernatural figures of this religious world were just as real to him as the authorities of the empire."

It was these "supernatural figures" that were represented in paintings. The guise in which they were represented was prescribed by tradition and ultimately codified in the "Books of Painting". To use a strange term, what was thus prescribed was "the setting"; but by this I mean even the smallest details of appearance and of dress, of the placing and attitudes of the figures.[77]

The mediaeval representation of the life of Christ had to be invariable and, above all, "accurate" because it was a reproduction of the Christian myth; only thus could it share in the myth and really "be" a certain episode from that life. Once this accuracy was abandoned, religious painting was destined to exist as a thing apart from the original "fact". It would no longer be identified with the myth. The "accuracy" of mediaeval painting was measured entirely in terms of this myth and not in terms of the outer world.

What did the Middle Ages understand by the "outer world"? It meant little enough to the simple people: it was a place in which they waited for that other life, the life eternal, which was represented on the walls of the church and appeared so much more important than the earthly life.

Even Villon puts into the mouth of his mother, "a poor little old woman", the words:

> "*Au moustier vois dont je suis paroissienne*
> *Paradis peint où sont harpes et luths*
> *Et un enfer où damnés sont boullus.*"

To attain the one and avoid the other:

> "*L'un me fait peur, l'autre joie et liesse*"

was the real object of life on earth, whose setting—that is to say, nature—counted, as a result, for very little.

The cleric and the scholar lived in a universe which they saw with the philosophical eyes of "Realism", a theory which must not be dismissed as mere speculation, for it really dominated the spiritual life of the Occident from the fifth to the twelfth centuries, and mediaeval Christianity is unthinkable without it.

This conception of the world—of neo-Platonist origin—passed into the Christian world through the pseudo-Areopagiticus and through St. Augustine, who wrote: "The Platonists indeed saw the truth fixed, stable and unfading, in which are all the forms of all created things."[78]

Following the lead of St. Augustine, Realism would not allow that the tangible world had any real existence. The only true reality was God, though a sort of diminished reality was conceded to the "Universals", which were, according to Bréhier,[79] the "Voices" of Porphyry, that is to say, the pre-figuration of things and beings according to the genus and the species which are their substance. The tangible world which reproduced the Universals in series was only an illusion and not worthy of any degree of study. At the very best it might be the symbol of another world. When Physiologus speaks of animals, he shows no zoological interest in them, but is intent simply to attribute to them a significance in terms of things divine.

Without going so far as to assert that painting attempted to represent the Universals, there is at all events no question that artists painted concepts; that is to say, they painted what they knew in general about the object signified, but not the appearance of some particular object. And even when, at the beginning of the Renaissance, some degree of direct observation first became evident, it was directed for quite a while not to individual objects but to species. Thus, in his *Libro dell'Arte*, Cennino Cennini recommends making drawings of fragments of stone before painting a mountain.

As one may well imagine, an art so introvert made no study of space. Indeed, space played no part at all in mediaeval painting. The relative positions of figures and objects is indicated by juxtaposition and superimposition, but they are not swimming in space. Bodies are discreetly modelled in a special form of chiaroscuro which, instead of giving them "roundness" by *shading*, very often creates a form of relief by high-lighting, by the use of lighter colour. However, despite modelling, the bodies are disposed on a *flat surface* and never in depth. Thus, mediaeval painting is like a form of writing whose graphic emblems simulate a certain degree of relief (though it wore thin between the ninth and eleventh centuries) while remaining inscribed on an absolutely flat surface.

It was not until the thirteenth century that the tendency to explore into space began to make itself felt. One hundred years earlier belief had already begun to waver, and with it the whole fine edifice of mediaeval thought began to topple. In philosophy Nominalism triumphed. Aristotle succeeded Plato as the guiding spirit. Eyes turned from heaven to earth, and the latter was granted an existence of its own. So there came into being an art devoted to the investigation of the tangible world, every manifestation of which was studied. But it was not until the fifteenth century, that is to say two hundred years later, that this form of *extrovert art* came into contact with that other extrovert art practised by the Greeks of the fifth century B.C., from which it then proceeded to borrow. To those whose con-

L'Intransigeant · 1915

ception of art history ruled out the possibility of any "faithful" representation of the outer world other than that of the fifth-century Greeks, the word "Renaissance" signified the re-birth not only of the art of antiquity but also of naturalistic art, which was to them the only possible form of art.

Yet, like every form of plastic creation, mediaeval art had resembled Nature for the contemporary spectator, as one can read in so many of the texts which praise its "reality". The mediaeval Christian surrendered absolutely and without reserve to the painted image of that natural world which was in itself so indifferent to him. One might almost say that his aesthetic vision was blind to the outer world, which he considered as non-existent. Equally, the sacred images could not stimulate an "aesthetic contemplation", because that would have been an insult to the holy person of whom the image was but a projection. The real change, therefore, that took place was not the birth of a so-called naturalistic art, nor yet the adoption of a different manner of representing the outer world, but a complete transformation of the relationship between man and this outer world. Abundant proof of this change—dating from long before the discovery of Greco-Roman art—can be found in thirteenth-century literature as well as in the plastic arts. In my own essay *Vom Sehen und Bilden*, to which I have already referred, will be found several instances. There I have pointed out the almost total absence of descriptive passages, whether dealing with people or places, in the Chansons de Geste, and in the *Tristan* of Béroul or Thomas of Brittany (striking evidence of the introversion and blindness of the period as far as the outer world was concerned), and the sudden change that occurred with Dante, Petrarch, and the *Tristan* of Gottfried von Strassburg, who burst into wide-eyed description.

In an age like that in which the outer world was discovered, and which may be called "scientific", not to say materialist, painting is assigned the more profound task of *exploring the outer world*, which is credited with a material existence, discernible by and the same for everyone. The painter attributes his emotion to a cause outside himself and makes every effort to analyse it. Thus, it is natural that he should also tend to give a picture of the setting in which the bodies which he seeks to imitate live, and be led thereby to a representation of space. I shall consider later the development of the representation of space and of the element—atmosphere—with which it was gradually filled.

We must not be deceived by the apparent survival in such a period of an aim which seems outmoded; there was no true religious painting after the Renaissance. Reproduction of a fixed, invariable myth ceased. With the Renaissance, the idea of the "Theotokos" or the "Sedes Sapientiae" died, and the Virgin became a young mother lavishing tender care on her child; the idea of the "Pantocrator" or the Supreme Judge gave place to Christ as a man suffering on the Cross. The conception "holy" disappeared from the plastic arts. The painter believed that he was carrying out his commission, but involuntarily he was obeying the dictates of the true spirit of the time. Instead of painting God, he painted men and women whom he had "seen". And so the importance of religious painting went on decreasing until, after one last brilliant flare-up in the seventeenth-century Baroque, which was the art of the Counter-Reformation, that is to say the recrudescence of Catholicism, it ceased altogether in the eighteenth century.

For four centuries the emphasis was on narrative painting, and by this I mean just as much the

Fruit-bowl and Newspaper · 1918

J.G

painting of history, in the fullest sense of the word (in which logically portraiture must be included), as *genre* painting, which is "fictional history" painting. Then, in the nineteenth century, the apparent and the deeper purposes of painting almost united in landscape and still-life, which are disinterested studies of the outer world and devoid of epic or narrative value. Painting ceased to be narrative after 1850, when photography (and later the cinema) took over this function. However, we must be clear about this. The invention of Niepce and Daguerre was not the *cause* of this revision of the apparent purpose of painting: their invention had become necessary precisely because painting tended more and more to devote itself, openly and exclusively, to the deeper purpose of completing the analysis of the visible world.

This investigation reached its conclusion in the developments of pictorial art between 1860 and 1920; that is to say, between the Impressionists and the Cubists. *Cubism began the change-over to the antithesis.* Having been pushed to its limits, painting began to destroy belief in the material existence of the outer world, the study of which it had so eagerly taken up. The imagination of the creative artist was once again given control.

It is one of the objects of this book to show how this change-over was effected by the Cubist painters, and the degree to which Juan Gris contributed to their success.

I. MADRID

What was there for the young José Victoriano Gonzalez, who was studying at the Escuela de Artes y Manufacturas, to look at in that depressing Madrid of 1900 when he began to devote himself to painting? I remember that when I first went there as a tourist, in 1906, it seemed to me like a town which had been asleep for fifty years. There were primarily the treasures of the Prado, where El Greco still occupied only a humble position. And then the work of contemporaries: the painting of the Madrid

Academy, which was perhaps more slick but certainly not better than any other academic painting of the period. He was given his grounding, as we have seen, by an old academic painter; but one can well imagine that he derived no satisfaction from his master's style of art. Where should he look? Then, as now, all the "advanced" artists of Spain left the country, most of them for Paris. Not that the innovations of Zuloaga, Yturrino, and Anglada Camarasa were very terrible, but even they decided that the atmosphere of Spain was intolerable. Picasso, too, had arrived in Madrid from Barcelona as a young man—he still called himself Pablo Ruiz—and had spent some time there before leaving for Paris. He had even founded a short-lived review called *Arte Joven*. But his passage through the capital had been without much effect.

There remained foreign influences. What foreign influences were at work in Madrid at this time? Paris was the place to which most of those who left the country went in search of the source of Europe's living painting. There painting was dominated by the work of one great living artist—Paul Cézanne— and of two who were dead—Vincent van Gogh and Georges Seurat. But they were still very little understood; they were unknown to the majority of people and admired only by a few. On the other hand, the Impressionist painters—all still alive with the exception of Sisley—were at the height of their fame among art-lovers, though they had not yet been generally accepted. In fact their work had ultimately penetrated into the museums of France; for the opening of the gallery in the Musée du Luxembourg containing the Caillebotte legacy marked their entry by the back door. In Germany they had been freely admitted to the museums of Munich and Berlin by Hugo von Tschudi, in the face of opposition both from the academic painters and from William II himself. But it was not the influence of the Impressionists which was felt in Madrid, and even less the influence of the three great painters whom I have named. Indeed, Impressionism never caught on in Spain, not even with the Spaniards who came to Paris; and though certain Catalans like Rusiñol did borrow a little from it, what they took was not the essential. Picasso never fell for it; nor for that matter did Gris. Therefore neither of them subsequently went through a period of "Fauvism", that final flicker which heralded the death of the painting of light. It is an open question whether this national immunity should be attributed to defensive instincts working in the Spanish genius to protect its passion for draughtsmanship and composition against the formless mist of colour and the slice of life offered by Impressionism; or whether what led the artists of Madrid to shun French painting was the fascination of German science and philosophy, to which the whole of Spanish culture had been enthralled for a hundred years. The fact is that the chief influence on the painters of Madrid around 1900 was German.[80] It was the influence of Munich; and the means by which it penetrated were two weekly illustrated papers, *Jugend* and *Simplicissimus*. That is to say, the influence was *Art Nouveau*, or as it is more precisely called in German— *Jugendstil*.[81]

I do not think there is any question that, when Juan Gris started to draw, these two weekly papers provided him with his first contemporary stimulus, and that *Art Nouveau* was the first style he was tempted to adopt. Besides, the German artist Willy Geiger, a friend of Gris in Madrid, was a regular contributor to *Jugend*, and Gris himself told me of his own enthusiasm at that time for these two papers.

95

In any case one has only to study the drawings he made during this early part of his professional career to discover immediately the influence of *Simplicissimus*, and in particular of its contributor Bruno Paul. The *Témoin*, of which Gris was later one of the principal contributors, might even be a French imitation of *Simplicissimus*.

The draughtsman who signed himself José Gonzalez could be temporarily content with the modest degree of modernism in *Simplicissimus*. Some of the contributors to this paper had a tendency in their drawings to distortion; but they distorted for satirical and not for plastic effects. That is to say, their distortion was pre-eminently expressionistic, anti-academic, and it was, I am sure, one of the seeds from which the Expressionist Movement in Germany later sprang. But whereas, for a draughtsman, *Simplicissimus* represented a sort of revolt, which was echoed in the paper's subversive political and social tendencies, the *Jugend* was wretched lukewarm fare for a painter despite the so-called novelty of its *Jugendstil*. What, in effect, was this *Art Nouveau*, which we now call "The 1900 Style"? In no sense was it an attempt—as with Impressionism in the hands of Cézanne, van Gogh, and Seurat—to face up to the eternal problems of painting and the creation of a new conception of pictorial art. It was simply a form of *stylisation* which rejected straight lines. Its sinuous line, its serpentine appearance, could be grafted on to any style of painting, whether academic or modernist. For this line did not originate in painting but in architecture and ornament. It came in with the use of new materials, when architects and decorators, reacting against the rigidness of stone, were inspired by the plasticity of concrete and the pliability of steel to indulge in an orgy of curves. This element was completely alien to painting and was more like a parasitic climbing plant which formed no integral part either of the architecture or of the *pictorial* writing. At the very most one might talk of the existence of a pseudo-symbolist "atmosphere" in a certain type of painting around 1900; but this "atmosphere" was more a product of the period than of *Art Nouveau*, and appears exclusively in the choice of subject. For a short time Gris was subject to the influence of this "atmosphere". In Paris the 1900 hall-mark is undeniable and is visible in the work of a pitiable creature like Mucha, as well as in certain posters by Lautrec and the early work of Vuillard; but it does not in any way change the real significance of the

Illustration for
"Alma America" by José Santos Chocano · 1906

art of any of them. In Munich the *Jugendstil* was a sort of transparent mask covering the sham truculence of the Academy in the days following Boecklin and Lenbach. Such was the pictorial nourishment that Gris could find in *Jugend*. It was not much, and it soon proved insufficient. He turned his eyes elsewhere, like many another before him. At the age of nineteen he left for Paris.

II. FIRST CONTACTS WITH PAINTING

Paris had for the last hundred years been the centre of all creative painting. The Renaissance had to its astonishment discovered the outer world where the previous eight centuries had seen merely a pale reflection of the Universals or, at best, the gloomy antechamber of a world beyond, which was all that mattered. Painting's role in the investigation of this new world had been optical research. Nor had it failed in the task assigned to it in the spiritual life of the European community. The outer world had been made to appear real in man's eyes. *The solids* came first. *Light* was not omitted; but it was simply the means by which bodies were made visible. Its effect on bodies was simulated in the form of chiaroscuro. Then the bodies had to be exactly "situated" in relation to each other, and thus *space* began to come into its own. Every effort was made to give full expression, both to it and to the bodies with which it is filled, by means of linear perspective, an invention of the scholars. Next came the discovery that space is filled with air; then the attempt was made to render the discoloration of objects seen at a distance through this "atmosphere". From the fifteenth century onwards, distant objects no longer retained their "true" colour, that is to say their "local colour", but were given a bluish tint, a technique later called "aerial perspective". And so, having thus taken stock of space and what was in it, the interest inevitably shifted to light, by which it is illuminated. Light then became a study in itself.

Caravaggio, the Brothers Le Nain, Georges de La Tour and Rembrandt were the first to devote themselves to this new investigation; sunlight was treated as a thing in itself and thereupon assumed a more and more important place in painting.[82] Thus, what these painters really did was to complete the investigation of the outer world by trying to take in the whole of it. We should note that it was they, too, who looked around them and painted religious subjects in terms of daily life, in which the beggars, soldiers, peasants and Jews of their own day take part in biblical scenes.

By the end of the nineteenth century this new investigation had almost run its course. Not only had the disinterested study of the outer world ended by becoming the only (hidden as well as visible) aim of painting—in landscape, which dominates the second half of the century, as well as in still-life which, particularly in the hands of Cézanne, assumed more and more importance—but also the representation of *light and atmosphere* had become more important than the representation of solid bodies. The Impressionists had made it their business to record light in all its most fugitive aspects. Monet observed its appearance at all phases of the sun, on haystacks and cathedrals and in the mists of the Thames; but the solid bodies, the haystacks, the cathedrals or the buildings of London, disappeared because the painters seemed to have no interest in them. Nor did they appear to have any greater interest for space as a thing in itself. The position of objects was no longer defined primarily by careful draughtsmanship and linear perspective, but much more by aerial perspective, which relies on tonal values to indicate remoteness or proximity. Thus, the solid bodies which, five centuries earlier when this period of research began, had been the subject-matter of painting seemed now to have been discarded, whereas light, which had previously been a means, had become the subject-matter. That subtle element air had found its way into space (which, for the original investigators, had been simply a meeting-place of various bodies) and had transformed space into atmosphere; and it was this "air" which the Impressionists thought worthy of representation in paint.

This was indeed the logical conclusion of that tradition which had set out to study the world. It was the Impressionists, the "revolutionaries", who were the real continuers of tradition, and not the products of the Ecole des Beaux-Arts who without any justification claimed this privilege for themselves. In *Un Ménage de Garçons*, Balzac describes Joseph Bridau—one of the three or four great painters in the *Comédie Humaine*—painting the portrait of his brother Philip, a Major in the Imperial Dragoon Guards, who poses for him "in full uniform, mounted on one of those stuffed horses such as one finds at the saddler's and which had been hired by Joseph". What a ridiculous scene it must have been in the gloom of a studio on the Rue Mazarine, more especially if one thinks that this warrior was supposed to be charging across a battlefield. However, it gives us some idea of the degenerate state of painting, content simply to go on mouthing clichés and capable of drawing inspiration from the pseudo-reality of a stuffed and immobile model. The symbol is the lay-figure which satirises academic art in Courbet's *Atelier*.

The Impressionists, who hated all clichés, had only one wish: to compete with the outer world. They really wanted to represent it in what appeared to them to be its reality, that is to say, "just as they saw it". They were not the ones to arrange an open-air scene inside their studios; truth for them meant sitting down in front of the actual scene. They despised conventional art, but they felt that even among the great painters of other generations only very few had succeeded in preserving unaltered the appearance of the world as they saw it. The Impressionists carried on the investigation of the world which had been begun in the Renaissance, but their attitude to the outer world was different. The art of Courbet, for all that it called itself realist, was for them too "abstract", too much based on image-memories and second-hand information. Courbet did, of course, paint what he knew about an object; and for all the veil of mist in which Corot wrapped objects they certainly preserved their individuality. As a matter of fact the aims which the Impressionists set themselves, namely to set down only what they discovered about a subject during a single observation, had only previously been realised in a few little canvases by Bonington and in sketches by Constable and Turner. They made no use of image-memories to "complete" the picture of a house or a tree; they tried to depict them just as they saw them, that is to say, at the mercy of air and atmosphere. Admittedly the public, whose visual sense had become set to accept only the outmoded art of the Ecole des Beaux-Arts, had already had difficulty in following Delacroix, Corot and Courbet; but at least it had been able to read their pictures. The new factor was that the public no longer saw shocking "distortions" but simply a series of painted canvases which were illegible. The sensualism of the Impressionist painters was entirely disconcerting; they trusted only their own sensations to inform them about the outer world, and never for a moment doubted the excellence of their means of knowledge, nor questioned, therefore, the identification of these sensations with the outer world. Thus, it would be wrong to attribute to them the beginning of that introvert mentality which we shall have to discuss later in the case of the Cubists. Here we have to deal with the concluding phase of an extrovert mentality, striving to grasp reality in what it believes to be its full truth, freshness and bloom. What the Impressionists did, however, was of very great importance. For they undoubtedly arrested for some time to come the petrifying process to which our vision of the outer world was subject; by insisting that only subjective sensations counted they refused to accept any one form of vision as having eternal validity. Thus, they opened the way for Cézanne, van Gogh, Seurat, Matisse, the Cubists and their successors.

It is worth noting that, at the start, Impressionist painting was compared by contemporaries to a type of poetry which, although it too was an innovation, now seems diametrically opposed to it. Even if the story of Victor Hugo calling Mallarmé "*mon cher poète impressionniste*"[83] is apocryphal, it nevertheless throws a certain light on the tendency of the time. Why did the people of taste and refinement indulge in this parallel? We are given some insight into their reasons in a letter from Mallarmé to Henri Cazalis, dated 1864:[84] "At last I have begun my *Hérodiade*; with terror, for I am inventing a language which must spring out of my very new poetic conception, which I can define in a few words: *to describe not the thing itself but the effect it produces*. Therefore the verse must be composed not just of words but of intentions, and the language must yield before the sensations."

Contemporaries subsequently justified, by Mallarmé's reflections, their theory of a connection between the art of the Impressionists and Mallarmé. They were wrong.

The objection may be raised that the Impressionists too were trying to express just their visual sensation. But what Mallarmé meant by "sensation" was not a visual sensation. He was referring to the various emotions which are provoked by the visual sensation—what he calls "the effect the thing produces". The following passage from *Crise de Vers*[85] is a good example: "*Abolie, la prétention, esthétiquement une erreur, quoiqu'elle régit les chefs-d'œuvre, d'inclure au papier subtil du volume autre chose que par exemple l'horreur de la forêt, ou le tonnerre muet épars au feuillage : non le bois intrinsèque et dense des arbres. Quelques jets de l'intime orgueil véridiquement trompetés éveillent l'architecture du palais, le seul habitable ; hors de toute pierre, sur quoi les pages se refermeraient mal.*" Here it is clear that we have to deal with something totally different from the Impressionists who, though they undoubtedly painted "their sensations", believed that in so doing they were painting the outer world, the "*bois intrinsèque et dense des arbres*", the true stone of the palace, in their one and only recognisable existence. Their contemporaries were content to see a connection between Mallarmé's allusions and Impressionism without enquiring further. A parallel exists between Mallarmé and the Impressionists: whereas Mallarmé distrusted words, Monet and his friends distrusted "ready-made" forms. This reveals a common desire for freedom. That, however, is the full extent of their similarity. Naïvely the Impressionists

Still-life before an Open Window (La Place Ravignan) · *1915*

attempted "to paint what they saw". Humbly, and with superb patience, Mallarmé intended to set down in a rigidly pure art form only his sensation, leaving it to the reader's imagination to re-create the object which had stimulated the poet's emotion. Mallarmé's chief concern was for the work of art in which this emotion was communicated to the reader; he was a classical artist in the noblest sense. What is more, the Impressionists, despite their admiration for Mallarmé, never even divined the incredible nature of his contribution in his mature work. They were completely oblivious of the *incantatory* character of his art, of his desire to *create* a reality.

Their art relied more on observation than any earlier form of art, for the Impressionists attempted to imitate directly the image which was the optical sensation. They aimed primarily at spontaneity, and this seemed to them synonymous with truth. They set out to record a given landscape as they saw it, say on November 25, 1888, at four o'clock in the afternoon. Everything else was subservient to this aim. The only sculptor among them, Medardo Rosso—whose name is now almost forgotten— was so obsessed with the idea of preserving the fugitive moment, of not removing objects from the atmosphere in which he had seen them, that he ended by destroying them almost completely: objects lost their outlines and tended to be swallowed up in the surrounding air. In order to achieve this Medardo Rosso was obliged to abandon the true form of sculpture—sculpture in the round—and take to relief; he was obliged, that is to say, to use a pictorial technique. The same danger faced Rodin, but thanks to the force of his instincts he nearly always evaded it.

The Impressionists sacrificed the permanent to the transient. But it had serious consequences; for, while Monet sat in front of his *motif* searching for spontaneity and starting a new canvas with each change of hour, the balance swung heavily against the work of art. The Impressionists were Romantics; and this can be proved not only by the essential plastic criterion, namely the predominance of emotion over the work of art, but also by their lineal descent. For were they not the true descendants, *via* Géricault and Delacroix, of those great English landscape painters who so truly reflected the England of the romantic and pre-romantic days, when poets like the Countess of Winchilsea and Dyer waxed enthusiastic over the scene before them and thus introduced into poetry landscapes which were beautiful without having either mythological or archaeological interest? Admittedly the Impressionists them- selves, like their friends the Naturalist novelists, imagined that they were quite the opposite of the French Romantics; but the only difference was in their choice of subject, not in their basic conception. To-day we realise that Zola was profoundly romantic and that Naturalism, like Impressionism, was simply another of the eternal manifestations of romanticism. The Impressionists were lyrical. They spoke of their love for light, yet all that appeared on their canvases was an arrangement of colours held together by the brittlest of threads—their harmony. The work of art with a unity and existence of its own had ceased to exist. It is, of course, essential that the colours should be harmonised; but unless there is also a formal harmony to which this colour harmony is related the only quality of a picture will be its pleasant appearance.

Renoir, the greatest of the group, was able to produce works of lasting value because he abandoned the Impressionist aesthetic. On the other hand, the works of Monet, who always remained true to

Impressionism, are gradually fading (actually as well as figuratively) because there is no construction to hold together their rather indistinct graphic signs; and therefore his message is becoming less comprehensible to spectators.

Vincent van Gogh, who worked furiously for a few years before committing suicide, made a heroic attempt to transform into pictures his extraordinary ecstasies over light. Realising that emotion could not be communicated by servile imitation of the optical sensation but only by a new creation, he invented images which record the thrill he felt on seeing the landscape of Arles and St. Rémy; in so doing, he produced works of art whose forms are convulsed and twisted by a breath of ecstasy. Romantic art really only comes to life in the hands of one inspired, of one possessed; the minor romantic masters are little worth. That is why, in days to come, van Gogh will be far more representative of the cult of the sun, which we call Impressionism, than the Impressionist painters themselves.

Out of Impressionism came Pointillism; this took luminism a step further and, abandoning the idea of an exact imitation of the optical sensation, attempted to render the vibration of light by a scientific procedure—Divisionism—based on complementaries. Here even the last trace of life which the Impressionists had permitted, the emotional touch in the handwriting, was obliterated by a laborious procedure. However, it was used by one great and pure painter, Georges Seurat, who devoted himself during the few years of his life to one of the fundamental problems of painting: non-imitative representation on a canvas which has two dimensions of figures which have three. Seurat, like the Cubists who came after him, was not content to simulate volume by chiaroscuro, that is to say high-lighting one side of a body and placing the other in shadow so that it appears round. Seurat projects forms on to a flat surface in much the same way as the Egyptians did. This solution is irreproachable when line-drawing is the technique employed, and Egyptian painting was more drawing picked out with colour than real painting. On the other hand, Seurat's Divisionism, despite his personal innovation, was technically in the line of oil-painting as it had been practised since the Renaissance. And because of this, Seurat's array of silhouettes is incompatible with the technique he employed, a danger which I shall explain later. But during his struggle to solve the problem of the third dimension Seurat, with his clear intelligence, rediscovered pictorial "architecture". In his work the parts were governed by the whole and had to conform to a general rhythm. He had only had time to complete a small number of noble and lucid works when death carried him off, and the line he began has never been followed up. It may be that it was a dead-end.

Georges Seurat was the one and only *classical* artist of his time. His emotion was entirely subject to the overriding law of the work of art in which it was given form. It is, however, pertinent to consider whether the danger of stylisation was not latent in his later work, a stylisation which in the hands of his disciples became ornamental and decorative. I have already referred to the vague suggestion of *Art Nouveau*, to the foretaste of "the 1900 style" which is apparent in his curves. That in no way detracts from the great value of his works; it is merely a warning signal for anyone who would continue along the same line. Perhaps that is why no-one has tried.

Paul Cézanne, the third of the great painters whom I mentioned above, had just died when Gris arrived in Paris. He had been a boyhood friend of Zola, had been intimate with the Impressionists to the extent of exhibiting with them and having his name coupled with theirs; and yet there was no more solitary figure. One only has to read what his so-called friends, worthy writers like Duret who took up the defence of Impressionism, have written about him. They praised his colour, but they were horribly embarrassed by what they took to be the poor man's lack of skill. "I cannot manage to realise," he used to say; and his champions accepted what he said literally, whereas he was referring to an ambition of which they were not even aware. What embarrassed them were his "distortions", his "overlapping planes" (that is to say, his use of a different form of perspective from that invented during the Renaissance), the patches of white canvas on which there was no paint. It has been claimed that Zola was thinking of Cézanne when he created Claude Lantier in *L'Œuvre*. There does not seem to be much doubt, especially after the researches of Herr Rewald, that this is untrue. Nevertheless, Cézanne did really appear to his friends to be a gifted failure, one who was incapable of "realising".[86] Now what sort of painter was he in fact? A Romantic like themselves. This is evident in his early works, and even in his choice of subject (*Bacchanale*, *The Temptation of St. Anthony*, *The Murder*). These epic themes were followed by a period of lyricism; then he discovered for himself that his sensation would never be conveyed to others except in the form of a work of art which had strength and unity. But he wanted to express *the whole* of his sensation; that was his life struggle. And a gigantic struggle it was. For he did not want just to transmit a little sensation of light on objects. He wanted to transmit the whole of his spontaneous emotion, which took in the objects illuminated, with their volume and their position in space. In addition he wished to preserve in his pictures all those accidental modifications of the appearance of objects which are caused by light. That was what he meant when he referred to "doing Poussin over again after nature". It never seemed to him that he succeeded in expressing to the full the perhaps excessive complexity of this sensation. He was hurt to see it suffer, to see it diminished during this process of trans-substantiation. That was what he meant when he said that he could not manage to realise. He failed to find the spontaneity, the whole of his emotion in the finished work. And so this lyrical romantic never ceased regretting his sensation, which he believed had not been communicated intact to others; yet he never gave up the fight, although he was almost the only person who was aware of the stake.

Scarcely ten years before Gris became aware of French painting, a new generation had begun to realise the importance of Cézanne. Maurice Denis painted his *Hommage à Cézanne*, in which his friends the Nabis[87] were grouped around the great painter whom they had just discovered. Then came the copies of Cézanne. And from 1900 on, both the Indépendants and the newly founded Salon d'Automne began to teem with what the critics of that time called "Three apples on a ramshackle table". Next came the retrospective exhibitions of Cézanne.

At first his work suggested the possibility of representing the outer world in its three dimensions by a different means from that of the Impressionists or their predecessors, a means which enabled one to avoid, by virtue of what Cézanne called "colour modulation", servile imitation of the effect of sunlight on solid bodies. It was about 1895 that Bonnard and Vuillard became aware of this. However, although this discovery coincided with the break-up of the group of Nabis—of which they, like Denis, Roussel, Sérusier and a few other painters, were members—and caused them to abandon the decorative tendencies of the Symbolist painters, which they themselves had pushed almost to stylisation, it did not mean that they had fully understood. On the contrary, they remained blind to the majority of problems that had preoccupied Cézanne. For the moment they concentrated on spontaneity, and gaily accepted any sort of fortuitous silhouetting or bizarre composition into which this might lead them. Thus, they ended simply in a compromise which involved the tacking of Cézanne's "modulation" on to the Impressionists' "slice of life". There is good reason for calling these painters the Post-Impressionists.

Maurice Denis was unfortunately devoid of those gifts which make a real painter, but in his writings from 1890 onwards he did make an effort to define the fundamental problems of painting. True, he owed a great deal to that other painter and his disciples, who for a short while formed the Pont-Aven School.[88] This painter, Paul Gauguin, who had been a friend of van Gogh, had an undeniable talent and noble aspirations, but was very largely responsible for falsifying the lesson of Cézanne. "He wanders around on mail-boats with my little sensation," said Cézanne. Of an unsettled temperament, Gauguin wandered from Brittany to the Antilles, from Tahiti to the Marquis Islands, decking out Cézanne's uncouth humanity in the tinsel of picturesqueness, adulterating what, with Cézanne, was the natural cadence of the picture's own rhythm, adapting it to ornamental, decorative ends. Paul Gauguin was a dangerous master. If one needs convincing, there is ample proof in the careers of his friends and disciples from Schuffenecker to Séguin, from Filiger to Paco Durio. It was his influence, too, which contributed to the deflection of *Fauvisme*,[89] a movement which was launched shortly before the arrival of Gris in Paris.

Henri Matisse was—and is—the undisputed master of this movement, which counted among its adherents Derain, Vlaminck, van Dongen, Marquet, and three painters from Le Havre—Friesz, Dufy, and a younger man, Braque. Matisse, who was intelligent and eloquent, had already passed beyond the Post-Impressionism of Bonnard and Vuillard (they were a few years older) when he made the acquaintance of the two giants from Chatou—Vlaminck and Derain. Their art had its roots in the exacerbated form of Impressionism left by van Gogh.[90] Matisse taught them all about picture-making, for after he had given up the Post-Impressionist idea of spontaneity he spent some time thinking about composition. Evidence of this is to be found in the series of reflections which he published in the *Grande Revue*. In exchange, Derain and Vlaminck fired Matisse with their love of daring and their youthful ardour, qualities inherent in the strident brilliance of their works. Vlaminck used to boast of using pure colour, just as it came out of the tube.[91] As a result his pictures acquired weight, density and, I might almost say, a structure which was completely lacking in the patchwork of Bonnard and Vuillard or the dots of Cross and Signac. This formal element was even more strongly to the fore in the work of Derain, who drew expressive silhouettes with a heavily charged brush.[92] Out of the work and the ideas exchanged between these painters grew what one may call the doctrine of "The Fauves".

"To render light by colour" was the aim they claimed; and this clearly meant turning their backs on the sort of illusionism practised by the Impressionists, since it was no longer a question of imitating light but of finding its equivalent through colour. In short, they were to follow van Gogh, who often spoke in his letters (which were then very little known) of using colour in a way which one might call symbolical.[93] But they reflected another influence besides the wholesome one of van Gogh: a picture, they declared, had to be "synthetic and decorative". Synthetic: this meant that the forms and colours in a picture need not be copied from but should signify the object which it was intended to represent. Who does not recognise here Gauguin's old tag "*Vive la Sintaize*"? Decorative: this meant that the work as a whole had to be pleasing to the eye and should embellish the place where it would be hung. I do not think I am wrong in claiming that, at the back of this second adjective and its interpretation, lay once again that distortion of Cézanne's doctrine for which Gauguin was responsible.[94] Cézanne, with every single brush-stroke, strove only to make his emotion visible while always showing respect for the unity of the picture itself. The Fauves, on the contrary, thought of the spectator and tried to fascinate him by arranging things so that the picture had as pleasant an appearance as possible.[95] This naïve hedonism aroused the enthusiasm at that time of architects and decorators, for whom a picture is just an ornament with which to complete an interior; but its nefarious influence reappeared much later in the form of so-called "abstract painting", a contemptible form of decoration which just flatters the spectator and relieves the painter of his true role, namely that of perpetuating his emotional experience in the shape of "the being for others", the picture.

Certain Nabis—Denis and Sérusier, for example—have claimed that they were the precursors both of the Fauves and of the Cubists. We shall see presently that this latter claim is ridiculous. But one might feel differently about their claim in regard to the Fauves if all one knew were the writings of Denis, Sérusier and their friends, or just their early works. "In the early part of 1905 the war-cry went up from studio to studio: 'No more easel pictures! Away with useless bits of furniture! Painting must not usurp a freedom which cuts it off from the other arts! The painter's work begins where the architect decides that his work is finished! Give us walls and more walls to decorate! Down with perspective! The wall must be kept as a surface, and must not be pierced by the representation of distant horizons. There are no such things as pictures, there is only decoration.'" I cannot think of any more accurate or more vital description of the state of mind in the studios of 1905. But I have made a deliberate error; in reality my quotation should begin: "In the early part of 1890..." and is extracted from *Tourment de Dieu*, a book of youthful reminiscences in which Dom Willibrard Verkade, O.S.B., the Nabi who became a monk, tells of his conversion.[96] Anyhow, one can feel that there was a strange similarity between the artistic climate of 1905 and that of the early days of the Nabis. Nevertheless I do not think that they can truly be called the ancestors of the Fauves. It is vain to plead Gauguin's so-called lack of culture; the fact is that he, and he alone among the Synthetists, has left behind a body of work which will live, no matter how much he may be open to criticism. One cannot say the same for the miserable Emile Bernard, nor for any of Gauguin's companions at Pont-Aven and Le Pouldu. As for the Nabis, they intended to follow Gauguin when the group was formed; but, after painting a few early works which depended directly on Gauguin, they changed their direction.[97] Bonnard and

Vuillard, the most gifted of them, edged away in pursuit of the "spontaneity" of the Post-Impressionist slice of life, Denis and Roussel fell into a new conventionalism, fanning with a touch of modernism the dying embers of French academicism. Verkade, and after him Sérusier, rallied to the moth-eaten banner of the Beuron School, which was nothing better than a very stuffy poor relation of the German "Nazarene" group. Thus, none of them ever took their place in the line of descent which led to the Fauves. Tendencies exist and make themselves felt by representative works. The Fauves were descended *directly* from Gauguin and van Gogh; what is more, they never attempted to conceal either their dislike of the later work of Vuillard and Bonnard, which seemed to them lacking in structure, or their contempt for the other Nabis, who had fallen back into the clutches of the Ecole des Beaux-Arts.

One may consider Gauguin's theories disastrous, but at any rate they exist. Nothing that the Nabis painted was derived from them. The ideas of the School of Pont-Aven came to glorious fruition and reached their apogee in the work of Matisse; he inherited the "synthetic and decorative" tendencies of Gauguin, tendencies which, in the work of Vlaminck and Derain, were combined with the expressionism of van Gogh. The Fauves never completely understood Cézanne; Gauguin they understood better than his closest disciples, and van Gogh better than all their elders.

This is perhaps the time at which to make clear that the Fauves were not a link in the chain that led to the Cubists, who descended directly from Cézanne. The line started by Gauguin ended in *ornament*, the line started by Cézanne in the exaltation of *art as the creation of the visible world*. Gauguin and the Fauves meant to decorate, to make painting subservient to an already existing or imaginary wall, which it was their intention to embellish. The Cubists, following in the footsteps of Cézanne, always insisted on the *independent existence* of the work of art. They talked about "*le tableau-objet*", an object which could be put anywhere. (Like many of my painter friends, I have a taste for pictures standing around on the floor.) As I shall mention later, the Cubist poets used also to talk of "*le poème-objet*". In establishing the autonomy of works of art the Cubists were (unconsciously, of course) aspiring to that *integritas* which is claimed by St. Thomas Aquinas as the first essential *ad pulchritudinem*. The pictures which they made had to be "individuals", and the word was used in its most precise sense: that is to say, something organic which cannot be divided without ceasing to be the same person. Each of these "persons" had a unique "personality", and each took its place in history.

When Juan Gris arrived in Paris the *new* painting which he saw was the work of the Fauves. Their triumph was at the Salons des Indépendants of 1905 to 1907, where they exhibited large canvases such as Matisse's *Le Bonheur de Vivre* and *La Baigneuse Couchée*, Derain's *Taureau* (destroyed by the artist in 1908) and *Baigneuses*, and smaller works by the other Fauves. These large pictures were an expression of the decorative tendencies of Fauvism. They were not altogether devoid of composition, but there was evidence of the confusion brought about by Gauguin. For, in effect, these pictures were no more than charming arabesques composed with human bodies draped across the canvas. They wanted to be decorative, to please the spectator. What gives them a quality is their radiant youthfulness, their jubilant assertion of life and light, elements which are expressed even in the title of Matisse's picture already mentoined: *Le Bonheur de Vivre*.

Gris was, as one may imagine, not very enthusiastic about these pictures. He was by nature too fond of order and discipline to be in sympathy with this riot of colour; the harmonies were rich and pleasant, but expressive spontaneity meant a weakening of the whole structure. No doubt his innate Spanish aversion to riotous colour prevented him from even seeing the real effort at liberation which was implied by the term "synthetic", and which was particularly apparent in the smaller Fauve pictures. In these there was a real effort at plastic invention, and an attempt to create new and significant graphic signs capable of renewing the outer world. Gris found a spiritual nourishment more in keeping with his background and temperament in the company of Pablo Picasso, his compatriot and neighbour at 13 Rue Ravignan.

Picasso, who had for a time followed many a Parisian will-o'-the-wisp, had quickly come back to a form of painting which seemed almost anachronistic in the Paris of Post-Impressionism and Fauvism. At least that is how it appeared to me when I saw his work for the first time. The only influence which is discernible at the beginning of Picasso's "Blue Period" is once again that of Gauguin. When Gris met Picasso the latter was at work on a series of pictures which were then called "Pompeian", but which are now called his "Pink Period". The former name was an expression of the classical feeling which his contemporaries sensed in these pictures. I do not know whether Gris was entirely satisfied by these works, or whether, like Picasso, he felt that their "retrospective" appearance was after all not sufficiently in keeping with the emotion of the hour. What is certain, however, is that he followed with great enthusiasm the work which Picasso began at the end of 1906. It was this work which was to revolutionise the plastic arts.

III. THE BIRTH OF CUBISM

To my eyes Picasso's paintings had appeared anachronistic. It was not until much later that I realised why. In 1907 it was the problem of *colour* which seemed to me all-important. Its solution appeared to be the aim of those contemporary painters whom I admired. Now Picasso, except for a few youthful attempts when he was only eighteen and newly arrived in Paris, never seems to have concerned himself with this problem prior to Cubism. At any rate, it played no part whatever in his work between 1902 and 1907. The pictures of his Blue Period were camaïeu paintings; those of the Pink Period coloured drawings. The essentially *linear* character of all Picasso's work in the *classical* style, in 1906 as much as in 1921, is a noteworthy fact. Since 1923 he has abandoned a classical style in painting, and has only used it for graphic work—drawings and engravings.

When, during the winter of 1906–7, Picasso painted the large canvas later known as *Les Demoiselles d'Avignon*,[98] he seems no longer to have been unconscious of the problem which so deeply pre-occupied all those around him. For in this picture he tackled the problem of colour as well as that of form. The three female figures on the left of the picture are still in the manner of the Pink Period

The Check Table-cloth · 1915

and are painted in a pinkish camaïeu. But they are no longer coloured drawings and their appearance is not classical. The forms are firmly modelled and the bodies, as the first bewildered spectators said, are "hewn with hatchet-strokes". On the other hand the two female figures on the right, the one standing and the other crouching, show that he was engaged on far more daring experiments. They are painted in violent colours, not applied in broad areas but laid on in parallel strokes, so that the form is not created (as on the left) by chiaroscuro but by drawing, by the direction of the brush-strokes. The foundations of Cubism[99] were laid in this right-hand section of *Les Demoiselles d'Avignon*.

Cubism (together with Derain's experiments at that time) was the first serious attempt to carry on the work of Cézanne. His subject-matter and the appearance of his pictures had been imitated, but without any comprehension. The Fauves had interpreted him through Gauguin. Only now was he understood.

The problem, in short, was to reconcile the unity of the picture with the closest possible representation of the coloured forms of the outer world as they appeared in the artist's emotion. I shall be told that this is the problem of all true painting, and I do not deny it. What in effect the Cubists had to do was to follow Cézanne and *rediscover painting*, which had been mangled by Impressionism and its sequels.

It is important not to overlook the first part of this definition—"the representation of coloured *forms*". Cubism did not attempt a precise representation of *space*—as has been stated by many writers who do not realise that the representation of space depends entirely on representation of the bodies which inhabit it—but of *volume*, of the density of solids. It was this aim which distinguished the Cubists from the Symbolist painters (that is to say, those in Gauguin's more or less immediate circle) and the Fauves. Maurice Denis writes:[100] "Thus Sérusier revealed to us Gauguin's message as the still un-known conception of the *flat surface covered by colours arranged in a certain order*. In other words, one should not copy or reproduce nature as one sees it, but 'represent' it by transforming it into an interplay of vivid colours set out in a simple, expressive and original arabesque which is pleasing to the eye: this meant a return to the flat colours of the religious print and the 'tuppence-coloured', to the hieratic attitudes of the Egyptians, the Byzantines and Roman frescoes, to the art of child-like peoples."

It is not my purpose to criticise Denis' statement, nor to show that he does not seem really to have understood the art of the painters he invoked, most of whom had quite other aims. The programme he outlines is, in any case, that for a school of hedonistic decorators who think that their arabesques "represent" what they call "nature" by virtue of a "miraculously expressive quality".[101] He was not concerned with the study of bodies in terms of three dimensions, since mystery and equivalence covered everything. The study and representation of volume was, on the other hand, the first problem that the Cubists had to face.

Paul Sérusier, it appears, claimed to be "the father of Cubism". But he was a most unnatural father in every respect, since on February 15, 1915, he wrote to Denis:[102] "Now that the Kubist fraud is collapsing, I think we shall be allowed to indulge in a simple form of flat geometry, in an essentially French spirit of pure Christian simplicity." Sérusier clearly misunderstood the essentials of Cubism, and Raymond Escholier was similarly mistaken when he wrote:[103] ". . . he [Sérusier] made use of the laws of mathematical construction before even the first Cubists." But "the first Cubists", namely Braque and Picasso, never made use of such laws. They were not "geometrical" either in mind or in make-up. Those art historians who have taken seriously the contemporary journalistic references—facetious, in fact—to the mathematician Princet, and who have credited him with being the Cubists' mathematics master, have merely displayed their lack of curiosity. Who was this mysterious mathematician Princet? He was an employee of an insurance company, a frequent table-companion of painters, but, and for this I can vouch, he never had the slightest influence on Braque or Picasso, nor, for that matter, on Gris, who had made his own study of mathematics. Léger did not move in Montmartre circles and probably did not even know him.

The presence of straight lines and regular curves in Cubist works has been solely responsible for the growth of a belief in its geometrical basis. Actually it has nothing of the sort. These regular lines and curves, the reflection of the very basis of all human visual perception, are in fact to be found in every plastic work of art in which there is no longer any attempt at direct imitation. It may well be, as Escholier goes on to claim, that Roger de La Fresnaye, who is certainly a charming painter, transposed "natural forms geometrically and harmoniously"; but Roger de La Fresnaye is not as Escholier calls him, "one of the champions of the most delicate French Cubism". This painter has nothing to do with Cubism; he was a follower of Gauguin and, possibly, of Paul Sérusier, his teacher at the Académie Ranson. I should add that the same applies to a number of the earliest followers of Picasso and Braque, also to almost all those who subsequently exhibited at the Section d'Or and to every exponent of "Abstract Art" in whatever form. The latter, with their passion for angles and numerical relationships, betray not only their dependence on Sérusier's first master, Paul Gauguin, but also on his second, Father Desiderius (Peter Lenz), founder of the Beuron School and champion of the "sacred proportions". This type of painter has only perpetuated the errors of the Symbolists, and also of the Fauves. They have merely produced stylisation, for they are completely ignorant of the real problem which Cézanne considered fundamental and which later became the Cubists' main preoccupation, namely *the representation on a canvas with only two dimensions of solid bodies which have three.*

It would be unjust of me not to emphasise the importance of Derain's contribution in 1907, although he has since renounced his earlier noble aspirations. He turned away from Fauvism because he was vividly conscious of the problem with which painting after Cézanne was faced. He tackled it simultaneously with Picasso and Braque, and was only prevented from succeeding by a retrospective element in his vision. Derain's pictures always had an "old master" appearance, which was in complete contradiction both to the aim he set himself and also to the eternal purpose of all painting—the "re-creation" of the outer world. He wanted, he said, to "hide the framework". I once called Derain "a Classical artist".[104] At that time he was one in intention at least, for his aim was certainly classical. Yet he could not be successful with the means then at his command, and even less with those he tried to use. We shall see how, fifteen years later, Juan Gris was successful with new means.

Cubism was never in any sense a "museum" art. From the beginning its novelty lay in the fanaticism with which it tackled simultaneously the two aspects of the problem which emerged from Cézanne.

It strove to make of the architecture something firm, a real unity by virtue of which the subject-matter would be subordinated to the rhythm of the whole. It strove to produce a complete image of the objects signified by the emblems which formed this entity, but an image which should be at the same time devoid of everything ephemeral and accidental, retaining only what was essential and permanent. Here one can feel Cubism taking up the attitude which stamped its character historically, even at that date, in the eyes of the informed spectator: it was, that is to say, a profound reaction against Impressionism. The latter had tended towards spontaneity, attempting to record the most fleeting aspects of the outer world. Every visual impression seemed worthy of capture; all that mattered was to present it in all its freshness. Cubism disregarded appearances. Unsatisfied by the fortuities of a single visual impression, it endeavoured to penetrate to the very essence of an object by representing it, not as it appeared on a given day at a given time, but as it exists ultimately composed in the memory. For example, the transient appearance (in snow, fog, or rain) of landscape was rejected by the Cubists in horror.

In describing objects a kind of classification of their properties was established, according to whether they were judged essential or accidental. I would emphasise, in passing, the fact that none of these painters (nor any of the literary or other figures in their circle) had any philosophical training, and that they were unaware of any possible parallels (with Locke and Kant in particular); their classification was instinctive rather than reasoned. The essential for them was the form (outline and volume) of an object, regarded as a permanent quality. After that, its colour: but their approach to this was distrustful. It had to be purged of ephemeral qualities and presented in its permanent hue: "local colour" had to be separated from all accidental "discoloration".

These preoccupations immediately explain the Cubists' choice of subject. They wished to represent their subject completely. To begin with, therefore, it was easier to deal with very simple bodies: houses like cubes, trees, glasses, bowls, bottles, dishes and, somewhat later, musical instruments. It is obvious that this choice also offered considerable advantages to the spectator since, in the study of what was for him unquestionably a new handwriting, simple emblems were much easier to interpret.

I have said that Cubism was born in the right half of *Les Demoiselles d'Avignon*, and in so doing I have indicated another of this movement's primary objectives. I mean the attempt to avoid the imitation of light. Light was mistrusted. Had not the Impressionists fallen under its spell? By disregarding it, the Cubists hoped also to dispel from their representation of objects most of what was accidental. For, was not the constantly changing appearance of the outer world caused by variations of light?

Admittedly this first attack miscarried, and after attempting, in the right half of *Les Demoiselles d'Avignon*, to solve the problem of representing forms by means other than chiaroscuro, Picasso was for a while forced to revert to using effects of light to emphasise them.[105] Yet, although the attempt to eliminate light entirely was temporarily abandoned, Cubism took a step by which it disassociated itself from the traditional conception of painting. Light once again became just a technical means; this implied renunciation of the practice of the preceding centuries and a return to an ideal abandoned by western painting since Caravaggio. After this long period of "luminous" painting, light was made subservient, reduced to a means for making solid bodies visible. This was the first crack in the fabric of imitative art; one element of the outer world, light, was excluded from research. Thus, the more acute investigation of bodies put an end to the examination of light as a thing in itself.

I have already spoken of the Cubists' aversion to representing the chance appearance of objects due to changes in weather or the time of day. From this it can be inferred that "atmosphere" was no longer a subject of their study. They only recognised "space", in which bodies exist. In works such as the landscapes of 1908 and 1909, by Braque and Picasso, there is no longer any question of indicating the relative distance of an object by its colour. The position of any one body in relation to others is indicated by drawing alone.

Using light as a means, Picasso then set out on his course. He strove to simplify the forms he depicted, and thus rediscovered Cézanne's conception of the cube, the sphere and the cylinder. He rigidly maintained the predominance of the whole over the parts, and in this was joined by Georges Braque. It is a remarkable fact that whereas Picasso, in inventing Cubism, tried to introduce colour into his work, Braque, coming as he did from the Fauves' orgy of colour, strove to control their disorder by rigid draughtsmanship. Thus, both painters were enriched by the invention of Cubism, for it enabled each to acquire something he had hitherto lacked. Each arrived at Cubism in his own way, and the vague resemblance between Braque's landscapes painted at L'Estaque in the spring and summer of 1908 and at La Roche-Guyon in 1909, and those painted by Picasso at Rue-des-Bois (Oise) in 1908, and at Horta de Ebro in 1909, merely confirms the inevitability of their pictorial revolution. For though these two artists had similar aims, they only knew each other slightly in 1908 and were working in quite different places.

In my book *Der Weg zum Kubismus* I have tried to describe the struggle of these two painters towards the goal they had fixed for themselves. I shall limit myself here to a brief description of their difficulties. Cubism was above all a realistic art, since it aimed at as accurate a form of representation as possible. In the first place, therefore, it came up against what we have called the picture's own rhythm, which tended to "distort" the forms which the artist tried to integrate into this rhythm. The aim was to represent objects with their own, that is to say their "local" colour, which was regarded as the only true and permanent colour; but the need for modelling forms by chiaroscuro was an attack on local colour. At the same time, local colour was "discoloured" by the necessity for adjusting individual hues so that they would harmonise with the general tonality of the picture. This general tonality had been the only unity still respected by the Impressionists. It was also very important in Cézanne's painting.

What happened in face of these difficulties? In the conflict between subject and canvas (or handwriting and architecture, contents and container, part and whole) the Cubists sided resolutely with the canvas against the subject, and completely subordinated the part to the whole. By draughtsmanship the graphic emblems were bent to the strongly emphasised rhythm of the architecture. The colour of an object was totally disregarded in favour of a general tonality which, to begin with, was reduced to monochrome. Colour was not sacrificed voluntarily, but because, despite all sorts of experiments (such as that already mentioned, Picasso's use of a sculptural technique), no solution had been found to the conflict between local colour and volume. Therefore a compromise had to be found, and this consisted in strongly modelling objects in camaïeu and forgoing local colour.

For this reason, Picasso's painting (more than Braque's) often has the character of a painted imitation of sculpture, of *his own* sculpture, such as the bronze *Head of a Woman* for example, done at the beginning of 1910. In this sculpture light is "directed"; the artist was not content to let light shine normally on the outer surface of his *Head*, but broke up the surface by means of small protuberances which force light to play on it as he wished. One can see the same protuberances (like sculpted forms) on the objects and figures represented in his pictures painted in 1909 and at the beginning of 1910. After 1910 the emphasis on rhythm becomes so marked that the pictures are often difficult to read. The emblems are so distorted by the architecture that they are almost illegible. This was the so-called "hermetic" period.

The difference between the Cubism of Picasso and Braque and the painting of Cézanne was chiefly the fact that the role of light was reduced to that of a means for modelling objects. Although Cézanne tried hard to use light as a means for creating volume, he was nevertheless a man of his time and a friend of the Impressionists, and was interested in light for its own sake. He proposed to use landscape forms to render light filtered through atmosphere. His objects are enveloped in atmosphere and are "realised" in a colour harmony of "discoloured" local colour; but this did not worry him. Then, whereas Cézanne, like the Impressionists and their predecessors, made his pictures "limitless" (to use Focillon's expressive neologism), and drew the spectator's eye into a false depth, Picasso and Braque *limited* their pictures,[106] thus re-creating what Focillon calls the "monumental space" of Giottesque painting. They renounced both "geometric space", which had been used in western painting since the Renaissance, and also the linear perspective developed by Leon Battista Alberti. Their pictures were firmly enclosed by a fixed background against which the objects stood out, creating a shallow space which was carefully filled. Within this enclosed space, aerial perspective was entirely suppressed.

A letter from Cézanne to Emile Bernard is often acclaimed as the herald of Cubism. The text is as follows: "Treat nature by the cylinder, the sphere and the cone, everything in proper perspective, so that each side of an object or plane tends towards a central point. Lines parallel to the horizon give breadth, that is to say a section of nature, or (if you prefer) of the spectacle which the Pater omnipotens aeterne Deus has spread out before our eyes. Lines perpendicular to this horizon give depth. Now nature, for us men, is more depth than surface; hence the need to introduce into our vibrations of light, represented by reds and yellows, a sufficient number of blue tints to give the impression of air."

Cézanne unquestionably shows himself to be the lawful father of Cubism by affirming the importance of depth and specifying as the means of handling volume (which he considered fundamental) the three basic forms of our spatial perception, the cylinder, the sphere and the cone. And in order really to understand his thought, one must read very carefully his strange definition of "nature", in which he limits our knowledge to the spectacle which God spreads before our eyes. Yet he aspired nevertheless to an *illusionist* figuration of this "spectacle", and declared his means: normal linear perspective and aerial perspective.

From the very start of Cubism, Picasso and Braque strove to break with any form of *imitation*. They showed this in their works by the absence of all aerial perspective and the use of a linear perspective very different to that propounded by fifteenth-century theorists. Thus, their pictures began to look less and less like those of Cézanne, although partaking of the same spirit. To contemporary spectators they appeared strange and even exotic.

The years 1907–9 have been called Picasso's "Negro Period". This name is regrettable because it suggests an imitation of African sculpture, whereas in reality there was merely an affinity between the aims of negro sculpture and those of Picasso and Braque at one stage in their personal evolution. The artists certainly collected negro sculpture, but only later. As with the Italian artists of the Quattrocento and Greco-Roman sculpture, the Impressionists and Japanese prints, creation came first, and it was only subsequently that ancestors and collaterals were discovered.[107]

Somewhat later still, the aesthetic and technique of these forbears were investigated. There is no doubt that their study of African and Pacific sculpture was invaluable for the Cubist painters, but the results of it only appeared years after. Gris' reply to a questionnaire about Negro Art in 1920[108] shows that he understood its aesthetic and was aware of a close relationship with his own. As for technique, I shall quote only one example, to which I have already referred in *Der Weg zum Kubismus*. In Picasso's sculptures of 1913 the hole of the guitar is represented by a cylinder or cone *in relief*; this was unquestionably inspired by the eyes in certain Ivory Coast masks. So it is obvious that the real *influence* only showed itself long *after* what is wrongly called "the Negro Period". What in fact inspired this name was merely the crude simplification of forms and the colour of Picasso's figures at that time. People thought they were looking at negroes. Only the other day I found in a catalogue the reproduction of a *Man's Head* of 1908, which had been given the title *Head of a Negro*.

But whereas in origin this designation was simply a naïve expression of scorn, it gave rise to a theory based on a scientific error, unless it, too, is indicative of the same attitude. I refer to the theory of "Primitivism in Modern Painting". The confusion which permeates this whole question of "primitivism" in art is considerable. Let us consider a well-known authority on the subject: *L'Art Primitif* by G. H. Luquet.[109] I must first say that the mentality of the author, a "civilised being" who would doubtless indignantly repudiate as unscientific the confusion of the "microcosm" with the "macrocosm", is "mythical" and primitive to the point of still believing that the so-called "ages of humanity" reproduce the ages of man. And so he is led to deduce the "origins" and "development" of painting from the evolution that he has observed in drawings by his daughter and other children.[110]

Luquet overwhelms the reader with examples of "Primitive Art", three-quarters of which are not art at all and the remainder not primitive. According to him they are all products of that "intellectual realism" on which he believes primitive art to be based; against this he sets "visual realism" which forms the basis of "the classical art of the civilised adult"[111] (by which he means the academic art of the nineteenth century). To this, as a second criterion, he adds certain differences that he claims to have discovered in graphic narration and which result from this fundamental difference. Now, what Luquet has done is to confuse *formative writing* with *pragmatic writing*, thus depriving his evidence of all value. In his list there are works of art so widely different in spirit as the products of the Stone Age, of Egypt,

Crete, mediaeval Christianity and African negroes, etc., side by side with simple "communications", which have no existence of their own, such as pictographs, children's drawings and graffiti. It is obvious where such lack of method leads.

Basically, Luquet judges a painting or drawing to be primitive from its appearance alone, according to the amount by which it differs from things as he sees them. Here then is another instance of the presumptuous attitude characteristic of "civilised man", who regards as "inferior" any form of representation other than his own, for this is the only one he accepts as a "true likeness". Odd as it may seem, those who believe in and even enjoy the so-called "Primitivism in modern art" are reacting in exactly the same way. They, too, base their judgement on appearances (instead of inquiring into the causes of this appearance), just as an earlier generation talked of a "Negro Period" and lumped Cubist paintings together with negro sculpture. Now I do not think that art can be classed as primitive just by its appearance. If one considers as a whole those works which are undoubtedly "primitive" one will discover that they differ widely in appearance and include paintings currently called "naturalistic" (the palaeolithic rock-paintings of Altamira and Font de Gaume, for example), as well as the most "unnaturalistic" paintings and sculptures imaginable (for example, New Zealand sculpture); between these two extremes there is no limit to the possible forms of expression. It would be interesting to study the causes of this diversity, but that is not possible here, and I must limit myself to saying that, to my mind, in primitive cultures as in others, the appearance of the work of art is determined by the *practical purpose* imposed on the artist by his spiritual community. It is conceivable that the palaeolithic rock-paintings served the same function as those of the Dogon tribe investigated by Marcel Griaule. The Dogons told Griaule that their representations of animals were painted to protect them from the evil "Mana" of the animal killed by their huntsmen, which wanders about alone and is therefore dangerous. The Dogons, however, did not always portray a freshly killed animal. The event (the slaying of the animal) happened in the mythical past; and this explains the character and style of these paintings which, since they perpetuate a myth, necessarily tend to conform exactly to an established type of representation. This is certainly not true of the rock-paintings at Font de Gaume, Altamira or any of the other Franco-Iberian caves which contain paintings, for their style is admirably free. It does not seem unreasonable to explain the origin of these "naturalistic" figurations as an earlier stage of the belief referred to by Griaule, a stage at which fixation of the "Mana" took place, possibly after the death of each animal, but certainly at very frequent and short intervals, so that it was directly connected with the tribe's hunting. This would explain not only the imitative nature of these paintings (the painter having in mind a specific animal which had been recently killed and not an animal-type valid for every hunt), but also the numerous palimpsests in these caves, where one animal is painted on top of another. With the Dogons, as with Stone Age man, purpose accounts for the unusual places in which these paintings are found (almost inaccessible corners of unlit caverns) since it was wise to conceal these images as much as possible.

At the other extreme of representation, the form used by the natives of New Zealand, the idea was to reproduce as faithfully as possible the person who represented the myth—an ancestor, for example,

Siphon, Glass and Newspaper · 1916

who was not some specific father or grandfather but a mythical ancestor whose type was handed down by tradition in a stereotyped art-form.

Thus, no art can be classed as primitive by its appearance, since this can be so infinitely varied and can often resemble a non-primitive art. Art can only be called primitive if we can show that it is undeniably the expression of a primitive mentality. With one exception, Henri Rousseau, I very much doubt whether this can be proved against any western painter prior to 1910. Rousseau's work, the miraculous flowering of popular art, is, like all true primitive art, historically outside time. Rousseau lived from 1844 to 1910; we met him and knew him, but his art owed nothing to our own period, nor indeed to any other. He was ignorant of Delacroix, Courbet, Corot and the Impressionists, just as he was ignorant of Cézanne, Seurat and van Gogh. His painting owed nothing to them. One can, if one likes, call him an isolated primitive, but I incline to think of him as a touching spokesman for a whole stratum of society which even to-day has retained a certain primitive element. I am even inclined to think that his works depict some of the myths of this element of society—rather vague myths perhaps which are more like fables: the virgin forest in which Arabs on horseback are set on by tigers, the desert in moon-light, where a lion comes sniffing at a sleeping gipsy, all those distant countries with their inhabitants and strange beasts dreamed of by the child and the simpleton.[112] Such art is part of folklore. Rousseau himself is already almost a myth. Art historians try to situate him historically, arguing his acceptance by museums and his influence on other painters; but his contemporaries were not mistaken, they knew him simply as "*Le Douanier*".

There is nothing primitive about the other painters of our time. They have taken their place in history and have been subject to the influence of others. They have responded to the spiritual desires of a layer of society which is not in the least primitive. I shall attempt to describe the ends towards which these desires tended, both with Juan Gris and with the other Cubists, and then I think it will be clear that they contained no mythical element. But one should, I think, consider whether a *mythical* element did not subsequently invade western art. I shall try to give a brief answer to this question in a later chapter, and also to determine whether this mythical element is at the same time primitive. I hope, however, that I have made it clear that with Picasso and Braque there is no justification for deducing a primitive or mythical element from the appearance of their work even during what is so wrongly called "the Negro Period". Until the beginning of 1910 these painters dealt with purely plastic problems. They were, in fact, entirely concerned with composition. At that date no-one had challenged the Renaissance ideal, the investigation of the outer world; and this was the basis of all their work. Far from being primitive, their painting was simply a continuation, an enrichment of the western tradition, from which it hardly diverged even in appearance. The attack on illusionism was still feeble. There was the jagged surface of Picasso's sculpture, which he began to imitate in his paintings in 1909, but for a while this was the full extent of the change. And I think it is equally evident that there is no justification for using the word "primitive" about the works of the following years, since they were more and more dictated by plastic considerations and are not primitive even in appearance.

In 1910 a new factor was introduced, which is of great importance because it completed the break with imitation of the optical sensation. This was the introduction of several views of the same object juxtaposed in one picture. Thus, the split between the already difficult painting of the hermetic period and illusionism grew. I mean by "illusionism" a method of representation which employs all the means of plastic writing but in its result never renounces the possibility of identification with some optical sensation in the tangible world. Now here, although the aspects of the object presented were still derived from visual impressions, there were several of them together, whereas the imaginary spectator in the outer world would only be able to see one of them at a time. This is the startling novelty which one has to realise. Comparisons have, I think, been made between these multiple aspects of one object and pictures by artists of the Trecento and Quattrocento in which scenes from the life of some Saint are arranged round his central figure. But such comparisons are superficial, for the different scenes in the Saint's life were not intended to be read simultaneously but in sequence. They were an assembly of several different pictures. There was nothing like this in Cubism: the various aspects which make up a Cubist picture are intended to be seen simultaneously and to compose together a single object in the eyes of the spectator.

It is equally wrong to imagine that there is a precedent for these "multiple aspects" in the symmetrical repetition of the same form in decoration. This mistake is made, for example, by the authors of *Indian Art of the United States*, Frederick H. Douglas and René d'Harnoncourt,[113] when, discussing a Haida drawing of a whale, they write (refuting the idea that it might be some strange monster) that both sides of the animal are shown in this drawing and that this betokens a tendency to realism. Now it is easy to see that this double representation is simply an example of the universal tendency of decorative art towards symmetry, which is often achieved with reversed animals, as in the "abstract" designs of Persian carpets. This applies to all decoration, to all forms of ornamental petrifaction; it occurs as soon as there is no longer any question of recording an emotion. For then one is merely reproducing a stereotyped symbol, which ends by losing all meaning and becomes an aspect, an agreeable object. It is in fact certain, from the psychological point of view, that bilateral symmetry is one of the most effective ways of pleasing the spectator. All decorative art, being purely hedonistic, makes use of this formula. It is curious that Douglas and d'Harnoncourt have not observed that a "tendency to realism" never produces two *similar* images of the same object. A realistic approach expresses itself through *different* images of the same object; and this was the method of the Cubists. To put it in terms of handwriting: in order to signify a complete "glass" they presented simultaneously several emblems of "a glass", one signifying "a glass from in front", another "a glass from one side", a third and fourth "a glass in cross-section" and "a glass seen from above". This is what has since been called *analytica Cubism* (and I believe that Gris was the first to use this expression). By not limiting themselves to the reproduction of a single visual impression of an object, they hoped to express it more fully. They showed it from various angles, from above and from below; they broke it, in order to show it in cross-section or from inside. Fantastic constructions thus came into being within the *grisaille* of their pictures. No solution, however, had yet been found either for the problem of representing forms without chiaroscuro or for the problem of local colour.

IV. JUAN GRIS BEGINS TO PAINT

Juan Gris was six years younger than Picasso and Braque, and arrived in Paris long after them. At first he was content to work and reflect in silence. After some years of hard work he was able to free himself from the habits and tricks of newspaper illustration. In 1910 he painted several still-lifes, carefully done from nature in water-colour. In 1911 he first showed some oil-paintings (also still-lifes) to his friends. They were extremely simple, modest works: in no way spectacular, they revealed Gris' integrity. Each object was depicted with minute care, its form brought out by chiaroscuro and its colour indicated but changed to fit the general tonality. The background, however, was still rather fluid, yet it was not a dead surface and was articulated by objects and spaces through the repetition of forms, justified from the imitative point of view as shadows or reflections. The perspective was no longer that of the Renaissance, although in some ways similar to what is known as isometric projection: the objects were shown as if seen from slightly above.

It was not until 1912 that Gris' painting clearly revealed itself. He grasped the problems of his day and sought his own solution. He was aware of his progress since, for the first time, he now publicly exhibited his pictures (Salon des Indépendants and "Section d'Or"). His paintings were also at this time almost monochrome. The form of each object stands out clearly and the use of chiaroscuro is reduced to a minimum, since drawing was used as a substitute. The general appearance was rigid, "geometrical", to the eyes of contemporary spectators, and dominated by regular forms, particularly circles. This was indeed analytical Cubism; but by striving to simplify, to say the essential in the clearest and most precise way, it sometimes happened that he invented forms which foreshadowed synthetic Cubism. What undoubtedly worried Gris in his friends' work was the complexity, the confusion of lines—only apparent, it is true, but troublesome for the reader of canvases which justly claimed to be representational and realistic. This smacked of the "ambiguity" which he detested. His own contribution was clarity, purity and a hatred of falsehood. Picasso and Braque always proclaimed that they disdained tricks of brushwork; but, carried away by their emotions, they often yielded in spite of themselves to their technical gifts. Only Gris made his hand completely subservient to the will of his very clear mind.

In his work done in the spring of 1912, it was the composition which still reminded one of his youth in Madrid and the influences of that period. The rhythm is nowhere broken, but it has a sort of 1900 flavour. The folds of materials, even the silhouettes of the objects, contribute to this impression. It was the last spasm of a malady of his youth and it disappeared during the second half of the same year; for Gris, more than any other, was to widen the gap between stylisation (which still crept into his pictures) and plastic invention, whereby objects are no longer imitated but re-created within a composition which is not mechanical and external but organic and internal.

At the beginning of 1912 he painted numerous still-lifes, landscapes and portraits: one of Picasso, exhibited at the Indépendants under the title *Homage to Picasso*, which is a significant indication of Gris' modesty and youthful enthusiasm; one of his mother, painted from memory, for after leaving Madrid

224, 225

237

23, 29, 238–245

241

242

243

he never saw her again; others of Germaine and Maurice Raynal, and of Legua. Need I add that they were perfect likenesses? Gris would never have thought of painting a portrait that was not a real portrait. He *painted* no more after this (with the exception of two portraits of Josette which I shall mention later). The development of his painting, tending as it did towards the type, turned his mind away from observation of the individual. So Gris restricted his future portraits to line drawings.

He *drew* a number of portraits at various times, particularly in 1915, 1921, 1922, 1923 and 1926, of which, apart from those referred to in the text, I would like to mention here those of Reverdy, Vincente Huidobro, Boris Kochno, Ford Madox Ford and his Self-portrait.

V. THE END OF ANALYTICAL CUBISM

The last traces of stylisation vanished from Gris' work during the second half of 1912. From then on, everything was said without decorative emphasis. The picture as a whole was homogeneous and retained its unity; but there was no longer an empty ornamental unity acquired to the detriment of the initial emotion. Instead there was an ensemble, grouping and harmonising the multiple elements that the painter wished to transmit to the spectator.

During this period, his friends Picasso and Braque were experimenting with a technique which I have called "superimposed planes". In 1910 this technique emerged from their urgent desire to express the third dimension, depth (or, in other words, the volume and density of objects), by other means than effects of light—that is to say *trompe l'œil* and chiaroscuro. The attempt was made to express this density by an overlaying of planes. Gris never used this technique; chiaroscuro doubtless seemed to him as good a method as any other. Or did he realise that these superimposed planes were only leading to another form of *trompe l'œil?* Instead of being an imitation of nature, they were an imitation of the sculpture from which they derived, just as Picasso in his pictures of 1909 and 1910 had imitated his sculpture of that period. I do not believe that Gris was fully aware of this, since I do not recall any conversation in which he raised this objection; and it was only much later that I myself realised that it was an "imitation of an imitation". It was in their *sculptures* (that is to say, in the reliefs made with paper, iron and wood) that Braque and Picasso had discovered the means of substituting, for relief modelling of a continuous surface, independent planes superimposed one over the other. This was a new solution perfectly suited to relief and was moreover of fundamental importance, since it broke down closed forms and permitted the substitution in sculpture of transparent constructions holding their own in space. When transposed on to flat canvas, however, it lost the greater part of its meaning. Gris evidently felt this (if he had not actually reasoned it out), for it was a technique which he avoided. In any case he would have had to take it over at second-hand, since he had not made any of the reliefs which produced it.

Having got over the stage of decorative composition, Gris strove to break away from monochrome.

He wanted to represent objects as completely as possible, to tell the spectator everything about them. Each object was depicted from different angles, its colour was recorded, often on only one part of its surface, and even its substance was indicated by imitations of wood, marble, etc.—a technique used by Gris as well as by his friends.

248–252

I have tried in *Der Weg zum Kubismus* to show the part played by this craftsmanlike technique of illusion. The main purpose originally was to introduce "real details" into pictures which were particularly hard to read, and thereby, on the principle of *pars pro toto*, to stimulate the spectator's perception, to bring the whole object into focus. In my earlier book, I have explained at length the psychological process by which the object forms around one legible detail—a process called *Hineinsehung*—as well as the history of these "real details" in Cubism. The first example occurred in 1909, when Braque painted a nail in *trompe l'œil* in a still-life. There followed in 1910 the introduction of printed letters. These "stereo-forms", introduced into a canvas as "real details", "qualified" (to use a word from Gris' vocabulary) the objects for the spectator.

Jean Paulhan, in *Les Fleurs de Tarbes*,[114] discusses Paul Bourget's use of "commonplaces" or "clichés". The Cubist painters used clichés and commonplaces deliberately, on the one hand as a reaction against "artistic handwriting", and on the other to provide the beholder of these constructions (which were difficult to decipher) with signs which he could read easily, with threads for his guidance. Imitations of wood and marble were first used in the paintings of 1912. We shall see later in this book the extraordinary importance both of this technique and of the "real details".

One method which was imitated later by other painters was peculiar to Gris: the objects, whose form, colour and even substance he tried to express, were frequently completed by a sort of projection in the form of a black silhouette. But he did not make a system of this. Sometimes the "projection" alone was left to represent the object: for example, a pipe placed on the imitation wood of a table. At other times a tumbler was painted only once, carefully painted and modelled with shadows, as if seen in a sort of super-isometric projection (to coin a phrase), that is to say from a balcony or gallery.

249
258

It is particularly important to note during this period the beginning of the *dissociation of line and colour*. In fact, it was at this time that Gris gave up colouring the whole of an object's surface and left the spectator to re-create the object in the fullness of its colour, of which he only gave a sample. We shall see later that this was the first step towards an even greater freedom, which enabled Gris to isolate handwriting from architecture. But, as yet, there was nothing approaching this. The line itself (that is to say, the handwriting) ended by forming the architecture, which resulted from the fusion of all the emblems into a whole. The independence of the colour meant simply that it could be harmonised within the picture, that chiaroscuro was possible and that the spectator was informed of the object's local colour. Now, because this hue was used independently, it could be used without any "discoloration" and with the veracity to which Gris aspired. Another innovation of this period, which was unique to Gris, was his use in a composition of what I shall call a "polyphonic element".

35

We have seen that objects are often represented several times in his pictures, as in those of his friends; but the method peculiar to Gris was the arrangement of the supplementary views of the several objects

252 in a second composition, making a second picture (often placed obliquely) which is integrated with the first. Generally speaking, the first view shows the objects upright; the second shows them at an angle. The painter has combined the two architectures, the second being superimposed on the first, and they melt into each other in the unity of the picture.

247   During the summer of 1913, which Gris spent at Céret (Picasso and Manolo were also there), his painting matured. Gris had never spent a holiday in the country since he arrived in Paris, and he felt at his ease on the borders of Spain in this atmosphere of work. Several still-lifes, Catalan landscapes and

47, 246 figure pictures (*The Smoker*, *The Torero*) were the fruits with which he returned in the autumn to the Rue Ravignan.

    What strikes one in these canvases is the extreme intellectual rigour in the application of the theories he had adopted after mature reflection. The best account of the clarity of mind to which he had already attained can be read in Pedro Luis de Galvez' description of his visit to the Rue Ravignan some months earlier,[115] in which, humorously but not without a certain respect, he quotes some of Gris' opinions. He refers to the "painting of ideas" (this, as I shall soon show, was an illusion of the period, for it had not in fact yet been reached). Gris, however, clearly envisaged leading up to a true "painting of ideas". He explained, for example, that the eyes which one always thinks of in full face can equally be represented full face in a profile head. Nor is it surprising to learn that Gris insisted that this was an old idea, like every other he expounded. Thus, he proved himself, once again, a true follower of tradition, clinging to history. As Galvez wrote in his surprise, far from being a "*follia di Parigi . . . il Cubismo, al contrario, ha una storia vecchia come il mondo*".

VI. PAPIERS COLLÉS AND SYNTHETIC CUBISM

Guillaume Apollinaire in *Les Peintres Cubistes*[116] describes the Cubism of 1912 as "conceptual" painting, an expression much used by the Cubists themselves at the time. This is important because it shows that the Cubist painters were conscious of their goal, although Apollinaire was mistaken in calling their painting at that time "conceptual". In their painting of that period Gris and his friends did not express "concepts", objects conceived by the mind, but gave a great variety of information, derived from previous visual impressions, about a single object. There was talk of "conceptual" painting, but in 1912 the painters were still empiricists and were therefore directly in the tradition of the Renaissance.

    In the Middle Ages painting was frankly conceptual, and it is a characteristic of Christian Art to which I have already referred. The trees and buildings in the paintings and mosaics of those days were objects conceived by the mind and not observed with the eye. What could be less empirical than to represent the river Jordan by parallel wavy lines, or the four rivers of Paradise by four interwoven lines springing from under the feet of Christ and frequently identified by being labelled with their names? Inherent in this sort of painting there was, of course, always the danger of petrifaction, of a formative handwriting becoming pragmatic, of the concept hardening into a stereotyped emblem whose conventional meaning was invariable. That is to say, that the emblem would be predetermined and not created anew by each artist. There was also the risk that this conventional emblem would in turn end by losing all meaning and so become an ornament, an empty calligraphic flourish. Mediaeval miniatures did succumb to this danger but the large-scale paintings retained their character as formative handwriting.

There is, however, another form of conceptual handwriting—*children's drawings*—sometimes mistakenly referred to as "child art"—which has no formative character whatever. This is a conceptual, pragmatic handwriting—ideographic and not pictographic; one child's drawing resembles another so closely that one cannot avoid the conclusion that the signs are conventional. The emblems are not continually re-invented; the pictures have no autonomous existence; there is no trace of that architecture by which the graphic emblems of formative handwriting are held together and through which the picture lives objectively. The vague decorative arrangement of which a child is capable must not be mistaken for architecture. Children do not attempt to imitate things, they "describe" and record details by a conceptual graphic notation. The head is a circle which contains two other well-defined little circles for the eyes and a larger one for the mouth; the hand and arm are like a five-pronged rake at the end of a long handle. These are concepts—I would even call them *pure* concepts—in which image-memories play no part, for they are formed from *practical memories* connected with forces and not with forms. Thus, there is every reason for excluding children's drawings as an artistic manifestation, since the formative factor is absent in them. I remember, in about 1907, Matisse saying to his children, who were painting and scribbling as all children do: "You'll never get anywhere until you have mastered objects." He could see that his children were on the wrong lines as far as painting was concerned and that they should be encouraged to try another method, to look around them and make compositions out of image-memories.

This is not the place for me to explain how, almost simultaneously with the Cubists, Paul Klee, a lone but important figure, evolved a conceptual art of his own which has often been wrongly confused with children's drawings. All I want here is to explain the nature of conceptual art before discussing what it became in the hands of the Cubists. In a previous volume[117] I have referred to the year 1907 as "one of the turning-points of art history": and so it was in the limited sense that it witnessed the break with illusionism. But it seems to me now that the real turning-point was between analytical Cubism, an empirical form of painting, and synthetic Cubism which, as I shall explain, is real conceptual painting. The break with the empirical spirit of the Renaissance did not occur until then. Thus, synthetic Cubism is related, at the distance of several centuries, to mediaeval painting, though its aims and motives are quite different.

Juan Gris began to move towards conceptual painting in 1914 when he tried in his pictures to describe objects with as little complication as possible. Having pushed analysis to its extreme, he ended, in *The Smoker* (painted at Céret in the summer of 1913), with innumerable views of the man's head 246 displayed fanwise, and even the most knowing spectator has difficulty in fusing them in his perception.

The Violin · 1916

After 1914 Gris made every effort to say the maximum with the minimum of means, and this led him more and more towards invention, towards synthesis. As his composition became stronger, it became increasingly less mechanical. Gris who, as we have seen, was never associated with the researches of Braque and Picasso into the representation of volume by means other than chiaroscuro, no doubt felt at this time that some use of illusionist technique was essential and that nothing would be achieved by substituting one form of illusionism for another. Like Braque and Picasso, his pictures of this period are limited by a flat background against which the objects stand out in relief, being superimposed to indicate their relative positions. Instead of the eye being led inwards into an apparently limitless but artificial depth, the objects are placed in an enclosed pictorial space and arrange themselves by "coming out towards" the spectator.[118]

65, 73

Gris tended from this time to reduce more and more the "monumental space" of his pictures and began to collect all his forms on the flat surface. This was a step towards the realisation of his special conception of painting (*vide* his lecture in Part III) as "flat, coloured architecture".

81, 254, 255, 257–260

The year 1914—in Paris in the spring and later at Collioure—saw Gris, in company with Braque and Picasso, making great use of the technique known as *papier collé*. This was no more than a new development of the "real details", the introduction of which in the form of imitation wood and marble I have already discussed. Now these artists introduced into their pictures and drawings pieces of newspaper and wall-paper, printed matter of one kind and another, engravings, oilcloth etc., with the idea of abolishing more completely tricks of brushwork and of replacing the "hand-painted" surface by the "ready-made". At the same time, incorporation of the actual object in the picture was intended as an act of realism: it also proved the solidity of an architecture which was able to absorb such foreign bodies.[119]

And here I would draw attention to a rather curious fact which, so far as I am aware, has passed almost unnoticed. Between 1908 and 1914 Picasso and Braque hardly ever signed their pictures (or drawings) on the *recto* but always on the *verso*. Gris followed the same practice during the years 1913 and 1914, although previously he had signed on the *recto*, sometimes even with an inscription, as in the case of the *Portrait of Picasso*. After 1914 this practice was abandoned by all three painters, and in 1915 Gris again began to sign his pictures and drawings in the traditional manner, frequently with the full date (month and year). What was the reason for this unusual practice which was so soon given up? Was it the idea that a signature was a foreign element incapable of being absorbed into the composition as a whole? It might appear so; and the painters themselves used to say that a signature "looked wrong". And yet . . . Braque and Picasso followed this practice for several years, whereas in Gris' work it coincided exactly with the period of *papiers collés*. Now, during this period he was filling his compositions with the most heterogeneous elements; and so one cannot help wondering why a signature should not have been absorbed into the architectural unity just like any other element. My own belief is that the suppression of the visible signature was a deliberate gesture towards *impersonal* authorship, arising out of a conviction that the painter's "hand", his individual "handwriting", should not be visible in the finished product. And what is more "personal" than a signature?

242

262–264

This also explains why the habit of signing on the *verso* could be abandoned after 1914 by Gris as well as by his friends. As they developed, their handwriting became more and more "personal" (though this may not have been known to them), no matter what Gris may say. Later on, Picasso and Braque felt differently and agreed, when asked to do so by collectors, to put an additional signature on the *recto* of pictures of the "heroic period". But this did not mean that they had recanted; they no longer "felt" the necessity to which they had responded at the time and which prevented them signing across the painted surface. In retrospect I can see for myself that, even at the time when they were most concerned with an impersonal form of execution, the works of these painters bear the stamp of their individual "hands". For future generations these signatures on the *verso* present something of a material problem. All paintings on canvas end by being re-lined sooner or later, and the only way to avoid covering up these signatures is to leave a hole in the second canvas. But this imperils the whole operation. An additional complication is the fact that the whole surface of the canvas is not always covered, so that it will be impossible to transfer these pictures on to other canvases.

To get back to *papiers collés*, however. Braque only used this technique with drawings, some of which, on canvas, are fairly large. Picasso used it in a great number of drawings, and also in a very few paintings. On the other hand, Gris, whom it suited better than either of the others, for the double reason that it contributed to the honesty of the representation and assisted the dominance of the whole over the parts, made use of it only in paintings. Even in the early days, in 1912, he used pages from books and pieces of mirror in his pictures; but whereas, with Picasso in particular, the newspaper was often used simply as a piece of material, with Gris the fragment of mirror represents a mirror, the printed book page is itself, and so is the piece of newspaper. In support of this statement I would like to quote something he said to Michel Leiris some ten years later, and which was reported to me at the time. Gris was explaining the reasons which led him to stick pieces of mirror on to the canvas in two of his pictures. One of these pictures, *The Dressing-Table*, was exhibited at the "Section d'Or" in October 1912, where, as I well remember, it caused a good deal of criticism, not to say a certain scandal. But Gris had no intention of causing a scandal; he was, as usual, being simply honest. "You want to know why I had to stick on a piece of mirror?" he said to Leiris. "Well, surfaces can be re-created and volumes interpreted in a picture, but what is one to do about a mirror whose surface is always changing and which should reflect even the spectator? There is nothing else to do but stick on a real piece."

It is quite obvious why Gris used the technique of *papier collé*, and also how he used it. Picasso's motives for using it were, on the other hand, quite different. He was really concerned to be master of his means, to make his grip felt, to debunk the idea of "noble means", to prove that the painter can express his emotion just as well in terms of paper and cardboard (at a later stage, he used a piece of linen nailed to a board) as in oil paint or gouache. It was one of those romantic, ironic gestures calculated to display the pre-eminence of the creator's personality over his creation. Picasso wants one to feel that he is always there, just like Jean-Paul, who wraps his novel up in a network of bizarre complications —the dog-postman of *Hesperus* etc.—and continually breaks into the narrative with personal interventions.

241

Gris hid behind his works; *papier collé* was, for him, no more than another step towards anonymity. In 1913 he used it in only a few pictures. In 1914 (at Paris and Collioure) he executed a series of large paintings making use of wall-paper, newspaper, engravings and "imitation-wood" paper. Over these coloured papers he drew, sometimes in gouache but more frequently in oil paint, the outlines of an object seen from several points of view, thus making it stand out clearly.

250, 251
253–255, 257–260
55, 65, 73, 81

At the same time, in common with Picasso and Braque, he used another trick, that of thickening his paint with sand or ashes. This "solidification" of the colour was intended to diminish the viscous appearance of oil paint and so restrict the possibility of virtuosity in the execution.[120]

By the beginning of 1915, when he returned to Paris, Gris had begun to feel dissatisfied with the technique of multiple aspects. He wanted to find some other way of expressing himself. He wanted to make his painting richer, and he thought he had found a way. And yet, during the summer, he was overcome with doubts. He began to paint in quite a different spirit. Hitherto his pictures had always been absolutely *static* (they became so again later), and this was one of the very qualities which distinguished him so completely from Picasso and Braque, both of whose paintings—but especially those of the former—were *dynamic*.[121] Apparently Gris' ideal of architectural grandeur can only be realised with a static subject. But during the summer of 1915 he produced a series of pictures which are full of movement. The most important of the series—and this fact is significant—is an oval inscribed on a rectangular canvas. The objects no longer stand upright on the base of the rectangle, solid and motionless as usual, held in place by the frame; they have lost their footing on the slippery surface of the oval and are whirling around like mad things. One cannot even recognise what they all are. Some are seen from head-on, others from above. There are a number of black silhouettes, and there is even a suggestion of light effects playing on the surface and adding to the general confusion.[122] Was it an expression of Gris' disturbed state of mind due to the war? Or was it, as one might be led to think from the sort of ornamental effect of the whole, one last lapse into *Art Nouveau?* Or was it that Gris played for a moment with the idea of so-called abstract painting and forced himself to create "forms in movement"? If this last is the case he must have retreated from disaster very quickly for, in the works that followed, the objects found their feet again and stopped moving. Something similar happened too with the colour, which passed through a phase of being broken up with hatching and dots before regaining his habitual sobriety, though with an added gravity. Light reverted to being a technical means. Synthetic Cubism was built on a lasting foundation. Gris finally gave up presenting the beholder with a great variety of information (acquired by empirical observation) about the objects which he displayed. He now offered a *synthesis* : that is to say, he packed his knowledge into one significant form, a single emblem. True conceptual painting was born.[123]

107, 265

263–266

267

Of course, conceptual painting brought about a complete transformation of the relationship that exists during work between the painter and the outer world. There could no longer be any question of working from models in the studio—academic painting—nor of working on the *motif* like the Impressionists. This modification had come about gradually. Cézanne and Seurat had done both; van Gogh, for whom spontaneity was all-important, had only worked on the *motif*. Except in their large compositions, the Fauves followed van Gogh's example in that way as well as in others. Picasso and Gris, because of their starting-point, began by working from models. Braque, on the other hand, worked until 1907 in the open air. Braque's landscapes of 1908, and even those of 1909 by Picasso, are conceived as if they were painted on the spot, which in some cases they actually were. In 1908, following Braque's indications, I photographed the *Houses at l'Estaque* (coll. Hermann Rupf, Berne) from the spot from which he had "seen" them. The same was done in the following year for one of Picasso's landscapes of Horta de Ebro. There is an astonishing similarity between the photographs and the pictures. In 1910, at the height of the "hermetic" period, when Picasso painted my portrait, I had to pose at least twenty times. I have already mentioned the still-lifes that Gris painted from nature in 1910.

Now, neither Gris nor his friends could think of anything but working alone in the studio. Their approach was more akin to the sensuousness of the Impressionists than to the materialism of the Ecole des Beaux-Arts. However, they no longer sought to reproduce a unique optical sensation. What these painters did was to recall all their visual perceptions of a given object and then attempt to re-create it by means of a new emblem.

Henceforth, the emblems which Juan Gris invented "signified" the whole of the object which he meant to represent. All the details are not present. The emblems are not comprehensible without previous visual experiences. But the justification for calling this conceptual painting is the fact that the picture contains not the forms which have been collected in the visual memory of the painter, but *new forms*, forms which differ from those of the "real" objects we meet with in the visible world, forms which are truly emblems and which only become objects in the apperception of the spectator.

Gris' painting became more and more a "writing". It contained undisguised graphic emblems invented by the painter with no thought of imitation. These emblems are endowed with the power to create in the reader's imagination images which signify for him the outer world. Here was the tool which was to make possible the full realisation of his "great design".

Technically, the next stage in the development of Gris' art owed its birth to Cézanne, with whom originated the conception of a picture as a self-contained organism. Spiritually, however—and about this there should be no doubt—it derived from Mallarmé. I am convinced that the courage which these few painters required to re-invent conceptual painting, to believe themselves capable, that is to say, of performing acts of total creation, can only have come about through their discovery of the incantatory quality of Mallarmé's later poems. And Juan Gris certainly was concerned with acts of total creation; from now on, the emblems which he began to design were not endowed by convention with a meaning learnt in advance. So he broke completely with illusionist painting and with pragmatic hand-writing. He "objectivised" or, to use his own language, "qualified" the coloured forms of this picture in order to produce the most efficient emblems. He was convinced that these emblems would re-create the reality which he imagined, deprived of all incidentals, of any imitative recollection of the emotion in which it had its origin. "*A quoi bon,*" wrote Mallarmé,[124] "*la merveille de transposer un fait de nature en sa presque disparition vibratoire selon le jeu de la parole, cependant ; si ce n'est pour qu'en émane, sans la gêne d'un proche ou concret rappel, la notion pure ?*"

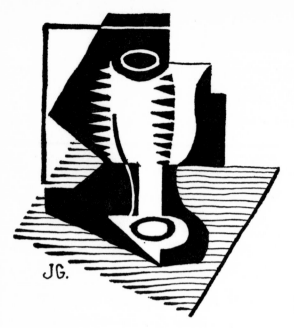

Glass · 1918

"*Je dis : une fleur ! et, hors de l'oubli où ma voix relègue aucun contour, en tant que quelque chose d'autre que les calices sus, musicalement se lève, idée même et suave, l'absente de tous bouquets. . . .*"

This was the sublime lesson that Gris had learnt. In talking of contemporary painting the phrase "magic realism" has sometimes been used, and there is actually no objection to it provided one does not fall into the trap of occultist musing, and always provided one realises that it is merely another name for what I call "conceptual painting".

In an earlier chapter (p. 108) I referred to the Neo-Platonism of the self-styled Symbolist painters. On this subject Maurice Denis[125] has written: "Like Sérusier himself, Symbolism was neo-Platonist. Both writers and painters were in agreement in affirming that natural objects are the signs for ideas, that the visible is just a manifestation of the invisible, that meanings, colours and words have a miraculously expressive value, quite apart from all representation or from the literal meaning of words." I have already remarked that there seems to be no reason why the paintings of the Symbolist painters —both those of the School of Pont-Aven and the Nabis—should have needed a "miraculously expressive value". The "distortion" of these pictures may perhaps have been shocking; but, coming after the Impressionists and Cézanne, they were certainly "legible" to any spectator, for they were composed of figurative signs which had, through familiarity, acquired a conventional value. A closer study of Denis' text suggests indeed that he was thinking more of some symbolic value of the colours (the forms are not even mentioned) than of the evocative power of the emblems to create "reality" without recourse to imitation; that is to say, without recourse to image-memories generally associated with these signs. I feel sure that the Symbolist painters were really only thinking of some sort of emotive halo which surrounds objects and which they intended to preserve; the philosophical jargon which they employed was taken over from the poets. For it is clear that these painters merely tacked themselves on to the Symbolist *poets* and appropriated their vocabulary without actually understanding what the words meant. The true significance of Mallarmé's "incantation" escaped them. Indeed, Mallarmé, like Cézanne, was not understood until after 1900.

Gris never intended to rely idly on the "mysterious equivalence" which Gauguin and his friends invoked with so little success to justify their conventional figurative arabesques. He knew that Mallarmé had resorted to incantation because his labours had ended in a *trobar clus*, the only approach to which was through the new evocative power with which his "words", his immutable materials,[126] had been endowed. Now the painter can renounce conventional signs. And so Gris was able to invent new emblems to signify "table", "guitar", or "violin"; but he was determined that these emblems should incorporate the whole of his knowledge about the plastic qualities of the solid bodies which they represented. There was no question of repudiating the researches which had led to analytical Cubism; his idea was simply to condense into one sign the multiplicity of information which had previously been offered. Gris was certain that this sign was the total figuration at which he was aiming; but the example of Mallarmé alone could give him the assurance that others would share his conviction, that the spectator would rediscover the complete object which it was his intention to represent, although transported to a higher plane as *"idée même et suave"*.

VII. ARCHITECTURE

The period that followed was one of the most fruitful and beautiful in the whole of Juan Gris' work. Indeed, many of those who admire his pictures consider the years 1916 to 1919 as the peak of his achievement. Certainly the works of this time have an austere grandeur and a manly vigour. Gris had come to maturity and was in full possession of the resources of an art which he had also mastered intellectually. And yet I do not think that one can be said to have fully understood Gris' art unless one recognises the progress which he continued to make after 1920. I even wonder whether the fact that these admirers are less enthusiastic about his work during the years 1920–26 is not due to an old misunderstanding of Cubism. Just as in 1908 the name "Cubist" was first used in the erroneous belief that the pictures of that time consisted of geometrical forms (that is to say, the essence of Cubism was thought to reside in its transient appearance), so with Gris it seems that only the period before 1920, with its harder lines and more pronounced angles, is considered by some people authentically Cubist. Far be it from me to deny either the severe grandeur, the impressive plastic solidity of Gris' canvases during these four years, or the increasing lucidity of his thought. From the purely technical point of view it was certainly the most rigorous period of his life. Stately and firm, his paintings had become the "flat coloured architecture" of which he talked. Everything was restored to the flat surface; the objects inscribed thereon were emblems which he invented, true "concepts". He abandoned multiple descriptions of objects. Line and colour were more closely associated, for his preoccupation with "local" colour apparently diminished. The emblems themselves rise one above the other architecturally, and they are controlled by the general structure, which causes their "distortion" and "discoloration". It might almost be more accurate to say that it is the architecture—the whole construction—that governs their form and their colour. During these few years Gris came very near to the pole of "unity". The form of the work mattered to him more than the detail of his emotion. The objects which he created are no longer those we meet with on a given day at a given time; they have been raised to the dignity of the type, redeemed from particular fortuities. Look, for example, at *The Miller* and *The Man from* 282, 283 *Touraine* (both of 1918), the various *Pierrots* and *Harlequins* (of 1919), and also the numerous bottles, 287 glasses and fruit-dishes in the "absolute". These figures and objects remind one of the Platonist 149, 155, 290, 291 "idea".[127] The one touching exception is in the two portraits in oil (the only ones done after 1912) 269 of Josette (1916), the woman he loved.

These pictures have all the characteristics of classical art. Gris revealed himself at this time as a classical painter: lucidity, purity, the preponderance of the work of art itself, the predominance of the general, the static quality, all the symptoms are there. He is classical too in the way he subordinates his emotion to the work in which it is expressed. In art as in life he was too modest to undress in public; and modesty is surely one of the characteristics of classical art.

There is further evidence of Gris' purity and modesty even in the words he chose for self-expression. "There is something equivocal about it"—this, as I have said, was his most damning criticism. Again, the use of the word "brilliant" to describe some artist meant condemning him as superficial; a work of art which pleased him particularly by its solidity he referred to as "well furnished". And even the word "ingenuity" had something of a pejorative flavour for him; he applied it to what seemed to him minor forms of invention. But, for invention he had the very greatest respect.

The passions which he had to control in these majestic works were not lightly to be dismissed. It was not always easy to apply the brake of reason to his ardour, but his obsession with purity and order won the day. And in this Gris may be compared to a kindred spirit, Hölderlin, so often wrongly classed with the Romantics, who wrote:[128] "*Es ist nur ein Streit in der Welt, was nämlich mehr sei, das Ganze oder das Einzelne?*" And again:[129] "*Ich glaube durchaus gegen die excentrische Begeisterung geschrieben zu haben und so die griechische Einfalt erreicht.*" Hölderlin, too, stood for the subjection of the part to the whole, for avoiding an "eccentric enthusiasm". Whether he was excited, upset or in love, he has only transmitted to us the sublimated emotion. He refuses to lay himself bare; and yet we can find the whole of him in his poems, we can even recognise Hyperion and Diotima. Of Gris the same is true. His pictures are neither theorems for the erudite nor subtle intellectual exercises. They partake of his flesh and blood: those who knew him can read the whole of his life in them, although he has made every effort to hide the least trace. He thought he could hide behind the world that he created, but this world was himself. How modest is the chaste grandeur of such an art. The Romantic is determined to be master of the world which he creates, and even escapes from it occasionally to affirm his supremacy. The classical artist—a Hölderlin, a Gris—thinks only of the work of art in which he and the world are united. This is the meaning of that sublime cry of submission, that echo of Christ, which Bettina von Arnim records Hölderlin as uttering over one of his own works: "*Nicht wie ich will, sondern wie du willst.*"[130]

Still-life on a Chair · 1917

Mallarmé, another "burning classical artist", said much the same:[131] "*L'œuvre pure implique la disparition élocutoire du poète, qui cède l'initiative aux mots, par le heurt de leur inégalité mobilisée ; ils s'allument de reflets réciproques comme une virtuelle traînée de feux sur des pierreries, remplaçant la respiration perceptible en l'ancien souffle lyrique ou la direction personnelle enthousiaste de la phrase.*" And Gris, I think, was saying the same in a less grandiose way when he remarked to Michel Leiris: "I like painters who paint in the present participle."

The Romantic, the immodest artist—for example, Picasso—is quite the reverse. He is continually tortured by the need to expose himself, to let everyone know about his troubles, even about his love affairs; and this typical romantic attitude leads to a lyrical form of expression. The romantic artist, when he is lyrical, thinks of himself, and of himself only. He creates no strange creatures who are charged with the transmission of his message, and those he does create are just himself. Picasso's "Minotaur", who fights, carouses and makes love, is Picasso himself. It is his intention to give himself, naked and unashamed, so that the communion may be complete. So one must not be deceived by those of Picasso's works which appear classical: even those containing objects derived from Greek antiquity are romantic in *spirit*. I shall be told, I know, that Picasso was one of the originators of the Cubist revolution, and that its spirit seems to be profoundly classical.[132] So it is; but Picasso is always opening up possibilities and then abandoning them. The well-worn path is intolerable to him; he feels he must be entirely free to wander where he will. The second great protagonist of this revolution—Georges Braque—is also a romantic. Of this there is no better proof than his own aphorisms. The best known dates from 1917: "I like the rule that corrects the emotion."[133] With him it is the emotion that counts; it must be corrected, certainly, in order to be integrated with the form, but one must only talk of the rule by which this correction is made with the respect and humility due to an inevitable discipline. And what would Gris, the classic, have said? "I like the emotion that corrects the rule." Deep in his heart the rules were there, but he delighted in the emotion which softened them. Then, too, there is Braque's other utterance in 1938:[134] "Art is made to disturb us, science to reassure us." I cannot help thinking that Gris would have inverted this too, for his art is not meant to be disturbing.

Insofar as Cubism was a reaction against the romantic excesses which ended in Fauvism, there is no doubt that Gris was its purest exponent. Gris was more imbued than any with the spirit of this movement which tended to reinstate the picture as a thing in itself. Admittedly his pictures, "like all works destined to become classics" (to use his own phrase), have no resemblance to the pictures in museums; yet more than any others his pictures form the bridge, across the effusions of romanticism, between Cubism and the periods of order and clarity.[135]

This is for me the real merit of his work during the years 1916–19, a period of "great painting". Gris knew this when he said to me: "I am the good workman"; or again, "My work may be bad 'great painting', but at any rate it is 'great painting'." And if I am asked for my definition of "great painting" I cannot do better than reply in the words of another painter, André Masson: "Great painting is painting in which the intervals are charged with as much energy as the shapes which determine them."[136] This is a very clear and precise definition of what Gris meant by "coloured architecture"; that is to say, painting in which every part of the picture contributes to its unity.

In conclusion I would like to indicate the special character of the "classical architecture" of these four years. The work of Juan Gris was always solemn, but his work during the war was distinguished by a peculiar austerity and sobriety which is as evident in the design as in the colour. But his Castilian ardour has merely draped itself in black, denying all display; only superficial beholders mistake it for coldness. Gertrude Stein has stated very well[137] how easily Gris was seduced by everything French. During these four years he lived on his national heritage, and disclosed to us unwittingly his "artistic atavism", which to him was identical with what is called "quality".[138] This period proves him to have been a Spaniard. After 1920 he began to study French painting more and more intently. The rare copies (which are interpretations) he made of pictures by other masters were not of Zurbaran (with whose work Gris' pictures of 1916–19 have been compared) but of French painters—Corot and Cézanne. Now he attempted to combine his own painting with what he had learnt from studying the plastic art of the country in which he had settled and which he loved more than any other. During the last few years of his life, his studio was decorated entirely with reproductions of the works of French painters: Fouquet, the brothers Le Nain, Boucher, Ingres.

277–280

VIII. POETRY

Gris, it will be remembered, wrote to me on August 26, 1920: "I don't know how it will be with my painting, and am keen to begin. I think it will be impossible to take up my work again exactly where I left off more than three months ago." When he once more took up his brush, which illness had obliged him to drop at the beginning of May, he felt that he had first of all to reconsider the problem of *technique*. The last picture he had painted before his illness, *Vase with Lilies of the Valley*, closed a period whose technique he felt he had exhausted. As early as December 14, 1915, he had written to me: "I never seem to be able to find any room in my pictures for that sensitive, sensuous side that I feel ought to be there." As he lay in bed, he thought a great deal about his art and felt that he had discovered a solution. As always with Gris, the new manner which he adopted was the result of mature consideration and not of a sudden decision or a weakening due to his illness.

293

The change (I had almost said advance) which one notices is above all a change in *technique*, for in appearance the difference is not great. Gris still refused to indulge in little tricks of the brush, but he now replaced the areas of flat colour with something more skilful. He did not go so far as to copy the glazes of that master technician whom he most admired, Chardin; but he now began to prepare his canvas with an under-painting over which he painted at once. This meant that he could make his tones warmer or colder as he wished, that he could give them an intensity and a richness which were unobtainable in any other way. Indeed, the technical experiments on which he embarked were the cause of a few mishaps in about 1924, when some of the paints began to crack. During this period Gris was unquestionably attempting to make his painting more complete by the assimilation of that "sensitive, sensuous side" that he felt to be lacking.

It will have been evident from Gris' letters that he was in the habit of working on several pictures at the same time, taking them up one after another according as the paint dried. His new technique made this method of work more necessary than ever. Braque, too, works in this way; with Picasso it is the exception, for many of his canvases are completed in a single day.

It is not a sign of self-confidence to limit oneself to one particular manner. A powerful artist is the richer for acquiring what he feels to be lacking in himself; and I am convinced that Gris was not misguided when, from a desire to increase and lighten his palette, to intensify his tones by a more subtle technique, he plunged into the great line of French painting.[139] However, there was another factor (besides his desire for self-completion) which caused the change in his work about 1920. As the classical spirit matured in Gris' work the balance swung over in favour of the "whole", which naturally meant that the "detail" suffered. Now "distortion" is alien to the true classical spirit, and so we must be clear about what Gris really wanted. "Abstract painting" was as much anathema to him as the monstrosities[140] which flaunted their brutality with such candour under the banner of Expressionism. Nor could he, with such faith in his art, swallow the nihilism of Dada. He disapproved, even among the Cubists, of any sort of "witty" draughtsmanship, which he felt approached the monstrous; he also disliked "constructivist" distortion, though it worried him less than that of the Expressionists.

Picasso said to me one day—and he meant it as a criticism—that, in his opinion, Gris, if he had lived, would have tended to make his pictures more and more legible. I am sure that Picasso was right, but at the same time I cannot agree with him in disparaging this tendency in Gris. Gris had a most strict, logical and scrupulous mentality and his work as a whole is entirely homogeneous; but he had no system. This is apparent, for example, in his unconcerned attitude towards chiaroscuro; he felt no obligation to prefer one method rather than another. He never looked on Cubism as a system but as a way of feeling and thinking which left him free to choose his own technique.[141] He had scruples of another sort; he wanted the appearance of his pictures to be as unobtrusive as possible; he wanted manifest simplicity.[142] Very often he would say to me: "There's nothing monstrous about that violin, is there? It must not be an oddity."

In short, what he most feared was that the beholder reading the emblems he had invented might be confused because of a lack of conformity between the new image and earlier image-memories. Constructivist distortion, and Gris considered no other, causes merely a passing sense of visual uneasiness; the "oddity" is quickly absorbed by the beholder's mind. But Gris felt that even this short disturbance conflicted with his need for purity. I have already remarked that Gris hated hermetism—even if it was involuntary—as a form of equivocation. This was one reason why he attempted to loosen slightly the grip of the whole composition on the individual object. Another was the fact that he was becoming more and more interested in objects. A new element—*the poetic element*—entered his painting and dominated it from 1920 until 1923. Gris was aware of it: "This painting is to the other what poetry

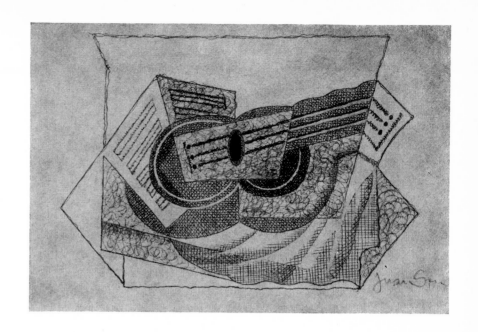

Guitar on a Table · 1923

is to prose."[143] In *Der Weg zum Kubismus* I had already defined Cubism as *lyrical* painting, and it was an intense pleasure for me to hear Gris confirm the poetic character of his painting. It is more difficult than ever, now that we have experienced Surrealism, to explain what is meant by poetic painting, by plastic lyricism, a lyricism of forms and not of ideas. For the Surrealists (and, I should add, for the uninstructed) poetic painting means "literary" painting, an adjective used without a derogatory meaning. In other words, the poetry of a picture by Masson is created by an association of ideas and feelings, of literary and other memories, which are produced in the spectator as he digests the picture; the poetry is quite separate from the purely plastic element. This conception is fundamentally opposed to that of Gris. Masson writes:[144] "It is all-important not to forget that the saying of Delacroix '*une œuvre figurative doit être avant tout une fête pour les yeux*' is still absolutely true." But Gris in his austerity would, I fear, have interpreted this as the thin edge of the wedge of hedonism; and the idea of expressing "those things which are at the root of all human beings, hunger, love and violence"[145] would have seemed a heresy as great as any expressionistic frenzy.

Gris had been opposed to such ideas since 1919, although they had first raised their head in the early days of Cubism. I remember a conversation in about 1912 between Braque and a young German expressionist painter who criticised him for the absence in his pictures of that extra-plastic element which, according to Masson, is lacking in all Cubist painting.[146] "But that's all understood," Braque replied. Gris, I think, would have given the same answer, for at that time the Cubist painters were all agreed that the plastic element in painting was sufficient in itself and that the message transmitted thus was complete. Indeed, the Cubists felt that the "expressionism" which the young German painter looked for in their works was foreign to painting; they condemned it as "literary", a word which had for them only a pejorative meaning.

This young German was aware of a discrepancy which the supporters of Expressionism in his own country had not realised, for they treated Cubism as another aspect of the Expressionist movement.

Indeed the Expressionist painters thought of themselves as fellow-travellers with the Cubists. This is immediately apparent in official publications like *Der Blaue Reiter*[147] (Munich, 1912). To-day it is obvious that they were mistaken in their conception of the aims of Cubism, but their misunderstanding necessitates an exact definition of Expressionism so that we can be clear about its limitations. I have frequently referred already to "expressionist distortion", a violation of form in favour of expressiveness. Derain's remark which I have already quoted (Note 92) is a typical example of the psychological process which leads to this form of distortion. "The telegraph wires must be made enormous," he wrote to his friend Vlaminck in 1901, "so much goes on along them." It was not the subtlety of their span standing out against the sky that Derain wanted to depict. He wanted the spectator to feel them as an agent of fate carrying thousands of tidings, good and bad. Here the painter is no longer interested in *form*, but only in a *force*.[148] However, with Derain this interest was not exclusive; that other considerations also played their part one can discover by reading the rest of his letter. This cannot be said for the German Expressionists who were, for the most part, entirely concerned with forces to the utter neglect of form. They lived in a world where nothing existed but forces; forms simply served to "express" them visibly. In the past, "expressionist distortion" had nearly always served to signify very simple "forces". For this reason, it had, as we have seen, seldom passed the stage of a graphic trick. The German Expressionists aimed at something totally different: the expression of a whole host of "forces", both physical and psychic. It is, therefore, easy to see why the Cubist painters reproached them with the "literary" (that is to say, non-plastic) spirit of their work: inevitably the plastic element was reduced to a minimum.

There are certain similarities between Fauvism and Expressionism. The influence of Matisse was considerable in Germany; this came about partly through his studio in the Couvent des Oiseaux,[149] where he had several Germans among his pupils. One notices particularly in Expressionist painting the same sort of decorative arrangement posing as composition which one finds in the pictures of the Fauves, and also the same riotous colour. How then can the confusion have arisen that linked Cubism with Expressionism? First of all one has to remember that there existed among the German painters a sort of feeling of *avant-garde* camaraderie. And then, in their ignorance of the true aims of Cubism, these painters "mis-read" Cubist pictures. Because they confused "constructivist distortion" with "expressionist distortion", they thought—albeit in good faith—that the Cubists had the same aims as themselves and that their "distortions" were evidence of a concern for the "forces" which they too intended to make visible.[150] That this was not so, we have seen.

The question may be asked whether the "forces" can be identified with the "existential" element of which Masson speaks. I do not think so; the Expressionists can only claim to have anticipated one element of Surrealism—the literary element. I even doubt whether many of their works will survive the test of time. The plastic poverty of so many of them will be the main reason for their playing no part in the history of art, and the same can be said of the majority of surrealist pictures.

Only one member of the *Blaue Reiter*—Paul Klee—succeeded in evolving an idiom attuned to his tender, sarcastic vision. The importance of his achievement is very considerable; he took an opposite course to Cubism, with its architectural discipline, and gave free rein to the unforeseen contingencies of his fancy. He was the first to achieve that "liberation of the subconscious" of which the Surrealists talked so much. But the astonishing thing is that his scrawls have an autonomous *plastic existence*. Miró's debt to Klee, for example, is obvious. One can say more: anything worth-while in the evolution of the plastic arts since 1920 has had its origin either in the work of the Cubists or in that of Paul Klee. Dada contributed nothing: it was entirely nihilistic and destroyed even its own creators. Many is the time that I have heard Gris deplore Marcel Duchamp's waste of his considerable gifts. Chirico's legacy to Surrealism was a taste for "the disquieting"; but that is a taste which is quickly exhausted. For the rest, he set an example in academic technique. All that counts in Surrealist painting derives, I am convinced, either (like Miró) from Paul Klee, or (like André Masson) from Cubism. The European tradition is being carried forward by these two painters, while most of the others are caught in the academic rut. Even madness often takes a lamentably conventional form.

The majority of the Surrealist painters are just naïvely perpetuating the errors of Expressionism; that is to say, they are not concerned with the real, the plastic existence of a picture. Thus, their works never come to life. For the most part these artists are closer to a debased form of academicism than to Cubism. But this is not the case with André Masson, who is most conscious of what he has called "the necessity of knowing the pictorial means most suitable for the art of this time".[151] And in his opinion the "means" have been furnished by Cubism. What then is the nature of the profound difference between the generation of 1880 and that of 1900, which uses the means of its predecessor to such different effect? Masson cares little for what is considered of prime importance by the official Surrealists: "Automatism, the investigation of the powers of the unconscious, dreams and the association of images only provide the materials."[152] Masson's attitude is romantic, unquestionably; but we have discovered romantics within the ranks of the Cubists. And it would be dangerous to insist on the irrationalism of the younger generation in contrast to the so-called rationalism of their elders, which would be so difficult to demonstrate. It seems, therefore, that the only real difference—the explanation of the fact that Gris and Masson mean two such different things by the phrase "poetic painting"—lies in the introduction of what I have called "the existential element".

The difference is not just that between two men but between two generations. However, I would insist that we are not in the presence of a new *Weltanschauung*; the world-picture has not changed, its forms are the same. The transformation that has occurred is in the attitude of man to this world. Cubism, like the poetry and philosophy of that time, felt that it should ignore the powers of darkness which govern the universe, that it should confine itself to recording the unchanging image of the world which it was re-creating for us. But the new generation is more wild and feels incapable of resisting whatever may batter at the gates of thought. Violence and death have been admitted into the sacred precincts. Freud is merely an accidental aspect of the whole. It is my belief that in the work of Masson —and also of Suzanne Roger—there is revealed above all the mentality of a generation which has more admiration for Kierkegaard than for Nietzsche, and whose philosophers are Heidegger, Jaspers and Sartre. Is it the apocalyptic period through which we are passing that makes people more receptive to a doctrine based on *Weltangst,* on the primordial anguish of man trembling under the blows of an implacable fate? It is the feeling of tragedy which dominates the life of this generation and fills its art. Its art is that of poetic tragedy. And so the definition for which we were looking has come of its own accord. Cubism is essentially a lyrical art; the work of Masson and of his contemporaries is essentially tragic. Nor is this invalidated by the case of Picasso. He is never tragic; he has none of the harshness and cruelty of the tragic artist, he is animated by tenderness and pity. These are his sentiments towards the beggars, the blind, the cripples and the street-girls of the "Blue Period", just as they are towards the victims of Guernica. On the rare occasions when his sentiments are not simply lyrical they are never those of a tragic artist. I remember how, in 1933, he often talked to me of a painting which would express "the grand sentiments". He was contemplating David's *The Oath of the Horatii.* That, however, was not a move in the direction of tragic but of epic art. There is no sign there of man meekly submitting to a fate which he is powerless to change; it is an affirmation of human grandeur, of man's opposition to fate.

I cannot, perhaps, do better here than quote Hölderlin's excellent definition of the three forms of poetry:[153]

"*Das lyrische, dem Scheine nach idealische Gedicht ist in seiner Bedeutung naiv. Es ist eine fortgehende Metapher eines Gefühls.*

"*Das epische, dem Scheine nach naive Gedicht ist in seiner Bedeutung heroisch. Es ist die Metapher großer Bestrebungen.*

"*Das tragische, dem Scheine nach heroische Gedicht ist in seiner Bedeutung idealisch. Es ist die Metapher einer intellektuellen Anschauung.*"

We are not likely, I think, to find any definition as accurate or as profound of the difference between the lyricism of a Gris and the tragedy of a Masson. Yes, the meaning of a picture by Gris is ingenuous. It is the never-ending image of a single emotion. The same goes for Braque; also for Picasso, for I do not think that (except for *Guernica*) he actually painted the epic pictures—"Images of great aspirations"—which he at one time contemplated. Gris' art stands imperturbable outside that stream of becoming which has swallowed up the work of Masson.

It is not, I think, as paradoxical as it at first seems to talk of the ingenuousness of Gris' art, or for that matter of all Cubist art. When Cubism was born, the poet Apollinaire perceived this aspect of its character most clearly. Now Apollinaire is often wrong when he states facts or constructs theories, of which he has only understood the first principles; but he is admirable when he allows his poetic genius full freedom. So, with the fraternal sympathy of a contemporary creative spirit, he reacted to the artlessness of the Cubist painters and to their will to cut themselves off from life, which was in itself an expression of artlessness. In the Preface to the Catalogue of Braque's Exhibition at my Gallery in the Rue Vignon in November 1908 (that is to say, on the occasion of Cubism's first public appearance), he wrote this short and perfect definition of the state of mind of a Cubist painter: "*Un lyrisme coloré et dont les exemples sont trop rares l'emplit d'un enthousiasme harmonieux, et ses instruments de musique, Sainte Cécile même les fait sonner. Dans ses vallons bourdonnent et butinent les abeilles de toutes les jeunesses et le bonheur*

Fruit-bowl, Pipe and Newspaper · 1917

de l'innocence languit sur ses terrasses civilisées. Ce peintre est angélique. Plus pur que les autres hommes, il ne se préoccupe point de ce qui, étant étranger à son art, le ferait soudain déchoir du paradis qu'il habite."[154]

The lyrical form of expression is the purest and the least ornamental. The Cubist painters attained to a lyrical form of painting by straining to recover what is essential in painting and to discard the accessories. The Impressionists had already banished what they called "narrative"; the Cubists in their turn also banished any form of "plastic narrative", the transient, the accidental.

Henri de Régnier describes a lunch at Valvins[155] with Elémir Bourges and Mallarmé at which the poet said: "Poetry has followed entirely the wrong line since Homer's great original error."

"And what was there before Homer?" answered Bourges.

"Orpheus," came the reply.

Whether consciously or unconsciously, the Cubist painters dreamed of a return to the same kind of source. The naked lyricism to which they attained in their painting, free from all tragic or epic elements, was the preliminary stage which entitled them to envisage an art with the same magical powers of creation as Mallarmé conjured up by his invocation of Orpheus.

What is the quality which distinguishes the lyricism of Gris from that of the other two poetic painters? Why does he say with such insistence that his painting is to the other as poetry is to prose? Poetry to him meant purely plastic poetry, and I hope I have made clear what he meant by that. I think it is possible to demonstrate in the "handwriting" the difference between this plastic poetry and that other form of poetry whose meaning is deliberately dependent on elements of a different nature. The signs which Gris uses are "emblems". They *are* a knife or a glass. They are never symbols, for they never have a dual identity, as is so often the case with Masson. They *are* the objects which they represent, with all the emotive value attaching to them; but they never signify anything outside of these objects. It would be a mistake to imagine that the "rhymes", which I shall discuss shortly, in any way imply a dual identity as symbols do. These "rhymes", like every other rhyme, are a form of repetition: the repetition of two forms, each of which retains its own unique identity.

Gris' poetry is in the forms of the picture and the relationships between them. The rhythm of his "poem" is dependent on the cadence of these relationships.[156] Bettina von Arnim has recorded for us what Friedrich Hölderlin, before his madness, said to his friend Sinclair: "*Nur der Geist sei Poesie, der das Geheimnis eines in ihm eingeborenen Rhythmus in sich trage, und nur mit diesem Rhythmus könne es lebendig und sichtbar werden, denn dieser sei seine Seele, aber die Gedichte seien lauter Schemen, keine Geister mit Seelen.*

"*Es gebe höhere Gesetze für die Poesie, jede Gefühlsregung entwickle sich nach neuen Gesetzen, die sich nicht anwenden lassen auf andere, denn alles Wahre sei prophetisch und überströme seine Zeit mit Licht, und der Poesie allein sei anheimgegeben, dies Licht zu verbreiten, drum müsse der Geist und könne nur durch sie hervorgehen. Geist gehe nur durch Begeisterung hervor. Nur allein dem füge sich der Rhythmus, in dem der Geist lebendig werde.*"[157]

This apologia of rhythm might, I think, almost have been written by Gris. For it is a defence of that rhythm which is not mechanical but which proceeds from within the very depths of its creator, which is re-born as something different with each new emotion, which creates its own laws each time afresh and is the actual manifestation of the spirit. It is this rhythm which infuses the poetic emotion of their creator into Gris' pictures; but we can take the analogy with written or spoken poetry further. In the years which followed, Gris was to make use of a device for emphasising the cadence of this rhythm, namely the "rhymes" to which I have already referred. These were intended by Gris as plastic metaphors to reveal to the beholder certain hidden relationships, similarities between two apparently different objects. Rather like rhymes in a poem, two forms, generally of different sizes, are repeated.[158]

289   In 1920 these metaphors are fairly evident and are based on the simplest objects (playing cards, glasses etc.). Then a bunch of grapes is compared to a mandolin (1921). Finally, objects of increasingly disparate character are reconciled through more inventive "rhymes". In the *Portrait of a Woman* of 1922, for

300   example, the woman's head is repeated in reverse in her hand. In *The Nun* of 1922, the whole figure

301   is repeated in reverse in the clasped hands and the folds of the sleeves. In *Three Masks* of 1923, the rhymes have become still more numerous and the head of each figure is repeated in the folds of their garments, their arms, etc.

This is no mere sport. It is a genuine case of poetry finding expression through the means so often used to emphasise the metre and capture the reader. In the *Introduction à la Poésie Française*, by Thierry-Maulnier, is the following: "*Le poème n'existe que là où existe cette prise de possession implacable de l'âme dont le rythme est l'instrument : il n'existe que là où l'âme, maintenue par les chocs répétés et réguliers d'un mécanisme exact dans une sorte de torpeur vigilante analogue à la nuit réceptive des voyants, s'anéantit à tout ce qui n'est pas en chaque instant la pure attente de ce qu'elle ne saurait prévoir.*"[159]

Gris' claim that his painting has the quality of poetry is fully justified by the introduction into his works of an "exact mechanism", and because he attained to that "implacable taking possession of the soul". Thierry-Maulnier, admittedly, seems to be talking only of a rhythm in time, but there is no doubt that rhythm exists also in space—rhythm of forms—because that is the emotive basis of architecture. Rhythm, whether in time or in space, is a taking possession of the soul, but I think that the distrust engendered by the equivocal "vigilant torpor" makes us unwilling to accept the idea of suspense. For acceptance of this rules out the psychological effect of spatial rhythm—I cannot accept that there is an evolution of rhythm in time as the result of the eye travelling across the picture. The eye, in fact, sees a picture in one glance.[160] The formal rhythm, the inescapable cadence of Gris' pictures, which we are made to feel by the "rhymes" as in ordinary poetry, creates the detachment, the disinterestedness which, according to Schopenhauer and many other philosophers, is the condition of aesthetic contemplation. Most probably we have to reckon here with a particularly forceful assertion of the continuity of the work of art, in opposition to the discontinuity which reigns in the tangible world. By this means the artist frees the spectator—or the reader—from discontinuity.

Gris' lyricism burst forth with particular freedom in a kind of picture which he painted with increasing frequency in these later years: I mean the series of *Open Windows*, in which a table loaded with objects is placed before a window which is open on to the world. The still-life is thereby united with the landscape. There are those painted at Bandol (winter 1920–21) with a sombre Provençal landscape, and

294, 295   those at Céret (winter 1921–22) in which the light is cristalline with the snow of the Pyrenees. It seems surprising, perhaps, to talk of "light" after I have described how the imitation of light had ceased; but in these pictures it was not really a question of imitating light. For the beholder, every picture which succeeds at all in creating a reality is filled with a space and light appropriate to that reality. Man cannot imagine bodies without space, nor space without light to illuminate the bodies. So even a painter like Gris, who traced his emblems on a flat surface which he intended at all costs to preserve, must end by creating a complete world in the beholder's imagination.[161] In this way his emotion is re-born; it remains complete, retains all its constituent elements. Once again it is the emotion transmitted which shows that it is a message which unites the creator with the beholder, and not more or less doubtful theorems. For it is Gris' own *Erlebnisse* at Bandol and Céret, which are thus re-created for us in works which are not imitative.

In the *Open Windows* the two elements of the picture—still-life and landscape—interpenetrate on the flat surface. This was a great advance on the conception of "monumental space". More and more Gris' work became "flat coloured architecture", and objects were freely grouped on the flat surface without regard to the distance which separates them in nature from the spectator. Their respective positions are determined by their lyrical importance and not by the fact that "in reality" one would see them better or worse or only in part. In *The Bay of Bandol*, "Le Journal" is written across the mountains, and the form of the table is carried on in outline across the waters of the bay. The hills and the sky have penetrated into the room and are depicted on the walls. The sailing-boat is resting on the table. The picture surface has become a sort of unperforated "lyrical plane" on which are assembled the objects of the painter's inspiration.

From about this time Gris also made occasional use of a curious trick for creating volume; one sees it particularly in the *Harlequins* and *Pierrots* of 1922. I refer to a sort of undulation imposed on flat 298, 299, 301
surfaces which is rendered by line and a certain degree of shading. In a later chapter, dealing with Gris' sculpture, I shall show that this is a *sculptural* idea—what I call "the activation of the flat surface"— and it is the only occasion on which Gris (though it often happens with Picasso) is caught imitating his own sculpture. I shall also discuss the purpose for this "corrugation" of the flat surface in his sculptures.

Space was no longer simulated by imitative means. The position of objects is indicated principally by intersection but, as we have just seen, the degree of their lyrical importance prevails even over this imaginary "spatial classification".

What happened then after Gris recovered from his illness and began to work again? We have seen that a great change occurred in his painting in the year 1920, and I have attempted to explain the spiritual causes which were at work. It is reflected also in his own writings.

In his reply to the questionnaire of *Valori Plastici*[162] at the beginning of 1919, Gris' only claim for Cubism was that it was painting based on intellectual elements, that is to say non-imitative painting.

By April 1920 already (in his reply to *Action's*[163] questionnaire) he defined the method of Negro Art (and it was the method he was to adopt himself) as "individualising generalities, each time in a different way".

Finally, in 1921 (in *L'Esprit Nouveau*),[164] he formulated his new theory clearly. "I want to arrive at a new specification," he wrote; "starting from a general type I want to make something particular and individual."

He wanted, as he said, "to humanise" the architectural side of painting, which he had finally mastered in the years just past. He no longer attempted to arrive at a generalisation: he now started from generalisation with the idea of creating a special type. One might almost say that he considered his previous work too "abstract"; he wanted to make it more "concrete". But he was not prepared to become an empirical observer, because be always clung to an invented reality, defined and "qualified" in a more precise way. And he was careful to specify that he wanted to "construct particular individuals"; he did not want to imitate any existing individual.

Thus, for Gris himself, it meant first and foremost a change of method. To use his own phrase again: his method had ceased to be "inductive" and had become "deductive". Nor is it too much to attribute this change to the poetic emotion that he was attempting to express. But, at the same time, it was also the natural outcome of his Platonist mentality.

His art remained classical but, to quote his definition of Negro art, it was "the reverse of Greek art, which started from the individual and *attempted to suggest* an ideal type".[165] For the Greek way of attaining to the classical ideal Gris substituted his own; but he followed Greek art in not imitating what is individual simply because it is accidental. One form of classical art can differ from another not only in appearance but even in working method. The fundamental character of Gris' art was not in any way affected by his lyrical urge.

IX. POLYPHONY

It seems, however, that the new vein of lyricism also had its dangers. Pictorial unity, the law which Gris considered fundamental, was threatened. Admittedly no picture has survived in which this unity was violated; but in the winter of 1923-24, during his wearisome sojourn at Beausoleil with its unpleasant wranglings with the world of the Ballets Russes, it did occur in certain pictures. Then Gris recovered himself and destroyed them.

He wrote to me on November 5, 1923: "I have worked little. I have only finished three small canvases and am working on the same number. Gertrude [Stein], who arrived on Saturday, found them very attractive. This has encouraged me as I had my doubts. As soon as I have finished what I have on hand I will send them to you. There is also my portrait, which is nearly done: this time I find it a fair likeness."[166]

Then, on November 26: "I am sending seven small canvases to you to-morrow or the day after. I am waiting till they are quite dry. Also four drawings. Please tell me what you think of them as I am rather worried. I look at them every day and find them good and bad in turn."

Finally, on December 9: "I am grieved at your opinion of my paintings. Alas, it only confirms my fears, for I was afraid of having taken a wrong turning. Thank you for telling me the truth, for it will save me from starting on a false trail. And above all don't hesitate to destroy them if they reflect badly on my work.[167] I feel very discouraged and exhausted... I am all too aware that I am going through a bad phase. Nothing gives me any confidence, and I haven't any of the necessary assurance to work."

December 12: "I am a bit happier as my work seems to be going better."

December 15: "I am working quite hard and am fairly content. I thought I was finished."

December 20: "I am going to send you four drawings and four canvases on which I am now working. If you like one of them, please accept it as a Christmas present."

Through his letters one can follow the development of this crisis, one of the most serious in Gris' life, almost from day to day. He felt that he was on the wrong track, but was not quite certain. As soon as he was certain, he did not hesitate to destroy the pictures which dissatisfied him, even though they represented the work of several months and therefore an important element in his budget. Then he went back to work, painfully at first, gaining courage later and finally becoming convinced once more hat he had something to say.

It was at this time that he laid the foundations of the method that culminated in the masterpieces of his last years, which sum up the whole of his earlier work.

The end of his short life was drawing near. It seems—is it imagination or is it true?—that a great artist who is to die young—Raphael or Mozart, Novalis or Seurat—makes one supreme effort to pour his whole genius into his last works. So it was with Gris from 1924 to 1927. Whereas from 1916 to 1919 the balance had swung in favour of Architecture (the mould), and from 1920 to 1923 in favour of Poetry (the content), the arms of the balance now stood level. He achieved equilibrium. Architecture and Poetry were blended in what I have already called Polyphony, and his work attained a magnificent amplitude. Gris' main preoccupation had always been structural research. He rediscovered many of the compositional devices used by painters prior to the period of plastic disorder.[168] He himself often pointed out to me some of these devices, notably in pictures by Corot, whose knowledge he greatly admired and whose *Woman with a Mandolin* he copied. He also copied, in pencil and in oil, works by 277, 278–280 Cézanne. These researches led him to a new method of work.

For many years he had been guided by certain fundamental ideas on painting. Now they suddenly took form in a coherent and rigorous method. He had been pondering over these ideas ever since analytical Cubism had given way in his painting to synthetic Cubism; in fact they had been the cause of this change. The first time Gris clearly formulated them for me was in a conversation on March 13, 1920—unfortunately the only conversation of which I have kept notes. We had just met again after an interval of more than five years, and we discussed his method of painting.

"I begin," he said, "by organising my picture; then I qualify the objects. My aim is to create new objects which cannot be compared with any object in reality. The distinction between synthetic and analytical Cubism lies precisely in this. These new objects, therefore, avoid distortion. My *Violin*, being a creation, need fear no comparison."

Still-life with Plaque · 1917

So it is evident that for some time he had been clearly conscious of the fundamentals of what now became a fruitful method of creation.

It is difficult to say anything useful about his method after Gris' own masterly exposition of it in his lecture. But I shall try to explain it with the help of what I learnt from him in conversation. His starting-point—which will seem strange to anyone who regards him simply as a logician[169]—lay in the depths of the subconscious. A proportion (for example, a Golden Section) would be the springboard from which his imagination leapt towards what seemed to him an *abstract* "coloured architecture".[170] He began with drawings, which he later destroyed. Before his death, he asked Josette and myself to burn those which he had not had time to destroy; this we did. Next came the canvas, in which the rhythm begun in the drawings was extended to coloured forms. For the part played in this creation by his technical conception of colour, the "warm and cold hues", one must read his lecture. I myself could only clumsily repeat what Gris explains with such clarity.

He then proceeded to "qualify" (as he called it) the coloured forms for the spectator by giving them an objective significance. Thus, one can see that the basis was a sort of "automatic drawing", an irrational motivation. This automatic drawing was, however, provoked by a conscious choice: the geometrical "spring-board" to which I have referred. This culminated in the picture's architecture. After this the creative imagination consciously intervened in order to objectivise this construction for the spectator. We can call this the logical stage of the creative process. It is interesting to find Gris—who seems to be quite the opposite of a Surrealist—using a creative process based on automatism, which played such a large part in surrealist technique.

May I try to clarify this? Gris' method in the hands of a cold artificer would only produce soulless constructions. I am not proclaiming it as the philosopher's stone of painting, capable of transforming base metal into gold. What impresses me is that it suited Gris' aesthetic as well as his temperament. I am struck by the meeting, in a mysterious no-man's land, of these coloured forms with the image-memories floating in his memory. I have so often seen figures and objects of which Gris had spoken to me with emotion objectivised in a coloured architecture.

The advantages of the method that Gris thus invented for his work are plain. It did away with the most troublesome obstacle that he had met: the conflict between the part and the whole. Instead of starting with the detail and laboriously building up an ensemble, he started with the ensemble, whose rhythm he allowed to develop freely. From this rhythm sprang, in their turn, the objects. A few simple "stimulants" sufficed to make the spectator "see" the desired object. Parallel lines drawn on a white surface changed it into a page of music; lines of type turned it into a newspaper; a flatly drawn ring made it into a plate. The object thus furnished by the spectator's imagination had no "constructivist distortion" to fear; nevertheless Gris' emotion had given it unshakeable reality.

This must also be explained in terms of handwriting. What really constitutes the peculiarity of formative writing is the autonomous value of the thing itself. Gris now made the creation of this thing—the picture-object—his primary concern. The emblems were then defined within this pre-established unity without its structure being changed. Gris felt in this way that he had solved the

Study of a Violin · 1913

problem of figuration within the heart of the architecture, which could thus develop without hindrance. The polyphony was built up firmly like a fugue, and was no longer obliged to unite with the forms of the emblems of which it was constructed. Thus, through their rigour, these constructions could attain complete symmetry. One should not, however, expect the symmetry always to be immediately apparent. It often lurks slantwise in the picture, inclined at an angle. The polyphony supports the general architecture and enriches it by multiplying the rhythm; but it remains invisible to the beholder who has not time to look for it.

307

In employing the term "polyphony" to define the construction of Gris' works at this period, I am not merely inventing an ingenious label. It is worth examining some of these "architectures" closely. In these "double compositions", which can be found in Gris' work from the start (cf. p. 120), it is no affectation to talk of "independent voices". Thus, one can describe Gris' method as "contrapuntal". "The fact is that since the fifteenth century counterpoint has been understood to be *the simultaneous development of independent lines of melody*," writes René Leibowitz, in a book to which I shall refer again later (Note 197). No definition fits Gris' compositions better.

155

32

I have spoken of the Cubists' desire to preserve the independence of the creative effort during the *material* birth of a picture. Gris' contrapuntal work remained completely free and unhampered since the canvas (the architecture) was built up organically from a core (the "spring-board") which was the foundation of the whole construction, and was only revealed (as writing) as the image of the painter's emotion when it was complete. Spontaneity and rapture could take a free course during the whole creative process; no "rule", no thought of imitation restrained them.

Gris was never the victim of a hollow and pedantic method which bound both his mind and his hand. He never experienced a "revelation" like that which came to Sérusier[171] in Hohenzollern, in the upper valley of the Danube, in 1897, a revelation of "a completely new aesthetic, a new hieratism and theories of art based on mathematics, numbers and geometry, theories taught by the large and flourishing Benedictine college at Beuron". Father Desiderius (the Munich sculptor Peter Lenz) and Father Willibrord (the Dutch painter Jan Verkade, a friend of Gauguin) were undoubtedly holy men; but, like Sérusier himself, they were miserable painters. The reader will perhaps be surprised that I have thought it necessary to draw a distinction between their theories—which never produced any works of value—and those of Gris. But the Beuron theories have influenced a number of painters, often mysteriously and without their knowledge, for they were probably as ignorant of Father Desiderius' work as of his writings. In particular I would instance several of the minor Cubists, Jeanneret and Ozenfant during their "purist" period, and practically every exponent of "Abstract Art". These artists all believed in a calculable "beauty"; they believed that "beauty" could be produced by mathematical means. I am not concerned here with proving the weakness of such a theory, which ends in a belief that after adequate instruction "beauty" can be industrially produced. All I want to point out is that the art of Juan Gris, logical, reflective, but vibrant, is infinitely removed from this formal conception of beauty. Gris never thought of his mathematical basis as an aesthetic guarantee for his picture. It is important to insist on the arbitrariness of his choice of starting-point. Gris needed a spring-board, not a strait-jacket. Having found it—apparently by chance—he did not indulge in calculations and never fetched out his dividers. Far from curbing his instinct, his one thought was to free it even from the fetters of "handwriting", so as to allow the completely independent development of that rhythm set up on the whole canvas by the confrontation of the parts created by the painter's first act. If there is an element of mathematics it did not extend beyond this first act: for him it was merely a primary stimulus. The monks of Beuron and their direct and indirect disciples wanted, in their pride, to catch beauty in a geometrical net. Gris, convinced like them of the transcendency of "beauty", but not of the possibility of creating it at will, humbly hoped that it might lend its aura to his work. He strove to be "true"; that is to say, to preserve the integrity both of his emotion and of the canvas on which it was made perceptible to others. He was determined to violate neither. His method of work during the last years of his life was an expression of this fundamental concern for honesty. But it also had another result.

Gris achieved what Derain had attempted with inadequate means: he disguised the framework. Derain had tried to camouflage it under the traditional appearance of occidental painting, but this had ended by stifling the composition. With Gris it was disguised (like the letter in Poe's short story) by its very obviousness. The "real" picture (the picture-object) was the flat, coloured architecture at which Gris aimed; but the picture which was "read" (the picture as a message, as an active force) appeared, in the spectator's imagination, to be composed of objects which were signified by the emblems born within the unity of this architecture.

Guitar and Fruit-bowl · 1919

The works thus created suggest a comparison with another art: the majestic musical compositions of Johann Sebastian Bach. I know how inexact historical parallels are, but they sometimes serve to place things better than epithets. Bach is perhaps not superior to certain other musicians in the invention of melodic "line", nor in the "colour" of his harmonies. What makes him incomparable is the polyphonic architecture of his works, which is based on rhythm and mysteriously embraces the whole musical emotion. The role of the "architect" is less showy than that of the draughtsman or the painter. That is why Bach's fame suffered a long eclipse until he was rediscovered by Mendelssohn. That is why so many fervent admirers of Picasso and Braque have remained indifferent to the works of Juan Gris, and have only perceived by degrees the austere magnificence of his art, which turns its back on attractiveness as foreign to its monumental, consciously poetic aim.

Towards the end of his life Gris attained to the noblest simplicity of which painting is capable: not a bloodless classicism, but a true classical spirit, imbued with controlled emotion. In this there was no system, but perfect freedom in the choice of means. With the desire for purity which rejects all system, even the rhymes appeared less and less frequently and finally disappeared. His technical mastery is amazing, but it is merely the visible expression of that spiritual mastery which leaves nothing to chance. No longer was there either geometrical or monumental space. Everything was arranged with such ease that the forms of the objects appear to be inscribed without effort on the flat surface as pure graphic emblems. Nor is there any sort of projection, accompanied by stylisation, as in Egyptian painting or the work of Seurat: he has invented signs which, by themselves and by their inter-relationship, create a plastic reality. It seems to me that a comparison can be made between this representation of three-dimensional form (volume) without imitation and the way in which the same problem is solved by line drawing.[172] Indeed, since Masaccio and Uccello, line drawing also has often moved in geometric space for the creation of complicated compositions; that is to say, whenever space has to be represented. It could not divorce itself from the mentality—the *Weltanschauung*—of the various epochs. But nevertheless it always carried within it a germ of revolution, which has been manifested by the way in which bodies have been represented directly—without chiaroscuro, without "imitation"—when nothing else was involved. All that was necessary was a favourable atmosphere in which this germ could flourish, and I believe it found life in the solution discovered by Gris, which I have already explained. This was made possible by the divorce of line from colour; now it was freed from the last of the shackles with which it was encumbered in traditional oil painting and re-established in its original independence. Line drawing within an oil painting thus became possible, and the way was open to a form of re-presentation capable of signifying objects without artifice, whilst within the supporting framework, the independent architecture, there arose a grandiose polyphony. The position of objects was made clear by simple intersections. When it was important to give a complete view of an object in the background, the intersection was marked by drawing only the outline of the foremost object, so that the object behind is "situated" without dissembling. As we have seen, the beginnings of this invention appeared in 1921 in the *Open Windows*, in which the walls often do not conceal what appears essential   294, 295
in the landscape. Gris still used chiaroscuro sparingly in certain pictures. It served to indicate the volume   169, 311

Woman with Fan · 1925

of minor details (grapes, for example). Finally, in certain pictures (such as *The Yellow Guitar*) he renounced all imitative means: the form was simply created by drawing on the flat surface. Here was the "flat" and coloured "architecture" to which he aspired. But what must be emphasised here is that in every sense he lived up to that definition of painting with which this book began, namely *handwriting employing graphic signs*. The Middle Ages had made good use of graphic emblems, but although they were inscribed on a flat surface, they were endowed with a false plastic density. The Cubists always tried to give their painting that character of "flat writing" which is its true quality. Gris attained this goal without recourse to any subterfuge.

A third problem, that of space, was thereby also solved. Gris realised that this was not a problem. We must distinguish carefully between two concepts which are all too frequently confused: volume and space. The Cubists did not invent a new way of representing space (as has often been said) but a new way of representing solid bodies. From the beginning of the movement, space became again what it had been for the mediaeval painter: the place in which bodies meet. Gris understood that there was no need to represent space, because, if the assembled bodies were truly represented, the beholder would himself place them in space and they would immediately group themselves. The graphic emblems of formative writing create, in the spectator's imagination, not only the bodies but also, through the mere disposition of the emblems, the space without which man cannot conceive of them. This is in fact the test of formative writing; for ornamentation, which is not writing but decoration, always fails to create for the spectator bodies existing in space.[173]

187

Once again Gris revealed himself as a neo-Kantian, though he had never read Kant. He discovered for himself that space exists *a priori*, that it is, in Kant's words, "like a subjective and ideal diagram, originating according to a fixed law, in the nature of the intellect which enables the co-ordination of all objects in the sensory world". We must not look for space outside ourselves; it is the very structure of our visual perception.

Gris' clear and direct mind thought out again the problems besetting the painter and found its own solution. Conflicts and contradictions were resolved. In his studio at Boulogne-sur-Seine, and during visits to Toulon (winter 1925–26) and Hyères (winter 1926–27), Gris painted his final works. There is no need to stress their classical spirit; one might almost say that their appearance betrays this, although I do not think that the uninitiated spectator will see that connection with Pompeian frescoes[174] and the Ecole de Fontainebleau[175] which Gris himself explained to me, and which is indeed true.

I should like to have said that the serenity of his last works indicated a world at peace. It was but the fine, cloudless evening of one short life; for Gris succeeded to the end in keeping the world of art apart from bodily suffering. Death was already waiting in the wings, but nothing in his work announced its approach. There was no trace of that "stiffening", for which apparently he was on the look-out from the moment when, knowing that he was ill, he was led to think of such things. "Sick men," he said, "paint stiffly." It is only given to poets to reveal the beauty of a picture by a lyricism which re-creates it. Apollinaire has done this for Picasso, Limbour for Masson, and, before them, Baudelaire for the "romantic painters". The rest is mere verbiage, and I am no poet. I can only confess my admiration and faith, and add that I consider Gris' last works to be one of the summits of pictorial art. A firm hand, serving a pure soul and a clear mind, created the supreme inventions of an ardent sensibility before it became still for ever.

Ihr *dürft leben,*
Solang ihr Othem habt; ich nicht. Es muß
Beizeiten weg, durch wen der Geist geredet.
Es offenbart die göttliche Natur
Sich göttlich oft durch Menschen, so erkennt
Das vielversuchende Geschlecht sie wieder.
Doch hat der Sterbliche, dem sie das Herz
Mit ihrer Wonne füllte, sie verkündet,
O laßt sie dann zerbrechen das Gefäß
Damit es nicht zu anderm Brauche dien',
Und Göttliches zum Menschenwerke werde.
Laßt diese Glücklichen doch sterben . . .[176]

Friedrich Hölderlin (*Der Tod des Empedokles*)

Gris made few sculptures, but those which he did make were, as I have already said, true sculptures existing in space. Gris would have considered "sculpto-painting" hybrid, verging on a detestable equivocation. The most worked of his sculptures dates from 1918, a year in which he saw a great deal of Lipchitz. It is a polychrome work in plaster: *The Harlequin*.[177] The figure is standing: it is an architectural composition of heroic simplicity. The objectivisation of light is severely controlled, not by a series of small dents and protuberances, as in Picasso's *Head of a Woman* of 1910, but by deep concavities of regular shape. The angles are sharp, the immobility absolute. Its general appearance and sombre colour links it stylistically with the paintings of the same period.

Gris regarded this sculpture as his most important; those which he executed in 1923 he considered as playthings and gave them away to friends.[178] Yet, plastically speaking, I believe these "playthings" had a message of which Gris himself was not fully aware and which has not been understood. They were made from pieces of sheet-iron, cut up, bent and painted; but this very bending gave them an intense reality in space. *The Man with Guitar, The Negro Boxer, The Gentleman, The Pierrot*, all these "occasional pieces" are, to my mind, of considerable sculptural importance. Picasso had "opened up" sculpture and exposed its inside: he had made "lines in space" with wire. Gris did something quite different. His small piece of flat, cut-out sheet-iron, as a result of the way in which it was bent, suddenly acquired a third dimension and lived in space as sculpture in the round. This "activation of a flat surface" brought new resources to sculpture. I have said earlier that Gris imitated it in his painting by rendering with chiaroscuro the undulations of the sheet-iron which created volume. I do not think any sculptor has yet followed in this path, which seems to me full of promise. It is different from the old forms of sculpture in which the surface is not broken; it is different from Picasso's "transparent sculpture"; nor is it the method of the Oceanians, who anticipated Picasso's invention without pushing it as far as "drawing in space". With Gris the flat surface came to life, twisting, curving and finally, by its activity, creating volume.

For the sake of completion I must mention the paper heads which Gris made for the two of us on the occasion of the "Bal Suédois" in 1923; these solemn cubic masks, worn with evening dress, transformed us into twin golems.

Besides the series of water-colours executed at the beginning of his career as a painter, Gris also made a number of other water-colours and gouaches. They differ from his oil paintings only in technique and size. They were not sketches but independent works, thought out with the same care as his pictures. Gris often told me that the smallest water-colour cost him as much hard work as a picture. The gouaches date mainly from the last six years of his life. A small number of pastels and coloured crayon drawings also exist, mostly of 1912 and 1923.

His drawings, too, are related to pictures contemporary with them. Before 1920, the majority were charcoal drawings; later he favoured pencil drawings, but towards the end of his life he used mainly pen and ink. I have already referred to the portrait drawings of his friends—in pencil—done at various

periods (1918, 1921, 1923). It seems that Gris conceived of line-drawing as something apart from the 18, 19
rest of his paintings and drawings. I have already referred to this distinction and its causes: volume can
be represented by line-drawing with non-illusionistic means, and this completely alters the face of the
problem. We have seen how reflection on this problem led Gris, in his final paintings, to make use of
a form of representation derived precisely from line-drawing.

The series of crayon drawings that he made in the summer of 1920, during his convalescence, must
also be placed in a separate category. One can, I think, connect these drawings—still-lifes—with his 167
portrait-drawings. Like the latter, they are clearly separated from preceding and succeeding pictures
by a similar use of line-drawing. As he recovered his strength, he seems to have been "portraying"
objects as, with amazement, he discovered them anew. These portraits are precise though free, simple
in their grandeur, and redolent of that "sublime familiar" which Maurice Raynal so rightly perceived
in Gris.

Gris took up engraving fairly late in life. His first lithographs date from 1921 and his first etchings
only from 1925. Six of his lithographs are portraits (1921) and are related to the line-drawings. The 323
others (illustrations for *Ne Coupez pas, Mademoiselle* by Max Jacob; *Le Casseur d'Assiettes* by Armand 324, 325
Salacrou; *Denise* by Raymond Radiguet and *A Book* by Gertrude Stein)[179] are all lithographic solutions 328, 329
(in crayon and ink) of the problems which preoccupied him and are related to his pencil and pen
drawings of the same period. Finally, the etchings (illustrations for *Mouchoir de Nuages* by Tristan 326–327
Tzara)[180] are closely connected with his pen and ink drawings of 1924 and later. These drawings,
carefully worked in an infinite gradation of black and white, anticipated by two years the etchings in
which they were to culminate. They already had the latter's appearance. One can but regret that Gris
only began to engrave shortly before his death: he would have excelled at it.

XI. THEATRICAL DESIGNS

The painters of the nineteenth century never made contact with the stage. Theatrical designs were the
work of specialists who painted nothing else and had no thought of being innovators. Such attempts as
there had been at theatrical reform were never designed to attract painters; the tendency was rather
to eliminate scenery and substitute simple hangings. In Paris, particularly around 1900, Lugné-Poë—the
one truly great actor-manager, who first presented the works of the men who were to leave their mark
on the theatre between 1890 and 1930—always despised scenery. For him, very properly, the spoken
word came first, and his finances would not run to lavish *décors*. True, friends such as Vuillard often
helped him; but neither they nor he attached much importance to this collaboration.

It was not until the arrival in Paris of Serge de Diaghilew that scenery designed by painters other
than specialists was first seen on the stage. The excitement (a little overdone perhaps) caused by the
scenery and *mises en scène* of Bakst and Benois is well known. This was the folklore period of Diaghilew's

Carafe and Fruit-bowl · 1919

Ballets Russes. Everything in his company was Russian—dancers, singers, painters and musicians—with the exception of a few older pieces of music, former successes from the operas of St. Petersburg and Moscow. The *Sacre du Printemps* was, from the musical point of view, the peak of this period; *Petrouchka* the most complete success. Then it was interrupted by the war.

When Diaghilew—after touring neutral and non-European countries—contemplated reviving his company, he seems to have realised that the public was beginning to tire of exclusively Russian ballets. Jean Cocteau, an admirer of the folklore style of the Ballets Russes, had just met Picasso and he introduced the two men. For composer they chose a great musician, Erik Satie, who had been alienated from the public and the concert halls by the novel purity of his work, the eccentricity of his titles and his personal touchiness. The result of this combination was *Parade*. It was first performed at the Théâtre du Châtelet on May 18, 1917. Following Picasso, all the other Cubist painters were to design theatrical settings: Gris for Diaghilew; Fernand Léger for Rolf de Maré's Ballets Suédois and, much later, for the Paris Opera; Braque—like Picasso—not only for Diaghilew but also for Comte Etienne de Beaumont's "Soirées de Paris", organised at the Cigale in 1924. Very soon not one well-known *avant-garde* painter was without a theatrical commission.

One might think that the Cubist painters, who revolutionised the plastic arts, would have been just as revolutionary in the theatre. But not at all. The *décors* which they created were as ephemeral as any other and were lost, bit by bit, during Diaghilew's tours in the two hemispheres. To-day only a few curtains survive. The direct influence of Cubism in this sphere was only superficial, and I cannot think of any important change on the modern stage which can be attributed to it.

The Cubists came as novices to the theatre. Avid readers and surrounded by poets, they cared little for the theatre and only went there occasionally. They were therefore not unnaturally ignorant of the theoretical writings of Gordon Craig, Appia, etc.... They went to the circus. But the circus (I can hear the objection) was the one spectacle which might have provoked a reform of the theatre precisely in the spirit of Cubism, for the circus is a three-dimensional spectacle. The acrobats, seen from all sides, are sculptures living in space; here was something very much akin to the Cubists' idea of a complete representation of volume. One could imagine them setting the spectacle in the middle of the audience, for example. If such an idea ever occurred to the Cubists not one of them ever mentioned it to me. They arrived in the theatre, ignorant of its particular laws, and found an existing auditorium and stage with which they had to come to terms.

In antiquity the theatre was sculptural in conception, not free-standing sculpture like the circus or the amphitheatre, but high relief. This high relief, without a frame, projected on to the proscenium and moved against a permanent background which limited the field of vision. The back-wall in the theatre at Orange gives one an idea of the importance of this permanent background. On the other hand, nothing separated the actors from the audience. The characters in a Greek or Roman theatre lived in real space, in the same space as the audience. The actor, therefore, had to be distinguished from the spectator by being shod with buskins, having his features exaggerated with masks and his chest and stomach padded out with breast-plates. In the same way, free-standing sculpture attempts to distinguish itself from the other inhabitants of a common space by its dimensions—larger or smaller than "nature"—and by its lack of colour; for, since its style is "illusionist", it will be immediately compared with the appearance of the other inhabitants of the outer world.

The high-relief character of the Mystery Plays performed against the façades of cathedrals need not, I think, be explained: their similarity with true relief is evident and generally recognised. This conception survives still in the Teatro Farnese at Parma (1618), whose proscenium projects far into the auditorium: the actor could be seen from three sides and was not enclosed in a box. The same idea predominated in the Elizabethan theatre, the prototype of which was the stage built on the Shoreditch Road in London in 1576 by James Burbage. A permanent set was built complete with a façade with balcony and doors. It is obvious that the general effect was reminiscent of a Cathedral Square with the high-relief quality of the "Mysteries" which were there enacted. Yet, almost at the same moment, a great architect had invented a very different stage. Palladio's "Teatro Olympico", at Vicenza (1580), was a revolution. There a *picture* was obtained by sculptural means. Perspective was created by the most insistent *trompe l'œil*, and the spectator's eye was taken along seemingly endless streets which were in fact only two or three yards in depth. Palladio thereby created the limitless stage, a pictorial conception—although executed with sculptural means—which completely replaced the sculpturally conceived stage of antiquity and the Middle Ages. In Italy more and more importance was attached to scenery. It had to be changed, the actors had to be able to wander through a great variety of imaginary places. The fixed setting of the Teatro Olympico was dispensed with and for it was substituted the painted curtain, with the appropriate machinery; thus the change-over from the sculptural to the pictorial conception was completed.

An engraving of 1641 depicting a scene from *Mirame*, a tragi-comedy performed at the opening of the new theatre of the Palais Cardinal, shows a stage beginning to be framed and hollowed out to contain scenery and machinery, but still connected with the auditorium by stairs. A sonnet by François Maynard, published in the *Recueil* of 1645, describes the French public's delight at the magic of the new theatre. Here is an extract:

"A Son Eminence"

"*Sur les machines de la Comédie Italienne*[181]
Jule, nos curieux ne peuvent concevoir
Les subits changements de la nouvelle scène
Sans effort et sans temps, l'art qui la fait mouvoir
D'un bois fait une ville, et d'un mont une plaine.

Il change un antre obscur en un palais doré
Où les poissons nageaient, il fait naître les roses
Quel siècle fabuleux a jamais admiré
En si peu de moments tant de métamorphoses."

A stage like that of our day appears in an engraving commemorating the first ballet production at the Académie Royale de Musique in Paris, the *Fêtes de l'Amour et de Bacchus*, a pastoral ballet by Lulli, presented on November 15, 1672. This stage had wings and a backcloth, and was enclosed by a gilt frame which gave it the effect of a picture. Since that date there has been no change. The modern stage is a picture and does not conceal the fact. This quality is also emphasised by the large gold frame which surrounds it. It employs linear and aerial perspective to produce depth, and its backcloth often creates an added false depth by means of a landscape painting. It is painting, and is therefore separate from the space in which the spectators live. Within its framed box, open only on one side, it creates its own artificial space which is faked by every means of perspective, *trompe l'œil* and lighting. The actors no longer move in general space like animated statues; the gilt frame cuts them off from this space as well as from the audience. They move around like silhouettes on the other side of the frame, in an imaginary space. Braque, when doing his first ballet, *Les Fâcheux*, was so conscious of this silhouette quality of actors that he had the idea of treating the dancers as silhouettes visible only from in front. This discovery was inspired by an idea which occurs frequently in his work. For example, his two small plaster sculptures of 1920 are treated as double silhouettes, front view and back view. The third dimension is not represented at all. As regards the dancers, he told me: "I shall make them into silhouettes and they will only be seen in full face; as for their backs, I shall choose a colour which will blend with the *décor*. Thus, when they turn round, they will disappear and won't be seen." It goes without saying that this very remarkable idea was suppressed by Diaghilew's dressmakers.

We know the sort of stage the Cubist painters found when they began to work for the theatre. It was defended by the die-hards of the theatre, who were determined that it should not be altered. Diaghilew was quite capable of permitting several little novelties (even though he rejected a great number) which seemed to him interesting eccentricities, so long as they remained on the surface and did not fundamentally alter his conception of the stage. If he had wished to be responsible for a real theatrical revolution, he would have needed a completely new theatre. This was manifestly impossible for a troupe whose tours involved a constant change of theatre. That is doubtless why the work of the Cubist painters, which was like a tidal wave in the plastic arts, caused only a superficial ripple in the theatre.

True, within the gilt frame bounding their scenic picture they created a closed space (which, like Focillon, I call "monumental space"), but the tendency to suppress "flats", which was under way before their intervention, was evidence of a similar research amongst professional designers. One might even say that a sculptural conception was tentatively developing in the arrangement of the stage in an *avant-garde* theatre like the Vieux Colombier, where the proscenium projects into the auditorium and comes down in a short flight of steps. It remains to be seen whether the theories thus put into practice owed anything to Cubism or simply appeared concurrently, springing either from the same need or from retrospective historical considerations. At any rate, one must admit that when the Cubists entered the theatre they made little use of their own theories. They did not even always strive strictly to limit their backgrounds. Picasso's *Tricorne* and Braque's *Les Fâcheux*, like Gris' *Colombe*, are evidence of this. They brought some new ideas into the theatre, they gave freely of their admirable gifts as painters, but they failed in the task of reforming the stage, doubtless for lack of time in which to study it. Also perhaps because they had no theatres which would have allowed them to put new ideas into practice.

To my mind, the theatre must ultimately be reformed. The part played by *décor* must be cut down, the stage-picture must be abolished by taking it out of its frame, and we must re-establish a plastically conceived stage the inspiration of which is sculptural. The very principles of Cubism, as they are manifested above all in sculpture, should be of great assistance in such an undertaking. It is infinitely regrettable that the only time when a sculptor—Henri Laurens—was entrusted by Diaghilew with a *décor* (*Le Train Bleu*) he was forced to make a stage-picture, enlivened by a few Chanel bathing costumes, where the only hint of the sculptor were a few details in relief.

The influence of Cubism is unmistakeable in the theatrical projects put forward by Pierre-Albert Birot in *SIC* in 1916;[182] that is to say, prior to *Parade*. Birot wrote: "As for the theatre (the building), it should be a circus, the centre of which is occupied by the public while the main part of the spectacle is unfolded on a revolving peripheral platform related to the audience by actors stationed at points within the enclosure." We must regard this as an attempt to unite actors and public in the same "space"; but to my mind Birot was probably inspired by the idea of our fathers' "panorama", which placed the spectator in much the same way in the middle of New York Harbour, or of some battle, that is to say, in a completely illusory, false space. Instead of placing actors and public, like sculptures, in "true" space, common to all, he would have brought the actors out of the stage enclosure and would have transformed the entire theatre (the circus) into a stage.

Pierre-Albert Birot's "*théâtre nunique*" is unquestionably the origin of Antonin Artaud's projects.[183] Artaud, too, would place the audience in the middle. He would have four stages, at the four cardinal points, connected by galleries, and wants in addition a "central site" which would not be a proper stage but would permit the most important part of the action to be grouped and concentrated whenever necessary. In short, the audience like the court of the seventeenth century would be moved on to the stage itself; but there would be no stalls and boxes, because the stage would be simultaneously the auditorium and the boxes would be occupied by the actors. I cannot help feeling that it is not so much a question of uniting actors and public in the same false space, as in Birot's project, but of creating four stages pictorially conceived, completed by a fifth—the central stage—which is sculpturally conceived. This is a hybrid solution, because the audience and the actors share the central stage, the "true" space, while the actors on the four other stages live in a false space.

Apart from certain spectacles in the circus itself which have made use of the orchestra well, the arena and the boxes—as in *On a enlevé la femme à barbe*, a very successful production at the Cirque Médrano around 1937—the principal achievement (later imitated)[184] has been Reinhardt's production of *Oedipus Rex* in about 1912 at the Circus in Berlin. There the actors moved in a space common to all and were "seen from all sides"—the realisation of one of the principal ideas of analytical Cubism. On the other hand, when Reinhardt produced *Everyman* in Salzburg, he merely imitated the production of mediaeval "Mysteries".

But to return to the Cubists' personal contribution. They gave the stage minor discoveries in abundance. *Parade* was already full of them—for example, the Managers who carried off bits of scenery as an integral part of themselves. Each of the Cubists contributed something, and we should have seen more had it not been for a certain lack of courage in Diaghilew. If he did not understand, he turned down any new ideas.

After a first unsuccessful contact in 1921, Diaghilew commissioned a *décor* from Gris in 1923. I must mention that Gris had already thought of doing a ballet, for which he had worked out the scenario; this developed from a single motif, and the *décor* was similarly based on a single form. I remember a semi-circular bench and a bicycle, but I cannot now link these scattered fragments in my memory. Maybe this ballet, which took hardly any account of the stage as it then was, would have brought about the desired revolution. I do not know. In any case, Diaghilew soon swept it aside and assigned to Gris the *décor* for a ballet to seventeenth-century music, which underwent several changes of name before it appeared as *Les Tentations de la Bergère ou l'Amour Vainqueur*.[185] In Part I, I have described how much 162, 163 this work suffered from Diaghilew's clever arguments. Nevertheless, Gris did not need to blush over what remained. Everything in it was sober, logical and at the same time nobly lavish. The curtain played a large part in the *mises en scène* commissioned by Diaghilew, and each artist painted a special curtain for his production. At the opening, the ordinary theatre curtain rose to disclose a painted curtain which the public greeted with applause or jeers. In some cases it was merely a gigantic picture, a sample of the artist's "style", which in no way fulfilled the function of a curtain. But the reader will not be surprised to learn that Juan Gris' curtain was not just an illusionist picture framed in the same gilt frame in which the second picture, the *décor*, was later to appear. Gris would never have accepted anything so nonsensical. His was a real curtain, on which the title of the ballet was inscribed, surrounded by draperies. The *décor* and costumes were all of one mould: Louis XIV, which Gris had studied at the Château de Versailles before he began. And so the whole, like the details, was based on one form which was developed and varied throughout. The palace bounded the back of the stage; depth was emphasised by practicables (staircases, fountains, etc.). The pillars of the proscenium—for Gris constructed a stage upon the stage—can even be regarded as an attempt to deflect the spectator's gaze from the frame surrounding the real stage in order to make it appear less of a picture, but these pillars failed to prevent the vision from straying into depth. The modern stage demands the creation of false space. Gris could not get away from this obligation. His shepherds and shepherdesses, his marquises and his Louis XIV revolved in this fictitious space while, on benches grouped round the pillars of the proscenium, sat the "spectators of their period". Nevertheless, Gris knew how to incorporate them into the *décor* and subordinated them, like every other detail, to the general effect of his conception.

Can the practicable scenery built by Gris for the "Fête Merveilleuse", organised by Diaghilew in the Hall of Mirrors at Versailles on June 30, 1923, be considered as an attempt at making a plastic setting? Yes, up to a point. For this construction of real staircases, rising almost to the ceiling of the Hall of Mirrors, was completely architectural and free from illusionism or *trompe l'œil*. Nevertheless, it was presented frontally—covering the whole width of the room—to the audience and thus, except for the

Harlequin · 1917–18

Page 162:

Costume designs for "Les Tentationsde la Bergère"

A Chevalier · 1923 (top left)

A Shepherdess · 1923 (top right)

A Maid of Honour · 1923 (bottom left)

A Nobleman · 1923 (bottom right)

Page 163:

Model of set for "La Colombe" · 1923

Model of set for "Les Tentations de la Bergère" · 1923

Mask for "Bal suédois" · 1923

Pierrot · 1923

Man with Guitar · 1923

164

absent frame, was very like an ordinary stage. Its depth—real and not simulated—was at first concealed by a curtain held up by men with poles, and its sudden disclosure later gave the impression of a picture at vanishing point, and not of high relief. One cannot say as much of the *décor* for *Nuit de Mai* (Red Cross Gala at the Nouveaux Magasins du Printemps, May 28, 1924). The architectural qualities of these colossal platforms had nothing in common with the stage of a theatre; the problem to be solved was quite different.

163   Gris also designed the scenery of *La Colombe*[186] for the Ballets Russes. I have already referred to this *décor*, in which the countryside is seen through a large window. True, the interior and the landscape were treated by Cubist means and not by linear perspective; but the effect produced was, nevertheless, a glimpse of the countryside; and so, the "monumental space" was injured by not being "enclosed".

During his visit to Monte Carlo for the rehearsals of *Tentations de la Bergère*, Gris did a third *décor*: *Une Education Manquée*.[187] He had to work quickly, and so, though his room was solidly constructed, it did not represent any new contribution. After this he had no further occasion to design scenery.

To resume: Gris succeeded no more than the other Cubist painters in transforming the modern stage. True, the appearance of his *décors* has since been copied, as have those of his friends; but, for the reasons that I have tried to explain above, Cubism did not carry into the theatre the revolution which it brought about in the plastic arts.

The collaboration of the painters with the Ballets Russes ended in absurdity. Diaghilew, on the look-out for "success"—that is to say, in reality, the victim of a whispering campaign—poured all that he had into the scenery studios of Prince Cherbachidje, including those painters who were least qualified to design scenery and least capable of understanding the requirements of the stage. The curtain that each of them painted—just a picture—ended by becoming the *pièce de résistance*, and the poor stage had to be content with a few bedaubed rags and some picturesque tinsel. In one production even original pictures by the two painter-designers were brought on to the stage. If ever Diaghilew had had any desire to reform the stage—which I doubt—that time was past. Everything lapsed again into a dull routine camouflaged by false daring. Then Diaghilew died in Venice, and his tradition was scattered by the hands of his former collaborators, who founded rival troupes.

XII. RECAPITULATION

We have now come to the end of this Life and Work, and I shall perhaps be told that I have said a great deal about other artists, particularly about Braque and Picasso. But I believe that it was necessary. The art historian should not display his hero like a botanical specimen mounted on a piece of cardboard. On the contrary, I think he should display him in his living reality, as he was, in that setting which always to some extent determines a man's work. In the case of the Cubist painters this is still more important. One must have lived those years between 1907 and 1914 with them in order to know the meaning of a collective effort by a number of great painters, in order to understand anything of the continual exchange of ideas (in which Derain shared for a time) and the atmosphere of exultant heroism. Many years later Picasso told me how much he missed its stimulation and support. This atmosphere was shattered by the first World War. "When mobilisation was decreed in August 1914," Picasso once said to me, "I accompanied Braque and Derain to the railway station at Avignon. We have never found each other again." Their ways parted; each one chose his own. Subsequently each became an individual centre of attraction. The *milieu* of Gris consisted of Gertrude Stein, Raynal, Reverdy, Lipchitz and Huidobro the Chilean poet; later he used to receive visits from Beaudin, Suzanne Roger, Masson, Lascaux, Salacrou, Leiris, Limbour and the younger Spanish painters like Borès.

I have attempted to describe Gris' origins, how he was influenced by the first Cubists, what he contributed to their effort, the nature of his profound originality and lastly his importance. Perhaps it will be said that I have not always clearly indicated who was the inventor of each of the new techniques employed by the Cubists. For every technique I could state by whom it was first used; but this would not be the same as naming the inventor. For in this *milieu* every idea was freely exchanged. To use an old judicial maxim in a slightly unorthodox sense, I would say: "*Is fecit cui prodest*"—the real inventor was the one who knew best how to make use of it.

In order to define clearly Gris' position, I feel obliged to resort once again to a comparison, albeit not very satisfactory. To me, the contrast between Picasso and Gris is like that between Michel-Angelo and Raphael. With Gris, as with Raphael, I feel a truly classical aspiration: the creation of a static art, painting which is measured, restrained, calm and pure, which resumes and yet renews the work of earlier times. Picasso, on the other hand, is tumultuous like Michel-Angelo, both of them dynamic and romantic. Nor, I think, is Picasso altogether unaware of this possible comparison; for one day when, as usual, he had been accused of responsibility for the latest false development in modern painting he replied: "And was Michel-Angelo responsible for Renaissance side-boards?"

I feel that to call Gris a classical painter is most completely to express his outstanding greatness. He had all the gifts of a great draughtsman and painter, but above all those of an "architect", in the sense of his own definition. Yet he was more than just a great painter; he was a great man. It is impossible to think of his aesthetic greatness without thinking also of his ethical greatness. He was the purest of mortals, incapable of compromise. I have discussed his horror of equivocation; this horror dominated his life as it did his art. His love of clarity and good order was no mere attitude; for him clarity meant purity, logic meant veracity. The really great classical artist needs moral purity as much as artistic gifts. None I am sure was more endowed in this respect than Juan Gris.

It is part of the art historian's responsibility, after dealing with the development of an artist in the light of his own time and personal circle, to define his influence on the succeeding generation. In this way he reveals the growth of one of those "links" with which he is concerned.[188] In the case of Gris we must distinguish between the legitimate lineal descendants—those who are attempting, at least in part, to carry on his work—and the illegitimate descendants—those who have merely adopted the appearance of his pictures, completely ignoring their meaning and real significance.

The first legitimate succession to Gris was attempted by Ozenfant and Jeanneret with "Purism", around 1918. They attached themselves to Gris at that period but did not follow him in what he was "becoming"; so their movement quickly dried up and was finally abandoned by its own authors. One sculptor, Jacques Lipchitz, was a friend of Gris. There were also some lesser Cubists, for example Maria Blanchard, who simply copied him. Yet Gris is an incomparable master, and his lesson truly understood will help any disciple to discover his own powers without having to copy the appearance of his master's pictures. Therefore, I consider that painters whose work does not in the least resemble that of Gris can be considered as his disciples; some of them actually knew him and listened to his words of wisdom. Others know only his work.

I have described the contrast between Gris and Picasso as resembling that between Raphael and Michel-Angelo. From Gris has come a New Mannerism which is full of style, from Picasso a New Baroque which is vibrant with passion. As far as I am concerned, Mannerism has no deprecatory meaning. Quite the contrary: by it I mean (and this was its original meaning) those painters who "have the grand manner", who produce "great painting", like Gris. And it will not, I think, be long before this word again loses its pejorative implication, like so many other words before it: "primitive", "baroque", "gothic", "rococo". I myself am very fond of Pontormo, Parmigiano and those other masters, both French and Italian, of the Fontainebleau School, for whom Gris too had a great admiration and with whom he felt a kinship. By The New Mannerism I would cover painters whose work appears to differ as widely as that of Beaudin, Lascaux, and Roux. And so that my meaning shall not be in doubt, I would add that under The New Baroque I include Masson, Miró, Suzanne Roger and Kermadec. There are, however, a number of points in common between these two groups. In 1922, for example, Masson like Gris thought it was "poetic" to make *partridge* "rhyme with" *pomegranate*; to-day his conception is totally different. Thus even The New Baroque is linked by certain threads to Gris. The

Still-life · 1920

New Mannerist painters still attempt to preserve as much as possible the autonomy of the architecture; those of The New Baroque admit man's passions and vicissitudes into their art. Both groups have been touched with the spirit of existentialism. Notwithstanding their different attitudes to life, all these painters are the legitimate heirs of Cubism—the former tracing descent from Gris, the latter from Picasso. The basis of their reality is imagination, and the means they use to paint it are derived from the Cubists.

Such is not the case with what I have called the illegitimate descendants of Gris. Disavowed by Gris himself, the so-called "abstract painters" make use of the technique of Cubism, but it is a mere façade behind which there is nothing. The misunderstanding out of which they have developed was already evident in early writings about Cubism. Even Apollinaire was careless enough to talk of "pure painting" and of "abstract painting", echoing the catch-phrases which he picked up in the *cafés* frequented by the hangers-on of the first Cubists. How could there be any such thing! To what does the work of Mondrian (to name only one of the leaders of this school) really amount? It is Gris' "flat architecture" imitated but not understood. Gris himself said that these painters' "pictures" were unfinished; in other words they are not even pictures. The greatness and novelty of Gris' architecture consists exactly in the fact that while it is mysteriously linked to the emotions experienced by the painter, it is yet capable of making the beholder share them because he is able to perceive the objects by which they have been caused. And so it fulfils the biological function of painting: namely, the re-creation of man's outer world. Cubism not only re-created the visual world, but by its very subject-matter it has made us "see" and love so many simple, unassuming objects which hitherto escaped our eyes (kitchen and household utensils, musical instruments, etc.).[189] It has increased the world of our aesthetic vision by introducing us to new objects. Every great painter has enriched our visual heritage in this way; even the Impressionists' observations of atmosphere contributed something. It is one of the great virtues of Gris' painting that he enlarged and beautified our outer world perhaps more than any other painter of our time. Being a Classical painter, Gris forced himself to discard the particular in favour of what is valid for all; so the forms that he created are sober, unassuming and marvellously apt to fuse with the everyday images which they revivify. The Cubists—like all true painters—always preserved that affectionate relationship between the painter and his subject which surpasses the formal aesthetic pleasure. Picasso said to me one day: "I think it's monstrous that women should paint pipes when they don't smoke them."

What the "abstract" painters have failed to understand is the eternal interdependence of painting and the outer world, a relationship which is fundamental. They have not created a handwriting. The lines which they use to produce a series of more or less rigid forms never fulfil their real function, because the forms do not "signify" anything. They are not emblems but forms with no meaning. These so-called painters have nothing to say, no message to transmit; they have not had an *Erlebnis*, they have experienced no emotion which they wish to perpetuate.[190] Mondrian's so-called paintings are unfinished because there is no means of finishing them; they are not painting, that is to say, writing. They never get beyond the preliminary stage, so that they are a kind of decoration. They never approach

Grapes · 1921

beauty; at best they are pleasant, for, with hedonistic intent, the colours and proportions are so arranged as to please the beholder. There is no action, no radiance; the surface is coloured and no more. No amount of pseudo-Pythagorean speculation can change this fact; this type of painting is all the more artificial for having no foundation. It is not based on an emotional experience (like painting), neither is it (like ornament) stylisation nor the repetition of worn-out emblems.

There is, however, another form of so-called "abstract" painting which is stylisation. Mondrian "invented" his coloured forms, and in this appears to have been following the method of Gris, though without understanding. The other branch of this movement derives from Léger and is a form of painting which, though it originates in an emotion, kills it by stylisation. The result is therefore a meaningless petrifaction like ornament, which excludes the possibility of transmitting the original emotion. Of this type Theo van Doesburg, another Dutchman, is as good an example as any. In the Catalogue of the exhibition "Cubism and Abstract Art",[191] held at the Museum of Modern Art in New York in 1936, there is a reproduction of one of his pictures with the source of its inspiration. It is a striking example of stylisation—the naïveté is unconsciously comic—demonstrated from its beginning (a photograph of a cow!) to its completely futile end as a shabby piece of ornamental arabesque. The emblem which exists in the first stage of its evolution loses its identity and becomes an anonymous patch of colour.

Let us hope that all "abstract painting"—which is neither painting nor abstract—will soon disappear. It has done a great deal of harm, for it has largely prevented Cubism being understood and has turned more than one painter and collector against real painting. It has absolutely nothing to do with real painting. There are, however, certain indications that those of its more ardent supporters who are painters may, in the end, make the necessary effort to return to real painting, to the creation of graphic emblems, which is the only means of communicating with other men. Several of them have already done so. An understanding of the work of Gris should be a great help. No real follower of Gris will ever be in danger of copying just the appearance of his pictures, and so fixing his vision; for Gris' pictures did not start from image-memories, but, on the contrary, from an assemblage of coloured forms—this allows the artist's vision full liberty while permitting him ultimately to re-create the outer world.[192]

No petrifaction of vision is ever wholesome. Some of us, in about 1910, dreamt of a Cubist Style (which never developed); but we never for a moment thought in terms of an invariable imitation of the appearance of Cubist pictures. For this sort of imitation, while admittedly avoiding the errors of the "Abstract Artists", would merely have led to a new academicism. As we have seen, the few genuine painters of the younger generation to-day who do not copy the appearance of Cubist works are infinitely closer to the Cubists than are those champions of "Abstract Art" who imitate the pictures of Gris and his friends.

Neither the New Mannerism nor the New Baroque can be described as a "Cubist Style". The emotions which the painters of the generation of 1900 are trying to express are no longer of the Cubists. The Existentialist philosophy (and I use the word "existential" to cover Heidegger, Jaspers, Klages,

Scheler and Sartre) is a clear statement of the mentality, not to say sensibility, of this new generation, which considers "humanity and historicity as the positive sources on which we live in reality and by which we can really live".[193] Needless to say, it was bound to turn away from the "general" (or, as I would prefer to say, from "ideas"), with which Gris, an unconscious Platonist, was concerned, and go back to the particular, the individual. Racked with anguish, these young men can no longer indulge in the proud metaphysical solitude in which Juan Gris and his friends developed their art. Yet, though as men they may be different from the Cubists, as painters they are carrying on the Cubist tradition. They have fully understood the significance of Cubism's pictorial revolution. Not one of them would think of imitating an optical effect in his pictures. Their conception of painting is inherited from Cubism; they use the technique of the Cubist painters and, thanks to their efforts, the spirit of Cubism is still active in painting to-day. The difference that exists between the two generations is not of an aesthetic order.

XIII. CONCLUSION

Carl Einstein said to me one day, some thirty years ago: "We know that we would never have been so excited about Cubism if it had not been something more than just an optical experience." This is extremely true.

Within the field of the arts, the "Cubist revolution" was not confined to painting.

I only mention decoration in passing—the appearance of Cubist pictures has often been slavishly imitated for decorative purposes—for, although it is often classed as "applied art", it is in fact not one of the fine arts; decoration is not creation, it is hedonistic ornamentation applied for the purpose of making some existing object more "pleasing"—this object may be natural like the human body or manufactured like furniture.

About sculpture I need not say much: I hope I have made it clear that our conception of it has been entirely renewed by the Cubists. The art of sculpture had ended by becoming almost indistinguishable, except for the means used, from painting; the Cubists, with their sense of its true nature, restored its real cubic existence in space. Think, for example, of those works by Rodin (who was nevertheless a forceful artist) which seem to cry out for a background wall to support them in their imaginary space. Ostensibly they are reliefs: *The Burghers of Calais*, for example. It was Cubism which re-created authentic sculpture in the round, the only true sculpture.

Present-day architecture, too, owes a debt to Cubism, which is evident in its appearance. In common with decoration this too might be due to superficial imitation or to the fortuities of "fashion". But such is not the case. The geometrical appearance of modern buildings is the result of those very same ideas and aspirations which originally produced Cubism in painting. Here, for example, is what Le Corbusier, a leading architect of our day, has to say:[194] "Would you believe it? *Proportion*, the key to all architecture, has been lost, forgotten. Time was when it was everything, when it solved every mystery; no-one thinks of it now, no-one cares. It has been abandoned. That's how it is to-day."

Le Corbusier has here formulated a plea for rhythm, that unifying principle which is the real existence of everything created by man. It was this principle which was at the root of Cubism. Le Corbusier's idea of rhythm is, as a matter of fact, slightly different from that of the Cubists; it is more rationalistic. Le Corbusier considers that proportion is calculable and at the same time transcendental; for the Cubists it is neither. But we must not forget that Le Corbusier is none other than the painter Jeanneret who, with Ozenfant, invented "Purism" in 1918. Granted a certain ideological difference—primarily due to intellectual dissimilarity—it is clear that, in practice, Le Corbusier is attempting in his architecture to create new entities based (as a whole and as parts) on unique proportions; and, like Gris, he respects the law of the rhythm set up at the beginning of the creative act, in which the objective existence of the work itself originates. His art is austere; it rejects all forms of subterfuge and parasitic ornamentation. But Le Corbusier is more than a mere inventor of forms in space, as he appears here; he is *a creator of space*. And inasmuch as the art of building has regained at his hands its full meaning he can be compared with the great Baroque architects.

"Briefly, we can also say that architecture is interior circulation," he has written,[195] "and the various aspects of the construction, that symphony which we must experience, should not be revealed to us exclusively by functional considerations (the problems of modern architecture—factories, administrative offices, public buildings—are so rigid that the architect is forced to arrange the various functions in the absolute sequence of a belt-conveyor) but by emotional considerations; for the various aspects only become comprehensible gradually as we follow our wayward feet, moving hither and thither, with our eyes fixed on the walls and the perspectives, meeting expectedly or unexpectedly with doors which reveal the secret of new spaces, with the succession of shadows, semi-darkness and light created by the amount of sunlight filtering in through the windows and the bays, with distant views of carefully planted trees or buildings as well as the equally deliberate arrangement of the foreground.

"The quality of the interior circulation will constitute the biological merit of the edifice—that is to say, the organisation must be seen in conjunction with the purpose of the building. Good architecture can be traversed both inside and out. That is 'living' architecture."

This interest in the "interior" is very close to the Cubist preoccupation with expressing fully the third dimension, a preoccupation which led these painters to exhibit in their pictures the interior as well as the exterior of the objects which they studied. Thus, in the end, they achieved "total representation" after experimenting with a variety of means during the different phases of Cubism. Of necessity it meant assembling a multiplicity of aspects in a single object destined to be "seen" at one glance by a spectator who was assumed to be static. This applies to all Cubist paintings: to Braque's paper reliefs and to Picasso's constructions in metal and wood, all produced during the years 1912 to 1914. In his only sculpture in the round executed between 1905 and 1913—the bronze *Head of a Woman* of 1910[196]— Picasso allowed for "external" circulation alone. It was not until *The Absinthe Glass* (a bronze of 1914) that he began to represent the interior of objects as well. Gris seems to have thought of sculpture

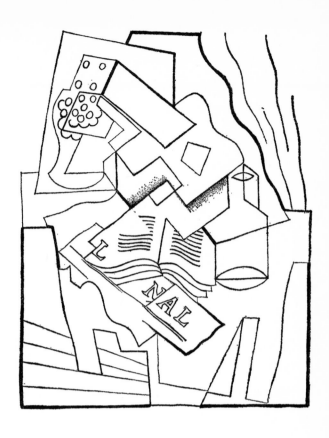

Guitar, Book and Newspaper · 1920

simply as the art of creating emblems in space (thereby remaining faithful to his conception of its original function), and so in his sculpture he paid less attention to representing simultaneously both the outside and the inside of an object. Even within these limitations the real problem seemed to him sufficiently difficult, for it involved the creation of emblems which would present a series of aspects to a moving spectator. Juan Gris was content to create forms in space, and the professional Cubist sculptors, almost without exception, accepted the same limitation. It was Picasso who, in 1925, began to concern himself with the *creation of space* in metal sculptures; but, as these sculptures were either small or only of medium size, "interior circulation" was out of the question. And so, Picasso solved the problem by making the forms and spaces simultaneously apprehensible by the beholder from outside. It was not that he never thought of making the space that he created traversable. I have already mentioned his projects of enormous sculpture-architecture, which, for want of a backer, never got beyond the painted canvas. Had they ever been executed they would have been traversable in Le Corbusier's sense.

It is important also to emphasise the connection between Cubism and the twelve-tone scale invented by Arnold Schoenberg and his disciples Anton Webern and Alban Berg. These composers found in music exactly the same sort of situation as confronted the Cubist painters and the architects of Le Corbusier's generation: namely, that their art was in a state of dissolution. In music, as in the other arts, very few men had attempted to react against and escape from the paralysing influence of academicism and the formlessness of impressionism. Gustav Mahler and Erik Satie did their best; but after them came a number of younger musicians—Strawinsky, Hindemith and the like—who, though at first they attempted to break out, finally relapsed, like Derain, into a dead traditionalism through which they wrongly hoped to re-discover *order*. Order does not, however, consist in submitting to a set of rules which has been for too long generally broken; it can only be produced by a new set of rules based on the fundamental principles of the art concerned.

Consciously, Satie and Mahler concentrated their efforts on discarding worn-out techniques, inventing new forms of expression and composition. Satie began by contributing a completely new and individual conception of harmony. His art is pure and modest and even his earliest works are remarkable (by contrast with the complex harmonies of the romantics, which progress in a conventional manner) because of his re-discovery of simple harmonies succeeding each other in a manner which is new and has no functional purpose. In his later works—*Socrate*, for example—his classical spirit is also expressed in the bareness of the melody, which appears linear after the flickering melodies of impressionist music. Mahler, though a neo-romantic, purged orchestral writing of those accompanying figures and super-fluous parts introduced by Brahms, Liszt and Wagner to increase the richness of sound of romantic music. There are few voices in Mahler's music, and each can be clearly followed because it is unencumbered. Mahler, in his symphonies, anticipated the modern chamber orchestra created by Schoenberg. Although his music is rarely polyphonic, the construction is nevertheless built up around the melody, and in Mahler's harmony there is already implicit a tendency made explicit by Schoenberg in his theoretical works: namely, that the difference between a consonant and a dissonant harmony is not an essential but a gradual difference.

About 1915, after attempting to achieve the maximum of expression in works like *Pierrot Lunaire*, Schoenberg (like the Cubists) resorted to a more rigorous architecture and subordinated the details to the ensemble. Schoenberg and his followers then adopted a structure which was both "horizontal" (in melody) and "vertical" (in harmony); they abolished the vague sentimental bond which, reinforced by the last traces of the tonal system, represented the precarious unity of impressionist music. Like the Cubist painters they broke with traditional technique, which had already lost its value (especially in the case of the tonal system), and substituted a new method more in the spirit of older musical traditions long forgotten and despised. Their conception of "the series of twelve notes",[197] whose intervals are the nucleus of the whole work, is reminiscent of the "proportions" and "relationships" at the basis of every painting of Gris. And I do not think it exaggerated to compare their austere technique of variation, recurrence, inversion (which is fundamental in twelve-note musical composition) with Gris' "rhymes". Like the Cubists and Le Corbusier, the masters of twelve-tone music appear simultaneously as innovators and traditionalists. For example, by atonality they were enabled to practise really pure counterpoint (simultaneous conduct of several independent "horizontal" lines of melody) unhampered by "vertical" harmonic restrictions. In rejecting the old-established tonal system and creating a basis for atonal music in its own essence, the series of twelve notes,[198] which became the foundation of a new musical architecture, they were affirming their double role of conservative-revolutionaries. This reform, which swept away all the impermanent technical means and preserved those that are essential, is closely related to what the Cubists achieved in painting. I will make one parallel: the Cubists

The Two Pierrots · 1922

rejected perspective in the form in which it had been codified (like the tonal system) at the beginning of the Renaissance. In its day it was adequate for every painter's requirements; but when the requirements changed it was no longer valid. Turning to what in music is valid for all time, a parallel exists between Schoenberg's orchestration[199] of Bach's Preludes, or his transcription as a Concerto for 'Cello and Orchestra of G. M. Monn's Concerto for Harpsichord and Orchestra, and Gris' copies after Cézanne and Corot, or certain of Picasso's drawings inspired by the Isenheim Altarpiece which one might call "Variations on a Theme of Grünewald".

I must now turn to a problem which was as acute for the painters as for the musicians and the poets: namely, the contradiction between the *Erlebnis* and the object in which this is made apparent to others. Let us for a moment consider the various attempts which were made to modify this antinomian duality. We are already acquainted with the method invented by Juan Gris. In their early Cubist works, Picasso and Braque accepted the "distortions" resulting from this duality; later they proclaimed their absolute confidence in their emotion and relied on it entirely to beget a construction which would be consubstantial. The Cubist poets, as I shall show presently, shared their faith in the creative force of the *Erlebnis*. These two painters, like the poets, felt that, if the emotional unity could be faithfully preserved, then the unity of the object-work of art, which was its "being for others", would be automatically guaranteed.

The atonal composers also tackled this problem of duality, spurred on by considerations not unlike those of Juan Gris. The primary *Erlebnis* remains hidden in the case of a composer: he knows only a secondary,[200] already "musical", *Erlebnis* which seeks to become a "being for others". And so the contradiction which results from the confrontation of the musical *Erlebnis* with a form may appear less. Yet the atonal composers felt that it was a major obstacle. They considered that by its own laws tonality, for example, threatened every time to distort their musical *Erlebnis*. René Leibowitz, who belongs to the group, writes:[201] "Every modal or tonal figure of sound contains in it the following duality: it is simultaneously independent of the mode or scale (since it is neither) and also tied to the mode and scale (since its very essence is conferred on it by them). In metaphysical terminology that is the same as saying that what exists (subject, common chord, etc.) can be subdivided into an external appearance (the intervals of which it is composed) and an interior being (the mode or tonality which constitute its essence). From this point of view twelve-tonal (indeed, every 'serial') thought has achieved a complete reversal. The act of composition is involved in the initial choice of a series of notes. This choice therefore appears linked *a priori* to the series, which is neither the subject nor the common chord, it is never a 'living' figure of sound; but all these things are contained in it, not only in appearance but also in essence. It is in itself already a *personification* by contrast with the same raw material of mode or tonality."

Painters and musicians faced the same problem—to make the *Erlebnis* coincide with the object-work of art. Their methods were different, but both aimed at ending this duality. They knew that their emotion existed; but they knew that their picture (or piece of music) existed also. This urge to analyse the creative act is peculiarly typical of the whole generation. Painters, architects and musicians alike, all those of the 1880 generation are intensely concerned with discovering the real nature of the art which is theirs and of building anew on a solid foundation based on the very essence of this art. Every one of these artists has attempted to create works of art which have as strong an autonomous existence as possible, to produce objects whose unity is ensured by the force of their rhythm and in which the parts are subordinated to the whole. To each of these objects, fruits of their emotion, they intend by its uniqueness to guarantee complete autonomy. They mean to practise their art as purely and as forcefully as possible. They are all of one mind with regard to the products of their work.

We must not forget, however, that architecture and music are "abstract arts", or rather "chaste arts". Admittedly it is impossible to conceive of an architect or a musician whose creation is not born of emotion; but these artists nearly always conceal from us their initial emotion, their "primary *Erlebnis*", even when (as so rarely happens) they are aware of it. This initial emotion bears no investigation; it is nearly always incommunicable in words. But even if it is, by chance, revealed to us, the process by which it is transmuted into a work of art remains mysterious. When a romantic composer like Beethoven informs us that he was thinking of "the awakening of cheerful emotions on arriving in the country" when he wrote the first movement of his Sixth—"Pastoral"—Symphony, or when we read that he composed his Third Symphony (called the "Eroica") in a moment of enthusiasm for "General Buonaparte", neither our understanding of the work nor our aesthetic pleasure is increased. In the same way the "programme" of the symphonic poems by Richard Strauss—for example, *Death and Transfiguration*—does not in the least explain, and certainly does not touch, the essence of his creations.[202]

What do we mean by "understanding" a musical or architectural composition? They are not signs,[203] and therefore "understanding" is not the same as "reading", which is the interpretation of signs. I hope I need not explain that by "understanding" I do not in this context mean a learned analysis in terms of the laws of the particular art. I would define "understanding" in this case as the coming-together in the perception of either the beholder or the listener of the real object created by the artist. It is only at that stage that this object will exist, for what is at first perceived is simply a mass of stone or waves of sound. The majority of people never get beyond this stage. One of the most striking examples of this is the first performance of some really new piece of music, which at first appears to the greater part of the audience to be cacophonous because they have failed to perceive either the melody or the rhythm and have mistaken the harmonies for dissonance. Can one say that people "know" this work because they have been present at a performance? Undoubtedly not. It is not the musical composition that they have "heard", but simply a collection of sounds. The work of art only exists in the apperception of that listener, beholder or reader who has "understood", that is to say, recreated it.

In the case of painting and sculpture—arts which are in themselves writing—there is no complete understanding unless they are read aright. The artist has sought to fix and transmit his emotion, his *Erlebnis*. Therefore the work of art can only live properly in the apperception of the beholder if the emotion too is revived. The same is also true of poetry. It follows therefore that, in the case of these three arts, we are not only able to study the products from the formal point of view, but also to get back to their source, to the *Erlebnis* which produced them; we can examine the *Erlebnis* itself as well as the ties which bind it to the objective work of art. The choice which the artist makes among his welter of emotions (choice of *motif* or *subject*) is perhaps the most significant and eloquent act, not only for the light it sheds on the message which may have crept into his work even without his knowledge, but equally because of what it implies with regard to his attitude towards his own emotions; that is to say, to the outer world. In the same way, his manner of transcribing his *Erlebnis* will teach us about his spiritual attitude. Indeed, one of the noblest tasks of the art (or literary) historian is to study the connection between the artist's *Erlebnis* and the work of art, its "being for others".

In the present case our study must necessarily be summary, for we are only dealing with literary and artistic production since 1907. But it should enable us to discover whether what, for want of a better name, we must call "the Cubist spirit", which is so much in evidence in painting, sculpture and architecture (and, as we shall soon see, in poetry), can be detected *at the very moment a graphic work of art is conceived*. And if, as a result, we discover that there are striking analogies at all stages of creation, shall we not have proof that the art and poetry of our time is no vain artifice, no arbitrary production, but is conditioned both in form and in essence by some factor common to but transcending them—that is to say by the imperious necessity of the spiritual message of our time? Or to put it more bluntly: a radical change in art and letters means that a radical change has taken place in human thought. It means that our *Weltanschauung* has changed.

In studying "the Cubist spirit" in literature we must first consider the movement called "Literary Cubism". Now this term is even more absurd than plain "Cubism", but Guillaume Apollinaire, Max Jacob and Pierre Reverdy tolerated it simply because, as friends of the Cubist painters, they felt that it drew attention to their community of thought. Yet the label affixed to this group of writers was in a sense a significant admission of the fact that at that time painting was leading the arts. A few ignorant journalists, believing all that they are told by some of Apollinaire's more over-zealous friends, still refer to the great poet as "the moving spirit" of Cubism. This is not so much an error as a distortion of historical fact. Apollinaire began in the circle of the *Revue Blanche*; that is to say, among the Symbolists, an influence which is even more strongly marked in those "*philtres de phantase*" of *L'Hérésiarque* than in his early poems. The spirit of Cubism, which was so opposed to the preciosity of Symbolism, was revealed to him by Picasso. Apollinaire had already tried to react against his *milieu* in the folklorist *Rhénanes*, which owes a certain debt to Charles Cros. And his book *Les Peintres Cubistes* is no proof that he was "the moving spirit". All the theoretical parts of each chapter were written—it is no exaggeration—with the assistance of the painter to whom that particular chapter was devoted. Nor was anything altered except where, as in the case of Gris, Apollinaire quarrelled with the artist between the time of writing and the day of publication and decided to make extensive cuts. Apollinaire was a magnificent spokesman for the Cubists; but he was no more. Even his more general aesthetic reflections are merely a repetition of what was said in *bistros* like Azon, where great battles of words were fought daily among the minor Cubists, quoting more or less accurately (as they have also done in their writings) the rare words which fell from the lips of the masters, who in those days took no part in discussions and never wrote a word. "It is forbidden to talk to the pilot," said Picasso one day in a moment of impatience.[204]

Apollinaire was content to set forth the ideas of these painters, and the beauty and value of his book consists in its sympathetic approach. The innermost thoughts of his friends were revealed to him by empathy, and his flights of lyricism in prose reflect, as they re-create, the art of these painters.

I do not wish to insinuate that Apollinaire, Max Jacob and Reverdy "imitated" pictorial Cubism. "Literary Cubism" did not begin until after the revolution had been effected by the painters; but the poetry of these three writers is a literary equivalent of Cubism in painting. Apollinaire died young, and is fully appreciated to-day; but he signed a number of manifestos in his time which are inclined to be contradictory. He was continually in need of renewing himself; and in this he was like Picasso, without the latter's staggering and unique creative genius. It is therefore more appropriate to look for the spiritual basis of "literary Cubism" among the theoretical writings of the other two great Cubist poets—Max Jacob[205] and Pierre Reverdy—who have not yet been accorded the position which they deserve. A few selections from their writings will make clear the close parallel which exists between the two forms of Cubism.

From the formal point of view, the Cubist painters insisted on the autonomous objective existence of the work of art as a unique, homogeneous creation. They spared no efforts to re-discover the very essence of pictorial art. Historically that implied first and foremost a reaction against the formlessness of Impressionism and the preciosity of Symbolism. The same considerations applied for the Cubist poets.

As a matter of fact, Max Jacob wrote in the Preface to *Le Cornet à Dés*:[206] "A poem is something constructed, not a jeweller's shop-window. Rimbaud is a jeweller's shop-window, and not a jewel: a prose-poem is a jewel."

And Pierre Reverdy formulated the same conception thus:[207] "The logic of a work of art is its structure. The moment the ensemble holds together and is balanced, it is logical." Naturally the Cubist poets never thought of adopting a ready-made mould. Reverdy, for instance, felt that the substance of a poem should determine its form. "Furthermore," he wrote, "I am not in search of some specific form; I do not know of any which I would like to fill. And even if I did know of one ready-made I should never have the courage to attempt to use it. The poet must look for the true poetic substance in himself and all around; it is this substance which imposes on him the only form which he needs."[208]

Reverdy insists on this osmosis of form and content: "We are experiencing in our epoch a fundamental transformation of art. It is not a change of sentiment but a new structure which is being born, therefore the aim is quite different. We have a new conception both of the form and of the inner meaning."[209]

Reverdy has noted that the new conception of form is only comprehensible if one is aware that it is the result of an equally new conception of the inner meaning. And so it is at once clear that the fundamental transformation of art of which Reverdy speaks applies to all stages of artistic creation.

We shall see from other quotations that the change that occurred at the very roots of this creative act required the self-same attitude to the "outer world" that we have already discovered in the Cubist painters. This is what Reverdy writes: "Those who see art only as imitation think that every work of art is easy.

"People are more accustomed to life than to art; hence, the success of those works which give an appearance of life. The presentation of a work which rises above this appearance demands a very considerable change of habit.

"I am talking of an art which is not descriptive, not of an art which is descriptive in fewer words.

"Now what is this work about? About itself; everything in it has been done for the sake of the work itself." [210]

And Max Jacob puts it this way: "A work of art stands by itself and not by virtue of the comparisons that can be made with reality." [211]

"A work is created when every one of its parts has been absorbed into the whole; it is objectivised when each of its movements—whether or not they resemble the earth's movements—takes place a long way away from the earth. There are few works which resemble the earth and are situated a long way away from it." [212]

It is clear then that, just like their friends the painters, the poets were intent on making their works autonomous. They, too, stood for renouncing all imitation and creating a new reality; they, too, repudiated a naturalistic aesthetic. They knew that neither a "slice of life" nor "nature" was the origin of their creation, but only their *Erlebnis*; that is to say, something in their conscience.

Max Jacob wrote: "Sincere is a word we reserve for work endowed with sufficient force to make the illusion real." [213]

"Art is the conflagration after a harmonious being has met with himself." [214]

"The world in a man; such is the modern poet." [215]

"Life can be understood through art but not art through life." [216]

This last sentence even suggests the idea of "creating the outer world", which as we have seen is the function of painting, and especially of Cubist painting. And there are some reflections by Reverdy on the need for the artist to attain to "reality" which Gris himself might have written: "And the deeper reality, *the* reality, is what only the spirit is capable of grasping, extracting and modelling; it is everything everywhere (even in matter) which responds to its attraction, accepts its domination and avoids and eludes the deceptive grasp of the senses. Where the senses rule, reality fades and disappears. Naturalism is an example of this submission to tangible reality. The result is of no interest because there is no question of making something true; what is true in art to-day is false to-morrow. That is why poets have never been concerned with truth but always only with reality." [217]

Reverdy makes it very clear that the pursuit of the "real" involves the condemnation of what is decorative, abstract. "The decorative is the opposite of the real. One must look for the true poetic substance within oneself, and then arrive at the form required by this substance. In order to penetrate to reality the artist's mind must disregard the fugitive appearance. It does not follow that his art must

Seated Harlequin · 1923

be abstract; on the contrary, by disregarding what is superficial and transient in appearances he has a guarantee which should lead him to the production of more substantial facts, more concrete works and a stronger real existence."[218]

It is significant that the Cubist poets shared the taste of the painters for subjects which were simple, familiar, and matter-of-fact. Max Jacob, for example, said: "Modern poetry no longer consists in evoking characters whom one believes to be poetic because of their costume, their name, or some other personal attribute. The *Midsummer Night's Dream* sort of poetry is a masterpiece of the past."[219]

"Look at what is around you; you can look at the rest later if you live long enough."[220]

Introversion is at the basis of Cubist poetry as it is of the painting, and after Reverdy's religious conversion he went so far as to repudiate the outer world.

"A prisoner of appearances, confined within this world, which is moreover purely imaginary although it satisfies the great bulk of mankind, he [the poet] gets over the obstacle and attains to the absolute, the real, where his spirit moves easily. We must follow him thence for what *is* is not this obscure body, humid and despised, which you knock listlessly against on the pavement—that, like every other, will pass away—but these poems, considered apart from the form of the book, these crystals deposited after the effervescence which occurs when the spirit makes contact with reality."[221]

It is therefore true to say that both the Cubist painters and the poets are in complete accord; they have the same conception of the structure of a work of art and of its content, the same way of objectivising the *Erlebnis* for others. And the objectivised *Erlebnisse* are so similar in type that we must accept them as evidence of tendencies common to both. But still more important is the fact that they all have the same attitude to the world.

The public reacted alike to the works of both painters and poets: they found them obscure. But this obscurity was not the wish of either the painters or the poets. About this they left no doubt, Max Jacob writing: "Modern poetry may seem obscure, but it is not Hamlet-like.[222] Modern poetry is objectified; Hamletism is the same as subjectivism, which is its essence. The one maddens by not being understood, the other would madden if it were."[223] And here is Reverdy's comment: "A work is not of necessity obscure because it is enclosed. Instead of beating against the walls in an attempt to get inside all one has to do is to find the opening through which the light penetrates. . . . Obscurity is very easily dispelled by the intervention of a little light; the air inside a closed room is just as transparent as that outside; all one need do to prove that these four walls do not surround a mass of blackness is to fetch a lamp or open the window. Obscurity must not be confused with cloudiness. Cloudiness is the result of adulteration, of impurity in the mixture. We believe that a work is only obscure if the reader or beholder directs the rays of his lamp—the mind—wrongly."[224]

As we have already seen, the difficulty experienced by the beholder of Cubist pictures was caused by the fact that the artists had invented new signs which at first no-one was able to read. Moreover, these signs melted into the architecture of the picture in such a way that the simple-minded beholder was frequently unable to isolate them individually and thereby read the picture more easily. These signs were, in effect, "distorted" by the rhythm of the whole.

What then was the explanation of the (momentary) obscurity of the Cubist poets? Had they, too, invented new signs? And if so, what is a new sign in poetry? Does it mean a word which is completely invented? What is a new form of linking up the signs in poetry? And does any such new form immediately imply the rejection of existing syntax? I remember Carl Einstein—whose position as a German Cubist poet I shall discuss in a minute—saying to me reproachfully that the French Cubist poets had neither invented new words, nor rejected the syntax of the French language. But, as I shall show presently, this reproach was based on a misunderstanding. What in fact had the French Cubist poets done? Nothing more than the poet's *real* job always has been; *they had given existing words a completely new meaning.* Knowing the incantatory value of words, which they had learnt from Mallarmé, they had no doubt achieved this with greater force and daring than many another poet. "It is only in that moment when words are freed from their literal meaning," wrote Reverdy,[225] "that they take on in the mind a poetic value. It is at that moment that they can be freely placed in the poetic reality."

"Now take care; words belong to everyone. And so you are obliged to make of these words something different from everyone else."[226]

The poets never upset syntax, but found new and, at first sight, disconcerting ways of associating words and phrases which did not accord with any logical development of thought but were freely dictated by the mind just as the "associations" came. Max Jacob said so bluntly: "Modern poetry defies every explanation."[227]

"Modern art is an association of ideas, they say. Admittedly; but how are yours associated? Imagination is nothing but the association of ideas."[228]

And here we must not overlook the similarity between the "association of ideas" and Gris' "metaphors". As a Platonist, "association of ideas" meant for Gris "association of realities". Now Reverdy is another Platonist whose intellectual approach is exactly the same as that of his friend Gris. As he has said: "The word '*like*' serves to bring two realities together while leaving the spirit free to register the comparison."[229]

"I have preferred to bring the various elements together more directly, simply by showing their connection and dispensing with any intermediary, for the sake of 'creating an image'."[230]

"An image is a pure creation of the spirit. It is not born of a comparison but through the bringing together of two more or less remote realities."[231]

"The characteristic of the strong image is that it results from the spontaneous bringing together of two very remote realities whose connection has been grasped *by the spirit alone.*"[232]

One cannot help noticing here the importance that Reverdy, like Gris, attributes in his work to images as a means not only of evocation but also of construction.

Here I must again quote an essential passage from Max Jacob. His definition of the prose poem, as he created it, is not only of value in our study of the aims of the Cubist group, but was fundamental in determining the "laws" of a type of literature which became more and more common in the following generation: I mean the "poetic novel", one of the most significant contributions of this generation. Max Jacob wrote: "The prose poem such as I conceived it in *Le Cornet à Dés*—and as it has subsequently been imitated—differs from the Fantasies of Aloysius Bertrand in this, that neither the subject nor the picturesque detail is of any importance. My only preoccupation was with the poem itself; that is to say, with the harmony of the words and images and their constant and mutual appeal:

"(i) The tone does not change from one line to the next as with Bertrand.

"(ii) If a word or phrase fits the ensemble I do not think of whether this word or phrase is picturesque, whether or not it fits the poetic anecdote. I have been attacked for being incomprehensible just because of that."[233]

Without any question, the importance he attached to the construction—to the unity of the work itself—is one of the causes of his temporary obscurity. And this phenomenon is comparable with "constructivist distortion" in painting. The Cubist poets, like the painters, had an absolute respect for the unity of the work itself, and it is important to realise that their conception of this unity was resolutely anti-rational. The "unity" is in no way demonstrable. It cannot be described in words, and there is no recipe for producing it. It cannot be formulated; it is subject to no "law". According to these poets it is born—and the extracts which I have quoted afford ample proof—of the unity of the feeling from which the work springs. The preservation of this unity will guarantee that of the work itself. And the Cubist poets, like the painters, conceive of this unity as something absolute, unshakeable and capable of absorbing any kind of heterogeneous element. In painting we have seen that knowledge of the power of the work's unity made possible the technique of *papiers collés*, which is the equivalent of using "ready-made" plastic phrases. We find a similar technique in some of the poems of Apollinaire. I am thinking of works like "*Lundi Rue Christine*" or "*Les Fenêtres*", poems composed of phrases supplied by friends sitting round a table in a bar or overheard in a café. And Max Jacob even went so far as to justify it theoretically: "The new spirit is based on rhymes which are too rich and the absence of rhyme, journeys, the names of streets and signs, literary memories, conversational slang, what happens on the other side of the Equator, unexpected changes of gear, a dream atmosphere, unexpected conclusions, the association of words and ideas. Our enemies call this incoherence. Why then are the best modern poets absolutely inimitable? Because they have a unity of sentiment and of taste. Modern poetry is a proof that, as far as poetry is concerned, only poetry matters. Every art is sufficient unto itself."[234]

With Apollinaire and Max Jacob, as with the painters, the idea was to use ready-to-hand material in order to prevent virtuosity, to escape from the drone of some pre-established rhythm.

Discussion of literary Cubism is as a rule confined to the French poets. This I think is wrong; for it always seems to me that the Cubist spirit is shared in English by Gertrude Stein and in German by Carl Einstein. In the case of Gertrude Stein this spirit seems so intense and rigid that sometimes one has the false impression that she has reached the point of abstraction. She makes use of existing words without inventing any, but she uses the raw material of language with absolute liberty dictated by the logic of her work (if I may so describe her imperturbable flow, which does not unfold logically) and not in accordance with pre-existing laws. She herself has written:[235] "I like the feeling of words doing as they want to do and as they have to do." This I am sure is an affirmation of her faith in the inner life and inevitability of the material which she uses for her creation, and goes beyond a belief in the necessity for established forms of language determined by the time and place of their use. I would add that though in the writings of Gertrude Stein the syntax of the English language is reduced to its simplest form it is nevertheless preserved. Gertrude Stein, who is as often praised as she is decried, has had a considerable influence on English and American literature. In some cases her influence has been formal, but in the majority it is at work at that moment when the emotion is transformed into the work of art. Thus, the younger American writers may have followed Mark Twain and Sherwood Anderson in their choice of subject—that is to say, in the words of Max Jacob, "by looking around them"—but it is from Gertrude Stein that they have learnt how to re-create their *Erlebnis*. It is not for nothing that Gertrude Stein has spoken of "a book which when you open it attracts attention by the undoubted denial of photography as an art".[236]

The time I think will come when the poetry of Carl Einstein[237] will be highly esteemed. He is generally classed as an Expressionist, but although the idiosyncracies of some of the Expressionists give them an occasional resemblance to Einstein, I prefer to class him separately as a German Cubist poet. Full-flavoured, dense and rigorously precise, the phraseology and construction (which is "architectural" and not anecdotal) of his novel *Bébuquin*, of his other prose works and of his poems, is certainly Cubist. They are best described in the words he uses in *Die Kunst des XXten Jahrhunderts* (p. 50), about synthetic Cubism: "*Form ist nicht mehr Ausgleich oder Weglassen widerstehender Teile aufgenommenen Motivs, Ausgleich zeitlich getrennter Wahrnehmungsteile, sondern Herrschaft des subjektiven Aktes.*"[238]

I have already alluded to Einstein's comment that the French Cubist writers had too much respect for the signs and forms of existing language. True, he invented numerous neologisms and treated syntax with a certain freedom; but the German language (possibly more than any other Germanic language), with its composite words and flexible syntax, makes possible experiments which would be unthinkable with a Latin language. Let us consider this in more detail. A poem is born, of the shock of the *Erlebnis*, in language, which in this case is the raw material in which the experience is made objective for others, just as with a painter it is coloured forms. The signs used for objectivisation can, up to a point, be invented in painting;[239] but in poetry it seems that the primary task (in all languages) is to give a new meaning to signs which are already known. Now this is achieved—to use a metaphor from Gris—by "re-qualifying" these signs; that is to say, by bringing together unexpectedly one or more signs not usually associated, so that their combination tends to change their meaning. Mallarmé is undoubtedly correct in assuming that meaning resides in "the phrase", so we can follow his example and talk of "new words", while reserving the expression "*mot total, neuf*" for an entire phrase. Mallarmé wrote:[240] "*Le vers qui de plusieurs vocables refait un mot total, neuf, étranger à la langue et comme incantatoire, achève cet isolement de la parole : niant, d'un trait souverain, le hasard demeuré aux termes malgré l'artifice de leur retrempe alternée en le sens et la sonorité, et vous cause cette surprise de n'avoir ouï jamais tel fragment ordinaire d'élocution, en même temps que la réminiscence de l'objet nommé baigne dans une neuve atmosphère.*" The question of the creation of new words now appears in a different light. In using Mallarmé's terminology, it is essential to state that every language demands that the poet shall use existing vocal signs. New words are born of the impact of vocal signs not previously associated. Therefore, according to the structure of the language, "new words" may be either real new words or signs born either by combining several established vocal signs in a single unit (as in German), or (as in French) in a phrase—"*mot total*"—the process in each case being the same. Even James Joyce, whose attempt to create new words was the most determined that I know, could not get away from this. Apart from his own language, Joyce made use of elements from three or four others as an expedient. He did not create words out of nothing, probably because he discovered that entirely new words, lacking even a minimum of recognisability, would have no meaning whatever for his readers. No matter how much one admires the baroque richness of Joyce's language, there is no denying that his experiment is only valid for and because of himself: it cannot be carried on by others.

Two French writers have attempted "the creation of words" in the more strict sense of the term. Fargue made use of invented words in *Ludions*. And in *La Nuit Remue*, Michaud has written some poems which are partly composed of invented words. These words do succeed in conveying some meaning, but the transmission of the author's thought is nevertheless rather vague. Neither Fargue nor Michaud has invented words which will be a permanent enrichment of the vocabulary of the French language; their words cannot become common property as is the case with the German poets.

In the poems of Tzara,[241] and in the very fine poems which Picasso has been writing since 1934, the syntax is frequently very loose, or at any rate very much simplified. Yet it would not be fair to speak of a tendency to destroy its traditional forms. The Futurists, however, with their "words at liberty" which were proclaimed and extolled in all the manifestos typical of this group, did want to destroy syntax. Yet, though they talked a lot about it, nothing happened. They made use of a collection of onomatopoeiac sounds, noise imitations and short phrases which were a sort of primitive rendering of some particular event. But, far from imposing itself on the anecdote, their language was adapted to suit it. In fact they merely practised an extravagant form of journalism. As Pierre Reverdy says in *Self-Défense* : "One must not confuse freedom of spirit and words at liberty."

The contrast between Cubism and Expressionism in painting repeats itself also in literature: the same aspirations, the same fervour, the same distrust of a pseudo-reality identical for everyone. Kafka is an example of this distrust; but, like his friends, Kafka used the language handed down by earlier writers, and there is no trace of the Cubist will to architecture in his writings.

I cannot however dismiss the achievement of Raymond Roussel, who really had a "will to architecture" as I have defined it. Roussel has given his own explanation of the conception and construction of his writings. But, so far as I am aware, no-one has yet noticed the similarity between his procedure, in which the content of a whole book develops out of a few words (they determine the anecdote), and that of Gris, who starts with a few coloured forms and ends with a "subject". It is, I think, only fair to say that Gris did not like Roussel's work. However, at that time Roussel had not yet divulged how his mind was set in motion by the play on words which led to the invented reality.

Perhaps it is now clear that certain ways of thought were in the air, as is always the case with any important spiritual development. Quite apart from the affinities of which I have spoken—in the concep-

Guitar with Sheet of Music · 1926

tion of *form*—there were others fundamentally as significant, in particular the manifestations of an introvert mentality in epic poetry. They are so numerous that everyone can think of his own examples. Here I will mention only two, which strike me as being particularly noteworthy because they gave rise to certain technical innovations. First of all the "interior monologue" of Joyce, which has been copied by a number of young writers in America and France. By reason of it a Faulkner, for example, is able, by giving a description of what appears in the minds of several different people, to depict a character or a scene "from several aspects". Again there is the "confession", the self-analysis, of Max Jacob's characters, who talk about themselves in letters and confidences addressed to some questioner. In both cases the writer shows reluctance to describe his characters "from outside". He gets under their skin in his determination to get away from the epic duality; he tends towards lyricism. No-one can overlook the large number of autobiographical novels, from Proust to the young writers of to-day; even more significant, however, are the great quantity of works which are frankly confessional in character, beginning with the works of Gide.

In this present volume I have not been able to do more than indicate the vast extent of that movement of which Juan Gris was one of the most important protagonists. But I hope I have made clear how widespread and serious it has been. It would be tempting to enquire into its repercussions in the latest literature; but that unfortunately is not possible here. We must get back to painting. The "Cubist revolution", which marks the beginning of that tremendous movement which started in the arts about 1900, was the outcome of a century of doubt and upheaval in the plastic arts. Gradually, their complexion changed until finally the strictures of a blinkered vision were severed, and the plastic element once more became supreme. What was the cause of this restlessness to which western painting fell a victim shortly after 1800? We have seen how the men of the Renaissance set out to explore that material world which seemed to lie open around them as far as the eye could see. They had no doubts about the solidity of bodies moving in three-dimensional space; they never questioned the existence of space itself. The Cartesian *Cogito ergo sum* seemed but a petty gesture incapable of shaking this firm edifice. Yet this edifice was knocked down by one man who distrusted everything outside of himself and declined to "accept as true anything which he did not know clearly to be so". With full knowledge, this man could discover only one proof of his existence—his own thoughts. What then is the value of that knowledge of the outer world which we receive through the medium of our poor senses? Berkeley expresses himself quite bluntly: solid bodies, space, are all illusion. All that we know is the content of our sensations; but for these he postulates an external cause—God. Finally came Kant who, in *The Critique of Pure Reason*, set out without prejudice and proved that the essence, the "thing-in-itself", of the outer world is not accessible to us. We shall never know more than its appearance. Despite all attacks and much incomprehension, this is the *Weltanschauung* which has dominated western thought for a century and a half, from Fichte and Hegel to Rickert, the Phenomenology of Husserl and the Existentialism of Jaspers. Since the beginning of the present century (coincidental therefore with the birth of Cubism) it has been adopted even in the field of the natural sciences, and under its influence physics has been transformed. For example, Max Planck, in refuting Positivism and seeking a wider basis for Physics, writes:[242] "It [the necessary step] consists in posing the hypothesis that our personal impressions do not as such constitute the physical universe; but that, on the contrary, they are merely evidence of another world which remains hidden behind them and does not depend on us." As a physicist he adds, however: "This amounts to an admission of the existence of a real outer world." The physicist must adopt a pragmatic attitude. The world with which he has to deal is not a world of appearances, as is the case with artists and poets, but a world of forces, that world in which every being has to struggle for life. And here is Planck's definition of the role of the physicist: "The physicist, too, must imagine that the real world obeys certain laws, even if he has no hope of ever achieving complete knowledge of these laws and possibly not even knowing with certainty what is their nature."[243]

Painters and sculptors do not need to ask themselves to what extent their outer world is real, for, since it is purely an appearance, it obeys no laws, physical or otherwise; it is divinely free, obedient only to its creators the artists. Nor do poets need to ask themselves such questions. One hundred years earlier than the Cubist painters, poets seem to have had a presentiment of a world created by the imagination as the supreme basis of all reality: I am of course thinking of the German Romantic poets. But the pathetic little painters who were their friends were quite incapable of translating such theories into plastic terms; so it took another century of philosophic and scientific preparation before a state of mind existed (in Cubism) which was capable of carrying through this great upheaval.

I am not attempting to establish a connection between contemporary painting and some definite philosophical system.[244] But whether, like Planck, the solution adopted has been that of transcendental realism, or, like Kant and his followers, that of transcendental idealism, the philosophical convictions of the last one hundred and fifty years have (except for the "analogical" musings of the Nature Philosophers) been restricted either to the conviction that the real world is inaccessible to us or to the conviction that the world outside of ourselves does not exist at all. Positivism, with its belief in "an immediate reality" based on sensuous perceptions, is no more in opposition to the contemporary attitude of the visual arts than is Stirner's Solipsism, which proclaimed the unreality of everything except the sensations of the "individual self". Only straightforward materialism has found no champions. This mistrust of the results of our perceptions, the supposite of "the real world", is really a different *Weltanschauung*, another conception of the world. A novelist like Proust could write (in *The Captive*): "The universe is true for us all and dissimilar to each of us ... it is not one universe, there are millions, almost as many as the number of human eyes and brains in existence that awake every morning."

It may be remembered that in a letter of January 3, 1922, Juan Gris picked on an erroneous use by Waldemar George of the terms "deduction" and "induction"; Gris maintained that his method of work—progressing from the general to the particular—was "deductive". Now, what has happened is that the inductive method—the progression from the particular to the general—which has dominated the thought of man since the beginning of the modern age has recently been abandoned in favour of the deductive method. And it is no over-simplification to link each of these methods, between which man's conception of his world alternates, with the name of one of the great Greek philosophers—Plato and Aristotle. For the moment it is Plato's turn.

We have moved a long way from that splendid but imprudent spirit of daring which, for so many centuries, was convinced of its mastery of the outer world, of its ability to know it. Time was when man walked unhesitatingly among the solid bodies which he touched and of which he therefore felt convinced. In a certain sense the introduction of the element of light into painting signified that the field of research was being enlarged. But, coming simultaneously with Descartes, may it not have been the first expression of doubt? Gradually light penetrated the solid bodies and caused their compact structure to dissolve. Impressionism caused them to crumble completely. In their courageous effort the Cubists returned to the study of solid bodies; it was their profoundest wish to be *realistic*, and their achievement was to substitute for the "realism" of the nineteenth century the "Realism" of mediaeval philosophy. To-day, conceptual painting is not the representation of an object "perceived", but the plain conception of that object. And so, whereas at the beginning the painters imagined themselves as simply in reaction against Impressionism, the Cubist revolution has carried them far beyond so narrow an aim. It has launched us on a new epoch in the history of art, just as our metaphysical conception—of which the plastic arts are but a visual expression—has changed. Indeed, Cubism is helping to disseminate this new metaphysical conception. The Renaissance spirit ended vulgarly in Materialism, which preached belief in an immutable and readily cognizable outer world; this was broken down by the Cubist painters and poets as it was by the philosophers and physicists. Unfortunately I cannot here pursue all the repercussions of this new introvert conception of the world.

In conclusion, I would like to sum up briefly the particular role played by Juan Gris in the revolution which has taken place in the plastic arts. First, I would emphasise the fact that at the crucial moment —when analytic Cubism gave way to synthetic Cubism—Gris had just reached maturity. There is, then, no escaping the conclusion that he was probably among the first to be aware of what was at stake, and that his adoption of an introvert form of art was deliberate. "I hope I shall come to express with great precision a reality imagined in terms of pure intellectual elements," he wrote on August 25, 1919.

Reading what Gris wrote, in conjunction with looking at his pictures, one becomes increasingly aware of the great part which he played. In his work are all the essential qualities which constitute the historic importance of Cubism. It is still too early to attempt any comparison of the aesthetic value of the work of each of the four great leaders of the movement. Léger abandoned his colleagues, with whom, anyway, his friendship was never very intimate. The influence of his work on the appearance of our cities has been enormous; but since 1923 he has ceased to practise Cubism in the sense in which I have defined it and has taken another turning which I cannot here discuss. As for the other two great Cubists, I have no hesitation in stating that neither the fanatically autobiographical production of Picasso nor the serious and intimate work of Braque, romantics both of them, represents the new spirit as clearly as the work of Gris. And we have defined this new spirit as being engendered by the philosophical conception of the tangible world as inside man, rather than of man as part (and this was the conception of the previous eight centuries) of the tangible world. The progress of Cubism is more clearly reflected in the work of Gris than in that of any of the other painters; particularly is this true at that decisive moment when the Cubist painters suddenly gave up taking stock of the outer world and decided to create a world of their own imagining.

Gris added to the stock of emblems by which man recognises the outer world a set of noble, simple, intense forms. Once painting had lost its epic and its tragic purpose, the artist was free to devote himself to his love of forms, to pursue a lyrical aim; Gris did this consciously and with complete success.

One need but look around to become aware of the profound influence of Cubism. It has transformed our vision of the outer world—and that means the outer world itself—more completely and profoundly than any other pictorial movement since the Renaissance, and it has had an immensely liberating influence. Proof of this can be seen in the variety of movements of greatly differing aspect which owe their origin to Cubism. In this respect, too, I think that Gris' influence was considerable. Time will, I am sure, increase the reputation of this modest genius, who received so little encouragement during his all too short life.

Juan Gris was with us for only forty years; he was painting during no more than seventeen of these. No obstacle was so great, however, that it killed his rapturous lucidity. That fragment of the world which he rescued from the destruction of suffering and stripped of all adventitious elements will survive in all its solemn and serene beauty.

"O Seele! Seele! Schönheit der Welt! du unzerstörbare! du entzückende! mit deiner ewigen Jugend! du bist; was ist denn der Tod und alles Wehe der Menschen?—Ach! viel der leeren Worte haben die Wunderlichen gemacht. Geschiehet doch alles aus Lust, und endet doch alles mit Frieden."

Friedrich Hölderlin (Hyperion)

"O soul, soul! The world's beauty! Indestructible, ravishing, eternally young, Thou art. What then is death and all of human suffering? Many an empty word has been said by these strange ones. Yet everything comes to pass through joy and everything has its end in peace."

INTRODUCTION

One day long after Gris' death, Picasso said to me in front of a picture by him: "It's grand to see a painter who knew what he was doing." This same lucidity, to which Picasso drew attention, is apparent in Gris' letters and is also characteristic of the few written papers he intended for publication. They are printed here in chronological order.

I

Artists have thought a poetic effect could be made with beautiful models or beautiful subjects. We, on the other hand, believe that we can produce it with beautiful *elements*; for those of the intellect are certainly the most beautiful.

Valori Plastici, Rome. February–March 1919.
Number devoted "*al Cubismo Francese*", p. 2.

II. ON NEGRO ART

Negro sculptures provide a striking proof of the possibilities of an *anti-idealistic* art. Religious in spirit, they represent precisely, but in different ways, great principles and universal ideas, How can one deny the artistic validity of a creative process which can thus individualise generalities, each time in a different way? It is the reverse of Greek art, which started from the individual and *attempted to suggest* an ideal type.

In answer to an enquiry.
Action, No. 3, p. 24. Paris, April 1920.

Juan Gris' family originates from Castile and Andalusia.

Juan Gris was born in Madrid on March 23, 1887.

General education.

Arts and Crafts.

Decided to be a painter.

Did not attend the School of Fine Arts.

Came to Paris in 1906.

Knowing nobody, he sought out Picasso (then at the end of his pink period and starting his negro period). Gris witnessed the birth of Cubism, adopted it shortly afterwards, and exhibited for the first time at the Salon des Indépendants in 1912.

1912, Section d'Or, Rue la Boétie.

The first admirers of Juan Gris' paintings: MM. Sagot, Kahnweiler and Léonce Rosenberg.

His aesthetic: "I work with the elements of the intellect, with the imagination. I try to make concrete that which is abstract. I proceed from the general to the particular, by which I mean that I start with an abstraction in order to arrive at a true fact. Mine is an art of synthesis, of deduction, as Raynal has said.

"I want to arrive at a new specification; starting from a general type I want to make something particular and individual.

"I consider that the architectural element in painting is mathematics, the abstract side; I want to humanise it. Cézanne turns a bottle into a cylinder, but I begin with a cylinder and create an individual of a special type: I make a bottle—a particular bottle—out of a cylinder. Cézanne tends towards architecture, I tend away from it. That is why I compose with abstractions (colours) and make my adjustments when these colours have assumed the form of objects. For example, I make a composition with a white and a black and make adjustments when the white has become a paper and the black a shadow: what I mean is that I adjust the white so that it becomes a paper and the black so that it becomes a shadow.

"This painting is to the other what poetry is to prose."

His method: "Though in my *system* I may depart greatly from any form of idealistic or naturalistic art, in practice I do not want to break away from the Louvre. Mine is the method of all times, the method used by the old masters: there are technical *means* and they remain constant."

L'Esprit Nouveau, No. 5, pp. 533 and 534. Paris 1921.

This biography and notes are signed "Vauvrecy", the pseudonym of Amédée Ozenfant, one of the editors of the review, but they were written entirely by Gris.

Paul Westheim reprinted them under the title "*Zu Meinem Schaffen*" in his *Künstlerbekenntnisse*, p. 150. Berlin, undated (1924?).

IV. NOTES ON MY PAINTING

"'The world from which I draw the elements of reality is not visual but imaginative.

"Though the way of looking at the world and the concentration on certain of its aspects—that is to say, the aesthetic—has varied from period to period, the relationship of one coloured form to another—that is to say, the technique—has always, so to speak, remained fixed. I therefore believe that my technique is classical, for I have learnt it from the masters of the past.

"It would almost be true to state that, with rare exceptions, the method of work has always been inductive. A given reality has been rendered pictorial, a picture has been made out of a given subject.

"My method of work is exactly the opposite. It is deductive. It is not picture 'X' which manages to correspond with my subject, but subject 'X' which manages to correspond with my picture.

"I call this a deductive method because the pictorial relationships between the coloured forms suggest to me certain private relationships between the elements of an imaginary reality. The mathematics of picture-making lead me to the physics of representation. The quality or the dimensions of a form or a colour suggest to me the appellation or the adjective for an object. Hence, I never know in advance the appearance of the object represented. If I particularise pictorial relationships to the point of representing objects, it is in order that the spectator shall not do so for himself, and in order to prevent the combination of coloured forms suggesting to him a reality which I have not intended.

"Now painting is foreseeing—foreseeing what will happen to the general effect of a picture by the introduction of some particular form or some particular colour, and foreseeing what sort of reality will be suggested to the spectator. It is, then, by being my own spectator that I extract the subject from my picture.

"I do not know if one can give to this aesthetic, this technique and this method, the name of Cubism. Anyway, I make no claim to represent any particular sort of appearance, be it Cubist or naturalistic.

"It is the appearance of the work as a whole which is its culmination, for this aspect is unknown to me. My subject, obviously, modifies the pictorial relationships without destroying or changing them. But it does not modify them any more than a numerical relationship is modified by the multiplication of both quantities by the same figure.

"Therefore I would say that a subject painted by myself is simply a modification of pre-existing pictorial relationships. Nor do I know until the work is completed just what modification it is, which gives it its character."

Der Querschnitt, Nos. 1 and 2, pp. 77 and 78, Frankfort-on-Main, Summer 1923.

These notes, addressed to Carl Einstein, were published by him wit the sub-title "From a Correspondence with Carl Einstein".

V. ON THE POSSIBILITIES OF PAINTING

In submitting for your consideration a few reflections on painting, which have come to me in the course of exercising my profession, I am above all afraid of three things: firstly, of boring you by talking of things that you already know; secondly, of not expressing myself clearly, and thirdly, of touching too closely upon my own work. For I consider that no man should talk of his own profession except with extreme caution or, better still, not at all.

For the sake of clarity in this talk, I have arranged my thoughts in a certain order, and therefore I have selected a starting-point, namely: in order to paint, one must understand the possibilities of painting.

One of my friends, a painter,[245] has written: "Nails are not made from nails but from iron." I apologise for contradicting him, but I believe exactly the opposite. Nails are made from nails, for if the idea of the possibility of a nail did not exist in advance, there would be a serious risk that the material might be used to make a hammer or a curling tong.

A painting is not made simply with canvas, brushes and colours. One can produce a landscape, a nude woman, gleaming saucepans, triangles or squares, but there will be no painting unless the idea of painting exists *a priori*. We must therefore try to find out what painting consists of and from what it springs.

Everybody knows that air of contemplation which is the pride of the bourgeois on his Sunday morning walk, or of the commercial traveller in a train, as they survey the scene. Three broad categories of contemplation can be distinguished:

Firstly: People whose emotive condition remains unchanged by a natural or industrial spectacle or by an artistic one.

Secondly: People who feel an intense emotion in front of an artistic manifestation.

Thirdly: Those who feel the same intense emotion in front of a natural or industrial spectacle as they do in front of an artistic manifestation.

This third category of spectators, then, feels a similar emotion before an extra-artistic spectacle to that which a spectator of the second category feels before a work of art. Now as the spectacle in itself is not changed, it is the spectator who has modified it during his contemplation. To use a simile, I would compare what is seen to a game of cards. The cards are the elements of which the spectacle is composed. When a man feels emotion at what he sees it means that he has made some personal modification in the arrangement of the cards or elements. Without abolishing or changing them, he has grouped them in a new way. He has shuffled the cards and sees them set out in a different manner.

Naturally, a pictorial emotion will only be produced by a collection of pictorial elements: that is to say, elements which belong to the world of painting. For every spectacle, even those resulting from art, can be considered in various lights.

An object becomes a spectacle directly there is someone to look at it. But an object can be looked at in innumerable ways. Thus, a housewife will consider a table from a utilitarian angle. A carpenter will note the way that it is made and the quality of the wood used. A poet—a bad poet—will find in it a symbol of the peace of the home. And so on.... For a painter, it will quite simply be a grouping of flat, coloured forms. And I mean flat forms, for it is more a sculptor's business to think of these forms in terms of space.

Thus, every object will offer a number of different professional aspects; but in addition to these professional aspects there is something which we might call the basic idea of an object. This idea or conception lies outside any profession and outside scientific truth. It is sometimes even a hereditary error. Scientifically speaking, all vertical lines converge towards the centre of the earth's attraction; humanly speaking, they are parallel. Despite its different aspects, the table of which I spoke just now is the same idea of a table for the housewife, the carpenter and the poet. The only difference is in the extract from it.

Now why should one expect a painter to extract from an object the elements proper to other professions? Why should he not be content simply with the elements proper to his own profession? The man who, when he paints a bottle, attempts to express its material substance rather than paint a group of coloured forms should become a glass-blower, not a painter.

The pictorial elements have altered according to the preoccupations of each period. At certain moments in history importance was attached to the pure elements of painting, and they were endowed with religious significance: at other times a scientific influence has been at work. We know that Leonardo thought of the chemical composition of the atmosphere when he painted the blue of a sky. The luscious living flesh of the Venetian painters' nudes, in which one can feel the blood pulsating beneath the golden skin, can only be explained in terms of the physiological advances of the Renaissance.

The sum of these elements, with the influences to which they are exposed, represent at any one moment the aesthetic outlook of the period; and there can be no doubt that a purely scientific discovery, applicable only to the technique of painting, such as the Italian discovery of perspective, has influenced every aesthetic creed since the Renaissance.

It is solely the need for some particular category of elements that causes a variation in the objects or models selected for painting. On the whole the choice falls on those which most clearly and most liberally provide the elements required by the aesthetic. The painter who works with elements conditioned by anatomical or physiological considerations will not choose the same models as the painter who uses elements conditioned by effects of light, or the one who employs elements conditioned by effects of perspective. But an emotion produced by a group of elements belonging to different worlds will be most impure and crude on account of the anomalous elements of which it is composed. To continue my simile, I would say that the cards which have been shuffled belong to different packs.

This leads us to the conclusion that, if an emotion is to be expressed in paint, it must, above all, be based on elements belonging to an aesthetic creed which has been produced by the period. Every aesthetic should bear a date. I shall show later that the same is true of technique, for though a work in paint may be inspired by a bizarre and anomalous choice of elements, this does not prove that it is a real painting. Nor will a work in paint be a real painting if the pictorial elements of which it is composed are not ordered and arranged by means of an appropriate technique. It is not enough to shuffle the right cards: one must also know how to deal them. And if the cards, or elements, are properly set out, they express the primary idea, a conception of the object which is human and common to everyone, and which, in our example of the table, is the same for the housewife, the carpenter and the poet. The representation of the substantial world (and I say substantial because I consider the idea of an object as substantive) can give rise to an aesthetic, to a choice of elements whose sole function is to reveal the world of ideas which exists purely in the mind. In all great periods of art one senses the desire to represent a substantial and spiritual world. The representation has been influenced and varied in accordance with the needs and obsessions of each age. The role of technique on each occasion has merely been to qualify this substantial world. Certain technical methods are common to all periods; others are less constant and vary according to the aesthetic. For example, the Italian use of perspective was simply dictated by the scientific requirements of the Renaissance aesthetic. Only the purely architectural element in painting has remained constant. I would even say that the only true pictorial technique is a sort of flat, coloured architecture.

There are several forms of architecture. All architecture is construction, but not every construction is architecture. Before a construction, whether intellectual, material, visual or acoustic, can be architecture it must fulfil certain conditions.

All constructions of the natural world, whether organic or inorganic, are architectural. The molecular structure of a body distinguishes it from other bodies and gives it individuality. The phenomenon of crystallisation provides fine examples of natural architecture, for the same body always crystallises in the same volume and form. When oxygen and hydrogen meet they combine in certain proportions to produce a certain quantity of new molecules, the quantity depending on the amount of each element introduced into the mixture, neither more nor less. Water can be produced synthetically which is identical both in quality and quantity with natural water. This is an example of chemical architecture, of real architecture, because the result of this mixture has a totally different unity, consistency and chemical proportions to those of the elements from which it is made. It has a new individuality. But the mixture of water and wine, for example, only produces a construction. The result has no new chemical properties, no unity, no consistency and no individuality. In short, it is not a synthesis.

A motor-car is not architecture, but a more or less perfect construction. It is only a synthesis insofar as it has a utilitarian value. It can be divided into a number of organs, each of which exists separately and has a very distinct personality. The engine, the wheels and the coach-work are too distinct and interchangeable as parts for them to possess a single and unique affinity. But in itself the engine, which is subtly conceived as a delicate arrangement of somewhat impersonal parts, comes nearer to being architecture. And the wheels, or rather the wheel in its simplest form, is one of the most perfect pieces of architecture created by man, on account of its unity, its consistency and its positive, synthetic character.

True architecture cannot be broken up into different pieces, each of which is autonomous and exists alone. A fragment of architecture will be no more than an odd, mutilated object which ceases to exist when it is removed from the one place where it belongs. Construction, then, is merely the imitation of architecture. The technique of painting is flat, coloured architecture, and not construction. It is based on the relationship between colours and the forms which contain them.

One can now say that whereas the aesthetic is the sum of the relationships between the painter and the outside world, relationships which culminate in the choice of subject, technique is the sum of the relationships between the forms and the colours they contain and between the coloured forms themselves. This is composition and culminates in the picture.

Every form in a picture has three duties to perform—to the element it represents, to the colour it contains, and to the other forms which, with it, make up the whole picture. In other words, it must correspond to an aesthetic, it must have an absolute value in a given set of architectural relationships, and it must have a relative value within the particular architecture of the picture.

Later on we shall see why it is necessary for a collection of coloured forms to correspond to a certain number of elements, to a subject. But for the moment I want to show how forms can correspond to colours. The first thing one notices on looking at a flat form is, obviously, that it possesses two basic properties, size and quality. I will explain this. Any given form, for example a perfect circle, will always have the quality of a circle no matter what area it covers. An equilateral triangle will always have the same quality no matter what its dimensions are. A form always has a quality and a size.

In the same way a colour also has two basic properties: quality and intensity; that is to say, red, green or blue, and the degree of such colour which it has. Blue is always blue, whether it be pale or dark. There is the hue and its shade. Thus, one cannot help immediately noticing one analogy between the quality of a form and the hue it contains, between its size and the tonal shade.

To take a fairly simple example which appears paradoxical: it can be proved that the size of a form which is very pronounced counts for very little beside its quality in the mind of the spectator. Thus, a section of the lower part of the Eiffel Tower seems larger to the mind than the whole tower. This comes of the mind being struck by the impressive dimensions of this fragment of architecture when seen from close-to. The mind has grasped a large, uniform area. On the other hand, it is only from a distance, or in pictures, that it is struck by the form which is characteristic of the tower; and it is the quality of the form that the mind has retained which finds its expression in dimensions so large that they can only be made credible by an effort of reasoning.

Thus, when a form is very pronounced, its size is not of great importance. A tonal shade can be its substitute. Hence, if we have two forms of similar quality but of different size—two squares, for example, one larger than the other but both of the same red hue—the smaller one will appear as large as the other if its shade is more luminous. But we must not let that deceive us. It is never possible to make up by tonal shades for a great discrepancy in size between forms. Where the contrast in size between two forms is great, our sensibility is more aware of the intermediate sizes than it is of the intermediate tonal shades linking two shades which are far apart in luminous intensity. For if the distance between two shades is too pronounced we end by seeing them as two different hues. Thus, dark Prussian blue is almost black, and one cannot say that it is the same hue as the very dilute Prussian blue in white, which is very luminous.

A very pronounced difference in shade changes the quality of the hue. Only a slight difference in shade can, without an alteration in the hue, make up for a slight difference in size between two forms. If the difference in size is too great you can paint square "A" in a shade as luminous as you like but it will never appear as large as square "B". On the other hand, with two squares of the same size, square "C" will appear larger than square "D" if it is more luminous.

We now have another analogy: some colours are more luminous and expansive, others darker and more concentrated. Some forms are also more expansive than others. Rectilinear forms are more concentrated than curvilinear ones, which are expansive. There is no form more expansive than the circle and none more concentrated than the triangle. These two forms correspond to the brightest and darkest tones on the palette.

Now a third analogy: some colours are warm, some are cold. Those going towards cadmium yellow are warmer than those going away towards cobalt blue. There are also warm and cold forms. Those approximating to geometrical figures are colder than those which tend away from them. Freakish and complex forms are certainly warmer. We can point to a fourth analogy: some colours are more dense and have more weight than others. Earthy colours are on the whole heavier and denser.

Some forms also have a very accentuated centre of gravity, whereas in others it is much weaker. Symmetrical forms are heavier in relation to their centre of gravity than complicated, asymmetrical ones. Geometrical figures and forms with a vertical axis have more gravity than forms with an unpronounced or non-vertical axis. These latter forms possess the same two properties and are therefore equivalent to those colours which are neither dense nor light. A fifth analogy is to be found in the opposition of two colours, which may correspond to a contrast between two different forms.

Now it is plain that we have here the very *basis* of a pictorial architecture, a sort of painter's mathematics. And only these mathematics are capable of establishing the composition of the picture. It is only this architecture that can give birth to the subject, that is to say, an arrangement of certain elements of reality called forth by this composition. It seems to me more natural to make subject "X" coincide with the picture that one has in mind than to make picture "X" coincide with a given subject. One must give arithmetical values to the terms of this algebraical equation which is the picture. This needs an explanation.

A picture is a synthesis, just as all architecture is synthesis. The aesthetic has analysed the pictorial world and has provided us with the elements. It is evident that these elements materialise by substituting themselves for the abstract forms which make up the picture, just as the simple bodies of hydrogen and oxygen substitute themselves to the formula H_2O to achieve the synthesis of water. To do the opposite would not make sense, for that way lies analytical art. Now analytical art is the very negation of art itself.

You may raise this objection: Why need one give these forms the significance of reality, since a harmony already exists between them and they have an architectural unity? To which I would reply: The power of suggestion in every painting is considerable. Every spectator tends to ascribe his own subject to it. One must foresee, anticipate and ratify this suggestion, which will inevitably occur, by transforming into a subject this abstraction, this architecture which is solely the result of pictorial technique. Therefore the painter must be his own spectator and must modify the appearance of the relationships between the abstract forms. Until the work is completed, he must remain ignorant of its appearance as a whole. To copy a preconceived appearance is like copying the appearance of a model.

From this it is clear that the subject does not materialise in the appearance of the picture, but that the subject, in materialising, gives the picture its appearance. I would insist on this point in order to dispel uncertainty. The architecture of picture-making—that is to say, the technique—enables one to assemble on a given surface, which has form and therefore colour, certain coloured forms which call for certain elements "X" drawn from the pictorial world. Our technical possibilities are fairly precise and our aesthetic world rather vague. It is a question of fitting this rather shapeless world into these formal necessities.

A philosopher has said: "The senses provide the substance of knowledge but the mind gives it form." Similarly the aesthetic is the substance and the technique is the mould. Hues and shades belong to the technique, local colours to the aesthetic. A substance should not become a colour, but a colour should become a substance. Style is simply the perfect balance between aesthetic and technique. Artists of considerable stature have sometimes lacked style owing to a bad choice of subject. Others, more modest, have possessed it.

In the so-called "decadent" periods of art, there is an over-development of technique to the detriment of the aesthetic. There is no selection, and the most variegated elements jostle each other in contemporary works. *Pasticheurs* imitate the accepted appearance of works of the past without understanding either their aesthetic or the higher laws by which they are ordered. For no work which is destined to become a classic can look like the classics which have preceded it. In art, as in biology, there is heredity but no identity with the ascendants. Painters inherit characteristics acquired by their forerunners; that is why no important work of art can belong to any period but its own, to the very moment of its creation. It is necessarily dated by its own appearance. The conscious will of the painter cannot intervene. An appearance which is deliberate and results from a desire for originality is sham; every deliberate manifestation of the personality is the very negation of personality.

Cézanne, a great architect of colour, has a personality stamped with the period in which he lived. His works could not be dated either before or after the time at which they were created.

Henri Rousseau, a clever constructor of painted surfaces, is not an essential link in the evolution of painting. His works could just as well have been painted either before or after the date they bear.

Certain issues still need to be defined after all that has been said. Painting for me is like a fabric, all of a piece and uniform, with one set of threads as the representational, aesthetic element, and the cross-threads as the technical, architectural, or abstract element. These threads are interdependent and complementary, and if one set is lacking the fabric does not exist.

A picture with no representational purpose is to my mind always an incomplete technical exercise, for the only purpose of any picture is to achieve representation. Nor is a painting which is merely the faithful copy of an object a picture, for even supposing that it fulfils the conditions of coloured architecture, it still has no aesthetic, that is to say, no selection of the elements of the reality it expresses. It will only be the copy of an object and never a subject.

Beside the emotional necessities for establishing an aesthetic and a technique, there are the professional exigencies. To achieve unity in a painting there must be homogeneity, there must be a connection between its constituent parts. The role of technique is to give cohesion to the coloured forms which make up the picture. It is essential that the elements of the reality they signify should belong to the same category or the same aesthetic system.

The role of aesthetic analysis is to break down the material world, in order to select from it elements of the same category.

Technique should serve to elaborate all these formal elements into a coherent unity. Its role is synthetic.

Every period has felt this need for unity in a picture. An analysis of a certain aesthetic of light, a certain technical method—perspective or composition, for example—has no other end except that of achieving synthesis.

Therefore I will conclude by saying that the essence of painting is the expression of certain relationships between the painter and the outside world, and that a picture is the intimate association of these relationships with the limited surface which contains them.

This lecture was published in full in: *Transatlantic Review*, Vol. 1, No. 6, pp. 482–488, Paris, June 1924, and Vol. 2, No. 1, pp. 75–79, Paris, July 1924.

Important sections of it were reprinted in French in the number of *Cahiers d'Art* partly devoted to Gris: *Cahiers d'Art*, Nos. 5, 6, Paris 1933 (pages unnumbered).

It was published in full in German in: *Der Querschnitt*, Vol. 1, pp. 32–40, Berlin, January 1925.

Important sections were published in Spanish (translated by J. de J. V.) in: *Alfar*, No. 43, pp. 24–30, La Coruna, September 1924. Also a short excerpt in: *Favorables Paris Poemas*, No. 1, Paris, July 1926.

VI. REPLY TO THE QUESTIONNAIRE: "CHEZ LES CUBISTES"

"Cubism? As I never consciously, and after mature reflection, became a Cubist but, by dint of working along certain lines, have been classed as such, I have never thought about its causes and its character like someone outside the movement who has meditated on it before adopting it.

"To-day I am clearly aware that, at the start, Cubism was simply a new way of representing the world.

"By way of natural reaction against the fugitive elements employed by the Impressionists, painters felt the need to discover less unstable elements in the objects to be represented. And they chose that category of elements which remains in the mind through apprehension and is not continually changing. For the momentary effects of light they substituted, for example, what they believed to be the local colours of objects. For the visual appearance of a form they substituted what they believed to be the actual quality of this form.

"But that led to a kind of representation which was purely descriptive and analytical, for the only relationship that existed was that between the intellect of the painter and the objects and practically never was there any relationship between the objects themselves.

"Moreover, this is perfectly natural, for each new branch of intellectual activity always begins with description: that is to say, with analysis, classification. Before the existence of physics as a science, men described and classified physical phenomena.

"Now I know perfectly well that when it began Cubism was a sort of analysis which was no more painting than the description of physical phenomena was physics.

"But now that all the elements of the aesthetic known as 'cubist' can be measured by its pictorial technique, now that the analysis of yesterday has become a synthesis by the expression of the relationships between the objects themselves, this reproach is no longer valid. If what has been called 'Cubism' is only an appearance, then Cubism has disappeared; if it is an aesthetic, then it has been absorbed into painting.

"So how do you think that at this moment I can even consider the possibility of expressing myself 'sometimes in the Cubist manner, sometimes in another artistic manner', since for me Cubism is not a manner?

"Cubism is not a manner but an aesthetic, and even a state of mind; it is therefore inevitably connected with every manifestation of contemporary thought. It is possible to invent a technique or a manner independently, but one cannot invent the whole complexity of a state of mind.

"But now I see that I have after all given you an approximate account of the development of my own painting, instead of strictly answering your questions."

This reply to a questionnaire sent out by the *Bulletin de la Vie Artistique*, Paris, was published in their edition of January 1, 1925 (sixth year, No. 1, pp. 15–17).

VII. REPLY TO A QUESTIONNAIRE

"My reply to your questions about Cubism is as follows:

"As I never consciously and after mature reflection became a Cubist, but by dint of working along certain lines have been classed as such, I have never had to think about it like someone outside the movement who was exercised in mind before taking it up.

"To-day I am clearly aware that, at the start, Cubism was simply a new way of representing the world.

"By way of natural reaction against the fugitive elements employed by the Impressionists, painters felt the need to discover less unstable elements in the objects to be represented. And they chose that category of elements which remains in the mind through apprehension and is not continually changing. For the momentary effects of light they substituted, for example, what they believed to be the local colours of objects. For the visual appearance of a form they substituted what they believed to be the actual quality of this form.

"But that led to a kind of representation which was purely analytical, for the only relationship that existed was that between the intellect of the painter and the objects, and practically never was there any relationship between the objects themselves.

"Moreover, this is perfectly natural, for each new branch of intellectual activity always begins with description, that is to say, with analysis, classification. Before the existence of physics as a science, men described and classified physical phenomena.

"Now I know perfectly well that when it began Cubism was a sort of analysis which was no more painting than the description of physical phenomena was physics.

"But now that all the elements of the aesthetic known as 'cubist' can be measured by its pictorial technique, now that the analysis of yesterday has become a synthesis by the expression of the relationships between the objects themselves, this reproach is no longer valid. If what has been called 'Cubism' is only an appearance, then Cubism has disappeared; if it is an aesthetic, then it has been absorbed into painting.

"And so now I cannot even envisage the possibility of expressing myself sometimes in the *Cubist manner* and sometimes in another artistic manner, since for me Cubism is not a manner but an aesthetic and even a state of mind.

"This being so, Cubism must inevitably be connected with every manifestation of contemporary thought. It is possible to invent a technique or a manner independently, but one cannot invent the whole complexity of a state of mind.

"Besides if, on looking at a painting, one is more conscious of the school to which it belongs than of the painting itself, then it is most probably not a good painting.

"This is said without reference to particular schools or movements for, to my mind, there is a tendency to-day to be very proud of not painting objects which resemble real objects, as the Impressionists did, but something which resembles those objects overlaid with the pictorial personality they have acquired with the passage of time.

"But perhaps, after all, I have dealt more with the development of my own painting, instead of replying impartially to your questions about Cubism.

"With apologies,

Juan Gris."

This text was first published in German under the title of "Reply" (translated by Walter Mehring) in: *Europa-Almanach*, pp. 34–35, Potsdam 1925, then in French with a foreword by Carl Einstein in: *Documents*, No. 5, pp. 267–273, Paris 1930. It amounts, in effect, to a somewhat elaborated re-statement of the reply to the questionnaire of the *Bulletin de la Vie Artistique*.

"To-day I am aware that up to 1918 my work was exclusively representational. Then came a period in which I concentrated on composition, followed by one dominated by colour. These three stages taken together represent a sort of analytical phase of my work.

"To-day, at the age of forty, I believe that I am approaching a new period of self-expression, of pictorial expression, of picture-language; a well-thought-out and well-blended unity. In short, the synthetic period has followed the analytical one."

This text was published in: *Anthology of Painting in France, from 1906 to the Present Day*, by Maurice Raynal, p.172. Aubier, Paris 1927.

[1] *Juan Gris* (Junge Kunst, Bd. 55), Leipzig, Klinckhardt and Biermann, 1929.

[2] *The Life of Juan Gris, The Death of Juan Gris*, Transition, No. 4, p. 162, July 1927.

[3] Salmon, Carco, Raynal, etc. . . .

[4] "Jeunesse": review of the book *Montmartre de nos 20 ans*, by Paul Yaki (in *Nouvelles Littéraires et Artistiques*, April 27, 1933).

[5] The annual rent of this studio was 450 francs.

[6] At the private view of the Juan Gris Exhibition at the Galerie Balaÿ et Carré.

[7] Gris was therefore of true Roman Catholic stock and not Jewish as M. Camille Mauclair claims in his "*Lettre sur l'Art*" in *L'Ami du Peuple* of April 25, 1929, where he speaks in glowing terms (he has revised his statement subsequently) of "the Jewish painters of all lands, Kisling, Soutine, Gris". In the same article he also refers to "the German Jewish aesthetician" Wilhelm Uhde, actually a son of an old Prussian Protestant family.

[8] I owe most of my information about Gris' early life to his sister Señora Antonieta Sanchez-Lefler.

[9] To-day this School is called the *Escuela Industrial*.

[10] *Vide* Part III of the present volume.

[11] Moreno Carbonero is, I suppose, the painter Jose Maria Carbonero who died in Madrid in April 1942 at the age of eighty-two. If so, he would not have been much over forty when Gris was his pupil. It often happens, of course, that the very young look on those of forty as old.

[12] It was not long, of course, before many of these painters deserted the banner of Cubism. Completely ignoring the honourable aspirations of the leaders behind whom they had ranged themselves, they had seen nothing but Cubism's external appearance, which they aped in an attempt to produce a picturesque division of the painted surface.

[13] *Vida de Manolo, contada per ell mateix*, Sabadell, 1928, p. 131.

[14] "Let us make old-fashioned verses around new thoughts."

[15] He is referring to the picture now called *The Smoker*.

[16] Picasso was at Avignon.

[17] This news was false.

[18] I received this telegram on August 17, at Siena, where I had moved to in the meantime.

[19] Gris has here used the word "*temporellement*", a mistake due to his writing in a foreign language.

[20] A local painter (1858–1922) who lived at Elne.

[21] Frank Haviland (F. Burty).

[22] He is referring to the German review of that name, which was edited in Berlin by Herwarth Walden. Walden was undoubtedly sincere and was doing his best, but his complete lack of aesthetic sensibility caused him to make the most extraordinary blunders in his choice of painters to reproduce. Moreover, as he was a real champion of the aesthetic doctrine of the German Expressionists, one can imagine how much Gris was exasperated by his review.

[23] It was just at this time that Severini saw a certain amount of Gris. It is therefore probable that some similar remark, misunderstood, is the basis for the purely apocryphal words which he has attributed to Gris: "We are all a generation of failures." It is not surprising that these words have been taken up by M. Camille Mauclair, "the words", as he calls them, "of another one who is dead, the Spanish Cubist Juan Gris, that equally abortive and unintelligible painter" ("Les Ratés" in *Le Figaro*, August 16, 1933). It is worth noting in passing that M. Mauclair had changed his opinion about Gris, of whom he had written in eulogistic terms but four years previously (cf. page 205, note 7). I suspect M. Mauclair, it is true, of having only a very vague idea of Gris' work either in 1929 or in 1933. But, in addition, it is a hobby of M. Mauclair's to make out that great artists thought themselves "failures". Consider, for example, the words he attributes to Mallarmé (*Mallarmé chez-lui*, p. 100): "But, Mauclair, we are all failures."

[24] The name of the house rented by Gris at Beaulieu.

[25] This is a reference to the illustrations for *Ne Coupez Pas,* by Max Jacob.

[26] I assume that all readers are familiar with the French system of classification of canvases from 1 to 200, there being three types of each: F for figure, P (paysage) for landscape, M (marine) for seascape.

[27] The butcher's name was Marmaronne. Shortly after this he took over an agency at the Paris *Halles*, and Gris met him again. His son—the "pupil" in question—was the model for the lithograph entitled *The Little Boy*. Gris owned two very pretty still-lifes by the body, who does not seem to have gone on with his painting.

[28] This is the lithograph entitled *Marcelle la Brune*, i.e., *The Dark Marcelle*.

[29] The lithograph of this woman is entitled *Marcelle la Blonde*, i.e., *The Fair Marcelle*. The one of her cousin is entitled *Jean le Musicien*.

[30] The ballet in question was "*Cuadro Flamenco*", for which, in the end, Picasso did the sets and costumes.

[31] Slavinsky.

[32] Maria d'Albaïcin, a Spanish gypsy.

[33] The Russian painter who devised several of the ballets. This drawing is now in the Museum of Modern Western Art in Moscow.

[34] In the end no lithographs were made and there were photographic reproductions of the originals in the programme.

[35] This refers to the article by Waldemar George which appeared in the *Cahiers Idéalistes*.

[36] See Part III of the present book, p. 193.

[37] "Jean has put on three kilos," Josette had written a few days earlier, "and it is clearly visible. He is developing a corporation and it gives him a self-satisfied air." Gris protested against these statements in the same letter.

[38] It was finally fixed at 3000 francs.

[39] *Vide* p. 153.

[40] The *décor* was by Marie Laurencin.

[41] Satie had returned from Monte Carlo as disgusted as Gris, and having quarrelled with Cocteau and Auric.

[42] It is only right that the name of Alfred Flechtheim should be associated with memories of Gris. The fame of this painter owed so much to the enthusiasm and zeal of this true lover of art, a great dealer of unrivalled energy, who, not content with merely acquiring numerous works by Gris, never ceased to extol their creator and to show his paintings throughout Germany. Alfred Flechtheim died in exile, gallant to the end, after having begun to prepare the way in England for the painters whom he had introduced to Germany. Amongst these Juan Gris occupied one of the highest places.

[43] One must, however, admit that some of the earliest and most ardent admirers of Picasso and Braque, such as Wilhelm Uhde and Roger Dutilleul, never grew to appreciate Gris. The fact is that, romantics themselves, they were caught by the romantic aspects of Cubism. In Braque and Picasso they responded to the brilliant technique, the lively draughtsmanship, the sensitive colouring and even the brushwork. They liked a dash and vivacity which the Jansenist art of Gris—that admirer of Philippe de Champaigne—could not and would not give them. Therefore they did not collect his pictures; thus proving that, in their reactions to painting, they followed the inclinations of their own temperaments and did not respond to outside influences.

[44] These were for needle-work chair-covers, designed by Gris, which my wife was making.

[45] The frescoes in the Wardrobe Tower.

[46] Ford Madox Ford, the English writer.

[47] They were designs for the above-mentioned embroideries.

[48] Georges Duthuit, the art historian.

[49] The German word *Erlebnis* describes, to my mind, most nearly the "experience lived", which I believe to be the basis of a work of art. Every *Erlebnis* includes "objects", whether perceived with a consciousness of "reality" or clearly of a subjective character.

[50] *Manuel d'Anthropologie culturelle*.

[51] *Loc. cit.*

[52] On the clothing of the Naskapi Indians of Labrador, F. G. Speek writes: "In brief, these designs are charms. According to the beliefs of their wearers, they act as a means by which their minds gain control over the minds of the animals which they hunt." (Lévy-Bruhl, *L'Expérience mystique et les symboles chez les Primitifs*, p. 229, Alcan, Paris 1938.)

These charms are "commands", but similar magic commands are frequent in painting, sculpture, and even decoration. Their presence alone is not enough to classify these garments as pictography, as there is no question of *information*.

[53] *L'Humanité Préhistorique* (*L'Evolution de l'Humanité*, Vol. 2, p. 271, Paris 1921).

[54] It seems clear that attempts were made to avoid these pictographical disadvantages in a form of representation frequently found in Australia: namely, the tracks of the animal in place of the animal itself. Lévy-Bruhl (*L'Expérience mystique et les symboles chez les Primitifs*, p. 176), quoting C. P. Mountford, mentions "Rock-paintings at Windulda, Western Australia", drawings "representing the tracks of the wallaby; these consisted of two broken, parallel tracks with a line between them, the broken lines representing the marks made by the animal's feet, the centre line by its tail. The wallaby as it hops strikes the ground with its tail, unlike the kangaroo. In general, the native who depicted an animal or a reptile only drew its tracks." Here then are signs which could be rapidly drawn by anybody and whose meaning was plain to any native. (Lévy-Bruhl, quoting Mountford, definitely confirms this.) These, however, are pictographic and not mnemonic signs, since it is clear that the image *track* evokes the image *animal*, and that the *idea* is secondary. I believe that this representation of the tracks is an example of pictography beginning to change into ideographic writing.

[55] *La Pensée Chinoise* (*L'Evolution de l'Humanité*, Vol. 25, Part II, pp. 54 and 55, Paris 1934).

[56] *Le Langage* (*L'Evolution de l'Humanité*, Vol. 3, p. 374, Paris 1921).

[57] "*Vom Bilde zum Buchstaben*": *Die Entstehungsgeschichte der Schrift. Mit einem Nachwort von Siegfried Schott.* (Untersuchungen zur Geschichte und Altertumskunde Aegyptens, Vol. 12, Hinrichs, Leipzig 1939.)

[58] *Loc. cit.*, p. 48.

[59] *Loc. cit.*, p. 52.

[60] *Loc. cit.*, pp. 54 and 55.

[61] There is no doubt that Mallarmé's *Coup de Dés* (as published in *Cosmopolis* in 1897) was the immediate starting-point for Apollinaire's experiment. Thus I have mentioned for the first time the name of the poet who, together with Cézanne, did most to create the atmosphere in which Juan Gris' art could take shape. Apollinaire, who was a great bookworm, was acquainted with the baroque poems in the form of a tree, a flower and a lyre, and perhaps even the graphic conceits of musical manuscripts, the cruciform and heart-shaped canons of the Renaissance; but without *Un Coup de Dés* he would not have thought of reviving them. Mallarmé, however, only created an atmosphere. He let a little air into the printed page; but he thought only of typographical effect and had no pictorial tendency.

[62] Granet, *loc. cit.*, p. 61.

[63] See also p. 184.

[64] Cf. my essay *Das Wesen der Bildhauerei*, in *Feuer, Jahrgang I*, Vols. 2–3, pp. 145–156, Nov.–Dec. 1919.

[65] The following passage, from *Problèmes de la Vision* by Armand de Gramont (Paris 1939), will show where such simplicity can lead. On page 79, he writes: "In fact, the painter is emmetropic or myopic, sometimes hypermetropic; he is more or less able to adapt his eye. His sight can be corrected by glasses corresponding to a fixed distance. The nature of the resulting halos will vary according to the particular plane of the landscape on which he focuses. This is doubtless one of the reasons for the different interpretations which painters can give of the same subject, provided they are sincere and assuming that they see colours normally."

Thus this physiologist claims to attribute, at least in part, the "different manifestations" of painting to the way in which painters' eyes differ—according to whether they are more or less "emmetropic, myopic, hypermetropic". According to him, therefore, if every painter had normal eyesight they would all paint an almost identical picture of the same landscape.

I should add, in the author's defence, that he at least, unlike some of his colleagues, recognises that what he calls El Greco's "elongation" is not due to astigmatism.

[66] I should add that the pseudo-antique works of the Siculo-Apulian proto-Renaissance are not empty, soulless attempts at imitation, but acts of spiritual impersonation, acts of admiration and love. For Frederick of Hohenstaufen, Rome came to life again and provided him with a dazzling model in the person of Julius Caesar.

Friedrich Gundolf writes (in *César—Histoire et Légende*, p. 87, translated by Marcel Beaufils, Rieder, Paris 1932): "Frederick was undoubtedly the first emperor to call himself Caesar, and not merely Imperator or Augustus, in official documents. In all but his administrative capacity the Emperor was often honoured with the name of Caesar during the Middle Ages. But Frederick, with a new feeling for the human personality, claimed the right, even in official documents, to add to his title of Emperor this heroic glory, which had a significance for the whole world, even beyond the sacramental magic of the name. The coins which were struck stand out, by their direct imitation of Roman profiles, from all the coins which were struck before or after his reign. They are the first Renaissance medals."

[67] Cf. my essay *Vom Sehen und vom Bilden* (Weisse Blätter, No. 7, Berlin, July 1919).

[68] Cf. also Gris' lecture "On the Possibilities of Painting" in Part III of this book, p. 195.

[69] The bastard origin of the "conventional" style has been clear to anyone of intelligence since the beginning of the schism. Eugène Pelletan, whom I quote from Tabarant (*La Vie Artistique de Baudelaire*, p. 72, Mercure de France, Paris 1942), wrote in Villemessant's *Sylphide* about the Salon of 1843: "The Institute is composed of men who were educated under the Empire; they are the poor remnants of David's school, the hollow shell of a thing which, at its peak, produced Gros, Guérin, Girodet and Gérard—the most false and futile of all schools. Now, happily for art, this school has been destroyed by M. Ingres in the field of draughtsmanship and by M. Delacroix in the realm of colour."

[70] Cf. his lecture on p. 197 in Part III.

[71] Rickert, *Der Gegenstand der Erkenntnis*, fifth edition, Tübingen 1921. I dare not translate this as "form-value", for fear of provoking a confusion which would place beauty in the forms of the work and thus make it identical with proportion.

[72] Mallarmé clearly explains the process of creation of one of his poems, *L'Azur*, in a letter to Henri Cazalis, January 12, 1864 (Henri Mondor, *Vie de Mallarmé*, Vol. 1, p. 104, Gallimard, Paris 1941): "It has caused me a great deal of trouble, because I wanted to keep ruthlessly to my subject and so banished a thousand lyrical graces and beautiful lines which ran ceaselessly through my brain. I swear that there is not a single word which hasn't cost me several hours of searching, and that the first word, which embodies the first idea, besides contributing to the general *effect* of the poem, is already an anticipation of the last one. What I search for is the *effect produced* without a dissonance or a grace-note, however lovely. I am sure now, having read these lines to myself some two hundred times, that I have achieved it. The other, the aesthetic side, still remains to be considered. Is it beautiful? Is there some reflection of beauty in it? I should be immodest if I talked about this, and it is for you to decide, Henri. . . ."

I have quoted Mallarmé as an example because he is a poet who talks a great deal about "beauty" and "the beautiful". His letter proves that he drew a clear distinction between the end he aimed at, the "general effect" of the poem over which he knew he was master, and "beauty", a "reflection" he says, which comes from another source and whose wonderful presence, not consciously evoked, should be mysteriously revealed to the reader.

[73] H. Taine, *Les Origines de la France Contemporaine: L'Ancien Régime*, 16me édition, p. 254, Paris 1891.

[74] A small number of early Christian sculptures in the round—for example, the bronze St. Peter in St. Peter's in Rome—have survived. A large number of others were destroyed by the Eastern Church during the iconoclastic outburst in the eighth century. These sculptures are evidence of a temporary survival of the pagan spirit, and therefore of pagan technique. They date from the days of Constantine and his immediate successors.

[75] *L'Esprit de la Philosophie Médiévale*, by E. Gilson, Vol. 2, p. 182, Paris 1932.

[76] *The Making of Europe*, sixth edition, pp. 108–109, London 1939.

[77] Cf. Van der Leeuw, *L'Homme primitif et la Religion*, p. 105, Paris 1940: "For primitive man, however, repetition has a quite different value. Primitive, mythical repetition is the same as reproduction. That is why it is of prime importance that each repetition should be accurate. It is essential that what has once happened should continue to happen in the same way. What is happening at this moment must 'participate' in what happened then on a single occasion."

[78] Sermon 141.

[79] *La Philosophie au Moyen-Age* (*L'Evolution de l'Humanité*, Vol. 45, p. 130, Paris 1937).

[80] Oddly enough this influence has never entirely disappeared in Spain. Even in 1937 the review *Gaçeta de Arte*, published in Sta. Cruz de Tenerife (Canary Isles), produced a monograph on the German painter Willi Baumeister rather than on Fernand Léger, who was the forerunner and undoubtedly the inspirer of Baumeister.

[81] Naturally, I cannot attempt here to investigate the origins of "the 1900 style". It is obvious that there are many other ways in which this style might have penetrated to Madrid. In Barcelona it found an outstanding exponent in the architect Gaudi. The Paris Universal Exhibition of 1900 was nothing if not a tribute to this style. It is not too much to claim that it was curiously anticipated in the stylisations of Seurat (*e.g. Le Cirque, La Parade, Le Chahut*), which Signac imitated in his early work (for example, his portraits of Fénéon).

On the other hand, the tendency to "decoration" in the painting of Gauguin and his pupils, the Symbolist Painters, had prepared the way as early as 1890 for its acceptance by the younger generation, as may be seen in the early works of the Nabis. However, one must remember that it had not reached the man in the street in Madrid. There it was only known in artistic circles, and even then only in its Munich form.

[82] It is a curious fact that the light which these painters now discovered as an autonomous factor had compelled recognition from architects four hundred years earlier. For, in fact, Gothic architecture is nothing more than the triumphal admission of light into the precincts of the mediaeval sanctum. The Romanesque church was the dark, mystic grotto which was marvellously constructed. Light was discovered about the year 1200. And in order to admit it walls had to be constructed with such perforation that it could flood in; this led to the invention of the ogival arch, to a redistribution of the thrusts and to the breaking up of the vault. It is a mistake to describe this as the spontaneous birth of a "style", which is the free exercise of technical virtuosity, or as a purely aesthetic innovation; it was simply a constructional necessity resulting from the victory of light.

The Gothic church is invaded on a grand scale by thousands of rays which form a grandiose pattern. Light counts for as much as the solid architectural body; the architectural space is the frame which blends the light rays.

In the Romanesque church, the stained-glass windows were simply pictures, just sufficiently transparent for the light to make them visible; in the Gothic church they became more and more translucent, for they had the secondary function of acting as a multicoloured filter through which the light had to pass as it streamed into the church.

By the seventeenth century light had already lost its fascination for architects, and at that time more than half the windows of Rome's basilicas were blocked up. The taste then was for semi-darkness, an equally diffused light not broken by beams, thus leaving the organic function of the structure to speak for itself. Baroque architecture set itself the task of *creating space*, as Brinckmann has demonstrated so effectively.

[83] Cf. Mondor, *loc. cit.*, p. 111. Mondor places the interview between Mallarmé and "the prophet" at the beginning of Mallarmé's career, that is to say about 1865. But there is a difficulty here. Duret, who was a friend of the Impressionist painters, states that the name only dates from 1874, and his story is generally accepted. He writes in his *Histoire des Peintres Impressionnistes* (p. 20, Floury, Paris 1906): "Claude Monet had sent some particularly characteristic works [to the exhibition of the Société Anonyme des Artistes Peintres in 1874], and it was one of these that gave rise to the name. He was exhibiting five pictures, one of which was entitled *Impression, soleil levant*, a view in a harbour.... Such a work was the epitome of the new art. Thus, by its title and also by the way in which it was painted, it suggested the name *Impressionists* as being the term which seemed most aptly to characterise these artists. This word, which came almost spontaneously to the lips of the visitors to the exhibition, was taken up and applied by *Charivari* (then run by Pierre Véron) on April 25. One of the editors, Louis Leroy, headed the article dealing with the exhibition on the Boulevard des Capucines *Exposition des Impressionnistes*. The new name was of course only used in a strictly unfavourable sense with an implication of ignorance and presumption. The term Impressionist passed into common usage on the occasion of the second exhibition (at the Durand-Ruel Gallery in 1876). During the exhibition they published

a paper with illustrations called *L'Impressionniste, journal d'art*."

It is therefore difficult to imagine Hugo calling Mallarmé "impressionist" several years earlier. At the same time it is no less evident that even the invention of this anecdote is significant.

[84] *Ibid.*, pp. 144 and 145.

[85] *Variations sur un sujet*: Œuvres Complètes de Mallarmé (N.R.F., Pléiade, 1945), p. 365.

[86] I was rather afraid that I was merely repeating commonplaces. But I have just read in *Cahiers du Sud* (Marseilles, April 1941) some extracts from a new work by MM. Henri Cotard and René Cerisier which makes it apparent that even the modern protagonists of Cézanne have not got anything on his friends. To quote: "His incapacity for spontaneous self-expression caused him to submit passively to the influence of those who thought of him as blind and gave him their means of expression in order to try and be helpful." Or again: "Having no connection with time or space their forms vacillate in an unbalanced world. However, although certain canvases of Cézanne seem to proclaim an interest in architectural construction, we must distinguish the qualities which are inherent in the work of art from those with which we endow it; for what enables us to differentiate the planes and introduce them unconsciously into the world of Cézanne is our habitual reaction in front of nature and our physical reflexes" (*loc. cit.*, p. 235).

Naturally I have only quoted these naïve lucubrations to show that the idea of Cézanne as a sort of madman still exists even in the minds of those who pretend to admire him. I do not feel, therefore, that it is a waste of energy to explain the real drama inside Cézanne, which caused him to say that he could not manage "to realise". It was neither a case of "repression" nor of "obsession", as the authors of the above passage, in their ignorance of the problems confronting a painter, seem to think. Need I add that they also make free use of phrases such as "lopsided houses and drunken jars", which were used by the critics between 1890 and 1910?

An article like this is a useful reminder that one is not tilting at windmills.

[87] I think it is worth while recalling the origin of this name, which speaks volumes about the state of mind of these painters when the group was founded (1889). The following is the account by Maurice Denis (*Paul Sérusier: A B C de la Peinture, suivi d'une Etude sur la Vie et l'Œuvre de Paul Sérusier*, by Maurice Denis, pp. 44 and 45, Floury, Paris 1942): "It was at this time of struggle and enthusiasm that Sérusier had the idea of calling us all together occasionally around a table in a modest eating-house in the Passage Brady, near Julian's studio. These were called the dinners of the Nabis or *Nabiim*, which means 'The Prophets' in Hebrew. Sérusier had learnt this word from his friend Cazalis, who was studying under Ledrain; I have already remarked that Sérusier's interest in the semitic

languages dated from his school-days. The name he chose for us implied that, as distinct from the studios, we were initiates of a sort of secret society, the ways of which were mysterious, and that we were permanently in a state of prophetic rapture."

[88] These artists originally appeared with a name of their own choosing: "*Peintres Symbolistes et Synthétistes*". The original members of the group exhibited at the Café Volpini during the Universal Exhibition of 1889.

[89] This name, like that of Cubism later, was invented by Louis Vauxcelles, then the critic of *Gil Blas*, who described the room where the pictures by these artists were hung at the Indépendants as being "the cage of wild beasts".

[90] It is essential to check very carefully such information as is given by Vlaminck in his various volumes of reminiscences. However, he can be believed when he states that he first saw the painting of van Gogh in 1901, and one is probably justified in thinking that Derain first saw it at about the same time. Cf. *Portraits avant Décès*, p. 30, Flammarion, Paris 1943.

[91] Vlaminck has not forgotten this, and refers to it in *Portraits avant Décès* on p. 37. On p. 72 of the same volume he also recounts Derain's objection to this really rather too simple procedure which Derain described as "a dyer's theory". According to Vlaminck, Derain used to say to him: "You will never get a red more red or a blue more blue than the one made by the colour-merchant." From this it is clear that Derain did not mean that he would get more "beautiful" colours there, but more "expressive" ones than those ready-made.

[92] From 1900 until 1920 Derain tended towards expressionistic distortion. In *Portraits avant Décès*, p. 33, Vlaminck quotes a letter from Derain, the exact date is not given, but which must have been written in the summer of 1901, since Derain mentions with dismay his imminent departure on military service. Writing from Pornic, Derain says: "... Here it is just like Garenne-Bezons with the sea ... impossible to work ... the sea is ridiculous ... it doesn't excite me any more. The only things I am interested in are the windmills. There is one particular spot with a windmill ... a road ... some telegraph poles; it's magnificent! especially for making the mill go round. I think it is all in the drawing ... the mill must be drawn out so as to get the right proportions between the sails and the height of the mill. ... The telegraph wires must be made enormous; so much goes on along them." This liking for unpromising sites was very characteristic of the painters from Chatou. Garenne-Bezons is an area west of Paris renowned for its flatness and ugliness; Derain and Vlaminck would have passed through it in the train between Chatou and Paris.

[93] Sérusier says that this use of "symbolical colours" was also advocated by Gauguin. It is my impression, however, that at least in this particular the majority of *The Fauves* were guided by the example of van Gogh; it is certainly true of Vlaminck and Derain.

94 "Decorative painting is true painting; painting was only created to decorate the blank walls of the human edifice with thoughts, dreams, and ideas." (Albert Aurier, art critic and friend of Gauguin, in the *Mercure de France*, March 1891, quoted here from *Les Etapes de la Peinture Française* by Bernard Dorival, Vol. 1, p. 107, N.R.F., Paris 1943.)

95 It should be clear that I am only trying to define in general terms a psychological aesthetic process. It never occurred to these painters to please *any particular* spectators among their contemporaries, the great majority of whom found the Fauve pictures simply hideous.

96 French translation by Marguerite Faure, p. 94, Librairie de l'Art Catholique, Paris 1926.

97 Gauguin was quite aware of this, for in a letter to Daniel de Monfreid, written from Tahiti in July 1898, asking him to organise an exhibition of his work, he says: "It is as useless to send [invitations] to the old gang Sérusier, Denis and company, as it is to send to the Press."

98 Formerly in the Jacques Doucet collection, now in the Museum of Modern Art, New York.

99 It seems pointless to describe once again the origin of the word (cf. *Der Weg zum Kubismus*, p. 15. I must, however, make one correction: Braque sent six pictures to the Salon d'Automne, all of which were rejected. Marquet "rescued" one, Guérin another. But Braque withdrew them all). Its originator was, needless to say (as in the case of *Fauvism*), Louis Vauxcelles who, doubtless copying a "crack" of Matisse, spoke of "*Cubes*" in his review of the Braque Exhibition at my gallery in the Rue Vignon (*Gil Blas*, November 14, 1908) and of "*Bizarreries cubiques*" (still referring to Braque) in the following spring, when he reviewed the Indépendants for the same paper (May 25, 1909).

Thus the name was invented by an adversary, as also happened with Impressionism and even with "Realism" in the case of Courbet. The latter wrote in his manifesto (on the occasion of his private exhibition in 1855): "I have been labelled a Realist just as the men of 1830 were labelled Romantics. Names have never given a fair idea of things: if they did, the works themselves would be superfluous."

Furthermore, "conscious and organised movements" which choose their own name are equally untrustworthy. In doing this they betray either their artificiality or their submission to the will of an ambitious leader. I am reminded of "Syntheticism", the "Nabis", the "Rose-Croix", "Futurism", "Musicalism", "Constructivism", and "Surrealism".

100 *Paul Sérusier: A B C de la Peinture, suivi d'une Etude sur la Vie et l'Œuvre de Paul Sérusier*, by Maurice Denis, p. 43, Floury, Paris 1942.

101 Denis, *loc. cit.*, p. 64.

I shall return later (p. 128) to these pseudo-neo-Platonic dreams of the symbolist painters, whose pictures in reality owed their "legibility" to the fact that the artists never invented any new emblems.

102 *Loc. cit.*, p. 100.

103 *La Peinture Française au XXme Siècle*, p. 14, Floury, Paris 1937.

104 *André Derain* (Junge Kunst, Vol. 15, Klinckhardt und Biermann, Leipzig 1919).

105 I have referred above to Picasso's attempts to use a sculptural technique to avoid chiaroscuro—but these attempts only began in 1909. There have been many precedents in the history of art for such an attempt; chiaroscuro is only one of innumerable means of obtaining relief in painting. I shall only mention here the "sunken relief" used by the Egyptians throughout the whole Pharaonic period.

"For sculpture exposed to a full light and visible from afar," writes G. Jéquier (*Manuel d'Archéologie Egyptienne, I, "Les Eléments de l'Architecture"*, pp. 83–84, Picard, Paris 1924), "they did not use ordinary relief but the process of sunken relief, which gives to figures an extraordinarily clear silhouette, with a line of shadow on one side and of light on the other. This makes up for the almost complete absence of modelling. . . . As in all Egyptian sculpture, vivid, flat colouring, which has now disappeared, emphasised the relief and gave life both to small scenes and large compositions."

In accordance with current terminology, Jéquier refers to these works as *sculptures*. Now if, despite the use of sculptural means, the ordinary Egyptian relief is really painting, then the graphic spirit is even more evident in sunken relief, which is *coloured drawing* and creates a false effect of volume by a technique related to sculpture. The extreme economy of modelling permits a comparison of this process with Picasso's experiment.

106 I have discussed this question of enclosed space in Cubist painting in *Der Weg zum Kubismus*.

107 Confusing art history with legend, ingenuous journalists have given credence to Vlaminck's story of how he was the first to purchase an African object. And so the tale of this painter's "discovery" of Negro Art, and of how he imparted it to his friends, who were amazed, has spread.

There had always been curio-mongers who bought the ornaments, sculptures and exotic masks assembled by retired seafarers. One shop, "*Au Vieux Rouet*", even specialised in this trade. It was owned by the late M. Heymann, "the slavedealer of the Rue de Rennes" as we called him, and it became our chief source of supply. However, the curio-lovers who had preceded us regarded their acquisitions only as picturesque freaks, and Vlaminck undoubtedly had nothing else in mind when he made his purchase.

To make a real *discovery* of African and Pacific art possible, it would have been necessary for Picasso's work in the autumn of 1906, prior to *Les Demoiselles d'Avignon*, to create the right atmosphere for this widening of the aesthetic horizon. Some of us made our discovery among the gloomy show-cases of the former Musée Ethnographique in the Trocadero (now the Musée de l'Homme). Vlaminck made no such discovery in a *bistro*: one only has to look at his pictures to be convinced of this. Sometimes his pictures had a "negroid appearance" (the figures of 1908, for example), but there was never that spiritual affinity with African and Pacific Art which existed in the work of those artists who saw beyond outward appearances.

In any case, it is not important to establish who first *acquired* a "negro" object, a word used by us for African and Oceanian objects alike. From personal knowledge I can state that there was a "Tiki" from the Marquis Islands in Picasso's studio in 1907. Braque, in 1908, possessed an African mask and Matisse had a collection of about twenty pieces from different places. Derain had the Congo mask to which Vlaminck referred.

[108] See Part III, p. 192.

[109] Doin, Paris 1930.

[110] This sort of assimilation is impossible even from a psychological point of view. It takes no account, in fact, of the circumstances in which the modern child grows up. From the moment it opens its eyes the modern child is surrounded by images: advertisements in the street, engravings, photographs, even the pictures and drawings in its room. When it starts to draw for itself, it will almost always be in response to the imitative instinct which inspires so much of its behaviour, for it will have seen grown-ups drawing, often for its amusement. The *decisive step*, and the only one which counts, is when it passes this stage and realises the *connection of the sign with the thing signified*. This is the crucial problem. The child will realise the meaning of the vocal sign through learning to talk, and that of the formative graphic sign by learning to see with the aid of picture-books.

It is as absurd to compare a child's first efforts at drawing with the origins of plastic art as it is to maintain that its first gurglings re-enact the birth of human language. In both cases, instead of creating from nothing, it receives the heritage of its parents, whereas the really amazing thing about the beginnings of any form of speech or writing is the *discovery* of the possibility of signifying things.

Luquet furthermore ignores the real problem. His examination of infant and primitive psychology never touches more than the fringe of *art*. The act of drawing does not turn a child into a painter any more than the act of speech makes it a poet, so long as the act is merely imitative. For the artist like the poet is driven by his daemon to create; both are possessed and, to explain the mystery of artistic creation, one must define the nature of their possession.

It is astonishing that such mistakes are still made to-day. In 1894 Grosse, in his *Anfänge der Kunst*, proved that there was no similarity between Primitive Art and the pseudo-art of children.

[111] *Ibid.*, p. 252.

[112] At one time Rousseau's visions were generally attributed to so-called recollections of his expedition to Mexico, where there are neither Arabs, nor lions, nor tigers. I do not believe that anyone still upholds this pseudo-historical explanation.

[113] p. 11. Museum of Modern Art, New York 1941.

[114] N.R.F., Paris 1941.

[115] "*Deviazioni Artistiche: Chi è l'Evangelista del Cubismo*", *La Domenica del Corriere*, Milan, July 27–August 3, 1913.

[116] Ed. Figuière, Paris 1913.

[117] *Maurice de Vlaminck*, Junge Kunst, Vol. 11, Klinckhardt und Biermann, Leipzig 1920.

[118] Therefore these pictures should not be framed in the Renaissance type of frame, which leads the eye into the picture, but in what is called "reverse section". Alternatively, these pictures can be given a simple edging and fixed to a background (a board, for example) without any frame, so as to make the objects stand out in relief. Habit unfortunately is causing more and more of these pictures to be framed in fine old frames which are quite contrary to their rhythm.

[119] Cf. Gris' letter of September 17, 1913, from Céret, in which he points out that a collector can, for example, exchange the engraving which is *collé* for a picture of himself without disturbing the unity of the picture: "You are right, as a matter of fact; in principle the picture should be left as it is. But, once M. Brenner has acquired the picture, if he wants to substitute something else for this engraving—his portrait, for example—he is free to do so. It may look better or it may look worse, like changing the frame on a picture, but it won't upset the merits of the picture."

[120] I do not wish to be misunderstood. This was not a case of "infantilism", nor of contempt for the technique of painting. It was, on the contrary, an attempt to discover a medium adapted to their new aim. The invention of oil paint originally became necessary because painters undertook a complete inventory of the outer world. The painters of 1912 felt that the medium created by the painters of the fifteenth century was no longer adequate to their purpose, which was so radically different from that of the Renaissance. I remember many conversations that I had at the time with Gris, as well as with Picasso and Braque, about this so-called unfitness; they were all of one mind in distrusting oil paint. And yet, in the end, they retained this medium, which apparently proved capable of adaptation.

[121] I am fully aware how difficult it is to prove that a picture is either dynamic or static. For example, Léger believes that his painting is dynamic, whereas to me it is static. So, when I say that Picasso and Braque are dynamic I am expressing what I know intuitively rather rationally. Yet there are certain very striking indications of this difference. In the whole *œuvre* of Gris, whether

painted or engraved, there is *not a single* example of a moving figure, not even in his book illustrations. There is no need for me to emphasise how frequently moving figures occur in the work of Picasso. Again: long before Calder began to make his "mobiles" Picasso had dreamt of sculpture which would be set in motion mechanically. This was about 1912, as I have recorded in *Der Weg zum Kubismus*. Picasso also had the idea of pictures which would begin to "move" like targets at a fair when a switch was pressed. Braque never went as far as that, but one can often find figures in motion in his pictures, as for example the *Bathers*. In his engravings and sculptures a chariot drawn by two rearing horses frequently appears. These facts are, I repeat, merely indications. It must be clear—and I shall return to this point in discussing Gris in a moment—that a Still-Life can be dynamic. But I believe that the psychological significance of a painter's predilection for, or aversion to, subjects in motion cannot be overlooked.

At the same time it is not enough just to paint figures in motion. That does not of itself produce "dynamic painting", despite the Italian Futurists who, in their first manifestos in about 1912, proclaimed that only the painting of movement was capable of expressing life to-day. It was their intention to paint trains, motor-cars and trams in motion; but the majority of them only succeeded in producing perfectly static pictures. And yet they created a special technique for this naïvely anecdotal form of imitation. Some of them were content to elongate the subject in the direction of its movement; others attempted something more subtle which, as I have remarked in *Der Weg zum Kubismus*, was, nevertheless, not capable of creating the effect they were after. These painters decomposed movement, a method which was also used by Marcel Duchamp at about the same time in his *Nude Descending a Staircase*. This figure is represented more than once at different stages of its movement. Duchamp's "Nude" is shown three times on three different stairs and in three different positions. What vitiates this procedure is the fact that the spectator sees three images of the "Nude" *simultaneously*; thus he sees three separate "Nudes", and not one "Nude" descending the staircase. In the case of the Stroboscope and the cinema the illusion is created by the fact that the images are presented *successively*; hence, all subsequent images are seen in relation to the original image, which thereby begins to "move".

[122] It would appear that Gris was not entirely conscious of this hiatus in his work. He wanted to get away from the multiplicity of aspects, and he wanted more than ever to make the detail subservient to the whole. Yet one can feel a certain confusion. On March 26, 1915, he wrote to me from Paris: "I think that I have been making some progress in the last few months and that my canvases are beginning to acquire a unity which they used to lack. They no longer consist of those inventories of objects which used to depress me so much. However, I have got

to make a great effort yet to attain what I have in mind, for I can feel that no matter how clearly developed my ideas are, I cannot say the same for my way of expressing them plastically. In short, I have not got an aesthetic, and only experience can give me that."

He worked hard, but he was often dissatisfied with the result. On June 1, 1915, just at the time when he was producing these "dynamic" pictures, he wrote to me: "I am working a great deal and not getting much done. Of every five pictures three are failures. All the same it is getting better, because my painting has become less dry, more plastic."

Then he recovered again, and on September 7, 1915, he wrote: "In the last few days I have done two or three pictures with which I am quite pleased. They will be of more value to me for development than because of their own importance."

[123] Gris was aware that he had taken an important step. On December 14, 1915, he wrote again from Paris: "My life is still the same; I fight boredom with work. It goes in waves; I work very hard until my enthusiasm and confidence are exhausted, then for a time there follows a deep depression. At the moment I have got a good period. Let's hope it lasts! I have no great hopes or aspirations for I cannot see the end of it all. The future probably holds many a frustration in store for me. However, I find consolation in my belief that I have made progress with my painting. It seems to me that it is settling down, that everything is becoming precise and concrete. That goes for the ideas as well as for their sequence; as for the pictorial side I cannot be sure. Sometimes everything I paint seems to me like so much folly (*sic*). I never seem to be able to find any room in my pictures for that sensitive, sensuous side which I feel ought always to be there. Maybe I'm wrong to look for the pictorial qualities of an earlier age in a new form of art. At all events I find my pictures excessively cold. But Ingres is cold too, and yet it is good, and so is Seurat; yes, so is Seurat, whose meticulousness annoys me almost as much as my own pictures. Oh, how I wish I had the freedom and the charm of the unfinished! Well, it can't be helped. One must after all paint as one is oneself. My mind is too precise to go dirtying a blue or twisting a straight line." He thus reproached himself apparently for that honesty, which he regarded as a weakness, but to which he always remained true.

[124] *Vide, Variations sur un sujet*; Œuvres Complètes de Mallarmé (N.R.F., Pléiade, 1945) p. 368.

[125] Paul Sérusier, *loc. cit.*, p. 64.

[126] *Vide* also p. 185.

[127] I do not think I am mistaken in identifying it here although I have denied its presence in the works of the Symbolist painters. Gris was not so voluble as the Nabis in pouring out a flood of pseudo-neo-Platonism. Nowhere in his writings can one find a mention of Plato, nor of Plotinus, nor even of the Occultists whom he enjoyed so

much and through whose works he came to know Platonist thought. It is nevertheless worth noting one reflection at the beginning of his lecture: "Nails are made from nails, for if the idea of the possibility of a nail did not exist in advance, there would be a serious risk that the material might be used to make a hammer or a curling tong." And the same conviction that the idea precedes creation is inherent in the formulation of Gris' method which he gave in 1920 when he said that he proceeded "*from the general to the particular*".

[128] Letter to his brother Karl written in the spring of 1801: "There is only one quarrel in the world: which is more important, the whole or the part?"

[129] Letter to Wilmans dated April 2, 1804: "I feel quite certain that I have written against my eccentric enthusiasm and that I have thus attained a Greek simplicity."

[130] In *Die Günderode*: "Not what I will, but what thou wilt."

[131] *Divagations*, p. 252, new ed., Fasquelle, Paris 1943.

[132] It is evident that the "heroic period" of Cubism was *classical*: this is proved by the rigid design, the ascetic colour and the fact that in any composition the parts are firmly subjugated to the whole. Not until 1914 did Picasso and Braque once more allow their romantic temperament to break out. Analytical Cubism was a purely classical period, for Picasso and Braque as well as for Gris. In the period of Synthetic Cubism only Gris remained classical. Not one of the painters doubted the classical nature of Cubism in 1911 any more than I did. By way of proof I would like to recall Picasso's remark at the time (previously quoted in my own little book on Derain): "Van Gogh: he's a cheap sentimentalist!" This remark was meant to imply all the censure of the Cubist painter, obsessed with order, simplicity and concentration, for the romantic who yielded to every impulse. Picasso has subsequently changed his opinion of van Gogh but I never heard Juan Gris say a good word about him.

As for myself, I never tired of emphasising the classical tendencies of Cubism. I remember a particular discussion with Léon Werth, who was a friend of Vlaminck and a supporter of post-Fauve painting. "Cubism," he said to me, "that's not Racine, but Mademoiselle de Scudéry." History, has not, I think, confirmed his judgement.

[133] *Nord-Sud*, No. 4, December 1917, "*Pensées et Réflexions sur la Peinture*".

[134] *Figaro Littéraire*, November 15, 1941; cf. *Verve*, No. 2, p. 7, Paris 1938.

[135] Gris realised that he was continuing the tradition of painting. Here is what he wrote to me from Paris on August 25, 1919, about his work of the last three years: "I held an exhibition last April with a certain amount of success. I showed about fifty pictures painted in 1916, 1917 and 1918. They looked rather well together and quite a lot of people came. And yet I don't really know quite how much they liked it, for there is so much admiration for the flattest mediocrity; people rave about the products of disorder, but no-one likes discipline and clarity. The exaggerations of the Dada movement and others like Picabia make us all look like classics: I can't say I mind about that. I should like to continue the painting tradition with plastic means, while bringing to it a new aesthetic based on the intellect. There seems to me no reason why one should not pinch Chardin's technique without taking over the appearance of his pictures or his conception of reality. Those who believe in abstract painting are like weavers who think they can produce a material with only one set of threads and forget that there has to be another set to hold these together. Where there is no attempt at plasticity how can you control representational liberties? And where there is no concern for reality how can you limit and unite plastic liberties? For some time I have been quite pleased with my own work, because I think that at last I am entering on a period of realisation. What's more, I have been able to test my progress: formerly, when I started on a picture I was satisfied at the beginning and dissatisfied at the end. Now the beginning is always rotten and I am fed up, but I get an agreeable surprise at the end. I have also been successful in ridding my painting of a too brutal and descriptive reality. It has, so to speak, become more poetic. I hope I shall come to express with great precision a reality imagined in terms of pure intellectual elements; this really means painting which is inaccurate but precise, that is to say the reverse of bad painting which is accurate but unprecise."

The importance of this letter must be evident. It contains everything: a reasoned condemnation of "abstract painting", as well as of Dada, a declaration in favour of "conceptual" painting, and finally the first reference to "poetic" painting, an idea which was shortly to assume great importance.

[136] *Peindre est une gageure*, Cahiers du Sud, p. 136, March 1941. This article appeared also in a poor translation in *Horizon*, Vol. 7, No. 39, March 1943.

[137] *The Life of Juan Gris; The Death of Juan Gris*, Transition, No. 4, pp. 160–162, July 1927.

[138] Cf. his letter of November 27, 1921: "As you know I like definitions and have a good idea of the value of words, so I have been thinking of what is really meant by *quality* in an artist, a word which I once told you I did not quite understand. Well, now I believe that the quality of an artist is due to the amount of the past that he carries in him, to his artistic atavism. The more of this inheritance he has, the more quality he has. This is quite apart from his natural gifts and his talent, that is to say his realisations or his style. The simulation of quality means falling into pastiche, and so does the exaggeration of what one has. One is always sufficiently like one's parents without having to put on their clothes."

This was Gris' explanation one year later of why he gave up wearing the "clothes" of his own parents in the autumn of 1920.

139 Cf. also his letter of January 8, 1920 (about the picture he was exhibiting at the Indépendants): "I am not displeased with the colour, but I am afraid on that account, for it seems to me my weakness."

140 Cf. his letter of December 2, 1919: "expressionism, that extravagant stylisation". On the subject of Dada there is a passage in the same letter and also in his letter of August 25, 1919, against "Dada and others like Picabia".

141 Cf. Part III, p. 201, "Reply to the Questionnaire: *Chez les Cubistes*".

142 Cf. his letter of August 25, 1919: "I should like to continue the painting tradition with plastic means, while bringing to it a new aesthetic based on the intellect."

143 Cf. Part III, p. 193, and "On the Possibilities of Painting", pp. 195–201.

144 Masson, *loc. cit.*

145 *Ibid.*

146 *Ibid.*

147 The instigators of this periodical were Kandinsky, Klee, Macke and Marc. It contains reproductions of numbers of Cubist pictures. Admittedly both Expressionism and Cubism were reactions against the same evil tendencies—academic torpor and impressionist deliquescence. The contribution of the German painters to this general movement of revivification was well in keeping with their country's spirit. The faith and enthusiasm of *Der Blaue Reiter* are quite touching, and even to-day one cannot turn its pages without feeling an emotion. It is a living record of a mighty movement which embraced all the arts, every kind of spiritual manifestation. Thus, one finds among the contributors that great artist Arnold Schoenberg, whose austere figure dominates the music of our time. In those days he was among the Expressionists and made use of a non-musical factor —words—to provide the unity of his longer compositions, all of which were then written around texts. It was not until a few years later that he started the new era in music (cf. p. 174).

148 I remember another conversation with Derain in 1920, in his studio at number 13 Rue Bonaparte, Paris, when he told me that in order to paint a plant one had to know about its properties. I should also mention another of his remarks (quoted by Raynal in *Anthologie*, p. 122): "I am not interested in reproducing an object, but in reproducing what used to be called its 'virtue'." His mind was still occupied apparently with the expressionist ideas of his youth, although to be sure it is not easy to find any trace of them in his work after 1914. Gris would have regarded this interest in "forces" (a category to which the "properties" of plants belong) as the curiosity of a chemist, not of a painter. For Gris, an object was simply a grouping of flat coloured forms, and he added: "The man who, when he paints a bottle, attempts to express its material substance rather than paint a group of coloured forms should be a glass-blower, not a painter" (*vide*, "On the Possibilities of Painting", Part III). This is, of course, the formulation of an idea produced by passing through "Synthetic Cubism". Originally Gris had attempted to indicate material qualities as well as others.

The difference between Expressionism and Cubism is that of the painter's object.

149 A former Convent at the corner of the Rue de Sèvres and the Boulevard des Invalides, which was taken over by the State following the laws against religious congregations. The building was due for demolition, but in the interval it was let out in sections to private tenants. As many of the rooms were large, it was a favourite place for painters. Matisse ran a studio there from 1908 till 1909. He had a number of German and Scandinavian pupils, including Purrmann, Rudolf Levy, Moll, Grünwald and Nils de Dardel. The American painter Bruce was also a pupil.

150 Despite noisy manifestos and expensively organised exhibitions, *Futurism* was only one form of Expressionism, an Italian form. The more gifted of the painters who belonged to this movement did their best to copy the appearance of Cubist pictures. The "force" which they intended to make felt was *movement*. After Boccioni's death in 1914, the group broke up. Carrà and Soffici reverted to academicism; and, after a few years spent in the wake of Cubism, Severini too had a similar end. Marinetti's elaborate selection of watchwords—of which the latest was *aero-pittura*, bird's-eye painting—served merely to rally a few second-class figures.

151 Masson, *loc. cit.*

152 *Ibid.*

153 *Vide, Über den Unterschied zwischen lyrischer, epischer und tragischer Dichtung.*

"The lyric poem, idealist in appearance, is ingenuous in its meaning. It is a never-ending image of a single emotion.

"The epic poem, artless in appearance, is heroic in its meaning. It is the image of great aspirations.

"The tragic poem, heroic in appearance, is idealist in its meaning. It is the image of an intellectual conception."

154 "A lyricism of colour, examples of which are too rare, fills his [Braque's] work with a harmonious rapture, and Saint Cecilia herself makes music on his musical instruments. In his valleys can be heard the buzz of the bees of all our youth as they gather honey, and the happiness of innocence languishes on his civilised terraces. This painter is angelic. Purer than other men, he ignores everything foreign to his art which might suddenly distract him from the paradise in which he lives."

155 *Vide, De mon temps*, p. 86 (quoted here from Mondor, *loc. cit.*, p. 683).

156 He felt this so strongly that he preferred his painting to be classed as decoration rather than have it mixed up with "images and symbols". On February 10, 1921, he wrote to me from Bandol: "You can't imagine how delighted I was to hear that you liked the pictures. I have no bad memories, either of them or of the remorse which so often seizes me after I have despatched some pictures.

Of course, it is decoration. One should never be afraid of a word once one knows its meaning: all painting always has been decoration. Only things which are images or symbols are not decoration."

It is evident from the context that Gris was here attributing to the word "decoration" the meaning of "autonomous composition destined to be hung on a wall"—the emphasis being on the word "autonomous". It is worth noting that, by affirming that *all authentic* painting is decoration, he was attacking a theory which is still current: that Cubism is decoration and therefore nothing to do with painting. He, on the other hand, refused to accept as painting anything which he considered to be imagery or literature.

[157] *Vide, Die Günderode.* "Poetry is that spirit alone which has in it the secret of an innate rhythm, and only through this rhythm can the secret become visible and vital, because this rhythm is its soul, whereas the poems are simply diagrams and not spirits with souls.

"Poetry obeys higher laws, and every emotion develops according to new laws, which cannot be applied to any other. For everything which is true is prophetic and floods its own period with light. To poetry alone is it given to spread this light, and for this reason the spirit should not and cannot be made manifest except through it. The spirit only manifests itself in rapture. Rhythm only obeys the man in whom the spirit comes to life."

[158] In a letter to F. Vielé-Griffin, dated August 8, 1891 (Mondor, *loc. cit.,* p. 616), Mallarmé wrote: "*Tout le mystère est là ; établir les identités secrètes par un deux à deux qui ronge et use les objets, au nom d'une centrale pureté.*" Gris, of course, had never seen this letter, but it gives a beautiful definition of his poetics.

[159] Page 32, Gallimard, Paris 1939. "The poem only exists where there is an implacable taking possession of the soul, for which rhythm is the instrument; it only exists where the repeated and regular shocks of an exact mechanism maintain the soul in a sort of vigilant torpor like the mysterious receptivity of a medium, so that everything is excluded which is not the pure suspense in anticipation of the unforeseeable."

If the meaning of the word "rhythm" is somewhat extended, this is a very pertinent definition of a poem. It is clear from the context, and from the choice of poems in the Anthology, that Thierry-Maulnier means by "rhythm" a submission to a pre-determined metre. Eluard too—using the terms in which Baudelaire defined the *prose* which he dreamt for his "little prose poems"—accepts this restrictive meaning of the word, for he writes that contemporary poetry is "poetic prose, musical, without rhythm and without rhyme, sufficiently supple and jaunty to adapt itself to the lyrical movements of the soul, to the modulations of musing, to the sudden starts of conscience". I must, therefore, make it clear that in talking of "rhythm" I do not mean to limit the meaning to a pre-determined metre which bridles the emotion. By "poetic rhythm" I

mean a cadence which is objectively indefinable, but which arises out of the confrontation of the poet's *Erlebnis* with the verbal forms which render this experience communicable. This is the sort of rhythm which I detect in the poems of Eluard or Tzara, whereas it is absent from many a poem in regular verse, possibly through lack of authentic experience, or because this experience has not managed to pass into the forms through which it is meant to be expressed.

With Gris, undoubtedly, one finds "the repeated and regular shocks of an exact mechanism". Although Gris made use of apt means (they were normal in poetry and only novel in painting) to "scan" his "poem" such, for example, as rhyme, the rhythm of every one of his works is none the less consubstantial with it and a completely free agent.

[160] In my opinion it is also a mistake to talk of the existence of a rhythm in time due to the spectator moving around a free standing sculpture or a building, or to his moving through the interior. The spectator sees a *plurality of appearances*, each perceived successfully, but not connected with one another in the spectator's apperception; for with each glance he registers only what he is seeing at that particular moment. It is not difficult to prove that a spectator frequently interrupts his movement in order to look longer at one particular aspect. He at once becomes static like the work of art at which he is looking.

A painter in his work can only offer a single aspect. But sculptors and architects must anticipate, prepare for and interrelate the plurality of aspects which their work will possess owing to its three-dimensional existence. Each of these aspects must be endowed with a unity which preserves the natural rhythm, a rhythm which can only be spatial.

[161] Gris put most faith, however, in the character of the *spiritual* reality of this creation or, to be more precise, in the spiritual reality of a pictorial fact. On March 30, 1921, he wrote to me from Bandol: "I have written a long reply to Ozenfant on the subject of his *Purisme* which he sent to me. I think you would have approved of the reply. It is just as grotesque to talk of a craftsman copying the objects in one of my pictures as it would be to talk of executing a Poussin or a Chardin in sculpture. More particularly since a picture should not be a plan which can be executed in three dimensions. If Picasso ever started this hare, so much the worse for him!"

Picasso did, as a matter of fact, entertain the idea in about 1911 that objects should be so represented in a picture that any technician could manufacture them.

[162] *Vide* Part III, p. 192.
[163] *Vide* Part III, p. 192.
[164] *Vide* Part III, p. 193.
[165] *Vide* Part III, p. 192.
[166] This picture was subsequently destroyed. It is, however, significant that he should have wanted to paint a portrait at that moment.

[167] Naturally, I did nothing of the kind. Gris, on his return, selected and destroyed the failures.

[168] Cf. J. M. Power, *Eléments de la Construction picturale*, Roche, Paris 1933 (Analysis V), for the analysis of one of Gris' pictures from the point of view of traditional composition.

[169] He was not just a logician; far from it. For proof I need only mention his study of occult subjects to which I have already referred. It is not possible to avoid the connection between what he read and the magical power of direct evocation with which he tried to endow his emblems by "qualifying" them. One must remember that Mallarmé also has been treated as a logician. But he, too, "never ceased to pay discreet but genuine heed to the quality of magic, the Cabbala" (Mondor, *loc. cit.*, p.673).

[170] Let me recall Schiller's phrase quoted by Henri Mondor (*Vie de Mallarmé*, Gallimard, Paris 1941), from Basch and Thibaudet: "When I sit down to write a poem, what I most frequently see before me is its musical element and not a clear idea of the subject, about which I am often not entirely clear myself." T. S. Eliot, to my mind, gives an even more significant description of the creation of a poem: "I know, however, that a poem or a section of a poem tends to appear first in the shape of a rhythm before developing into words, and that this rhythm is capable of giving birth to the idea and the image" (from a lecture delivered at the University of Glasgow on February 29, 1942). It is clear that with Eliot, as with Gris, the rhythm is the prime factor.

[171] *Loc. cit.*, pp. 74–76.

[172] One may perhaps recall a saying of Cézanne's quoted by Gasquet: "Drawing is complete abstraction..." Cézanne doubtless referred mainly to the absence of colour in drawing, which involves a "transcription" in black or red chalk and is thus a first "abstraction". However, he certainly had in mind also the strange faculty of pure line drawing to "make an abstraction" of volume by discarding chiaroscuro. Cézanne put his finger on the non-illusionist character of drawing, which exists directly it is no longer the simple transcription of a picture in black and white; that is to say, directly it is a strict line drawing. It was not mere chance that Juan Gris' "Portraits" after 1912 were all line drawings. The same goes for practically all Picasso's "occasional" work after 1924.

[173] Gris had this in mind when he referred to Léger's imitators as "shop-window painters"; they were not painters but decorators, who suspended the contents of their pictures in a void, and wrongly called them "objects in space".

[174] Letter from Toulon, January 24, 1926: "It has a Pompeian look, but deriving from David rather than from Poussin."

[175] Letter from Toulon, February 6, 1926: "Now it is finished, it is more like something from Fontainebleau."

[176] "It is granted to *you* to live so long as you breathe: not so for me. He through whom the spirit has spoken must leave early. The divine nature of the gods often reveals itself through certain men. By this the human race knows them in their many undertakings. But when the mortal, his heart bursting with their joy, proclaims them! Oh! Let them then break the vase, so that it be put to no other use and the divine may not become the work of man. Let the blessed die!"

[177] Now in the Philadelphia Museum of Art (Coll. A. E. Gallatin). *Vide* p. 161, present volume.

[178] Germaine Raynal, Madame Huidobro, André Simon, myself and my family.

[179] All published by the Galerie Simon (see Part III for details).

[180] Also published by the Galerie Simon (see Part III).

[181] This refers to the "Feste Teatrali", a performance of opera organised for the Court by Mazarin, in 1645, in the Salle du Petit-Bourbon.

[182] *SIC* Nos. 8, 9, 10, August, September and October, 1916, with the title: "*A propos d'un théâtre nunique*" (unsigned), followed in Nos. 21 and 22, September and October, 1917, by a signed sketch. Apollinaire deplored the absence of a theatre on these lines in the prologue to *Les Mamelles de Tirésias*.

[183] "*Le Théâtre de la Cruauté*" (first manifesto), reprinted in *Le Théâtre et son double* (Gallimard, Paris 1938, pp. 103 et seq.).

[184] There was, for example, Firmin Gémier's production of an *Oedipus* by Saint Georges de Bouhelier at the Cirque d'Hiver in 1919–20, and also another production. Gémier, who filled the arena with gymnasts, wrestlers and acrobats, really only managed to produce a super-circus which was hardly different from the great equestrian and nautical pantomime to celebrate The Circus in 1900.

[185] Music by Montéclair (Michel Pignolet de Montéclair, 1666–1737), arranged by Henri Casadesus.

[186] Opera by Gounod.

[187] Opera-bouffe by Chabrier.

[188] Cf. Daniel Henry "*Die Grenzen der Kunstgeschichte*" (*Monatshefte für Kunstwissenschaft, Jahrgang XIII*, Vol. 1, April 1920, pp. 91–97).

[189] To the extent that even the Cubists themselves did not "see" them until after they had painted them; that is to say, after they had been endowed with a real plastic existence. I remember Picasso saying to me: "First of all I painted mandolines. It was not until later that I thought of looking at them and buying them."

[190] "Art which is not born of an emotion is no art": Cézanne to Girieud, quoted by Gasquet.

[191] Page 144.

[192] Great confusion seems to exist between so-called abstract art and Cubism: witness the number of Cubist pictures which are labelled "Abstraction", especially in America. In many cases, this unfortunate use of a word which bears no relation to the artist's intention can be explained by the inability of the author of the Catalogue to "read"; and so, in the absence of any traditional title,

recourse is had to a generic. There is no denying the sad fact that, through indolence, Picasso did not oppose the use of this title for certain of his pictures exhibited at the Galerie Georges Petit in 1932; this has seemed to justify the abuse. For this reason it must be all the more energetically opposed. The works of Gris, of Braque and of Picasso are not "abstractions"; they have more right to be called "concretions", "assemblies of parts into a solid whole". An "abstraction" tends only to express *a single* quality, independent of the subject; the works of these painters on the other hand express primarily their subject, and of its qualities only that which is judged strictly necessary. I cannot help thinking that the first person (I do not know his name) to use the word "abstraction" really meant to write "concept". However, even if one entitles a canvas "Concept" one must give some additional description of what "concept" it is: "Concept of a Table", or "Concept of a Guitar". But this would be merely pedantic and precious and, what is worse, overlooks the real identity of the "concept" with the object represented to symbolise it.

This is not the first such appeal that I have made, and I do not know whether this time it will be successful; but I would beg all future editors of catalogues, when they do not know the original title of a picture, to put something descriptive, such as "Mandoline and Fruit-Dish" or "Woman with a Guitar" or "Kneeling Man", rather than "Abstraction". In this, at any rate, they will be in keeping with the painter's original intentions. Traditional names (even if they are apocryphal) should, of course, always be respected, provided they do not conflict with the spirit of the picture: for example, *Les Demoiselles d'Avignon* or *Guernica* in the case of Picasso, *The Man from Touraine* in the case of Gris. These titles were all invented by someone other than the artist, though generally by a friend.

[193] *Vide* Karl Jaspers, *Descartes et la Philosophie*, translated from the German by H. Pollnow, p. 109 (Alcan, Paris 1938).

[194] *Entretien avec les étudiants des écoles d'architecture*, p. 38. Denoël, Paris 1943.

[195] *Loc. cit.* pp. 32–33. I do not think that Le Corbusier intends one to think of this "circulation"—whether internal or external—as a rhythm in time. I have already said (Note 160) that I do not believe in the existence of any such rhythm in static constructions in space. It seems to me that Le Corbusier is insisting simply on the fact that, in order to be seen, the various aspects which he mentions all necessitate the presence of a spectator who can move freely. In any case, my subsequent remarks should be interpreted with this in mind.

[196] Another very small sculpture, *The Apple*, a plaster, had preceded this one and anticipated its tendency.

[197] "Each series of twelve notes is unique, a specific *Erlebnis*, and this gives to the melodies and harmonies born of it a particular character which varies, so to speak, between one musical work and another. But, at the same time, by taking in the atonal *whole*, that unique chromatic scale, this series acquires a universal character, because by virtue of this relationship its essence is identical with that of every other twelve-note series" (from René Leibowitz' *Introduction à la musique de douze sons*, Gallimard, Paris).

[198] "The series of twelve notes is nothing but the ensemble of the intervals of which it is composed" (*ibid.*).

[199] For further information about Schoenberg, I would refer readers to the remarkable book by René Leibowitz, to whom I am greatly indebted for much valuable advice during the writing of this passage about modern music.

[200] In short, this secondary *Erlebnis*, which is the only determinable one in the case of musicians—and architects—corresponds to "inspiration" in the other arts.

[201] *Loc. cit.*

[202] There is admittedly such a thing as applied music; music, that is to say, which follows some existing text. In this case—the Lied, the liturgical chant, oratorio and opera—there is no doubt that the reading of the text was the primary *Erlebnis* for the composer. So he attempts to re-create for the listener his own emotion. Berlioz expressed his happiness at hearing that several people had fainted during a performance of his *Requiem* at Lille. The terror that he had attempted to communicate in composing the *Dies Irae* had had its effect.

Pure music is not concerned with the sentimental or nervous reactions of the audience, any more than architecture is concerned with those of the beholder. Every listener is expected to collaborate actively in perceiving the work effectively apart from its outgrowths. According to Bettina von Arnim, Beethoven almost broke with Goethe for crying as he listened to him playing the piano.

[203] Musical notation is a form of "writing" composed with signs. But those who can read music are rare, and so generally when speaking of music we are referring to an actual performance, when the music is really heard.

[204] He was quoting a notice affixed to the bridge of the steamers which in those days plied on the Seine.

[205] Max Jacob, one of my oldest friends, was still alive when this was written. He was arrested at St. Benoit at the end of February 1944, and died, a victim of the crazy Hitlerian terror, in the concentration camp at Drancy on March 5, 1944.

[206] Privately printed, Paris 1917 (new edition, Stock, Paris 1923). Naturally I do not mean that all that can be said of the "*œuvre burlesque et mystique*" of Max Jacob will be found in his theoretical writings. His impulsive spirit was always capable of breaking the rule he had just made, just as he could (like Heine with his emotion) laugh at himself.

[207] *Self-Défense*, Privately printed, Paris 1919 (pages unnumbered). This booklet, dedicated to Juan Gris, bears witness in every line to the great affection which then existed between the two men.

[208] *Le Gant de Crin*, pp. 16, 17. Plon, Paris 1927.

[209] *Self-Défense.*

[210] *Ibid.*

[211] Preface to *Le Cornet à Dés.*

[212] *Art Poétique*, p. 46. Emile Paul, Paris 1922.

[213] *Ibid.*, p. 22.

[214] *Ibid.*, p. 26.

[215] *Ibid.*, p. 27.

[216] *Ibid.*, p. 27.

[217] *Le Gant de Crin*, p. 16.

[218] *Ibid.*, p. 57.

[219] *Art Poétique*, p. 23.

[220] *Ibid.*, p. 10.

[221] *Le Gant de Crin*, p. 15.

[222] For Max Jacob "Hamletism" meant the tail-end of Symbolism.

[223] *Art Poétique*, p. 23.

[224] *Le Gant de Crin*, pp. 31, 32.

[225] *Self-Défense.*

[226] *Le Gant de Crin*, p. 16.

[227] *Art Poétique*, p. 17.

[228] *Ibid.*, p. 34.

[229] *Self-Défense.*

[230] *Ibid.*

[231] *Le Gant de Crin.*

[232] *Ibid.*, p. 34.

[233] *Art Poétique*, p. 34.

[234] *Ibid.*, p. 17.

[235] *Narration*, p. 152. University of Chicago Press, 1935.

[236] "Descriptions of Literature", *Transition*, No. 13, p. 151. Paris 1928.

[237] Carl Einstein died in June 1940. He had returned to France after the Spanish Civil War in which he took part. I saw him frequently, for we had been friends for thirty-five years. He was as usual full of ideas. He showed me a synopsis for a projected book on aesthetics, and also for a history of art. I have read several chapters of a novel which he had been writing for a long time. At the time of the invasion in May 1940 he was interned by the French authorities in a camp in south-western France. At the approach of the Germans he was released; but for fear of falling into the hands of the Gestapo he drowned himself in the River Gave and is buried at Pau.

[238] "Form is no longer an arrangement or omission of contradictory parts of a selected subject; it is not an arrangement of things perceived at different times but mastery of the subjective act."

[239] In order that a work may be read there must, of necessity, be some connection, no matter how tenuous, between the new sign and signs which the reader has already experienced, which he habitually identifies with the object "represented". It is this limitation which aggravates Picasso. Michel Leiris has reported to me a remark made to him by Picasso in 1943. Leiris was commenting on the fact that in a sculpture Picasso had succeeded in making a bicycle saddle "represent" a bull's head. "That's nothing!" replied Picasso. "One should be able to pick up a piece of wood and make it into a bird."

[240] Preface to "*La Traité du Verbe*", by René Ghil (1884), reprinted in *Divagations*, new edition, p. 256. Fasquelle, Paris 1943.

[241] As a matter of fact Tzara believes that the poet can only play the part of an animator, since the transformation of language is a "mental attitude". He writes in *Grains et Issues* (Denoël and Steele, Paris 1935, p. 273): "*Quoique le langage ne puisse changer dans ses racines, mais seulement se transformer par dépassements d'états signifiés successifs et cela, lorsque la normalisation de ce qui actuellement n'est exprimable que par symboles bruts ou formules de signalisation sera devenu expérience vécue du domaine publiée, il incombe au poète de démontrer par l'acte qu'une certaine ductilité, un caractère de mollesse dans l'adaptation traduite, de laisser-aller voluptueux de la matière linguistique, rend possible cette transformation.*

[242] *Initiations à la Physique*, French translation by J. du Plessis de Grenédan, p. 209 (Flammarion, Paris 1940).

[243] *Loc. cit.*, p. 211.

[244] There will indubitably be some attempt at a future date to relate Cubism to a contemporary philosophy, and it seems to me probable that the name of Husserl will be selected; for phenomenology, for which he has been responsible, is a transcendental form of idealism. I cannot embark on any such investigation in the present book as it would carry us too far, but it is worth recording that neither Gris nor any of his friends had heard the name of Husserl at the time when they were working out their new form of art.

[245] It was Braque.

THE PLATES

Chest of Drawers, Pitcher, Carafe and Bowl · 1909

Plate, Glass, Bottle and Bowl · 1910

Beer-mug · 1911

Still-life with Pears · *1910*

Three Lamps · 1910–11

Place Ravignan · 1912

Still-life with Bottles · 1912

Portrait of Madame Germaine Raynal · 1912

Parfum de Chypre · 1911

Still-life with Coffee-pot · 1915–16

Still-life with Coffee-mill · 1916

Coffe-mill, Carafe and Glass · 1916

Carafe and Bowl · 1916

Bottle and Fruit-bowl · 1917

Open Book · 1917

Siphon, Glass and Spoon · 1923

Still-life with a Book · 1911

Still-life · 1911

Still-life · *1911–12*

The Bordeaux Bottle · 1912

Le Lavabo · 1912

Portrait of Picasso · 1912

Portrait of the Artist's Mother · 1912

Portrait of Madame Germaine Raynal · *1912*

The Man in the Café · 1912

The Smoker · 1913

Landscape at Céret · 1913

Grapes and Wine · 1913

Still-life · 1913

Glass of Beer and Playing-cards · 1913

Violin and Engraving · 1913

Violin and Chessboard · 1913

Chessboard · 1914

Grapes · 1914

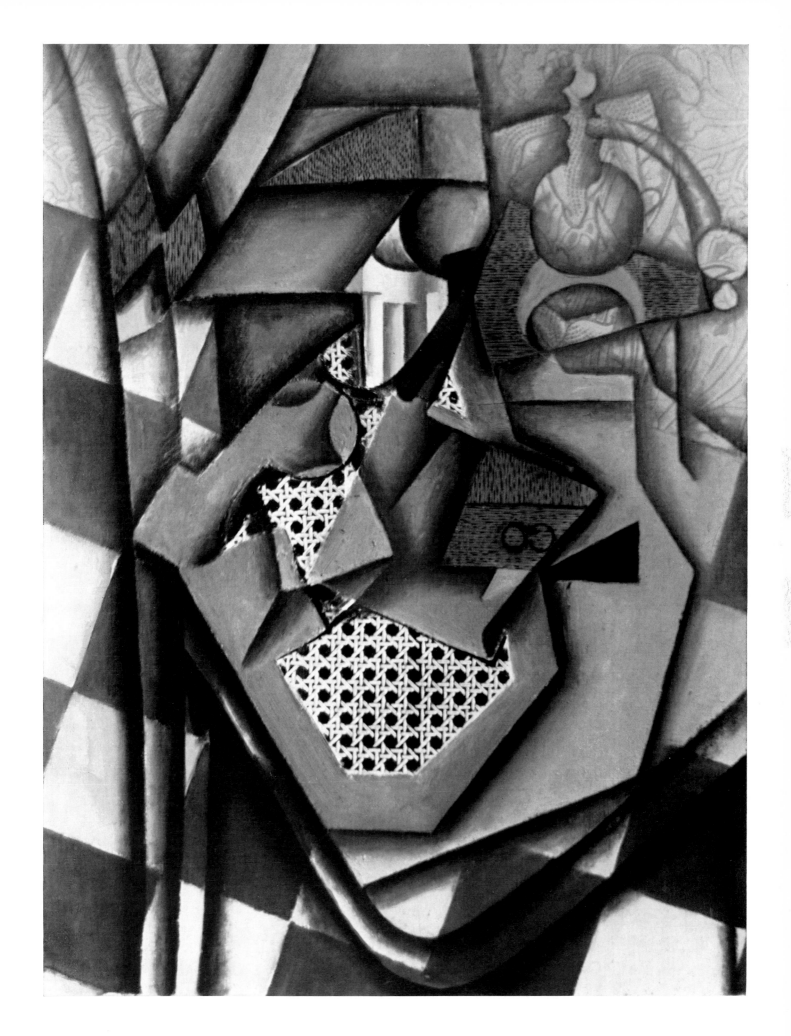

The Chair · 1914

The Bottle of Banyuls · 1914

The Marble Console · 1914

The Man in the Café · 1914

Still-life (Fantômas) · *1915*

Newspaper and Fruit-bowl · 1915

Still-life with Geraniums · 1915

JOURNAL

Breakfast · 1915

The Sun-blind · 1915

Carafe and Newspaper · 1916

Bottle and Fruit-bowl · *1915*

Portrait of the Artist's Wife · *1916*

The Open Window · 1917

Landscape · 1917

Carafe and Glasses · *1917*

Carafe and Pipe · 1917

Violin and Newspaper · 1917

Violin and Glass · 1918

Guitar and Bottle · 1917

Woman with a Mandolin (after Corot) · 1916

d'après Cézanne.

Bathers (after Cézanne) · *1916*

Portrait of Madame Cézanne (after Cézanne) · *1918*

House in a Landscape (Beaulieu) · *1918*

The Miller · 1918

The Man from Touraine · 1918

Man with Violin · 1918

Playing-cards and Fruit-bowl · 1918

Harlequin Sitting at Table · 1918

Pierrot · 1919

Guitar and Fruit-bowl · 1920

Guitar and Fruit-bowl on a Table · 1918

Still-life with Carafe · 1919

Siphon and Fruit-bowl · 1920

Vase with Lilies of the Valley · 1920

The Cloud · 1921

Le Canigou · 1921

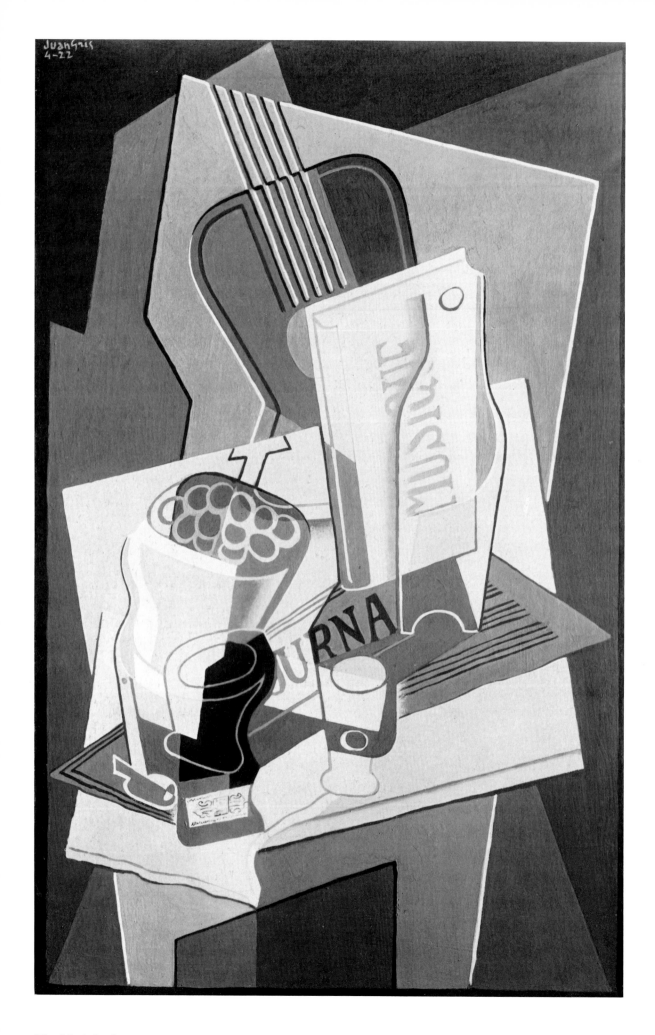

The Music-book · 1922

Pierrot with Guitar · 1922

Pierrot with Guitar · 1922

Pierrot · 1922

The Nun · 1922

Three Masks · 1923

Portrait of a Man · 1923

Woman with Clasped Hands · 1924

Pierrot with Guitar · 1925

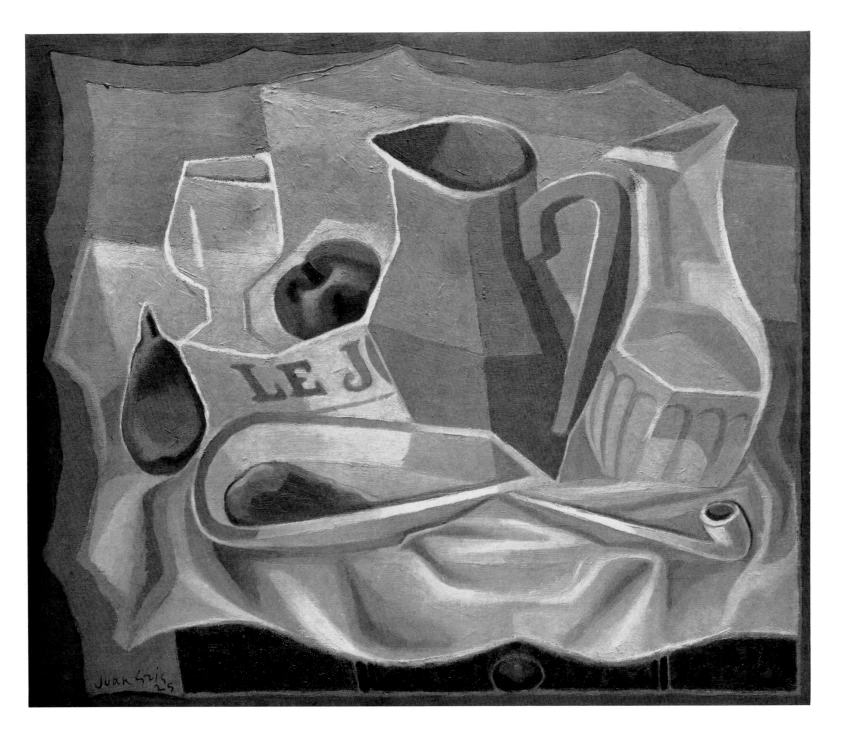

Pitcher and Carafe · 1925

Still-life : Table with a Red Cloth · 1926

The Musician's Table · 1926

Juan Gris 26

Fruit-bowl with Blue Grapes · 1926

Woman with Basket · 1927

1887   March 23: José Victoriano Gonzalez (later called Juan Gris) born in Madrid.

1902   Gris enters the Escuela de Artes y Manufacturas in Madrid.
Begins to contribute drawings to *Blanco y Negro* and *Madrid Comico*.

1904?   Leaves the Escuela to devote himself to art. Studies painting with José Maria Carbonero.
Friendship with Willy Geiger and George Kars.
Influence of *Jugend* and *Simplicissimus*: Art Nouveau.

1906   Arrival in Paris.
The Fauves dominant.
Gris goes to live at 13 Rue Ravignan, in the same house as Picasso.
Meets Guillaume Apollinaire, Max Jacob, André Salmon, etc.
Contributes drawings to *L'Assiette au Beurre* (Figs. p. 11), *Le Charivari* and *Le Cri de Paris*.
October 22: Death of Cézanne.
Picasso begins to work on *Les Demoiselles d'Avignon*.
The birth of Cubism.

1907   Picasso's so-called "Negro" period.
Kahnweiler opens his Gallery in the Rue Vignon, Paris, and makes Picasso's acquaintance.
Gris meets Raynal.

1908   Kahnweiler makes Gris' acquaintance.
Gris contributes also to *Le Témoin*.
Summer: Braque painting at L'Estaque.
Picasso painting at Rue des Bois.
Matisse and Vauxcelles refer to "the little cubes".

1909   April 9: Birth of Gris' son, Georges Gonzalez.
Picasso leaves 13 Rue Ravignan.
Summer: Picasso painting at Horta de Ebro.
Braque painting at La Roche Guyon.

1910   Gris begins painting seriously; naturalistic watercolours and drawings.

Braque and Picasso at the stage of "analytical Cubism".

1911   Gris' first oil paintings (Plates pp. 237–239).
Sells some pictures to Clovis Sagot.
Portrait of Maurice Raynal.

1912   Gris paints Picasso's portrait (Plate p. 242).
May: Picasso's first *collage: Still Life with Caned Chair.*
September: Picasso and Braque begin *papiers collés.*
March: Gris exhibits three paintings at the Salon des Indépendants.
April: He exhibits pictures at the Galeries Dalmau, Barcelona.
Gris tends towards analytical Cubism and makes first experiments with *collage* (Plate p. 241).
June: Gris exhibits at Cubist Exhibition of the Société de Peinture Moderne in Rouen.
October: Gris exhibits at the "Section d'Or". More intense colours used.
Kahnweiler makes a contract to buy all his work.
Josette comes to live with Gris at 13 Rue Ravignan.
First picture bought by Hermann Rupf of Berne.

1913   Braque and Picasso pass to "synthetic Cubism".
Publication of Apollinaire's *Les Peintres Cubistes.*
August to November: Gris and Josette staying at Céret.
Manolo also there.
The Smoker, The Torero and some landscapes (Plates pp. 246, 47, 247).
Pictures bought by Gertrude Stein and Léonce Rosenberg.

1914   Most of Gris' pictures contain *papiers collés* (Plates pp. 55, 65, 73, 81, 253–255, 257–260).
June 28: Gris and Josette leave Paris for Collioure (Rue de l'Église).
July: Kahnweiler leaves Paris.
September: Matisse arrives in Collioure.
Friendship between Gris and Matisse.
October 30: Gris and Josette return to Paris.

Financial worries; Kahnweiler's contract begins to lapse.

1915 January: Léonce Rosenberg tries to buy pictures from Gris.
June: Gris paints his first *Open Window*.
Summer: Gris' "dynamic" pictures.
Gris illustrates Reverdy's *Poèmes en Prose*.
December: Relations with Kahnweiler broken off.

1916 Gris' "architectural" period begins (Plates pp. 267, 268).
Léonce Rosenberg contracts to buy all Gris' output.
September: Gris goes with Josette to Beaulieu, near Loches.
Portraits of Josette; *Woman with a Mandolin*, after Corot (Plates pp. 269, 277).
November: They return to Paris.
Reverdy and Max Jacob are frequent visitors to Gris' studio.
Gris makes a contract with Léonce Rosenberg for three years.
Gris' friendship with Lipchitz.
Winter: *Harlequin* in polychrome plaster begun (Plate p. 161).

1918 March: *Portrait of Madame Cézanne*, after Cézanne (Plate p. 280).
April: Gris and Josette return to Beaulieu.
Visits from Lipchitz, Metzinger and Maria Blanchard.
The Man from Touraine, *The Miller* and landscapes (Plates pp. 283, 282).
November: They return to Paris.

1919 February: Publication of a text by Gris in the Italian review *Valori Plastici* (p. 192, I).
April: Exhibition of fifty pictures by Gris at the Galerie de l'Effort Moderne (Léonce Rosenberg), Paris.
Gris illustrates Reverdy's *La Guitare Endormie*.
May–June: Begins a series of *Harlequins*.
Alfred Flechtheim begins to buy Gris' pictures.
August: Kahnweiler resumes relations with Gris and attempts to make a new contract.

1920 January: Gris exhibits at the "Section d'Or", Paris.
February: Exhibits at the Galerie Moos, Geneva.
Exhibits at the Salon des Indépendants, Paris.
Kahnweiler returns to Paris.
April: Publication of Gris' text on "Negro Art" (p. 192, II).
May: Léonce Rosenberg's contract expires.
Gris quarrels with Rosenberg and makes a new contract with Kahnweiler.

Vase with Lilies of the Valley (Plate p. 293).
May: First illness.
Gris enters the Tenon Hospital.
August: Leaves the Tenon Hospital and goes with Josette to Beaulieu.
Gris makes a series of pencil and crayon drawings.
September: Gris begins to paint again.
Kahnweiler opens the Galerie Simon, Rue d'Astorg, Paris.
October: Gris and Josette return to Paris.
November: Gris and Josette go to Bandol (4 Rue Nationale).
The period of "poetic" painting begins.
December: At work on the illustrations for *Ne Coupez pas Mademoiselle* (p. 324).

1921 January: Begins a series of *Open Windows*.
March: At work on the four lithograph portraits, *Marcelle la Brune*, etc. (p. 323).
Léonce Rosenberg holds a Juan Gris Exhibition at his gallery.
April 14: Diaghilew asks Gris to come to Monte Carlo to do the *décor* for the ballet *Cuadro Flamenco*.
The project falls through; Gris does three portrait drawings instead.
April 29: Gris returns to Bandol.
Publication of Gris' text in *L'Effort Moderne*.
June 22: Gris goes to Le Cannet and subsequently returns to Paris.
July: Josette goes to Beaulieu.
Portrait drawings of Kahnweiler and his family (Plates pp. 18, 19).
October: Gris and Josette go to Céret (Hotel Garretta). Manolo is there.
December: Painting *Le Canigou* (Plate p. 295).

1922 January: Second series of *Pierrots* and *Harlequins* begun (Plates pp. 175, 297–299).
April: Gris and Josette return to Paris.
They move from the Rue Ravignan to 8 Rue de la Mairie, Boulogne-sur-Seine.
September: Gris in hospital after an operation.
November: Diaghilew commissions the *décor* and costumes for a ballet (*Les Tentations de la Bergère*) (Plates pp. 162, 163).

1923 March: Juan Gris Exhibition at the Galerie Simon, Paris.
Gris makes some small figures in sheet-iron (Plates p. 164).
June: Executes the setting for the *Fête Merveilleuse*, organised by Diaghilew, at Versailles.
Summer: Diaghilew commissions the *décor* for *La Colombe*, an opera by Gounod (Plate p. 163).
"Notes on my Painting", published in *Der Querschnitt* (p. 194).

October 9: Gris and Josette leave for Monte Carlo (and live at 3 Rue du Marché, Beausoleil).
Gris supervises the execution of his *décors*.
November: The "crisis" in Gris' painting.
December: Diaghilew commissions the *décor* for *L'Éducation Manquée* of Chabrier.

1924   January: *Premières* at Monte Carlo of *Les Tentations de la Bergère*, *La Colombe* and *L'Éducation Manquée*.
February 1: Gris and Josette return to Boulogne.
The "crisis" in his painting is past.
His "polyphonic" period begins.
At work on the illustrations for *Le Casseur d'Assiettes* (p. 325).
May 15: Gris lectures at the Sorbonne "On the Possibilities of Painting" (p. 195).
May 28: A Red Cross Fête with setting by Juan Gris, organised by Diaghilew, at the Grands Magasins du Printemps.
August 17–23: Gris and Josette stay at Nemours.

1925   January: Publication in the *Bulletin de la Vie Artistique* of Gris' text "Chez les Cubistes" (p. 201).
April: Juan Gris Exhibition at the Galerie Flechtheim, Düsseldorf.
August: Alphonse Kann begins to buy Gris' pictures.
Paul Rosenberg offers Gris a contract which he declines.
Gris' health begins to weaken.
Holiday with Armand and Lucienne Salacrou.
Publication in *Europa-Almanach* of Gris' "Reply to a Questionnaire" (p. 202).

At work on illustrations for *Mouchoir de Nuages* (pp. 326–327).
December: Gris and Josette go to Toulon (chez Mme. Ollivier, Bld. Sud des Casernes, Ste. Anne).
At work on illustrations for *A Book*, by Gertrude Stein (p. 329).

1926   February: Gris' health worse.
At work on illustrations for *Denise*, by Radiguet (p. 328).
March: Works on water-colours and gouaches.
April: Gris and Josette return to Boulogne.
Georges, his son, arrives from Madrid.
Summer: Gris' health improves.
November: Gris, Josette and Georges go to Hyères (Villa Germinal, Quartier Mont Fleuri).
December: Gris' health much worse.
His illness is diagnosed as asthma.
He is unable to work.

1927   January 22: Gris goes to Puget-Théniers.
His illness is diagnosed as uremia.
January 24: Gris, Josette and Georges return suddenly to Paris.
Gris takes to his bed. The first crisis.
February: Gris recovers sufficiently to get up.
Begins to work again.
The second crisis.
March: Gris recovers again and begins to work a little.
The third crisis.
May 11: Death of Juan Gris.
May 13: Burial of Juan Gris in the cemetery at Boulogne-sur-Seine.

Book Illustrations (pp. 324–329):

All illustrations were made especially for the books concerned, which were all first editions. After the printing of the illustrations, the stones and plates were cancelled or destroyed.

The copies numbered o and oo were made for the *dépôt légal*. They contain a set of illustrations printed from the cancelled stones or plates.

All copies are signed both by the author and by Juan Gris. They are paper-bound books with paper dust-jackets.

Dimensions refer to page size.

Lithographs 1–4 were made in 1921 and printed in 50 numbered and signed copies on Chinese paper. Numbers 5 and 6 also date from 1921, but it was not until 1946 that they were transferred to stone and printed in 50 numbered copies on Chinese paper. The dimensions of the lithographs refer to image size.

1. *Marcelle la blonde.* 1921. $11^1/_2 \times 8^3/_4''$.
Inscribed in the stone: Juan Gris 3–21 MARCELLE LA BLONDE.

2. *Marcelle la brune.* 1921. $11^3/_4 \times 9''$.
Inscribed in the stone: Juan Gris 3–21 MARCELLE LA BRUNE.

3. *Le gosse (The Boy).* 1921. $12^5/_8 \times 10''$.
Inscribed in the stone: Juan Gris 3–21.

4. *Jean le musicien (Jean the Musician).* 1921. $12^3/_4 \times 9^1/_8''$.
Inscribed in the stone: Juan Gris 4–21 JEAN LE MUSICIEN.

5. *Boris (Portrait of Boris Kochno).* 1921. $10^3/_4 \times 8^1/_8''$.
Inscribed in the stone: BORIS Juan Gris 5–21. Drawn on lithographic transfer-paper; transferred to stone and printed in 50 copies on Chinese paper, November 1946.

6. *Mahomet.* 1921. $12 \times 8^7/_8''$.
Inscribed in the stone: MAHOMET Juan Gris 6–21. Drawn on lithographic transfer-paper; transferred to stone and printed in 50 copies on Chinese paper, November 1946.

1

2

3

4

5

6

LE TRAIN

7

7–10. Max Jacob. *Ne coupez pas Mademoiselle ou les erreurs des P.T.T. Conte philosophique. Illustré de quatre lithographies hors-texte par Juan Gris.* Paris, Galerie Simon, 1921. 4 full-page lithographs, printed in several colours. 12³/₄×9″.
The total run of 100 copies (1–100) on Dutch van Gelder. 10 copies (1–10) with a set of the lithographs on Chine ancien. 12 copies *hors commerce* (I–X; o, oo; the last two printed in black from the cancelled stones).

LACARTELETTRE

8

9

ALCOFIBRAS
et
LA DEMOISELLE

10

L'APERO

11–15. Armand Salacrou. *Le casseur d'assiettes. Pièce en un acte ornée de lithographies par Juan Gris.* Paris, Galerie Simon, 1924. 5 lithographs *hors-texte*, one of which is on the jacket. $9^5/_8 \times 7^1/_2''$.

100 numbered and signed copies. 10 copies (1–10) on Japon ancien. 90 copies (11–100) on Vergé d'Arches. 12 copies *hors commerce* (I–X; o, oo; the last two printed from the cancelled stones).

12

ARMAND SALACROU

LE CASSEUR
D'ASSIETTES

11

13

14

15

16–24. Tristan Tzara. *Mouchoir de nuages. Tragédie en 15 actes ornée d'eaux-fortes par Juan Gris.* Paris, Galerie Simon, 1925. 9 etchings, one of which is on the jacket, 4 *hors-texte* (17, 19, 21, 23) and 4 in the text (18, 20, 22, 24). $7^1/_2 \times 4^7/_8''$. 100 numbered and signed copies. 10 copies (1–10) on Japon ancien. 90 copies (11–100) on Vergé d'Arches. 12 copies *hors commerce* (I–X; 0, 00; the last two printed from the cancelled stones).

19

20

21

23

22

24

25

25–29. Raymond Radiguet. *Denise*. *Illustré de lithographies par Juan Gris*. Paris, Galerie Simon, 1926. 5 lithographs *hors-texte*, one of which is on the jacket. $9^5/_8 \times 7^1/_2''$.

100 numbered copies, signed by Juan Gris. 10 copies (1–10) on Japon ancien. 90 copies (11–100) on Vergé d'Arches. 12 copies *hors commerce* (I–X; 0, 00; the last two printed from the cancelled stones).

26

27

28

29

30

31

30–33. Gertrude Stein. *A book concluding with as a wife has a cow. A love story. Orné de lithographies par Juan Gris.* Paris, Galerie Simon, 1926. 4 lithographs *hors-texte*, one of which is in two colours (No. 32). $9^5/_8 \times 7^1/_2''$.

100 numbered and signed copies. 10 copies (1–10) on Japon ancien. 90 copies (11–100) on Vergé d'Arches. 12 copies *hors commerce* (I–X; o, oo; the last two printed from the cancelled stones).

33

32

34. *Nature morte (Still-life)*. 1922. Stencil. $9^5/_8 \times 13^1/_8''$.
Published by *L'Esprit Nouveau* and distributed among
its subscribers on the occasion of new year 1923. Numbered
copies exist.

BIBLIOGRAPHY

by Bernard Karpel
The Librarian, Museum of Modern Art, New York

Several bibliographies on Juan Gris exist, ranging from a German booklet of 1929 to a French monograph of 1946 and its English edition of 1947, all by one distinguished chronicler, Mr. Kahnweiler. Probably the next major monograph is James Thrall Soby's *Juan Gris* for which the present compiler assembled the selected bibliography exactly ten years ago. Consolidating significant information since then, without necessarily cumulating all possible documentation reported below, provides an up-dated record useful to the researcher and scholar. Notes have been extended and references increased from 100 to almost 300 citations.

WRITINGS BY THE ARTIST

Main Collections

1. Les Écrits de Juan Gris. *In* Daniel-Henry Kahnweiler. *Juan Gris. Sa Vie, Son Œuvre, Ses Écrits.* Paris, Gallimard, 1946. pp. 274—292. Includes eight items, 1919—1927. Translated by Douglas Cooper in English edition below. Variant "titles".

2. Writings of Juan Gris. *In* Daniel-Henry Kahnweiler. *Juan Gris : His Life and Work.* New York, Curt Valentin, 1947. pp. 137—146. Eight selections of "papers intended for publication", 1919—1930. *French texts* in 1946 monograph above. Variant "titles".

3. *Letters of Juan Gris, 1913—1927.* Collected by Daniel-Henry Kahnweiler. Translated and edited by Douglas Cooper. London, Privately printed, 1956. Printed for Douglas Cooper. 300 numbered copies for distribution and sale.

Letters, Statements, Articles, Translations

4. [Unpublished letter to Kahnweiler. Dec. 14, 1951]. *Art News (New York)*, Feb. 1950, v. 48, no. 10, p. 18.

5. [Statement on "elements"]. *Valori Plastici (Rome)*, Feb.—Mar. 1919, p. 2. Special issue "al Cubismo francese". Translation see bibl. 1, 2.

6. [On Negro art]. *Action (Paris)*, Apr. 1920, no. 3, p. 24. "In answer to an inquiry." Translation see bibl. 1, 2.

7. [Juan Gris by Vauvrecy (pseud.)]. *L'Esprit Nouveau (Paris)*, 1921, no. 5, pp. 533—534. Essentially Gris' "*système esthétique et méthode*", these biographical notes were "signed" by an editor of the magazine (Amédée Ozenfant) although "actually written by the artist". Also extracts in "Quelques notes de Juan Gris sur ses recherches", *Cahiers d'Art (Paris)*, 1927, v. 2, p. 171. Translation see bibl. 1, 2.

8. [Notes on my painting]. *Der Querschnitt (Frankfort)*, Summer 1923, no. 1—2, pp. 77—78. *Notes sur ma peinture* addressed to Carl Einstein. Reprinted as *Zu meinem Schaffen* by Paul Westheim (Künstlerbekenntnisse, 1924?), p. 150. Translation see bibl. 1, 2. Reprinted in *Daedalus*, Winter 1947, v. 89, no. 1, pp. 82–83.

9. [On the possibilities of painting]. *Transatlantic Review (Paris)*, June 1924, v. 1, no. 6, pp. 482—488; July 1924, v. 2, no. 1, pp. 75—79. Original title: *Des possibilités de la peinture*, frequently re-published in whole or part: *Cahiers d'Art (Paris)*, no. 5—6 (1933); fully in German *Der Querschnitt (Berlin)*, Jan. 1925, v. 1, pp. 32—40; partly in Spanish *Alfar (La Coruña)*, Sept. 1924, no. 43, pp. 24—30; excerpted in *Favorables Paris Poemas (Paris)*, July 1926, no. 1; fully in English *Horizon (London)*, Aug. 1946, no. 80, pp. 113—122 (illus.). Translation see bibl. 1, 2; Seghers & Charpier, bibl. 139 (v. 3, 1965), p. 159, 193—202. Also note bibl. 149.

10. [Reply to the question: "Chez les Cubistes"]. *Bulletin de la Vie Artistique (Paris)*, Jan. 1, 1925, v. 6, no. 1, pp. 15—17. Translation see bibl. 1, 2. Quoted by Cassou (bibl. 42), pp. 216—217, who links the *Bulletin* and *Documents* infra as "intégral".

11. [Reply to a questionnaire]. *Documents (Paris)*, 1930, no. 5, pp. 267—273. Original title: *Réponse à une enquête sur le cubisme*. First published in translation by Walter Mehring: Antwort [auf einige Fragen ... über den Kubismus]. *In* Europa Almanach. Potsdam, 1925. pp. 34—36, illus., port. Later, with foreword by Carl Einstein in *Documents* (1930). Modified version of statement to *Bulletin de la Vie Artistique* (1925). Translation see bibl. 1, 2. Quoted by Cassou (bibl. 42), pp. 216—217.

12. [Statement]. In Maurice Raynal. *Anthologie de la Peinture Française*. Paris, Aubier, Éditions Montaigne, 1927. p. 172. Also American edition (Brentano, 1928). Translation see bibl. 1, 2.

13. ["Mitt sinne är alltför precist": utdrag ur Juan Gris brev]. *Paletten (Göteborg)*, 1957, no. 4, pp. 112—117, illus.

WORKS ILLUSTRATED BY GRIS

Books with Original Prints
(see Catalogue of Graphic Work, pp. 321—330)

14. Jacob, Max. *Ne coupez pas Mademoiselle ou les erreurs des P.T.T.* Paris, Galerie Simon, 1921. Four original lithographs.

15. Radiguet, Raymond. *Denise*. Paris, Galerie Simon, 1926. Five original lithographs.

16. Salacrou, Armand. *Le casseur d'assiettes*. Paris, Galerie Simon, 1924. Five original lithographs (one on jacket).

17. Tzara, Tristan. *Mouchoir de nuages*. Paris, Galerie Simon, 1925. Nine original etchings (one on jacket).

18. Stein, Gertrude. *A book concluding with as a wife has a cow. A love story*. Paris, Galerie Simon, 1926. Four original lithographs, one in two colors (one on jacket).

Books and Periodicals Containing Reproductions after Drawings and Gouaches by Gris

19. Chocano, José Santos. *Alma América. Poemas Indo-Españoles*. Madrid, Victoriano Suárez, 1906. XXIII, 341 pp. Cover decoration and 69 (71?) vignettes by Juan Gris. "These illustrations were the first work that he signed with his pseudonym of 'Juan Gris' just before leaving Spain for Paris" (Librería Mirto).

20. *L'Assiette au Beurre (Paris)*. No. 365—416. Mar. 28, 1908—Mar. 20, 1909 ff. Includes reproductions of 24 precubist drawings (some originals extant dated 1910). Similar illustrations for *Madrid-Comico* and *Blanco y Negro* (contemporaneous journals).

21. Dermée, Paul. *Beautés de 1918*. Paris, Éditions de "L'Esprit Nouveau", 1919. Jacket and three drawings.

22. Huidobro, Vincent. *Tremblement de Ciel*. Paris, Éditions de l'As de Cœur, Louis Tschann, no date. With a portrait of the author.

23. Peiper, Tadeusz. *Zywe Linje*. Krakau, 1924. Three drawings.

24. Reverdy, Pierre. *Poèmes en Prose*. Paris, P. Birault, 1915. With several drawings specially made for this edition.

25. Reverdy, Pierre. *La Guitare Endormie*. Paris, Éditions Nord-Sud, 1919. Four drawings and frontispiece portrait drawn for this edition. "Only exemplaires de tête are illustrated."

26. Reverdy, Pierre. *Au Soleil du Plafond*. Paris, Tériade, 1955. With 11 color lithographs printed by Mourlot after gouaches of 1916 by Gris. 45 copies with extra suite on Chine. Folio wrappers. Signed by the author.

BOOKS

27. Amberg, George. *Art in Modern Ballet*. New York, Pantheon, 1946. pp. 157, 238, 252, 762, illus.

28. Apollinaire, Guillaume. *Anecdotiques*. Paris, Stock, 1926. pp. 60—61.

29. Apollinaire, Guillaume. *Chroniques d'Art (1902—1918)*. Paris, Gallimard, 1960. p. 505 (index).

30. Apollinaire, Guillaume. *The Cubist Painters—Aesthetic Meditations, 1913*. New York, Wittenborn, Schultz, 1949. pp. 41—43. First edition, 1944, pp. 27—28. Bibliography on Apollinaire and cubism, pp. 54—64, by Bernard Karpel.

31. Apollinaire, Guillaume. [*Méditations Esthétiques*]—*Les Peintres cubistes*. Paris, Figuière, 1913. pp. 60—63. English translation, New York 1949 above, includes references to later editions in bibliography.

32. Balcar, Alexander J. *Knaurs Ballet Lexikon*. Munich-Zurich, Droemersche Verlagsanstalt, Th. Knaur Nachf., 1958. pp. 155. Original French edition: Paris, Fernand Hazan, 1957. Also English edition: *Dictionary of Modern Ballet*. New York, Tudor, 1959. Different editors.

33. *Ballets Russes de Serge de Diaghilev*. Paris, Théâtre des Champs-Élysées, May—June 1924. Catalogue includes "Les Tentations de la Bergère", programme for the ballet, photos of dancers, décor by Juan Gris (2 col. pl.).

34. Barr, Alfred H., Jr. *Cubism and Abstract Art*. New York, Museum of Modern Art, 1936. pp. 29, 42, 48, 77, 82—84, 211, 244—245, illus. Also reprint with Arno Press, New York, 1966.

35. Berger, René. *Discovery of Painting*. New York, Viking, 1963. pp. 79, 80, illus. Also London, Thames & Hudson, 1963; Lausanne, La Guilde du Livre, 1958.

36. Besson, George. *Masters of French Painting, 1850—1950*. London, Soho Gallery, A. Zwemmer, 1958. pp. 116—117, col. illus.

37. Bille, Ejler. *Picasso, Surrealisme, Abstrakt Kunst*. Copenhagen, Helios, 1945. pp. 75—77, illus.

38. Birren, Faber. *History of Color in Painting*. New York, Reinhold, 1965. pp. 69, 132, 133, 341, 343, illus.

39. Bouleau, Charles. *The Painter's Secret Geometry: a Study of Composition in Art*. New York, Harcourt Brace, 1963. pp. 242—244, illus. With a preface by Jacques Villon.

40. Bulliet, Clarence J. *The Significant Moderns and Their Pictures*. New York, Covici-Friede, 1936. pp. 142—143, illus.

Cahiers d'Art. No. 5—6, 1933. *See* Zervos.

41. Camón Aznar, José. *Picasso y el Cubismo*. Madrid, Espasa-Calpe, 1956. pp. 177—252 et passim, illus., col. pl. Also "Figuras, Juan Gris": pp. 8, 13—15, 18—19, 21—28, 30—35, 38, 85, 102, 104—168. Includes drawings from *Alma América*, 1906 (*see* bibl. 19).

42. Cassou, Jean. *Panorama des Arts Plastiques Contemporains*. Paris, Gallimard, 1960. p. 773 (index), illus. Ch. XIII: Les Cubistes, pp. 186ff. Quotes Gris, pp. 215—217.

43. *Les Clés de l'Art Moderne*. Paris, Éditions de la Table Ronde, 1955. pp. 44, 155—156. "Les Guides du Monde moderne dirigés par Georges Pernoud".

44. Cogniat, Raymond. *Histoire de la Peinture, II*. Paris, Nathan, 1955. Vol. II. pp. 159, 160, 162, 179, 275, 276, 277, 280 illus. (col.).

45. Colin, Mr. and Mrs. Ralph F., Collection. *The Colin Collection*. New York, Knoedler & Co., 1960. Gris, nos. 58—63, with notes and bibliography. Exhibition reviewed in *Connoisseur*, v. 145, pp. 206—209, 1960; similarly *Arts (New York)*, v. 34, pp. 28—29, 1960; *Art News*, v. 59, pp. 30—32, 1960; *Apollo*, v. 71, p. 123, Apr. 1960.

46. Cooper, Douglas. *Juan Gris, ou le Goût du Solennel*. Geneva, Skira, 1949. [14] pp. plus 15 col. pl. "Les Trésors de la peinture française" series; loose plates in cover.

47. Cooper, Douglas, ed. *Letters of Juan Gris, 1913—1927*. Collected by Daniel-Henry Kahnweiler; translated and edited by Douglas Cooper. London, Privately printed, 1956. 221 pp. Privately printed for Douglas Cooper. Only 300 numbered copies for distribution and sale.

48. Courthion, Pierre. *Art Indépendant*. Paris, Michel, 1958. pp. 25, 80—82, 88—89, 99, 123, 152, 183, 272, col. pl.

49. Delevoy, Robert L. *Dimensions of the Twentieth Century*. Geneva, Skira, 1965. pp. 42, 87, 92, 116, 136, 170, illus., col. pl.

50. Detaille, Georges and Mulys, Gérard. *Les Ballets de Monte-Carlo, 1911—1944*. Paris, Arc-en-Ciel, 1954. pp. 94—97, illus. "Les Tentations de la Bergère", 1924 showing costumes and maquette by Gris.

51. Diehl, Gaston. *The Moderns*. New York, Crown Publishers, [1961]. pp. 59, 71, illus. col. pl. Color plates same as in Modesti (bibl. 114).

52. Dorival, Bernard. *Les Étapes de la Peinture Française Contemporaine*. Paris, Gallimard, 1944. v. 2, pp. 246—252.

53. Dorival, Bernard. *Les Peintres du Vingtième Siècle*. Paris, Tisné, 1957. pp. 77, 84, 86, 96, 118—119, 129—130, illus. Also English edition: *Twentieth Century Painters: Nabis—Fauves—Cubists*. New York, Universe, 1958.

54. Dreier, Katherine. *Modern Art*. New York, Société Anonyme—Museum of Modern Art, 1926. p. 83, illus., port. Book issued to accompany the Brooklyn Museum exhibition, Nov. 1926; in effect, a *de luxe* version of the catalogue "composed by Katherine S. Dreier & Constantin Aladjalov". Preface by W. H. Fox of the Brooklyn Museum.

55. Du Colombier, Pierre and Manuel, Roland. *Les Arts*. Paris, Denoël & Steele, 1933. pp. 79—30. "Tableau du XXe Siècle", I.

Édouard-Joseph. *See* Gauthier.

56. Einstein, Carl. *Die Kunst des 20. Jahrhunderts*. 3. Aufl., Berlin, Propyläen, 1931. pp. 103—106, 368, 383, 639. Variable data in first (1926) and second (1928) editions.

57. Éluard, Paul. *Voir*. Geneva, Paris, Trois Collines, 1948. pp. 23—25, illus., col. pl. A poem: "Juan Gris".

58. Elgar, Frank. *Gris: Still Lifes*. New York, Tudor, 1961. [16] pp. (illus.), plus 15 col. pl. Little Art Library, no. 35. Originally Bibliothèque Aldine (Éditions Hazan, Paris).

59. *Encyclopedia of World Art*. New York, McGraw-Hill, 1959. v. 7, p. 174—175. Contribution by Robert L. Herbert. Bibliography.

60. Escholier, Raymond. *La Peinture Française du XXe Siècle*. Paris, Floury, 1937. pp. 82—83, illus.

61. *Europa Almanach*. Potsdam, Kiepenheuer, 1925. pp. 34—36, illus. (port.). Includes Gris "Antwort [über den Kubismus]". *See* bibl. 11.

62. Faure, Élie. *Histoire de l'Art: l'Art Moderne*. Paris, Crès, 1921. p. 469. Also English translation by Walter Pach (New York, Harper, 1924), and *Œuvres Complètes*. Paris, Pauvert, 1964. p. 253.

63. Fosca, François. *Bilan du Cubisme*. Paris, La Bibliothèque des Arts, 1956. pp. 39—44, 63—65, illus. Quotes Gris from Kahnweiler (1946), pp. 63ff.

64. Francastel, Pierre. *Nouveau Dessin, Nouvelle Peinture: l'École de Paris*. Paris, Librairie de Medicis, 1946. pp. 113 to 154.

65. Francastel, Pierre. *Histoire de la Peinture Française, II: Du Classicisme au Cubisme*. Paris, Brussels, Elsevier, 1955. pp. 131—151 (passim). Extensive biographical note by M. Bex.

66. Freedman, Leonard, ed. *Looking at Modern Painting*. New York, Norton, 1961 (c. 1954). pp. 22, 24, 25, 26—27, 78, illus.

67. Gallatin, A. E., Collection. *A. E. Gallatin Collection, "Museum of Living Art"*. Philadelphia, Philadelphia Museum of Art, 1954. pp. 36—37. Previous catalogues: New York, 1933, 1940.

68. Gauthier, Maximilien. *Gris*. In: Édouard-Joseph, René, ed. *Dictionnaire Biographique des Artistes Contemporains*. Paris, Art & Édition, 1931. pp. 149—150, illus. Includes Gris statements.

69. Genaille, Robert. *La Peinture Contemporaine*. [Paris], Nathan, 1955. pp. 53, 63, 74—77, 166.

70. George, Waldemar. *Juan Gris*. Paris, Gallimard, 1931. 63 pp., illus. "Peintres nouveaux" series. Illustrated books, p. 13.

71. Georges-Michel, Michel. *Chefs d'Œuvre de Peintres Contemporains*. New York, Éditions de la Maison Française, 1945. pp. 164—167, illus. Also his: *Les Grandes Époques de la Peinture Moderne*. New York & Paris, Brentano's, 1945, pp. 164—165, illus.

72. Georges-Michel, Michel. *From Renoir to Picasso*. Boston, Houghton Mifflin, 1957. pp. 98—99.

73. Gilson, Étienne. *Painting and Reality*. New York, Pantheon Books, 1959. pp. 44, 45, 55, 189, 254, 255, 276, 318—319, illus. Quotations from Gris.

74. Gleizes, Albert and Metzinger, Jean. *Cubism*. London, Unwin, 1913. 133 pp., illus. Original edition: Du "Cubisme". Paris, Figuière, 1912.

75. Gleizes, Albert. *Kubismus*. Munich, Langen, 1928. Bauhausbücher 13. Abbildungen, pp. 34—80.

76. Golding, John. *Cubism: A History and an Analysis, 1907—1914*. London, Faber and Faber; New York, Wittenborn, 1959. p. 204 (extensive index), illus. Chapter III: Picasso, Braque and Gris, 1912—14. Bibliography.

77. Gotoh, Shigeki [et al], eds. *Modern Painting*. [Vol. I]. Tokyo, Shogakukan Co., 1963. pp. 20, 64—65, 108, 118, 123, 128, illus., col. pls., port. English captions. Mainly Japanese text.

78. Grey, Christopher. *Cubist Aesthetic Theories*. Baltimore, John Hopkins Press, 1953. p. 185 (index).

79. Grüningen, B. von. *Vom Impressionismus zum Tachismus*. Basel, Birkhäuser, 1964. pp. 75—82, illus (col.). Also French edition.

Guggenheim. *See* Solomon R. Guggenheim.

80. Gullon, Ricardo. *De Goya al Arte Abstracto*. Madrid, Cultura Hispanica, 1952. pp. 99—111, illus.

81. Habasque, Guy. *Cubism. Biographical and Critical Study*. Geneva, Paris, Skira, 1959. pp. 63—69, p. 161 (index), col. pls. Translated from the French. Bibliography.

82. Haftmann, Werner. *Malerei im 20. Jahrhundert*. Munich, Prestel, 1954—55. V. I, p. 215—219, 500. V. II: 112, 127—131, illus. Revised editions, 1957, 1962, 1965.

83. Haftmann, Werner. *Painting in the Twentieth Century*. London, Lund Humphries, New York, Praeger, 1960. V. 1, p. 421 (index). V. 2, pp. 127—131 (illus.). New and revised edition: New York, Praeger, 1965.

84. Hamilton, George Heard. *Painting and Sculpture in Europe, 1880 to 1940*. Baltimore, Md., Penguin Books, 1967. p. 430 (extensive index), illus. Bibliography.

Henry, Daniel. *See* Kahnweiler.

85. Hess, Walter. *Das Problem der Farbe*. Munich, Prestel, 1953. pp. 14, 74—81, 99, 155—157, 161, 170. Originally published in mimeographed form as doctoral dissertation, University of Munich, 1950: "Die Farbe in der Modernen Malerei". Bibliography in both editions.

86. Hildebrandt, Hans. *Die Kunst des 19. und 20. Jahrhunderts*. Wildpark-Potsdam, Athenaion, 1924. pp. 392—393, 395, illus.

87. Huyghe, René. *French Painting: the Contemporaries*. New York, French and European Publications, 1939. pp. 31—39, illus (col.). Translation of: *La Peinture Française: les Contemporains*. Paris, Tisné, 1939.

88. Huyghe, René, ed. *Histoire de l'Art Contemporain: la Peinture*. Paris, Alcan, 1935. pp. 227—231 et passim. With text by Cassou and documentation by Bazin from *L'Amour de l'Art*, Nov. 1933. Reprint edition, New York, Arno Press, 1968.

89. Janneau, Guillaume. *L'Art Cubiste: Théories et Réalisations*. Paris, Charles Moreau, 1929, passim, pl. 7, 10, 19—20, 45.

90. Jardot, Maurice and Martin, Kurt. *Die Meister Französischer Malerei der Gegenwart*. Baden-Baden, Woldemar Klein, 1948. pp. 48, 53, illus., col. pl. Text on evolution of Cubism by Kahnweiler. Issued on occasion of exhibition in Freiburg, Oct. 20, 1947.

91. Jellett, Mainie. *The Artist's Vision*. Dundalk, Rundalgan Press, 1958. pp. 11, 79, 87.

Joseph-Édouard, R. *See* Gauthier.

92. *Juan Gris*. New York, Skira, [1958]. 4 pp. plus 6 col. pl. in folio. Unsigned text with notes on individual plates. Brief biography.

93. Justi, Ludwig. *Von Corinth bis Klee*. Berlin, Bard, 1931. p. 165, illus.

93a. Kahnweiler, Daniel-Henry. *I Maestri del Colore, 177: Juan Gris*. Milan, Fratelli Fabbri, 1966. [6] pp., illus., plus 17 col. pl.

94. Kahnweiler, Daniel-Henry. *Juan Gris von Daniel Henry [pseud.]*. Leipzig & Berlin, Klinkhardt & Biermann, 1929. 16 pp. plus 32 illus. Bibliography. "Junge Kunst", Bd. 55.

95. Kahnweiler, Daniel-Henry. *Juan Gris. Sa Vie, Son Œuvre, Ses Écrits*. Paris, Gallimard, 1946. 344 pp., illus., 51 pl. (col.), port. Exhibitions, pp. 296—309. Bibliography, pp. 312—326.

96. Kahnweiler, Daniel-Henry. *Juan Gris: His Life and Work*. Translated by Douglas Cooper. London, Lund

Humphries; New York, Curt Valentin, 1947. 178 pp., illus., 113 pl. (col.), port. Translator adapted and added to text. Bibliography of 103 items by H. B. Muller. Appendices: Collected writings of Juan Gris. — Juan Gris as engraver and illustrator. — List of exhibitions and articles in the press. — List of collections. — Chronology.

97. Kahnweiler, Daniel-Henry. *Mes Galeries et mes Peintres. Entretiens avec François Crémieux.* Paris, Gallimard, 1961. pp. 60—61 et passim. Reviewed by A. M. Mura, *Paragone*, no. 159, pp. 75—80, 1963.

98. Kahnweiler, Daniel-Henry. *The Rise of Cubism.* New York, Wittenborn, Schultz, 1949. Translation by Henry Aronson: *Der Weg zum Kubismus.* Munich, Delphin, 1920. Emphasizes Picasso, Braque, Léger.

99. Kepes, György, ed. *The Visual Arts Today.* Middletown, Conn., Wesleyan University Press, 1960. pp. 82—83. Special issue of *Daedalus*, v. 89, no. 1, Winter 1960, with text by Gris "Notes on my painting", from Kahnweiler, bibl. 95, 96.

100. Kochno, Boris. *Le Ballet.* Paris, Hachette, 1954. pp. 257—258.

101. Küppers, Paul Erich. *Der Kubismus.* Leipzig, Klinkhardt & Biermann, 1920. passim, illus.

102. Lake, Carlton and Maillard, Robert. *A Dictionary of Modern Painting.* 2nd rev. ed. New York, Tudor, [1964?]. pp. 150—153, 3 col. illus. "Second revised edition" also called "this third edition". Probably first is original French edition: *Dictionnaire de la Peinture Moderne* (Paris, Hazan, 1954?). — First English edition: New York, Tudor, [1956?]. Text by Jacques Lassaigne. Other references passim, e.g. "Cubism", "Kahnweiler", etc. New edition, bibl. 110.

102a. Landau, Rom. *Der unbestechliche Minos: Kritik an der Zeitkunst.* Hamburg, Harder, 1925. pp. 39, 81, 118, 138.

103. Lassaigne, Jacques. *Cent Chefs-d'œuvre des Peintres de l'École de Paris.* Paris, Éditions de la Galerie Charpentier, 1947. pp. 16, 22, 140, 142, 161, 188, illus. Includes an English translation by Frederic W. Stewart.

104. Lassaigne, Jacques. *Spanish Painting from Velasquez to Picasso.* Geneva, Skira, 1952. pp. 127, 138, 146 et passim. Biographical and bibliographical note. Also European editions.

105. La Tourette, François Gilles de. *La Peinture Française Contemporaine.* Paris, Librairie des Arts Décoratifs, 1937. pp. 7—8, illus. "Les Maîtres de l'Art Indépendant".

106. Leiris, Louise, Galerie. *50 Ans d'Édition de D.-H. Kahnweiler.* Paris, Galerie Louise Leiris, 1958. Preface by Kahnweiler. Exhibition and catalogue of *éditions de luxe* including the early Gris books (1921—26) issued under the imprint of Galerie Simon.

107. Lemaitre, Georges. *From Cubism to Surrealism in French Literature.* Cambridge, Mass., Harvard University Press, 1947 (c. 1941). pp. 71, 89, 142.

108. Lhote, André. *La Peinture.* Paris, Denoël et Steele, 1933. pp. 25, 155.

109. Lynton, Norbert. *The Modern World.* New York, McGraw-Hill, 1965. pp. 86, 98, illus., col. pl.

110. Maillard, Robert, ed. *Nouveau Dictionnaire de la Peinture Moderne.* Paris, Hazan, 1963. pp. 79, 150—153, illus. (col.). Also European and American editions. *Note* bibl. 102.

111. Marchiori, Giuseppe. *Pittura Moderna in Europa (da Manet a Pignon).* Venice, Pozza, 1950. pp. 123—127, illus. Bibliography, pp. 171—176.

112. Mendelowitz, Daniel M. *Drawing.* New York, Holt, Reinhart and Winston, 1967. pp. 226, 233, 237, 288, 289, 380, illus.

113. Miller Company (Meriden, Conn.). *Painting Toward Architecture.* New York, Duell, Sloan & Pearce, 1948. pp. 58—59 et passim. A collection of abstract art. Texts by Henry-Russell Hitchcock, M. C. Rathbun.

114. Modesti, Renzo. *Pittura Moderna nel Mondo.* Milan, Vallardi, 1961. pp. 35, 71, 203, illus., col. pl. Color plates same as in Diehl (bibl. 51).

115. Muller, Joseph-Émile. *Modern Painting from Manet to Mondrian.* New York, Castle Books, 1960. pp. 92, 105 to 106, illus. (col.).

116. Nacenta, Raymond. *School of Paris.* Greenwich, Conn., New York Graphic Society, 1960. pp. 30, 32, 81, 314, illus., col. pl. "The painters and the artistic climate of Paris since 1910." Also French, German, Italian and English editions.

117. Nicaise, Librairie. *Cubisme, Futurisme, Dada, Surréalisme.* Paris, Nicaise, 1960. Gris references (17, 96, 539, 579, 596, 751, 759, 810) in an excellent dealer's catalogue.

118. Olivier, Fernande. *Picasso et ses Amis.* Paris, Stock, 1933. pp. 158—159.

119. Ozenfant, Amédée. *Foundations of Modern Art.* New York, Brewer, Warren & Putnam, 1931. pp. 104—106, illus. Other editions: N.Y., Dover, 1952. Original edition: *Art* (Paris, Budry, 1929). German edition: *Leben und Gestaltung.* Potsdam, Müller & Kiepenheuer, 1930.

120. Ozenfant, Amédée and Jeanneret, Charles Édouard (Le Corbusier). *La Peinture Moderne.* Paris, Crès, 1925. Essays on cubism from *L'Esprit Nouveau*, pp. 89—131.

121. Petersen, Vilh. Bjerke. *Konkret Konst.* Stockholm, Rabén & Sjögren, 1956. pp. 30—31, 36—37, illus. English insert (4 p): Non-objective art.

122. Phillips, Duncan. *The Artist Sees Differently.* New York, Weyhe; Washington, Phillips Memorial Gallery, 1931. V. 1, pp. 51, 136.

123. *Pour Daniel-Henry Kahnweiler.* New York, Wittenborn, 1965. pp. 104—107, 305. Will Grohmann: Mit Kahnweiler bei Juan Gris (p. 104—106). Ms. letter by Gris mounted, p. 107 (letterpress transcription, p. 305). "Ouvrage établi sous la direction de Werner Spies. Copyright by Verlag Gerd Hatje, Stuttgart."

124. Power, J. W. *Éléments de la Construction Picturale.* Paris, Roche, 1932. pp. 53, 88—96, illus.

125. Prisme (Periodical). *Panorama de l'Art Présent.* Paris, Éditions d'Art et d'Industrie [1957]. pp. 22—24, illus. Reprints, from no. 3, May 15, 1956 of *Prisme*: D. H. Kahnweiler, "Une lettre inédite de Juan Gris" (refers to Ozenfant and Gris).

126. Pulitzer, Joseph and Pulitzer, Louise, Collection. *Modern Painting, Drawing* and *Sculpture. Collected by Louise and Joseph Pulitzer, Jr.* [Vol. I]. Cambridge, Mass., Harvard College, 1957. pp. 35—36, illus. Essay and catalogue by C. S. Chetham. Exhibited at Knoedler's, N.Y. (April—May) and the Fogg Museum (May—Sept.).

127. Rathbun, Mary C. and Hayes, Bartlett, H., Jr. *Layman's Guide to Modern Art : Painting for a Scientific Age.* New York, McKay, 1962 (c. 1954). pp. 70—71, illus. Based on exhibition *Seeing the Unseeable* at the Addison Gallery of American Art, Jan.—Mar. 1947.

128. Raynal, Maurice. *Anthologie de la Peinture Française.* Paris, Éditions Montaigne, 1927. pp. 171—180, illus. Statements by Gris included.

129. Raynal, Maurice. *Juan Gris. Vingt Tableaux.* Paris, Éditions de l'Effort Moderne, Léonce Rosenberg, 1920. 12 pp. plus 20 pl. "Les Maîtres du Cubisme." Reprinted: *Bulletin de l'Effort Moderne* no. 16, pp. 1—16, June 1925.

130. Raynal, Maurice. *Modern French Painters.* New York, Brentano's, 1928. pp. 93—100, illus. Translation from the French edition, 1927. Quotes Gris; bibliography.

131. Raynal, Maurice. *Peintres du XXe Siècle.* Geneva, Skira, 1947. pp. 22, 23; col. pls. 1, 27, 28.

132. Raynal, Maurice [and others]. *History of Modern Painting. [Vol. III] : From Picasso to Surrealism.* Geneva, Skira, 1950. pp. 66—68, 132—133, 196 et passim. Biographical and bibliographical notes. Translation: *Histoire de la Peinture Moderne* (1950).

133. Raynal, Maurice [and others]. *Modern Painting.* Geneva, Skira, 1953. p. 304 (chronology, bibliography); p. 329 (comprehensive index); col. pl. New revised edition, 1960. Compression of larger history (1950). Also European editions.

134. Rosenblum, Robert. *Cubism and Twentieth-Century Art.* New York, Abrams, 1960. pp. 109—125, 126, 130, 146, 149, 156, 176, 177, 192, 258, 260, 267, 284, 292, 305, 314, illus., col. pl. Bibliography. Also paperback edition.

135. Salmon, André. *La Jeune Peinture Française.* Paris, Messein, 1912, p. 57. Extracts printed in *Cahiers d'Art*, no. 5—6, 1933.

136. Salmon, André. *L'Art Vivant.* Paris, Crès, 1920. pp. 139—142.

137. Schmidt, Paul Ferdinand. *Geschichte der Modernen Malerei.* Zurich, Fretz & Wasmuth, 1952. pp. 136, 139, 140, col. pl.

138. Schmidt, Georg. *Juan Gris und die Geschichte des Kubismus.* Baden-Baden, Woldemar Klein; Stuttgart, Fink, 1957. 40 pp., illus. (col.). "Der Silberne Quell", Bd. 36.

139. Seghers, Pierre and Charpier Jacques, eds. *The Art of Painting in the Twentieth Century.* New York, Hawthorn Books, 1965. pp. 159, 193—202. Brief biography with Gris' text: "Some possibilities in painting" (Michelet Amphitheater, Sorbonne, May 15, 1924). Translated by Sally T. Abeles.

140. Shattuck, Roger. *The Banquet Years.* New York, Harcourt, Brace, 1958 (c. 1955). pp. 80, 218, 226, 253.

141. Skira, Albert. *Anthologie du Livre illustré par les Peintres et Sculpteurs de l'École de Paris.* Geneva, Skira, 1946. pp. 41—43, illus.

142. Soby, James Thrall. *After Picasso.* Hartford, E. V. Mitchell; New York, Dodd, Mead, 1935. pp. 8, 79, 80, 91, 92, 100.

143. Soby, James Thrall. *Juan Gris.* New York, Museum of Modern Art, 1958. 128 pp., illus. (col.), port. Also served as catalogue for exhibition in New York, Minneapolis, San Francisco, Los Angeles. Chronology. Bibliography by B. Karpel, pp. 120—124. Revised for Kahnweiler *Juan Gris* (New York, Abrams, 1969).

144. Soby, James Thrall. *Modern Art and the New Past.* Norman, Okla., University of Oklahoma, 1957. pp. 79, 85, 108, 110, 113.

145. Solomon R. Guggenheim Collection. *Art of Tomorrow : Fifth Catalogue of the Solomon R. Guggenheim Collection of Non-Objective Paintings.* New York, Solomon R. Guggenheim Foundation, 1939. pp. 124, 177, 2 illus.

146. Solomon R. Guggenheim Collection. *A Handbook to the Solomon R. Guggenheim Museum Collection.* New York, Solomon R. Guggenheim Foundation, 1959. pp. 69—71, 3 illus.

147. Stein, Gertrude. *The Autobiography of Alice B. Toklas.* New York, Harcourt, Brace, 1933. passim, illus.

148. Stein, Gertrude. *Portraits and Prayers.* New York. Random House, 1934. pp. 46—47. "Pictures of Juan Gris" partly reprinted: *Lectures in America* (1935), p. 82,

149. Sterup-Hansen, Dan, ed. *Juan Gris : Et Foredrag.* Copenhagen, Wivel, 1946. 23 pp., illus. Preface, with portions of "Des possibilités de la peinture" by Gris.

150. Sterling, Charles. *Still Life Painting.* New York, Universe; Paris, Tisne, 1959. pp. 107, 108, 110, 126, illus. Also French edition.

151. Sylvester, David. *Modern Art from Fauvism to Abstract Expressionism.* New York, Franklin Watts, 1965. pp. 63—65, 152, illus., col. pl.

152. Tharrats, Juan-José. *Artistas Españoles en el Ballet.* Barcelona & Buenos Aires, Argos, 1950. pp. 15—26, illus.

153. Terrasse, Charles. *French Painting in the XXth Century.* Paris, London, New York, Hyperion, 1939. pp. 20—21, 34, illus.

154. Théâtre de Monte-Carlo. *Programme générale de la Saison de Monte-Carlo. 1923—1924.* [Paris, Brunoff, 1923?]. passim, illus. (col.). Includes drawings by Juan Gris (cover and plates), dancers in costume, two maquettes, two color plates.

155. Toklas, Alice B. *What is Remembered.* New York, Holt, Rinehart and Winston, 1963. p. 135.

156. Thompson, G. David. *The Collection of Twentieth Century Paintings and Sculpture ... Public Auction.* New York, Parke-Bernet Galleries, 1966. pp. 46—47 (col. pl.). Note refers to traveling exhibitions, 1960—61 (Dusseldorf, The Hague, New York, Turin). Reproduces 1914 collage in color (no. 24).

157. Torres-Garcia, Joaquin. *Universalismo Constructivo.* Buenos Aires, Poseidon, 1944. pp. 513—520. Text dated 1936.

158. Uhde, Wilhelm. *Picasso et la Tradition Française.* Paris, Quatre Chemins, 1928. p. 83.

159. Westheim, Paul, ed. *Künstlerbekenntnisse.* Berlin, Propyläen, [1925]. p. 150. Text by Juan Gris: "Zu meinem Schaffen".

160. Wilenski, Reginald H. *Modern French Painters.* Glasgow, University Press; New York, Harcourt, Brace, 1954. passim. Other editions: 1940, 1944, 1949.

161. Yale University. Art Gallery. *Collection of the Société Anonyme, Museum of Modern Art 1920.* New Haven, Conn., Associates in Fine Arts, 1950. pp. 59—60, illus. Text by Marcel Duchamp; extract from Gertrude Stein (*Transition*, July 1927). Biography, bibliography.

162. Zervos, Christian. *Histoire de l'Art Contemporain.* Paris, Cahiers d'Art, 1938. pp. 236—240, 287—296, 304, illus.

163. Zervos, Christian, ed. *Gris—Léger.* Paris, Cahiers d'Art, 1933. Special Gris number of *Cahiers d'Art*, v. 8, pp. 178—208, issued in independent format for joint exhibition at Zurich. Texts by Apollinaire, Salmon, Ozenfant, Kahnweiler, Raynal, Gris, Zervos.

ARTICLES

No places are given for well-known and indexed magazines.

164. Adams, Philip R. The ill-starred troubadour of cubism. *Art News*, May 1948, v. 47, pp. 44—45, 55—56, illus. "The first show in a U.S. Museum."

165. Alloway, Lawrence. Round the London Galleries [Gris at the Marlborough]. *The Listener (London)*, Feb. 20, 1958, p. 330, illus. Similarly John Russell: "Master and manager" [Gris and Kahnweiler at the Marlborough]. *London Times*, Feb. 16, 1958.

166. Berger, René. Le cubisme. *XXe Siècle*, June 1962, no. 19, pp. 3—8, illus.

167. Breeskin, Adelyn D. "The painter's window." *Baltimore Museum of Art News*, Dec. 1943, v. 6, pp. 4—5, illus.

168. Brosse, La (pseud.). Silhouettes: Juan Gris. *Paris-Journal*, July 22, 1912. Cited by Kahnweiler (1947).

169. Bruguière, P. G. La présence de Juan Gris. *Cahiers d'Art*, 1951, v. 26, pp. 115—136, illus.

Cahiers d'Art. See also Zervos.

170. Caillois, Ronald P. Le cubisme classique de Juan Gris. *Critique*, 1947, v. 2, no. 12, pp. 411—416. "Compte-rendu du livre de M. Kahnweiler" (1946).

171. Clark, E. New York commentary [Gris retrospective at the Museum of Modern Art]. *Studio*, Oct. 1958, v. 156, pp. 120—122, illus.

172. Camfield, William A. Juan Gris and the golden section. *Art Bulletin*, Mar. 1965, v. 47, pp. 128—134, illus. Bibliography.

173. Camon Aznar, José. Juan Gris y sus etapes. *Goya*, Nov.—Dec. 1954, no. 3, pp. 156—163, illus. (col. pl.).

174. Casanyer, M. A. Juan Gris. *D'Aci i D'Ala (Barcelona)*, Dec. 1934, v. 22, p. 16—17, illus.

175. Cassou, Jean. Braque, Marcoussis et Juan Gris. *L'Amour de l'Art*, Nov. 1933, v. 14, pp. 227—231, illus. Reprinted in Huyghe's *Histoire* (bibl. 88), pp. 227—231.

176. Chamberlain, J. B. "Still-life with Guitar" acquired by St. Louis. *St. Louis Museum Bulletin*, Apr. 1940, v. 25, pp. 21—24, illus. Similar coverage: Juan Gris' "Still Life". *Minneapolis Institute of Art Bulletin*, May 23, 1953, v. 42, no. 21, pp. [1—3].

177. Clarke, Eliot. Milestones in modern art: 1. Guitar and Flowers by Juan Gris. *Studio*, May 1957, v. 153, no. 770, pp. 136, 153, col. illus.

178. Clay, Jean. Juan Gris, the broken destiny. *Réalités*, Dec. 1965, pp. 62—69, 8 col. illus. Also French edition.

179. Cooper, Douglas. Juan Gris, by Douglas Lord (pseud.). *Axis*, Autumn 1936, no. 7, pp. 9—12, illus.

180. Cooper, Douglas. Modern art and tradition, by Douglas Lord (pseud.). *In* Alan Campbell Johnson, ed. *Growing Opinions.* London, Methuen, 1934.

181. Courthion, Pierre. Les grandes étapes de l'art contemporain 1907—1917. *XXe Siècle*, May 1966, no. 28, pp. 79 ff., illus. (p. 94).

182. Davidson, Martha. Juan Gris, a pivotal figure of the School of Paris. *Art News*, Nov. 26, 1938, v. 37, pp. 13—14. A review of the Seligmann Gallery show.

183. Degand, Léon. Juan Gris [Exposition au Musée des Beaux-Arts, Berne]. *Aujourd'hui*, Jan. 1956, no. 6, p. 29, illus.

184. Diego, Gerardo. Devoción y meditación de Juan Gris. *Revista de Occidente (Madrid)*, Aug. 1927. Mentioned and cited by Gomez Sicre (bibl. 194).

185. Dorival, Bernard. Nabis et cubistes. *Bulletin des Musées de France*, May—June 1947, no. 5, pp. 9—18, illus. Acquisitions of the Musée National d'Art Moderne. Similarly: La donation André Lefevre au Musée National d'Art Moderne. *Revue du Louvre*, 1964, no. 1, pp. 33—37, illus.

186. Eisendrath, W. N., Jr. Painting and sculpture of the School of Paris in the collection of Mr. and Mrs. Joseph Pulitzer, Jr., of St. Louis. *Connoisseur*, Sept. 1962, v. 151, p. 31, illus.

187. Einstein, Carl. Juan Gris: texte inédit. *Documents*, 1930, v. 2, pp. 267—268, illus. Supplemented by pp. 243—248: "Exposition Juan Gris, Berlin."

188. Elgar, Frank. Une conquête du cubisme: le papier collé. *XXe Siècle*, Jan. 1956, no. 6, pp. 3—17, illus.

189. Elliott, Eugene C. Some recent conception of color theory. *Journal of Aesthetics and Art Criticism*, June 1960, v. 18, pp. 497—499.

190. Francastel, Galienne. The contemporary impact of Paolo Uccello. *XXe Siècle*, Christmas 1961, no. 17, pp. 27, 29 (illus.). Also French edition.

191. Gans, L. Juan Gris' vlakdeling. *Museumjournaal*, Mar.—Apr. 1959, no. 8—9, pp. 154—157, illus. (pp. 169—170). On 2 acquisitions by Stedelijk van Abbe-Museum, Eindhoven. French résumé, pp. 168, 171.

192. George, Waldemar. Juan Gris. *L'Amour de l'Art*, Nov. 1921, v. 2, no. 11, pp. 351—352, illus.

193. Golding, John. Juan Gris at Berne. *Burlington Magazine*, Dec. 1955, v. 97, pp. 384—386, illus.

194. Gomez Sicre, José. Notas de arte: En el aniversario de Juan Gris. *El Nacional-Domingo (Caracas)*, Nov. 23, 1947. Article dated Sept. 30. Reproduces 2 works from the Buchholz Gallery, N.Y. Quotes Gerardo Diego (bibl. 184).

195. Greenberg, Clement. The pasted paper revolution. *Art News*, Sept. 1958, v. 57, no. 5, pp. 46—49, 60—61, illus. On Braque, Gris, Miró, Picasso, Schwitters.

196. Ha mort Juan Gris. *Amic de les Arts*, May 31, 1927, v. 2, p. 40.

197. Habasque, Guy. L'atelier de Juan Gris. *L'Œil*, Jan. 1958, no. 37, pp. 28—35, illus. (col.). On the occasion of the Galerie Leiris (Paris) show.

198. Haftmann, Werner. Eine Lanze für Juan Gris. *Die Zeit (Hamburg)*, June 3, 1948, p. 5. Followed by: "Gedanken von Gris" (aus einem Briefe an Carl Einstein, *Der Querschnitt*, 1923). — *Westheim*, 1924. — *Curt Valentin*, 1947.

199. Heilmaier, Hans. Juan Gris. *Musaion (Prague)*, Nov. 1928, no. 1, pp. 25—29, illus. Also *Die Kunst (Munich)*, Nov. 1929, v. 61, pp. 63—65, illus.

200. Helot, Jean Valéry. Juan Gris vu par Maurice Raynal. *Beaux Arts (Paris)*, July 22, 1938, v. 75, p. 6. Reports talk by Raynal.

201. J., J. Juan Gris. *La Publicidad (Barcelona)*, Apr. 4, 1912, illus.

202. Juan Gris. *La Biennale di Venezia*, June—Sept. 1957, no. 28—29, pp. 33—34, illus.

203. Judkins, Winthrop. Toward a reinterpretation of cubism. *Art Bulletin*, Dec. 1948, v. 30, pp. 270—278, illus.

204. Kahnweiler, Daniel-Henry. Cubism: the creative years. *Art News*, Nov. 1954, v. 53, no. 7, pt. 2, pp. 106—116, 180—181, illus. "The Art News Annual", Vol. 24 [1955].

205. Kahnweiler, Daniel-Henry. Juan Gris. *Du (Zurich)*, Jan. 1952, no. 1, p. 32, port. (p. 30). Extracts from his "Juan Gris" monograph.

206. Kahnweiler, Daniel-Henry. Juan Gris. *In :* Biennale di Venezia. Esposizione Internazionale d'Arte: Catalogo. Venice, 1956, pp. 250—253. pl. 82—83.

207. Kahnweiler, Daniel-Henry. Der Tod des Juan Gris. *Der Querschnitt*, July 1927, v. 7, p. 558.

208. Kahnweiler, Daniel-Henry. Du temps que les cubistes étaient jeunes. *L'Œil*, Jan. 15, 1955, no. 1, pp. 27—31. "Un entretien au magnétophone."

209. Kahnweiler, Daniel-Henry. Une lettre inédite de Juan Gris. *Prisme des Arts*, May 15, 1956, no. 3, pp. 22—24, illus. Relates to letter from Gris to Ozenfant about article in *L'Esprit Nouveau* and Ozenfant's reply to the editor of *Prisme des Arts*, no. 8, Jan. 1957. Also in: *Panorama de l'Art Présent*. Paris, Prisme des Arts, 1957.

210. Keller, Horst. Sieg der Malerei über die Welt: Juan Gris. *Köln (Cologne)*, Dec. 1965, no. 4, [6 pp.], illus. (col.). On exhibit at the Museum am Ostwall; coming to the Wallraf-Richartz Museum, Jan.—Feb. 1966.

211. Kramer, Hilton. [Juan Gris exhibition at the Museum of Modern Art]. *Arts (New York)*, May 1958, v. 32, pp. 48—51, illus.

212. L., H. A. A note on Juan Gris and cubism. *Broom (New York)*, 1923, no. 5, pp. 32—35, illus.

213. Laporte, Paul M. Cubism and science. *Journal of Aesthetics and Art Criticism*, Mar. 1949, v. 7, pp. 243—256. Bibliography.

214. "Le Canigou" by Juan Gris. *Gallery Notes (Buffalo)*, Spring 1948, no. 3, pp. 25—26.

215. Legua, A. Portraits d'artistes: Juan Gris. *L'Intransigeant (Paris)*, Dec. 25, 1934.

Little Review. See Stein, Gertrude.

Lord, Douglas (pseud.). *See* Cooper, Douglas.

216. Louchheim, Aline B. Looking back at Gris, lyric cubist. *Art News*, Apr. 15, 1944, v. 43, p. 23, illus. Review of Buchholz Gallery show.

217. Michelson, Annette. Paris [and the Gris exhibition at Galerie Leiris]. *Arts (New York)*, Jan. 1958, v. 32, p. 16, illus. Refers to Kahnweiler's 1946 monograph, quoting Gris.

218. Nicholson, Benedict. Cubism and Juan Gris. *Horizon*, Mar. 1948, no. 99, pp. 225—227. A review of Kahnweiler's 1947 monograph.

219. "Numero dedicado a Juan Gris". *Arte Vivo (Valencia)*, May—June 1959, no. 3, [24 pp.], illus. Texts by D.-H. Kahnweiler, C. Einstein, M. Raynal. Also Antonio G. Pericas: El pensamiento estetico de Juan Gris. — Mercedes Molleda: "Los collages" de Juan Gris.

220. Ozenfant, Amédée. Juan Gris [par] "Vauvrecy". *L'Esprit Nouveau*, 1920, v. 1, pp. 533—534. Presumably written by the editor; "actually by the artist" (Kahnweiler).

221. Paul, Elliot. A master of plastic relations. *Transition*, July 1927, no. 4, p. 163—165.

222. Ragghianti, Carlo L. Revisioni sul cubismo. *Critica d'Arte*, 1961, v. 8, no. 46, pp. 1—16; no. 47, pp. 1—15; no. 48, pp. 1—11, illus. Works by Braque, Chagall, Delaunay, Gris, Picasso.

223. Raynal, Maurice. Juan Gris. *L'Esprit Nouveau*, Feb. 1921, no. 5, pp. 531—554, illus. (col.).

224. Raynal, Maurice. Juan Gris. *Bulletin de l'Effort Moderne*, June 1925, no. 16, pp. 1—16. Also in *Das Kunstblatt*, 1921, v. 5, pp. 364—372, illus.

225. Raynal, Maurice. La mort de Juan Gris. *Art Vivant*, June 1, 1927, pp. 431—432.

226. Raynal, Maurice. Juan Gris et la métaphore plastique. *Les Feuilles Libres*, Mar.-Apr. 1923, no. 31, pp. 63—65. Reprinted in his "Anthologie de la Peinture Française" (bibl. 128).

227. Richardson, John. Juan Gris en Suisse. *XXe Siècle*, Jan. 1956, no. 6, pp. 63—65, illus. On the occasion of the retrospective at Berne.

228. Rouve, Pierre. Portrait of the artist: Juan Gris. *Art News and Review*, Feb. 15, 1958, v. 10, no. 2, p. 3, illus.

229. Salacrou, Armand. [Gris paintings of 1927 stir memories]. *New York Times*. Dec. 22, 1957. Reminiscences by a close friend whose first book was illustrated by Gris.

230. Schmidt, Georg. Juan Gris. *Das Kunstwerk*, Jan. 1958, v. 11, no. 7, pp. 3—14, illus. (col.).

231. Seligmann, E. G., and G. Of the proximity of death and its stylistic activations: Roger de La Fresnaye and Juan Gris. *Art Quarterly*, 1949, v. 12, no. 2, pp. 146—155, illus.

232. Stabile, Blanca. Paul Klee y Juan Gris. *Ver y Estimar (Buenos Aires)*, Sept. 1951, no. 25, pp. 8—15, illus. Partly a review of Kahnweiler's study.

233. Stein, Gertrude. Juan Gris. *The Little Review*, Autumn—Winter 1924—1925, v. 10, no. 2, p. 16 plus 17 illus. Cover-title: "Juan Gris Number". Man Ray portrait.

234. Stein, Gertrude. The life and death of Juan Gris. *Transition*, July 1927, no. 4, pp. 159—162. German translation in Galerie Flechtheim, *Juan Gris*, Berlin, 1930, partly translated, *Kunst und Künstler*, Apr. 1930, v. 28, p. 308, Spanish translation, *Gaceta de Arte*, Oct. 1933, no. 20, pp. 1—2, reprinted Galerie Balaÿ & Carré, *Juan Gris*, Paris, 1938.

235. Storey, Benjamin. Juan Gris. *Emporium*, July 1956, no. 739, pp. 10—15, illus.

236. Sweeney, James J. Architect of the canvas. *Saturday Review of Literature*, June 28, 1958, p. 20. Review of and comment on J. T. Soby's "Juan Gris" (bibl. 143).

237. Tériade, E. Juan Gris. *Cahiers d'Art*, 1928, v. 3, no. 5—6, pp. 231—246 incl. illus. Illustrations, pp. 236—246.

238. Torre, Guillermo de. Apologia del cubismo y de Picasso. *Gaceta de Arte (Tenerife)*, Mar. 1936, v. 5, pp. 31—57, illus. Includes poem to Gris, p. 34.

239. Torre, Guillermo de. Juan Gris y Robert Delaunay, Reminiscences personales. *Revista de Ideas Estéticas (Madrid)*, 1963, v. 21, pp. 295—316.

Vauvrecy. *See* Ozenfant.

240. Venturi, Lionello. Piero della Francesca — Seurat — Gris. *Diogenes (Brooklyn)*, Spring 1953, no. 2, pp. 19—23. Also in *Paletten (Göteborg)*, 1954, no. 1, pp. 2—5, illus.

241. Vézelay, P. Juan Gris. *Artwork (London)*, Winter 1928, v. 4, pp. 258—261, illus.

242. Vincente, E. Gris: reality cubed. *Art News*, May 1958, v. 57, pp. 30—33, illus. On major retrospective at the Museum of Modern Art.

243. Warnod, André. L'esthétique de Juan Gris. *Comoedia (Paris)*, Mar. 17, 1923. Also "Juan Gris", May 13, 1927.

244. Zervos, Christian. Juan Gris et l'inquiétude d'aujourd'hui. *Cahiers d'Art*, Dec. 1926, v. 1, pp. 269—274, illus.

245. Zervos, Christian. Juan Gris. *Cahiers d'Art*, 1927, v. 2, pp. 170—172, illus., port. Notes on Gris just after his death, followed by "Quelques notes de Juan Gris sur ses recherches".

246. Zervos, Christian, ed. Juan Gris. *Cahiers d'Art*, 1933, v. 8, no. 5—6, pp. 178—208, 74 illus. Special number on Gris and Léger. Also issued as separate monograph (bibl. 163). Texts by Zervos, Apollinaire, Salmon, Ozenfant, Kahnweiler, Raynal, Gris.

CATALOGUES, EXHIBITIONS & REVIEWS: 1923—1967

Described as "all the exhibitions to which Gris contributed during his lifetime", Kahnweiler (1947) has published, pp. 150—154, an important chronological list from 1912 to 1928. It includes references to otherwise obscure catalogues and reviews in magazines and newspapers of the time. In spite of those details, the record is not complete. There is no mention of the *Exposicion Nacional de Bellas Artes* (Madrid, 1906) where two paintings were exhibited by Victoriano Gonzalez (Juan Gris) just before he left Spain, or special events like the *Premier Vendredi de Littérature* (Palais des Fêtes, Paris), Jan. 23, 1920, where canvases by Gris, Chirico, Picabia, etc. were on display. Since the "collective", "group" and "one-man" shows in which works by Gris have been exhibited, from 1928 to 1968, constitute a massive array of places and data, it has been necessary to restrict the following to a selective and representative cross-section in Europe and America.

247. Galerie Simon. *Exposition Juan Gris*. Paris, Mar. 20—Apr. 5, 1923. 54 works (1911—23), plus graphics. Reviewed by J. E. Blanche, *Revue Européenne* (Paris), June 1, 1923, pp. 69—70. Preface by M. Raynal; partly reprinted in *Cahiers d'Art* no. 5—6 (1933) and his *Anthologie de la Peinture Française* (1927).

248. Brooklyn Museum. *International Exhibition of Modern Art Assembled by the Société Anonyme*. New York, Nov. 19, 1926—Jan. 1, 1927. Nos. 206—209 by Gris. One painting reproduced upside down. Text by Katherine Dreier. Also *de luxe* publication (bibl. 54).

249. Galerie Simon. *Exposition in Memoriam Juan Gris*. Paris, June 1928. 66 paintings, 1 sculpture, drawings.

250. Galerie Flechtheim. *In Memoriam Juan Gris, 1887—1927*. Berlin, Feb. 1930. Gertrude Stein essay from *Transition*, 1927: Leben und Tod des Juan Gris. Biography, bibliography. Lists 90 works. Reviewed: *Art News*, Mar. 8, 1930, p. 14 (F. Turkel-Deri); *Der Cicerone*, Feb. 1930, v. 22, pp. 110—111 (W. Wolfradt); *Documents*, 1930, no. 4, pp. 243—248 (C. Einstein); *Kunstauktion*, Feb. 9, 1930, pp. 10—11 (O. W.).

251. Marie Harriman Gallery. *Juan Gris*. New York, Feb. 1932. Reviews: *Art News*, Feb. 13, 1932, p. 8; *Art Digest*, Mar. 1, 1932, p. 2.

252. Kunsthaus Zurich. *Juan Gris*. Zurich, Apr. 2—26, 1933. List of 147 works; preface by W. Wartmann. Special number of *Cahiers d'Art* (no. 5—6, 1933) issued as joint catalogue ("Juan Gris — Fernand Léger") with insert of Museum's checklist.

253. Julien Levy Gallery. *Twenty-Five Years of Russian Ballet from the Collection of Serge Lifar*. New York, Nov. 2—18, [1933?]. Nos. 33—36 by Gris. Foreword by Lifar. Collection now at Wadsworth Atheneum (1934).

254. Galerie des Beaux-Arts. *Les Créateurs du Cubisme*. Paris, Mar. 1935. Major retrospective and chronology. Catalogue by Raymond Cogniat. Gris: nos. 38—50, illus.

255. Mayor Gallery. *Juan Gris*. London, Nov. 1936. Reviews: *New English Weekly* (H. G. Porteus), Nov. 19, 1936, p. 115; *New Statesman and Nation* (C. Bell), Nov. 14, 1936, p. 771; *The Observer* (J. Gordon), Nov. 15, 1936, p. 16; *The Spectator* (A. Blunt), Dec. 11, 1936, p. 1038.

256. Petit Palais. *Les Maîtres de l'Art Indépendant, 1895—1937*. Paris, June—Oct. 1937. pp. 108—109, illus. 24 works, 1 plate, general preface by R. Escholier, A. Saurrat.

257. Galerie Balaÿ et Carré. *Juan Gris: Exposition*. Paris, June 13—July 3, 1938. 23 works (1911—20), all illustrated. Texts by M. Raynal, Gertrude Stein, Douglas Lord (Cooper). Reviews: *Art News*, July 1938, p. 19; *Beaux Arts (Paris)*, June 24, 1938, p. 16; *Cahiers du Sud*, Aug.—Sept. 1938, suppl. pp. 1—4; *Renaissance*, Aug. 1938, p. 44; *Revue Hebdomadaire (Paris)*, Sept. 1938, pp. 112—114 (J. Lassaigne).

258. Seligmann & Company. *Retrospective Loan Exhibition: Juan Gris*. New York, Nov. 10—Dec. 1938. 27 works. Texts by Gris, Raynal and Stein. Biography, bibliography. Reviews: *Art Digest*, Dec. 1, 1938, p. 6; *Art News*, Nov. 26, 1938, pp. 13—14.

259. Buchholz Gallery (Curt Valentin). *Juan Gris, 1887—1927*. New York, Mar. 28—Apr. 22, 1944. 40 works. Text by Gris (1926), preface by J. Lipchitz, bibliography. Reviewed in *Art Digest*, Apr. 15, 1944, p. 11; *Art News*, Apr. 15, 1944, p. 23. *Other exhibitions*: Apr. 1—26, 1947, 27 exhibits; text by Gris. — Jan. 16—Feb. 1, 1950, 46 exhibits; Gris letter to Kahnweiler.

260. Modern Art Society. *Juan Gris, 1887—1927*. Cincinnati, Apr. 30—May 31, 1948. Preface by E. H. Dwight. 64 works (illus.). Exhibited at the Art Museum.

261. San Francisco. Museum of Art. *Picasso, Gris, Miro: the Spanish Masters of Twentieth Century Painting*. San Francisco, Sept. 14—Oct. 17, Portland, Oct. 26—Nov. 28, 1948. Nos. 21—41 by Gris. Texts by R. B. Freeman, D. Gallup, D.-H. Kahnweiler, J. Larrea, Man Ray, Gris (*L'Esprit Nouveau*, 1921; *Der Querschnitt*, 1923).

262. Art Institute of Chicago. *20th Century Art from the Louise and Walter Arensberg Collection*. Chicago, Oct. 20—Dec. 18, 1949. A pioneer collection. Gris: nos. 93—97. Texts by K. Kuh and D. C. Rich. Collection now in Philadelphia; revised catalogue (1954).

263. Musée National d'Art Moderne. *Le Cubisme (1907—1914)*. Paris, Jan. 30—Apr. 9, 1953. Text by J. Cassou, chronology by B. Dorival, catalogue by G. Vienne. Gris: nos. 65—67, 88, 89, 124—127, 173—179, pl. 18, 46.

264. Kunstmuseum Bern. *Juan Gris*. Bern, Oct. 29, 1955—Jan. 2, 1956. 187 exhibits; chronology; bibliography. Foreword and catalogue by Douglas Cooper. Reviewed: *Museumjournal*, Feb. 1956, no. 7, pp. 122—124 (C. Giedion-Welcker).

265. Esposizione Biennale, Venezia. *XXVIII. Catalogo*. Venice, 1956. pp. 250—255, illus. Lists 29 works. Text by Kahnweiler.

266. Galerie Louise Leiris. *L'Atelier de Juan Gris*. Paris, Oct. 23—Nov. 23, 1957. 22 paintings (1926—27), all illustrated (9 col. pl.). Preface by Kahnweiler. Reviewed: *Arts*, Jan. 1958, v. 32, p. 16 (A. Michelson); *L'Œil*, Jan. 1958 (G. Habasque).

267. Marlborough Fine Art Ltd. *Juan Gris, 1887—1927. Retrospective Exhibition*. London, Feb.—Mar. 1958. 50 works, 4 illustrated books. Preface by Kahnweiler on Gris; preface on Kahnweiler by John Russell. Reviews: *Apollo*, Mar. 1958, p. 88; *Architectural Review*, May 1958, p. 348; *Arts*, Apr. 1958, pp. 22—23; *Art News*, Mar. 1958, p. 47; *Art News and Review*, Mar. 1, 1958, p. 8; *Connoisseur*, Apr. 1958, p. 115.

268. Museum of Modern Art. *Juan Gris*. New York, Apr. 9—June 1, 1958. Book by J. T. Soby serves as catalogue to major exhibition (123 pp., illus., col. pl.). Also shown at Minneapolis (June 24—July 24), San Francisco (Aug. 11—Sept. 14), Los Angeles (Sept. 29—Oct. 26). Reviews: *Apollo*, May 1958, p. 180; *Art News*, May 1958, pp. 30—33; *Arts*, May 1958, pp. 48—51; *Studio*, Oct. 1958, pp. 120—122.

269. Galerie Beyeler. *Le Cubisme: Braque, Gris, Léger, Picasso*. Basel, May—July 1962. 72 pp., illus. (col.pl.). Introduction by Georg Schmidt in German. Chronologies. Variant catalogue with text by C. Zervos: "Naissance du cubisme", issued for show at Knoedler, Paris, Oct. 9—Nov. 10.

270. Marlborough-Gerson Gallery. *Artist and Maecenas: a Tribute to Curt Valentin*. New York, Nov.—Dec. 1963. pp. 80—83, illus. Gris: nos. 147—154.

270a. Baltimore Museum of Art. *1914: an Exhibition of Paintings, Drawings and Sculpture*. Baltimore, Oct. 6—Nov. 15, 1964. 95 pp., illus. Texts by G. Boas, H. Peyre, L. Johnson, Jr., G. Rosenthal, C. Parkhurst. Nos. 77—80 by Gris (2 illus.).

271. Museum am Ostwall. *Juan Gris*. Dortmund, Oct. 23—Dec. 4, 1965. 181 pp. (illus., col.pl.); 170 exhibits. Chronology, bibliography. German texts by L. Reygers, J. Richardson, D.-H. Kahnweiler. Also shown at Wallraf-Richartz Museum, Dec. 29, 1965—Feb. 13, 1966.

272. Galerie Louise Leiris. *Juan Gris: Dessins et Gouaches, 1910—1027*. Paris, June 17—July 17, 1965. Preface by Daniel-Henry Kahnweiler. 72 illus. (4 col.), col. cover.

273. Rhode Island Museum of Art. *Herbert and Nanette Rothschild Collection*. Providence, Oct. 7—Nov. 6, 1966. Gris: nos. 57—64, 6 illus., 2 col. pl. Catalogue and text by G. Downing, D. Robbins.

274. Saidenberg Gallery. *Juan Gris: Drawings and Gouaches, 1910—1927*. New York, May 9—June 24, 1967. 48 exhibits; 21 illus.; preface by D.-H. Kahnweiler. Reviews: *Art News*, Summer 1967, p. 20; *Arts*, Summer 1967, p. 56.

INDEX

PHOTO CREDITS